The Kingdom of Armenia

THE
KINGDOM
OF ARMENIA

M. Chahin

DORSET PRESS
New York

This edition published by Dorset Press,
a division of Marboro Books Corporation,
by arrangement with Routledge
1991 Dorset Press

ISBN 0-88029-609-7

Printed in the United States of America

M 9 8 7 6 5

TO MY WIFE

Contents

Contents

Chronology of the Ancient Near East

Aegean & Greece	Egypt	Asia Minor	Syria & Palestine	Assyria	Babylonia	Iran	
	Egyptian writing hieroglyphs		Early Bronze		*Cuneiform writing* Uruk and Kish Rise of Nippur	*Proto-Elamite writing*	2800
	Old Kingdom Age of Pyramids		Ebla on site of Tel Mardik c. 2500. Destroyed by Sargon of Akkad c. 2300		Early city states		2600
							2400
					Sargon of Akkad Naram-Sin Quti		2200
	First Intermediate Period		Middle Bronze	Babylonian governors in Ashur	Ur III Dynasty Amorite invasions Sumer destroyed by Elam Isin-Larsa period	Babylonian governors in Susa	2000
Abraham at Ur c. 2000 ± 200. Mentioned in Ebla tablets							

	Egypt	Aegean	Anatolia / Syria	Assyria	Babylonia / Isin-Larsa	Elam
1900	Middle kingdom				Lipit-Ištar	Old Elamite kingdom
1800				Assyrian merchant colonies	Rise of Babylon Isin-Larsa continues until rise of Hammurabi 1792-50	
				Commercial expansion Shamshi-Adad I		
			Alalakh VII	Amorite dynasty in Assyria. Shamshi-Adad c. 1796	Hammurapi destroys Mari 1761 Beginning of Kassite invasions	
1700		Minoan Linear A	Old Hittite kingdom			
1600	New kingdom	Hyksos	Muršili I (Hittite king)		Hittite sack of Babylon 'Dark Age'	
1500						

	Aegean & Greece	Egypt	Asia Minor	Syria & Palestine	Assyria	Babylonia	Iran
1400	*Minoan Linear B* Destruction of Knossos			Alalakh IV Mitanni kingdom	Mitanni dominates Assyria. Nuzi, a Hurrian city with Biblical connections. (See Nuzi tablets)		
		Amarna Period: Akhenaten	New Hittite empire Suppiluliuma I	Mitannian Ugarit tributary	Ashur-uballit I	Kurigalzu II	
1300				*Alphabet*			
		Rameses II	Hattusili III *Hittite hieroglyphic writing* Urartu first mentioned 1275				
1200			Sea peoples Mycenae destroyed	Exodus Hebrew conquest	Tukulti-Ninurta I Shalmaneser I		
	Trojan War	XX Dynasty Ramases III		Philistines Joshua and Judges	End of Mitanni		
1100			Phrygians destroy Hittite empire		Tiglath-Pileser I	Nebuchadnezzar I	
	Dorian invasion			Sidon and Tyre			
1000							

	Kings of Urartu		Assyria	
900				
Phoenicians invent European alphabet *Greek alphabet*	Kings of Urartu	David Solomon		Aramaic invasions
	Arame Sarduri I Ishpuini Menua		Tukulti-Ninurta II Ashur-nasir-pal II Shalmaneser III	
800				
Homer	Argishti I Sarduri II Zenith of Urartian empire Rusa I	Fall of Samaria Deportation of Israelites	Tiglath-pileser III Sargon II	Merodach-Baladan II
Ethiopian domination				Assyrian domination
700				
Assyrian invasion	Argishti II Rusa II Sarduri III Epimena Rusa III	Hezekiah	Sennacherib Esarhadnon Assurbanipal Fall of Nineveh End of Assyria	Chaldean dynasty
				Medes Rise of Achaemenids
600				
Solon	End of Urartu 590	Fall of Jerusalem	Median domination	Nebuchadnezzar II

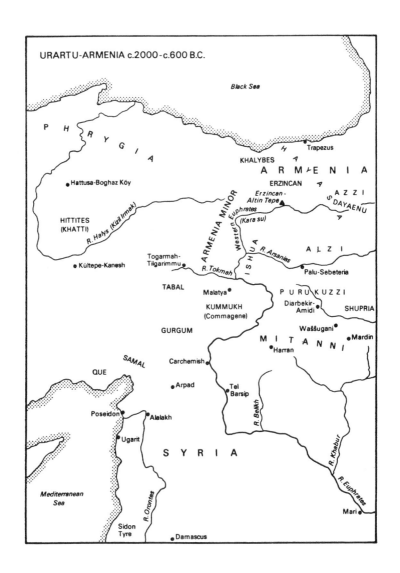

URARTU-ARMENIA c.2000-c.600 B.C.

Black Sea

P H R Y G I A

KHALYBES

Trapezus

A R M ʎ E N I A

Hattusa-Boghaz Köy

ERZINCAN

Erzincan-
Altin Tepe

AZZI
DAYAENU

HITTITES
(KHATTI)

R. Halys (Kızıl Irmak)

ARMENIA MINOR

Western Euphrates (Kara su)

R. Arsanias

A L Z I

Kültepe-Kanesh

Togarmah-
Tilgarimmu

R. Tokmah

ISHUA

Palu-Sebeteria

TABAL

Malatya

P U R U KUZZI

Diarbekir-
Amidi

SHUPRIA

KUMMUKH
(Commagene)

Waššugani

Mardin

GURGUM

M I T A N N I

Harran

SAMAL

Carchemish

QUE

Arpad

Tel
Barsip

R. Belikh

Poseidon

Alalakh

R. Khabur

Ugarit

S Y R I A

R. Euphrates

*Mediterranean
Sea*

R. Orontes

Mari

Sidon
Tyre

Damascus

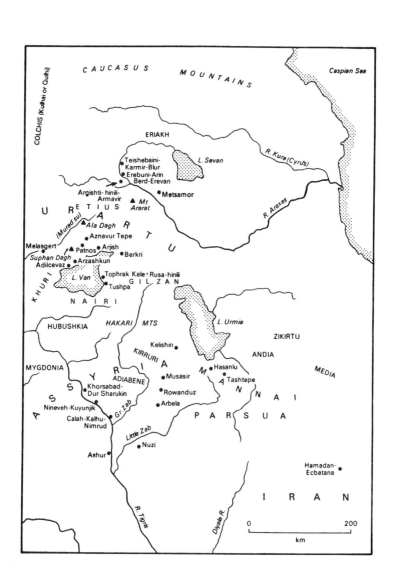

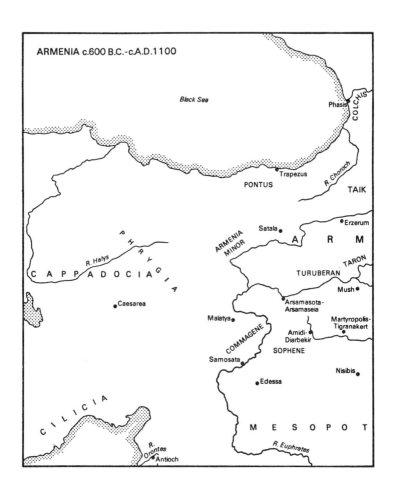

ARMENIA c.600 B.C.–c.A.D.1100

Black Sea

Phasis

COLCHIS

R. Choroch

Trapezus

PONTUS

TAIK

Satala

Erzerum

ARMENIA MINOR

A   R   M

TARON

TURUBERAN

R. Halys

P H R Y G I A

C A P P A D O C I A

Mush

Caesarea

Arsamasota-
Arsamaseia

Malatya

Martyropolis-
Tigranakert

COMMAGENE

Amidi-
Diarbekir

SOPHENE

Samosata

Nisibis

C I L I C I A

Edessa

M   E   S   O   P   O   T

*R.
Orontes*

R. Euphrates

Antioch

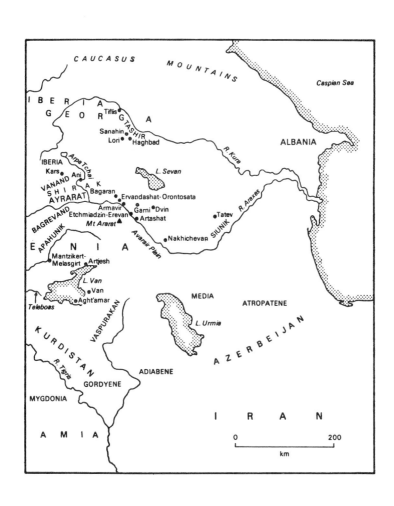

Preface

In the following pages I have given my reasons for attempting to write this history of Armenia. The few lines here were written after completion of the whole work. They are specifically intended to point out that in the Armenian — as distinct from the Urartian — section I have endeavoured to break away from the traditional view of Armenian subservience to its powerful neighbours for most of its long history. I hope I have shown that, contrary to such a negative view of its national history, Armenia enjoyed many centuries of independence and power. Lost or non-existent records chronicling the Armenian point of view mean that the period has been recounted and documented by its enemies. Those biased records have been passed down and accepted by most European and even by Armenian writers. A little research and the will to organise the facts out of intricate evidence, has I hope proved A.J.P. Taylor's comment, that history is not a catalogue but a version of events.

Introduction

This is a short history of a civilisation which was rediscovered in recent times on the eastern shores of Lake Van in Eastern Turkey. It bears the familiar, Biblical name of Ararat — the Kingdom of Ararat (Jeremiah LI.27) or, in Assyrian, Urartu. Its native name was Biaini. The documented history of Urartu begins in 1275 BC, and ends early in the sixth century BC, with the retreat of its aristocracy into the southern strongholds of the Caucasus, under the onslaught of the Medes and Armenians. Its continuance as the eighteenth satrapy (or governorship) of Darius the Great (522–486 BC) (Herodotus III.94) is recorded on the famous Rock at Behistun (or Bisitun), and is testified by Xenophon in his *Anabasis* (IV.3). Urartu's inexorable and bitter enemy was Assyria (northern Mesopotamia). Assyria itself was annihilated towards the end of the seventh century BC by the Medes and Babylonians. At the time of the destruction of Assyria, Urartu's successors, the Armenians (who are to the Urartians as the English are to the Britons or the French to the Gauls) occupied Urartu as a ruling aristocray. They have survived for over 2500 years, through many vicissitudes of fortune, to the present day.

In the 1840s, the impact of the spectacular discoveries of the sites of ancient Assyrian cities, such as Nineveh (all near modern Mosul), containing enormous sculptures and other monuments, not only overshadowed the less dramatic but equally valuable discoveries of Urartian antiquities first found at about the same time, but also prejudiced historians in favour of Assyria. Ararat (or Urartu or Biaini) was neglected for many years, a forgotten civilisation and it was only brought to the notice of archaeologists and historians at the end of the Second World War, through the efforts of such dedicated scholars as Dr Nicolas Adontz, whose works (some of them written in a Nazi concentration camp) were published in Paris; Dr R.D. Barnett, (Keeper of Western Asiatic Antiquities, British Museum, London), who listed and described many of the Urartian finds scattered in museums and private collections all over the world; and Professor B.B. Piotrovskii (Hermitage Museum, Leningrad); followed by Professor Konstantine Oganesian[1] (State Academy of Armenia, Erevan), whose special archaeological area is in the Soviet Socialist Republic

1

of Armenia, formerly a northern province of Ararat.

It is well known that historians seldom take a completely objective spirit. Thus, most Assyriologists in the past have tended to exaggerate the prowess in battle of the Assyrian monarchs, their organising ability, and the invincibility of their armies; and in writing of almost seven centuries of ceaseless struggle between Assyria and Urartu, they seem to gloss over the fact that no country has ever prevailed over another throughout its whole existence. This is certainly true of Assyria *vis-à-vis* Urartu, and is abundantly supported by the events of some 200 years — between 850 and 650 BC — when Assyria and Urartu were often equally matched, and Urartian military supremacy was assured for nearly half this period. But these achievements appear in small print as it were, while Urartu's greatness in the history of the Middle East is not sufficiently emphasised.

When I first considered writing this work, there was no book on Urartu in the English language. That was my reason for undertaking the project. In doing so, I had in mind the general reader who thinks of the study of history as an activity of deep and unending interest, rather than the few specialists in this field, to whom I am myself greatly indebted, having benefited from their articles in the professional journals *Iraq* (Journal of the British School of Archaeology in Iraq) and *Anatolian Studies* (Journal of the British Institute of Archaeology at Ankara). I refer especially to the articles by Dr R.D. Barnett, Mr Charles Burney, Professor Seton Lloyd and Mr James Mellaart. I also had recourse particularly to the late Dr Nicolas Adontz's *Histoire d'Arménie*, Professor B.B. Piotrovskii's works on Urartu and, for early Armenian history, to Professor Cyril L. Toumanoff's *Studies in Christian Caucasian History*. My thanks are also due to the writers and publishers of the books and articles listed in the references at the end of each chapter. Having made these acknowledgements, I ought to state that, besides one or two new contributions to Armenian history in the main text, Chapter 20 contains some controversial matter but interesting none the less, I hope.

The Prologue may be ignored by the impatient reader, or by those who are already familiar with the important events which, many scholars now agree, constitute the very foundations of western civilisation. In the context of the present work, its main purpose is to describe the historical background from which, over a period of several centuries, Urartu eventually emerged as a powerful kingdom; and how its development was, in many respects, influenced by the most ancient civilisations of the Near East.

The designation 'Armenia' is independent of political circumstances. It describes the region which was held politically and inhabited ethnically by Armenians, from *c.* 600 BC to the twelfth century AD. After that time, though not politically independent, the area was inhabited principally by Armenians down to the early part of the twentieth century. The region is loosely bounded by the Upper Euphrates, as it approaches Cilicia and Syria in the west (say, east of 38° longitude) and by the mountains beyond Lake Sevan, approaching the Caspian Sea in the east, and southwards, as far as the western border of Lake Urmia, and by the Hakari Range in Kurdistan (say, west of 46° longitude).

The geographical designation 'Anatolia', which, strictly, defines the peninsula from the Syrian border with Turkey to the western coast of Asia Minor (say, west of 36° longitude) has been used throughout the book to describe the whole of modern Turkey.

Some years ago, I visited Erevan (capital of the Armenian SSR), where I had the honour of an audience with His Holiness Vasgen I, Katholicos of all the Armenians, in his palace at Echmiadzin, near Erevan. It was through his kindness that I made the acquaintance of Professor M. Hazratian, Director of the Armenian State Historical Museum. I had the privilege of accompanying him and other Armenian academics to the Urartian archaeological sites of Karmir Blur and Erebuni. At Erebuni, I was introduced to Professor K.L. Oganesian, Director of Excavations, who very kindly presented me with copies of his books from which, with his permission, I have reproduced some illustrations. I am indebted also to T.C. Khachaturian and S. Amyrian for their unstinting helpfulness during my stay at Erevan.

I am grateful to the late Dr R.D. Barnett for having read my manuscript when he was Keeper of Western Asiatic Antiquities, British Museum, as it then stood, and for his authoritative suggestions. I am obliged to the Rev. Dr V. Nersessian, Curator of Armenian Manuscripts in the Oriental Manuscripts Department, British Library, for reading the manuscript. He made a number of valuable suggestions, particularly on aspects of post-Urartian Armenia. I am happy to acknowledge the consistent encouragement given to me over many years by my friends Mr Richard Batstone,

3

BA (Oxon) and the late Miss Jean Hickling, FLA, formerly Librarian, Medical School, Middlesex Hospital, London. My sincere thanks are due to Professor J.M. Cook, Emeritus Professor, University of Bristol, who, having recently read my article on *Some Legendary Kings of Armenia* (JSAS, 1985), in the true spirit of a teacher kindly offered his valuable comments, which I have applied wherever relevant in this work.

I wish to express my sincere appreciation of the interest taken in my work by Miss Judith Bridle, LlB, Mr Alan Edenborough, Mr Edward Gulbekian, MSc, Dr Edda Osterhild, Mr M. Pachaian, the Rev. Anthony Smith, Dr Anne Whitehead and other supportive friends, to many to name individually.

Any weaknesses or errors in this work are entirely my responsibility.

Note

1. This spelling is not phonetically correct, but it is the spelling used by other writers on the subject of Urartu. I have, therefore, also used it for reference purposes. The phonetically correct spelling is Hovannessian.

Method of References

Example: CAH I²iv — *Cambridge Ancient History*, volume I, part 2, section iv, under the chapter bearing the title of the article from which the quotation or information is taken.

JRAS — *Journal of the Royal Asiatic Society*.

J.As — *Journal Asiatique*.

AS — *Anatolian Studies*, Journal of the British Institute of Archaeology at Ankara.

IRAQ — *Journal of the British School of Archaeology at Iraq*.

Prologue:
Some Milestones in the Ancient
History of the Near East

As the ancient history of the Near East is still little known to the general reader, who usually associates only classical Greece (fifth century BC) with 'ancient history', it might be useful to touch upon some of the most important events which together developed, in the course of some 3000 years (from the first literate societies), into the complex historical tapestry within which the history of the Kingdom of Ararat (Hebrew) or Urartu (Assyrian) unfolded. That kingdom had collapsed by the sixth century BC, 150 years before the golden age of Athens.

Sumer

In southern Mesopotamia, where the Rivers Euphrates and Tigris together flow into the Persian Gulf, a group of primitive settlements were established in the sixth millenium BC, on the rich silt soil deposited each year by the ebbing rivers after flooding. These early, pre-literate societies developed their pictograms into the cuneiform (or wedge-shaped) script (*c.* 3100 BC) which is associated with the first literate civilisation of Sumer. A region of southern Mesopotamia, Sumer comprised a number of independent city-states — Uruk (Biblical Erech), Eridu, Nippur, Kish, Ur, Lagash, Isin, Larsa.

Sumer's cuneiform script (the importance of which cannot be over-emphasised) and language were used throughout the Near East, and persisted for nearly 3000 years, down to the second century BC, among the educated classes and in temple liturgy, just as Latin was used by scholars and in churches throughout Europe in the Middle Ages. Cuneiform was adapted to the various languages of the Near East, including those of Assyria and Ararat/Urartu (just as the Greek alphabet, much later, was used for the various European languages). Bilingual words and phrases were prepared, as well as grammatical texts, for the study of Sumerian syntax. Examinations were held for trainee scribes or teachers, and successful candidates were cautioned against the pompousness and arrogance of the academic.

There is abundant evidence, that the Sumerians traded with the peoples of the north who could easily be reached along the natural trade routes of the two great rivers and their tributaries. A skilfully and artistically conceived Sumerian statuette of a now extinct breed of a bull, cast in copper (*c.* 2300 BC), said to have been found near Lake Van and now in the British Museum, is witness to Sumerian presence there (see Plate 1). Gudea, Sumerian Governor of Lagash (*c.* 2100 BC) imported gold dust from Armenia. Viticulture was already known in Armenia — where the vine is an indigenous plant — and Armenian wine was served at the princely tables of Babylonia. The height of artistic excellence achieved by Sumer is exemplified by the artefacts made of precious metals and rare stones excavated at the royal cemetery at Ur (*c.* 2800–2600 BC) by Sir Leonard Woolley in 1922–29. The tombs themselves illustrate Sumerian ingenuity in the early use of the arch and the dome. At Ur (and no doubt at other cities of early Sumer), the Sumerians seem to have been deeply preoccupied with the question of life after death. It appears they believed in some form of reincarnation, as suggested by the gruesome sacrifices of large numbers of attendants and animals to serve the king and queen in the hereafter. Ur reached the peak of its civilisation during the third dynasty (*c.* 2100 BC), when it was the capital city of Sumer. It was destroyed by Elam, but rose again as a commercial centre, with spacious houses. (The Jewish patriarch Abraham lived there during that last phase of its history (*c.* 1800 BC).)

Semites and Babylonians

It was difficult to cross the central and most extensive part of the Syrian desert: travellers, whether on the king's business or for trading purposes, used the 'fertile crescent' route, made up of the valleys of the Euphrates and Tigris, the Orontes and Jordan; the last two rivers flow conveniently parallel to the Palestine–Syrian coast giving easy access to the sea ports of Ugarit, Byblos, Sidon, Tyre and Gaza. Semite nomads from Arabia appeared in the Syrian desert in the fourth millenium BC or earlier, and during the following centuries. As nomads and marauders, they attacked the weak city-states along the rivers, where they established their own chieftainships, principalities and kingdoms, which in time would become rich and powerful. Good examples are the wealthy and extensive kingdom of Mari, the recently discovered city of Ebla, and the Assyrian cities in northern and the Babylonian cities in southern Mesopotamia.

It was the Semitic city of Akkad (or Agad), probably situated near the site of Babylon on the Euphrates, which produced the first warlord, Sargon I of Akkad (*c.* 2371–2316 BC). He was a great administrator and was able to build and maintain an empire. The significance of such an empire is that it gave cohesion to extensive territories, so that travel became free and safe within its borders, encouraging commercial enterprise and quickening the accumulation of cultural wealth. Under Sargon, the city-states expanded into a larger 'national' unit, which rose to imperial proportions. Northern Sumer was thenceforth called Akkad and the south and north together called Sumer-Akkad. Akkadian, with its adopted Sumerian cuneiform script, became the international language of the civilised Near East during the second millenium BC. It is now increasingly believed that much of the Sumerian (non-Semitic) vocabulary was adopted by the Semitic Akkadian.

Sargon's two great successors, his grandson Naram-Sin (*c.* 2291–2255 BC) and the Babylonian king, Hammurabi (1792–1750 BC), developed his legacy of military power and the administration of vast territories. The most important contribution of Hammurabi was the marshalling and codifying of the existing laws, so that 'the strong may not oppress the weak'. The Sumero–Babylonian cultural legacy was appropriated by Aryan nomads — the Kassites — who had infiltrated Babylonia and seized power when the opportunity came. They remained masters of central and southern Mesopotamia for 500 years (1595–1157 BC).

Egypt

By 3000 BC, Egypt too was a unified kingdom, stretching from the Nile Delta to the First Cataract and beyond. The rich silt-soil deposited by the Nile assured an abundance of grain, as well as other flora and fauna. Egypt became literate soon after Sumer, its hieroglyphics possibly inspired by immigrant Sumerian scribes. Trade in antiquity very often followed migration or conquest, and it has been suggested, because of certain similarities in their early dynastic periods, that Sumer and Egypt had somehow come into contact. It seems that Sumerian traders and others migrated to Egypt and settled in the Nile valley:

> either by way of the Red Sea and thence by land through one of the wadis [perhaps the Wadi Hammamat] to the Nile Valley, or by way of Syria and the isthmus of Suez to the Delta[1] ... It can hardly be without significance that two of the earliest specimens of engraved cylinders found in Egypt are indistinguishable in style and decoration from some Mesopotamian cylinders of the Jamdat Nasr period [*c.*3000 BC] and the most probable explanation seems to be that they were imported from that country.[2]

Indeed, Egypt might well have imported other art and craft works from Mesopotamia, which in those early days she herself was incapable of producing.

If two peoples, separated by extensive desert land and the sea, contrive to establish not only a passing, exploratory association, but a continuous, commercial and cultural relationship with one another, how much closer must have been the links between the infant Urarto–Hurrian chieftainships and their southern neighbours, the great Sumero-Babylonian, all-pervasive civilisations, connected, as they were, by land routes and navigable rivers. This must have had a direct or indirect influence on the political and cultural attitudes and traditions of Hurri or Khurri-Urartians.

Egypt had a powerful priesthood, closely associated with the king, and a well-defined hierarchy of nobles. Like Sumer, she too believed in the afterlife so the preservation of the body, the abode of the spirit, was considered to be of paramount importance. In the process of disembowelling and mummifying the body of a dead king, priests and philosophers would have learned a good deal about anatomy. The great pyramids too are witnesses to their substantial engineering and architectural knowledge. The first of these vast monuments, the resting place of the Egyptian monarchs, is Pharaoh Djoser's (*c.* 2680 BC) Stepped Pyramid at Saqqara. But there must have been many smaller, experimental pyramids, starting in the fourth millenium BC, before the building of that great pyramid could be undertaken, unless immigrant Sumerian architects introduced their ziggurat-building skills which the Egyptians quickly developed. The architect of Djoser's stepped pyramid, Imhotep, who appears also to have been a physician and a scholar, was greatly respected during his lifetime and worshipped as a god after his death. His is the earliest name in the world of scholarship that we know. It is to the credit of the ancient Egyptians that they appreciated his work and perpetuated his name.

Politically, Egypt appears to have been content to develop within the natural boundaries set by the Sinai and the Libyan deserts, and to expand southwards into Nubia. However, in the seventeenth century BC, Egypt was invaded by hordes of horse-riding and chariot-driving Indo-Aryan and Semitic nomads. These were the Hyksos ('rulers of foreign lands'), who settled in the Delta region of Egypt (1674–1547 BC) while the true Egyptian Pharoahs continued to rule what was left of their kingdom from Thebes in the south. After more than 100 years of Hyksos rule, Theban Egypt produced a dynasty of powerful warrior-Pharoahs who expelled the foreigners, and then went on to invade Asia in order to secure their borders against future invasions. Thus, we find Tuthmosis III (1504–1450 BC), one of a number of great leaders of the eighteenth dynasty, ruling an empire extending into southern Syria and fighting the distant Mitannians, cousins of the later Urartians (see below) in northern Mesopotamia. At that time, the Hittites (see below), on the western bank of the Euphrates adjoining Armenia, were re-establishing their political stability after a palace revolution in 1590 BC, in which the king had been murdered. Hittite forces, which had ravaged, sacked and plundered the great city of Babylon far to the south, had to be withdrawn to the homeland. The political vacuum thus created was filled by colonists from the new Hurrian kingdom of Mitanni, on the eastern side of the Euphrates. It was Mitannian help to the small Palestinian states in the south, against Tuthmosis's aggression, that prevented that energetic prince from snatching an easy victory there. He was held up for no less than 17 years by the small Canaanite and Amorite principalities and chieftainships who barred his northward progress. However, he came to terms with Mitanni, and his successors enjoyed the fruits yielded by a great Afro-Asian empire.

Of those successors, the most famous are Amunhotep III (whose chief consort was Queen Tiy) who married a Mitannian princess, possibly the beautiful Nefertiti; and his son, Amunhotep IV (better known as Akhenaten) who married another Mitannian princess, and, on his father's death, took Nefertiti as a second, but principal, wife. Nefertiti supported (indeed she might have instigated) Akhenaten in his rebellion against the priests of Amun. He transferred his capital from the ancient temple city of Thebes to a new city which he called Akhet-Aten on the site of modern Tell el-Amarna where he established and honoured the monotheistic cult of the sun god, Aten. Akhen-Aten's Egypt is the first known monotheistic state. The Jews were at that time still in Egypt (but, since the departure of the Hyksos, only as 'hewers of wood and drawers of water'), and may well have been inspired by Akhen-Aten's monotheistic ideal. He secularised the personality of the Pharaoh, closed the temples of Amun, and curbed the power of the priests. Preoccupied with religious reform and the promotion of cultural activities, he neglected affairs of state and by the end of his reign (*c.* 1350 BC) Egyptian dominance abroad had seriously declined. After his death, the Amun priests re-established their power and did their best to obliterate the memory of Akhenaten and Nefertiti.

Amunhotep III and Akhenaten received many letters and despatches in cuneiform from King Tushratta of Mitanni (1300–1265 BC), father-in-law of the two Pharaohs. They are among the priceless Amarna tablets, found in 1887 on the site of Akhet-Aten, which are now distributed between the national museums in London, Berlin and Cairo. Tushratta's letters to his sons-in-law are expressed in the warmest terms, and the sincerity which becomes evident on reading them bridges the immense 3400 years time span between ancient Egypt and our own era.

The importance of Egypto–Mitannian relationships *vis-à-vis* Urartu is relevant to Urartu's cultural inheritance, to which reference is made below.

Assyria

The kingdom of Semitic Assyria, which never ceased to be Urartu's implacable enemy, was named after its founder-city, Ashur. This was also the name of the supreme Assyrian god. It is possible that its earliest rulers, during the last centuries of the third millenium BC, were the Indo-Aryan Mitannians. But the true founders of Assyrian power, the western Semites, overwhelmed northern Iraq and the southern regions early in the second millenium BC[3]. The Assyrian king-lists open after 2000 BC, with two Semitic names and a record of the building of temples in the city of Ashur for the gods Ashur and Adad and the goddess Ishtar. From Ashur, King Shamshi-Adad I (1814–1782 BC), an outlaw and a usurper, with the assistance of his two sons, annexed the great commercial city-state of Mari and its tribute-paying Mediterranean ports as far as Lebanon, establishing what

Table P.1: Approximate dates of the reigns of the kings of Mitanni, Egypt and Khatti

Mitanni	Egypt	Khatti
Shaushatar 1450-1440		
	Amunhotep II 1450-1425	
Artatama 1440-1420		
	Tuthmosis IV 1425-1415	
Shutarna 1420-1395	Amunhotep III 1415-1380	Khattusil I 1410-1385
Artashumara 1395-1385		
	Amunhotep IV	
	(Akhenaten) 1380-1365	
Tushratta 1385-1365		
		Shuppiluliuma 1385-1345
Mattiuaza 1365-1345		Mursil 1345-1320

Figure P.1: Family trees and marriages between the royal houses

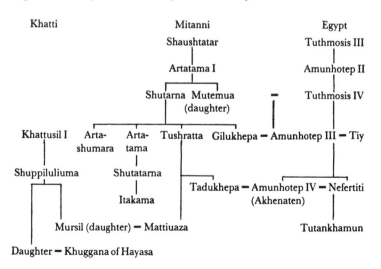

11

we now recognise as the first Assyrian empire. He was, however, troubled not only by the petty Hurrian principalities to the east of his kingdom south-west of Lake Urmia (western Urmia and northwards were the homelands of Hurrian Urartu), but also by the mighty King Hammurabi of Babylonia, who eventually took the powerful city of Mari (*c.* 1760 BC) and destroyed it, thus curbing Assyrian ambitions. It was not until the fourteenth century BC that a native Assyrian warrior, Ashur-uballit I (1365–1330 BC), once more seized the Assyrian throne from Mitanni and successfully conspired not only to overthrow the Mitannian yoke but, with the aid of a small northern ally in the Upper Tigris valley, called Alshe, divided the land of Mitanni between the two. Thus, Ashur-uballit ended Mitannian independence. His task was made easier by an earlier Hittite invasion of Mitanni and Hittite-inspired Mitannian palace intrigues, which had divided and weakened that kingdom — a ripe fruit, which ultimately fell into what became the capacious lap of Assyria. Ashur-uballit also forced the powerful Babylonian king, Burnaburiash (who had only recently complained to Egypt about Assyria's overmighty ways) to accept his daughter in marriage to the Babylonian crown prince. In time, the Assyrian had the satisfaction of witnessing the installation of his grandson on the Babylonian throne. Thenceforth, except during two periods of relative decline Assyrian might savagely dominated the Mesopotamian and Syrian political and military scene (though not the Anatolian, where Assyria was, after the tenth century, intimidated by the powerful kings of Urartu), until its own downfall and annihilation in 612 BC at the hands of the allied Medes and Babylonians.

The Kingdom of Mitanni

The warriors who overran eastern Anatolia and northern Mesopotamia in their horse-drawn chariots after 2300 BC, are known as Hurrians or Hurri — the Biblical Horites (Gen. XIV.6, XXXVI.20). They appeared prior to the horde which rode westwards later identified as the Indo-Aryan Khatti or the Hittites.[4] The first Hurrian tablet — and still the most significant one — was found among the Mitanni letters at Amarna. Their first settlement in the Middle East appears to have been in the hilly country south of the Caucasus, between Lakes Van and Urmia, where, much later (perhaps *c.* 1350 BC) the nucleus of the

Kingdom of Urartu was forged from a group of Hurrian chieftain-ships. The main body of the Hurrian invaders spread over the area between the River Euphrates and the Caspian Sea, later known as Armenia. But the ubiquitous Hurri appear in many places. There were Hurrians within the Hittite kingdom in central Anatolia; Hurrian names appear in the texts of the third dynasty of Ur (*c.* 2100 BC)[5]; in the time of the Akkadian kings (*c.* 2371–2230) the ruling class of Urkish (near modern Diarbekir, Turkey) was Hurrian[6]; the Hurrian Turrukians on the eastern bank of the River Tigris appear to have been at war both with Assyria's Shamshi-Adad (1813–1781 BC) and Hammurabi of Babylonia (1792–1750).[7] It is also possible that the Hyksos were partly of Hurrian stock. The Urartians, too, were Hurrians. They are first mentioned in 1275 BC in an Assyrian tablet, which implies a development period of many decades, or even centuries, before 1275 BC, when they dared to confront mighty Assyria. During the course of their forays into foreign lands and their conquests, the Hurrians transmitted Babylonian culture to the Hittites and indirectly to Greece, whence it travelled to Italy and Western Europe.

The first, and very important stronghold of Hurrian civilis-ation is known as the Kingdom of Mitanni (the Hurri-Mitan-nians). The Mitanni were an Aryan ruling aristocracy over the Hurrian settlments, and the names of Mitannian gods, such as Mitra, Varuna and Indra of the Hindu Rigveda, indicate their Oriental origin. That kingdom appeared in the sixteenth century BC out of a confederacy of small Hurrian principalities or chief-tainships in northern Mesopotamia. It included the city of Nuzi, as seen on Nuzi pottery (where documents describe certain social and religious traditions which are reflected in Hebrew legends, recorded in the Old Testament) and the rich grain-growing valleys of the rivers Balikh and Khabur, tributaries of the Euphrates. The kingdom seems to have extended north and north-east towards the River Arsanias (Murad su)[8] and Lake Van, adjoining and probably overlapping the lands of the later Hurrian kingdom of Ararat (Jer. LI.27 or Urartu) in Armenia. Mitannian presence in Armenia blocked any territorial ambitions east of the Euphrates that later Hittite rulers might have had.

Taking advantage of the collapse of Hammurabi's empire in the later part of the sixteenth century, which created a vacuum in northern Syria, the Mitannian warlords crossed the Euphrates, subjugated several principalities there, and exercised considerable political influence over the Amorites and the Canaanites in the south. That is probably the reason for the prolonged, 17-year campaign of the great warrior-Pharaoh Tuthmosis III in Palestine, before he could subdue that region (in *c.* 1465 BC) and claim victory over the Mitannian forces. An understanding seems to have been reached by the two powers to respect each other's territories, particularly as both countries were well aware of the threat of the aggressive Hittites in the north. Apart from

> Hurri-Mitannian political influence in Ugarit, in Qatna and indirectly, in Palestine, an even greater influence can be detected in northern Iraq [and Urartu, since north-east Mitanni overlapped the frontiers of the later Kingdom of Urartu], and there is reason to believe that all the kings of Ashur who reigned between 1500–1360 BC were the vassals of the King of Mitanni: when one of them dared to revolt, the Mitannian king Shaushatar [*c.* 1500 BC] we are told, plundered Ashur and took to his own capital, Washukkanni, 'a door of silver and gold'[9].

The mutual respect between Egypt and Mitanni was expressed by the successors of Tuthmosis III who married Mitannian princesses. 'Seven times' did Tuthmosis IV (1413–1405 BC) ask Artatama I of Mitanni for the hand of his daughter. It was a love match, for she became the Pharaoh's chief wife and his people called her Mute-mua, 'Mother-of-the-Sun'[10]. Their first-born and heir to the throne was named Amunhotep (the third of that name), and his reign (*c.* 1405–1367 BC) was among the most brilliant in Egyptian history.

An auspicious — if unprecedented — event, that marriage of an Egyptian king to a foreign princess was followed by the union of Tuthmosis's two successors with other Mitannian princesses, Gilu-Khepa and Tadu-Khepa[11], with the Pharaohs Amunhotep III (grandson of Artatama of Mitanni) and Amunhotep IV (Akhenaten), respectively (1367–1350). Princess Gilu-Khepa's arrival at the Egyptian court with 317 Mitannian maidens in her retinue was commemorated on a large scarab, copies of which have been found in Palestine and elsewhere. Such important events were widely publicised throughout the Egyptian empire.[12] It is said that after the death of Amunhotep III, his son Akhenaten (Akhen-Aten) married Gilu-Khepa, the youngest member of his father's large harem. As a reason for that second

14

marriage, it is suggested that Gilu-Khepa was none other than the beautiful, irresistible, and still very young, Nefertiti.

These demonstrations of friendship between Egypt and Mitanni were in addition to the extensive trade between the two kingdoms. Mitanni straddled the important 'fertile crescent' trade route in the north and it also controlled the tribute-paying port of Alalakh and, indirectly, the great port of Ugarit (Ras Shamra). Both ports traded regularly with Egypt across the Levantine Sea, as with other lands, and each influenced the other. Minoan and Egyptian influence can be detected in the design and colouring of pottery at Alalakh, which depicts papyrus and lotus stems. Vases, standing on slender feet, are more elegant than any others produced until that point in the Near East. Mitannian kings are represented in copper statuettes, wearing a crown and broad-bordered cloak, typical of the Hurri-Mitanni region. Most interesting of all, according to Egyptian accounts, Mitanni traded in willow, ash and hornbeam, from the Amanus mountains, which they shipped to Egypt where the timber was used in the construction of light chariots.

Ugarit was perhaps the greatest of the first international ports. Because of its geographical position, it held an effective monopoly as an entrepôt between Syria and the hinterland and the Aegean. Its busy quays must have teemed with merchants and traders, sailors and adventurers from Egypt, Crete, Cyprus, Rhodes, Samos and Mycenae. Importers in Alalakh and Ugarit no doubt purchased Mycenaean pottery through the entrepôt commercial centres of Rhodes and Cyprus for distribution in their own markets. Indeed, it seems that certain Mycenaean-type pottery was made in Cyprus for export to Syria and Palestine.

These cosmopolitan artistic and commercial factors are of paramount importance as influences on the development of the, as yet, nascent kingdom of Urartu, contemporary with, and probably to some extent involved in the commercial transactions of its great neighbours, particularly in those of its Hurri-Mitannian kinsmen. By that time, from small beginnings, Hurrian Urartu had grown to be important enough to be mentioned by name on the Assyrian King Shalmaneser I's tablet as a tribute-paying principality (or even, perhaps, kingdom) which rebelled against him in 1275 BC, the very year in which Mitanni suffered a fatal defeat at the hands of Assyria. Mitanni never recovered.

The Hittites

In *c.* 2000 BC a horde of horseriding nomadic Aryans appeared in Anatolia from the southern foothills of the Caucasus. Finding that area already occupied by another equally war-like tribe of Aryans — the Hurrians or Hurri — they continued to ravage their way westwards until they reached the Assyrian trading stations in Cappadocia. These migrants later became known as the Khatti or the Hittites, after the name of the indigenous people whose land they seized, and over whom they ruled. They seem to have infiltrated, rather than invaded these regions 'leading by degrees to a monopoly of political power — like that of the Semitic Akkadians in the Sumerian world of Mesopotamia, or later the Kassites in Babylonia'.[13] The capital, Hattusa (Boghaz Köy), was built within the bend of the River Halys (Kizil Irmak) in central Anatolia among the uplands, as befitted the rulers of a virile race of warrior-farmers and horse breeders. It was the centre of Hittite civilisation and the ancient religious and cultural traditions of its people were perpetuated within its walls: 'Its ruined palaces and temples, monumental sculptures and the four-mile circuit of its ponderously constructed walls cannot fail to leave one with the conviction that this city has been the cradle and home of a great imperial people.'[14] It was a great fortress-refuge and the most important religious centre of the kingdom, where large numbers of people and domestic animals could shelter in time of war.

Unlike some ancient civilisations, the Great King of the Hatti or Khatti at Hattusas was not deified in his lifetime. He was the high-priest of the sun-goddess Arinna and the storm-god Teshub.

> The Sun-goddess Arinna was exalted as 'Queen of the Land of Hatti, Queen of Heaven and Earth, mistress of the kings and queens of the Land of Hatti, directing the government of the King and Queen of Hatti'. She became the supreme patroness of the Hittite state and monarchy, and the king always turned first to her for aid in battle or in time of national danger.[15]

The eunuch priesthood, who were also votaries of the fertility goddesses, sacrificed their virility to them. The lesser native kings of the smaller centres which had developed around local shrines, were probably organised as a confederacy owing allegiance to

Hattusas. The newcomers were ultimately invaders, and although they adopted for themselves the name by which the region they occupied was originally known, they were a ruling aristocracy and their national assembly, the *pankush*, excluded the indigenous Anatolians. However, they do not appear to have abused their power. On the contrary, they seem to have been a liberal-minded class, 'preferring diplomacy as an alternative to military action, and their humane treatment of their enemies in the event of victory. As an example of the former, one might cite their predilection for arranging royal marriages.'[16]

Such a marriage is found in the royal chronicles at the zenith of Hittite power during the reign of the greatest of the Hittite monarchs, King Shuppiluliumash (1375–1335 BC). The annals record the marriage of the Hittite king's sister to King Khuggana of the powerful neighbouring country Hayasa-Azzi, east of Khatti. A letter from the Hittite king instructs his brother-in-law in etiquette, 'since', he writes amiably, 'your country is not very civilised'[17]. (According to an increasing number of scholars, Hayasa-Azzi was, partly at least, the original home of the Armenians [see Chapter 20].)

There must have been a good deal of trade between the Hittites and their eastern neighbours, especially with Hayasa-Azzi. The latter's territory extended eastwards, perhaps as far as Mount Ararat,[18] and so must have been rich in mineral resources including gold, silver, lead, iron, and copper and tin, the constituents of bronze (92 per cent copper: 8 per cent tin). Hittite merchants also traded with their western neighbours, the Luwian and Palaic-speaking peoples. Also, we are told, incidentally in a religious text, that 'copper was brought from Alasiya (that is, Cyprus) which contained the richest copper mines in the ancient world'.[19] Cyprus became a Hittite 'protectorate' (c. 1350 BC) and a colony in the thirteenth century BC for reasons of political and commercial expediency, for at that time, Shalmaneser I of Assyria destroyed Mitanni and crossed northern Syria, thus cutting off Hittite land communications with its important Syrian seaport colony of Ugarit, inherited from Mitanni. Alashiya (or Cyprus) was subsequently used by Hattusa as a route to and from Syria, Palestine, Crete and Egypt. Rebellions against the Hattusa erupted from time to time, but they were put down. The last one was probably that which took place towards the end of the thirteenth century BC, recorded in the recently discovered Boghaz Köy documents, which refer to a sea battle between the

Hittite and Alashiya fleets, when all Alashiya's ships went down in flames.

Interactions between the countries of western Armenia and the Hittite empire no doubt sowed the seeds of Hittite culture deep into the Hurrian countries to the east of Khatti, which later became part of the Kingdom of Urartu and must have had considerable influence upon the latter's development. As this is important to the history of Urartu as a whole, it should also be noted that the Hittite civilisation was itself greatly influenced by traders, travellers, settlers and military incursions into neighbouring countries by the enlightened and most ancient civilisations of Babylonia and Egypt, as well as by the contributions of Crete and the peoples of the great trading maritime city-states of the Levant, together constituting an inextricable webb of social, political and religious institutions, manners and mores, artistry and craftsmanship whose main (though not exclusive) roots were to be found in Sumer and Egypt.

The fourteenth century BC is a copiously documented period. Hittite, Assyrian and Babylonian annals, treaties, inscriptions and chronicles are found in abundance, and,

> above all, the three hundred letters written by the kings of Western Asia, great or small, to Amenophis (Amunhotep) III and IV and found at el-Amarna in Egypt, throw on these years of armed conflicts and subtle diplomatic moves the most welcome light. Moreover, these documents bring out with particular clarity some of the most powerful or fascinating personalities of the ancient Orient: Amenophis IV (Akhenaten), the mystic pharaoh more interested in religion than in politics; Kurigalzu II, the only Kassite king who could pose as a conqueror; Ashur-uballit, the shrewd prince who liberated Assyria and turned it again into a great nation; and surpassing them all in merit, the energetic Hittite monarch who imposed his mark upon the whole period: Shuppiluliumas.[20]

The Amarna letters of the Mitannian king Tushrata, to his Egyptian sons-in-law, Amunhotep III and IV, have already been mentioned.

When in 1372 BC Shuppiluliumash, an unknown commoner, seized the Hittite throne, he upset the balance of political power in the Near East, where the mighty, almost avuncular Egyptian Pharaohs (particularly Amunhotep III and IV) were closely connected by marriage and their gold with the two most powerful kingdoms of the time, those of Mitanni and the Kassites. They were also on good terms with everybody else. Even the Assyrians — no doubt with the permission of their overlords, the Mitannians — sent ambassadors to the court of Thebes. This harmony was upset irreparably when Shuppiluliumash invaded Mitanni from the north, plundered the capital, Washukkanni, crossed the Euphrates into Syria, and took Aleppo. He then fanned the flames of rivalry, jealousy and envy between the minor kings of the Syrian city-states, such as Ugarit and Alalakh, all of them either Mitannian or Egyptian colonies, so that it was impossible for them to unite in force against him. When in the south, he finally seized the key city of Kadesh, he came face to face with Egypt's might. The Amarna tablets are full of cries for help from the various colonial kinglets, Egyptian governors, generals and allies — cries for reinforcements, warnings of defections and uprisings and of the approach of enemies; all of which were unheeded by Amunhotep III, probably because he was too old and ailing, and by his impractical and indolent successor, Akhenaten (Amunhotep IV) who seemed not to care about Egyptian power and possessions in Syria, although apart from Syria, he continued his predecessor's foreign policy.

Akhenaten had married 'the youngest of his father's Mitannian wives, Tadu-Hepa — perhaps the charming Nefertiti — and remained on the best of possible terms with his contemporary, the Kassite-Babylonian Burnaburiash II (1375–1347 BC)[21], one of whose daughters he also married. As to Shuppiluliumash, having entrenched himself in Syria, broken Mitannian power and defied Egypt, he returned to his native land, where he was to remain for 20 years occupied with political issues and military tasks.

The texts found in the royal archives of the Hittite capital city, on the archaeological site of Boghaz Köy, might be described as the Hittite counterpart of the Egyptian Amarna tablets. They have enabled archaeologists to reconstruct the political and social organisation of the Hittite empire in the reign of King Shuppiluliumash, who opened the inscriptions with an account of his own political and military exploits. After the death of Pharaoh Amunhotep III (1367 BC), Hittite power under Shuppiluliumash in the Near East was unchallengeable. By the end of his reign, the frontiers of his empire had reached the southern coast of Asia Minor, Cilicia had been taken over, and the key city of Carchemish as well as Aleppo and the whole of northern Syria occupied.

Mitanni was still left as a tempting prize, but the Hittite king was too astute to risk a war with a still powerful and prestigious country. Yet, he was aware of an alert Assyria awaiting an opportunity to overthrow the Mitannian yoke, to invade and to destroy Aryan Mitanni and to replace it with its own Semitic power as far north as the foothills of the Taurus mountains, the frontiers of his own kingdom. Instead, he had recourse to intrigue. He enjoyed the friendship of no other than the Mitannian King Tushratta's brother, who plotted with him to depose or murder Tushratta, in favour of a prince with a more friendly disposition towards Khatti. In the end, Shuppiluliumash cleverly achieved his purpose, occupying Naharin (northern Syria), without actually going to war. Tushratta was murdered by his own son, Mattiuaza, and during the palace revolution that followed, Shuppiluliumash placed him, a pro-Hittite prince, on the Mitannian throne as a tribute-paying puppet of the Hittite king, and sealed the alliance by giving him one of his daughters in marriage.

Less than 100 years later, Mitanni, though supported by a Hittite army, succumbed to resurgent Assyrian military power under Shalmaneser I (1275–1245 BC) who built the city of Kalhu as his capital. The rebellious Mitannian king, Shattuara II, was decisively defeated and, although he himself escaped, 14,400 of his people were taken prisoner and blinded.[22] His cities and his palace were destroyed, his treasures were carried away, and the gold and silver doors, plundered by Mitanni from Ashur 200 years earlier, were restored to their original home.[23] Thus was Mitanni annihilated after 300 years of military domination of upper Mesopotamia, and Assyria acquired the trade routes leading to the Syrian and Anatolian Mediterranean ports, the wealth of the thriving cities, and the produce of extensive and fertile lands. The foundations of the second Assyrian empire had been laid.[24]

As we shall see later, King Shattuara, together with a following of a considerable force of the Mitannian aristocracy, their households, servants and retainers, escaped into neighbouring Urartu, to join their Hurrian kith and kin in their wars against Assyria, the common enemy. It is surely more than a coincidence that the Urartian rebellion against Assyria is recorded as having taken place at just this time (*c.* 1275 BC). In such a situation, the Mitannians would have introduced into Urartu their ancient and highly developed culture and social and political institutions.

After 1200 BC no more information is available from Hittite

sources. This coincides with great movements of peoples by land and sea whose territories had been (or were to become) certain countries and island states in the eastern Mediterranean. The end of the thirteenth century BC saw the close of the Bronze Age and the inception of the Iron Age — one of the watersheds of ancient history. The life-style of the iron-using, horse-riding Aryans was increasingly imposed upon, or adopted by, the more ancient and conservative peoples of Mesopotamia and the Levant. It was the time of the Trojan Wars, of the Etruscan migration to Italy, of Libyan and Philistine aggression against Egypt, of Philistine settlement in Palestine, and the appearance of the Greek provinces and city-states along the western coast of Asia Minor.

The last mentioned of these movements seems to have been caused mainly by the appearance of the Dorians, a Greek-speaking tribe, who blazed their way through the Balkan peninsula, burning and pillaging, and eventually reaching the Peloponnesus where they met the Mycenaeans, whom they uprooted, dispersed or dominated. This gives us the measure of Dorian savagery, for the Mycenaeans (Homer's Achaeans) were themselves, in many respects, very barbaric. Other Greeks from the mainland migrated to the Asia Minor littoral and became known as the Ionians, who founded the city-states south of Smyrna, such as Miletus and Ephesus; and the Aeolians, who occupied the coastal region north of Smyrna including, at first, Smyrna itself.

Another Aryan people, the Phrygians, who had come from Illyria, where they were known as Bryges and had lived in 'fenced cities' in Thrace, were forced across the Hellespont by other Illyrians from their original homeland in what is now Yugoslavia. The Phrygians settled for a time in the vicinity of the River Sangarius and subsequently encountered the forces of the Hittite kingdom. They appear to have swarmed upon the riches of Hattusa and expelled the Hittites from their homelands, which they themselves appropriated. Thenceforth, their Midas kings ruled in central Anatolia, west of the Euphrates (Firat) for 500 years. The Assyrians referred to them as 'Mushki' (see Chapter 20). According to Herodotus (VII.73), the Armenians were one of the Phrygian tribes. There appears to be some evidence that they settled in Tabal with its main city of Togharma, on the west bank of the Euphrates. The refugee Hittites re-established themselves in a group of neo-Hittite city-states in northern Syria, of which the most important was Carchemish, which dominated the important crossing-point of the Euphrates.

The peoples of central Anatolia

surviving the collapse of the Hittite Empire and the blows of the Land and Sea Raiders, their kings made terms with the immigrant Phrygians and other tribes, stood firm on the Taurus and Amanus line, and succeeded in passing to the West the tradition of Anatolian arts and culture until they were successively pressed back, then finally defeated, destroyed and obliterated by the Assyrians, whose custom, as was later said of the Romans, was 'to make a desert and call it peace'.[25]

Notes

1. L.E.S. Edwards, 'The Early Dynastic Period in Egypt', CAH I².vi, p.44.
2. Ibid., p.42.
3. Georges Roux, *Ancient Iraq* (George Allen & Unwin, 1964; Pelican, 2nd edn, 1980), pp. 177, 239.
4. W.F. Albright, 'The Amarna Letters from Palestine', CAH II².iii. p.110 'There can be little doubt that they [the Indo-Aryans] were bracketed in Hebrew tradition with the Hurrians [Horites]. According to the Septuagint, the prince of Shechem (who was also called 'father of Shechem') and the Canaanites of Gibeon were also Horites. Similarly the Boğazköy texts call both Indo-Aryans and Hurrians by the latter name. Evidently the Indo-Aryans migrated into the south-western Asia in such small numbers that they became submerged in the Hurrian mass, in spite of their obvious pride of family and their preservation of Indo-Aryan names as a token of nobility.' For the character of the Urartian language see E.A. Speiser, *Introduction to Hurrian (Ann.A.S.O.R.20)* (New Haven, 1941); J. Friedrich, *Einführung ins Urartaische* (MVAG 37,3) (Leipzig, 1933).
5. Margaret S. Drower, 'Syria *c.* 1550–1400 BC', CAH II².i. p. 417.
6. Ibid.
7. J.R. Kupper, 'Northern Mesopotamia and Syria', CAH II¹.iv. p.22.
8. A. Goetze, 'Struggle for the Domination of Syria', CAH II².i.
9. Roux, *op. cit.*, p. 236.
10. H.R. Hall, *Ancient History of the Near East* (Methuen, 1963).
11. It is interesting that the names of both princesses end with the name of the Hurrian goddess Hepa, Khepa or Kheba, just as those of the Pharaohs sometimes begin and sometimes end with the name of their chief god, Amun, as in Amun-hotep, Akhen-Aten, Tutan(kh)amun. In Babylon a number of kings appended Marduk, their chief god's name, to theirs (Marduk-zakir-shumi); as did some Assyrian kings (Ashur-nasirpal, Ashur-banipal).

12. Margaret S. Drower, 'Syria *c.* 1550–1400 BC' CAH II¹.iv.

13. Seton Lloyd, *Early Highland Peoples of Anatolia* (Thames & Hudson, 1967), pp. 58-9.

14. Ibid.

15. O.R. Gurney, *The Hittites* (Pelican, 1976), p.139.

16. Lloyd, *op. cit.* pp.68-9.

17. Nicolas Adontz, *Histoire d'Arménie* (Paris, 1946), p.29.

18. James Mellaart, 'Anatolian Trade, Geography and Culture', AS XVIII.

19. Gurney, *op. cit.*, p.86.

20. Roux, *op. cit.*, pp. 237, 238.

21. Ibid.

22. J.M. Munn-Rankin, 'Assyrian Military Power, 1300–1200 BC', CAH II².ii.

23. Ibid.

24. Ibid.

25. R.D. Barnett, 'Phrygia and the Peoples of Anatolia in the Iron Age', CAH II².xxx. p. 442.

Part One:
The Kingdom of Urartu

1

The Land of Armenia

The Kingdom of Ararat (as in Hebrew tradition — Genesis VIII.4; Jeremiah L1.27), Urartu (as known to the Assyrians) or Biaini or Biainili (as the natives called their country), was situated to the north and the south-east of Lake Van.[1] The fusion by conquest or treaty of a number of Hurrian chieftainships (see Chapter 2) had produced, by the thirteenth century BC, a powerful kingdom which, after the tenth century BC, under a succession of vigorous kings, expanded and occupied the region between the Upper Euphrates in the west and the Caspian Sea in the east (c. 46° longitude), the Caucasus mountains in the north and the Taurus Range in the south. Since c. 600 BC when the Armenians, a branch of the great Indo-European linguistic people, succeeded the Urartians, that area has been described as Armenia. I must emphasise, however, that it is thus described as a geographical, not a political region. Armenia's political extent fluctuated enormously over a period of some 2000 years, down to the fifteenth century AD, subject to the vicissitudes of war and peace. After that, in spite of 500 years of Turkish occupation, the geographical area defined above continued to be called Armenia, just as, for example, Poland, though occupied in turn by Germans or Russians for centuries, has sustained its geographical and, like Armenia, its ethnic and linguistic identity.

The land of Armenia, then, is situated largely on an extensive plateau, surrounded by high mountains, well watered by rivers which perpetuate its natural fertility. The legendary Mount Ararat dominates the valley of the River Araxes, and its majestic mass overshadows the city of Erevan, capital of the modern Soviet Socialist Republic of Armenia, a northern remnant of the mighty empire of Urartu and its Armenian successors. Further south tower the volcanic massifs of Aladagh, Süpandagh and Hakkari Hills, encircling Lake Van. A series of escarpments extend the massif southwards into the Mesopotamian steppes, whereas to the west, the massif remains consistently high, as far as the Dersin, and some of the highest and most inaccessible peaks in the world are to be found there. The massif is the watershed which feeds the great Euphrates and Tigris, flowing southwards into the Persian Gulf, and the Araxes and Kura which empty into the Caspian Sea. South-eastwards, this mountainous land-system is broken by the extensive Lake Urmia, and then continues through Ustan Cheharum and the wild mountains of Kurdistan (the watershed of the Greater and Lesser Zab rivers, tributaries of the Tigris) to join the Zagros mountains, the protective eastern wall behind which the early civilisations of the 'Fertile Crescent' developed.

The severe Armenian winters are fortunately followed by hot summers which help the rapid growth of vegetation (barley grows as far as, and beyond, the 6500 ft tree-line). There are excellent mountain pastures and extensive fertile valleys. Agriculture was always one of the main activities of the Armenian people, the valleys yielding their abundant crops of wheat, barley, millet, rye, sesame and flax, as well as vines. The uplands encouraged the breeding of sheep, goats and cattle, and the region was famous for its fine horses. Dairy farming was an occupation of the summer months.

Agriculture, then, appears to have been among the principal sources of state revenue. The rich land, with its great forests, generous mineral deposits and an invigorating climate, coupled with the fact that it lay astride the trade routes between Further Asia and western Anatolia and the Mediterranean, was always a tempting prize for the ambitious kings of the south and the west, as well as for the barbarians of the north and the east. The rulers of Armenia from its earliest Urartian period (*c.* 1400 BC) down to the fifteenth century AD had to be powerful enough in battle to withstand the hostile pressures on their borders; also, they had to possess above-average organising skill and considerable aptitude in the art of diplomacy to control the petty chiefs and princes in the many valleys and inaccessible mountain strongholds of their country, and to bring them and their warrior peoples within the hegemony of the kingdom. They were greatly assisted in this task by the east–west aspect of the Armenian Alps and the Taurus Range, which prevented an easy penetration of enemies from the south and the north. However, the same geographical features offered convenient routes not only to traders and their caravans, but also to invaders, particularly from the east and the west. Another important geographical factor which determined the country's long political and cultural history is that since it is one of the important Eurasian crossroads, it is intimately interwoven with those of its changing neighbours.

Some Sources

A.H. Sayce, 'The Kingdom of Van (Urartu)', CAH III.i. 'Biainas or Bianas, "the town of Bia", written Byana by Ptolemy, is now pronounced Van.'

R.N. Frye, *The Heritage of Persia* (Weidenfeld & Nicolson, 1965). 'The term Urartu is widespread but various forms of the name cause problems. It is found in several places in the Bible as Ararat, and in the Qumran "Dead Sea" texts as *(h)urat-*, further in the Babylonian version of the Behistun inscription as Urashtu (where Old Persian and Elamite have Armenia), in Armenian as Airarat, and in Herodotus (III.94 and VII.79) as Alarodi. The Urartians, in their almost four hundred preserved inscriptions, called their entire country Biainili, probably an ancient indigenous term.'

Urartians are referred to by Xenophon (IV.3, V.5) as Chaldaeans. The spelling here should be *Chaldians* — worshippers of the god Chaldi or Khaldi — to avoid confusion with Chaldaea, a province of Babylonia. 'As early as the sixteenth or seventeenth century BC, the Babylonians knew of the Armenian highlands as Urdhu, probably the contracted form of Urardhu.' For my source of this last statement, see note 2, Chapter 3.

As to the areas which have been called the derivative 'Urartu' or Nairi, Dr R.D. Barnett 'Urartu' (CAH III¹) writes: 'It is to the south-west of Lake Urmia that we find the most archaic portion of the Urartian kingdom or confederacy, the kingdom of Musasir' (p. 339). 'The site of Musasir has now been located with maximum plausibility at Mudjesir, eighteen kilometres north of Rowanduz, a little west of Topzawa' (p. 339). 'Was there a single tribe, one among eight closely related tribes or 'lands', named Uruatri or Urartu, whose name the Assyrians seized on in the early thirteenth century (it is on a stele of Shalmaneser I (1275 BC) that 'Uruatri' is first mentioned) and singled out to designate all? ... only one thing however is certain. The Urartians never speak of themselves as 'the people of Urartu' or use the term at all; when their inscriptions first begin some years later, they use either the term Nairi, or the name Bianili. For the Assyrians on the other hand, henceforth the 'Nairi lands' and Urartu become synonymous and interchangeable.' Earlier on the same page, Barnett refers to a text of Assyria's king Adad-nirari II (911–891 BC) which 'is significant as providing the first occasion that Nairi and

Ur(u)atri, later Urartu, are mentioned together (as is frequent later) ...
and it certainly seems to show that the original homeland of the people
... was well to the south-east of Lake Van, an area from which they seem
to have moved to concentrate around the more easily defensible area of
the lake itself.'

2

The 'Lost' Kingdom of Urartu

The existence of Urartu (the pre-Armenian, pre 600 BC civilisation) was unknown, a 'lost' civilisation, until 1823, when a French scholar, Jean Saint-Martin, chanced upon a passage in the *History of Armenia* by the fifth century AD Armenian historian, Moses of Khoren (Movses Khorenats'i)[1], which aroused his curiosity. It tells the well-known Armenian legend of the unrequited love of Queen Shamiram (the Semiramis of Greek legend)[2] for Ara the Beautiful, a legendary king of Armenia. Her pride wounded, Shamiram went to war against Armenia, but in spite of strict orders to her warriors not to harm him, a stray arrow killed Ara. The distraught queen decided to remain in Armenia, the land of her hero. The story continues colourfully:

> After these events, Shamiram remained but a short time on the Plain of Armenia, which is called, after Ara, 'Ararat'. She travelled southwards, while it was still summer, journeying leisurely through the valleys and the flowering countryside. Impressed by the scenery around her, the purity of the air, the limpid springs which gushed out everywhere in abundance, and the gentle murmur of the rivers, she said: 'In this delightful land, where the climate is so temperate and the water so pure, a city shall be built, our royal residence in Armenia, where we shall spend one quarter part of the year; the remaining months, consisting of the colder seasons, we shall pass in our city of Nineveh.' Searching carefully for a suitable site, Shamiram came upon a valley as she approached it from the east; its western extremity skirted the shores of the great salt-lake Van, where she observed an oblong-shaped mountain, its northern slopes gently falling towards the valleys, while the

southern, cliff-like face rose sheer to a high peak, pointing towards the sky. Not far to the south, a flat valley bordered upon the eastern side of the mountain, and extended towards the shores of the Lake, where it broadened out like a gorge. Across this land of marvels, crystal-clear waters tumbled down the mountain sides into the valleys and ravines below and united at the broad base of the mountain to form a great river. To the east of that smiling mountain-side, there was a smaller hill. Here, the energetic, sensual Queen Shamiram, inspired by the beauty of the region, decided to build her city. She caused 12,000 workmen and 6,000 skilled craftsmen to be brought from Assyria and from other parts of her empire, to work on wood, on stone, on bronze and on iron. By forcing the pace of the workers she completed in a short time a magnificent city (which she called Shamiramakert) consisting of wonderful palaces, each of two or three storeys high, made of stones of various colours. Each district of the city had a distinctive colour, and each was separated from its neighbour by a broad street. There were also artistically designed and decorated baths in the midst of the city. Part of the river was diverted by canals to supply the city's domestic needs, to water its gardens, orchards and vineyards and to perpetuate the fertility of the earth. She then had a magnificent palace built for herself and she peopled the city with a huge population. The whole city was girt with immense walls for its protection. Now, the eastern side of the mountain had such a hard surface that even an iron-pointed stylo could not impress a single line upon it; yet, palaces, long galleries and strong-rooms for the queen's treasure were hewn out of its side. *Over the whole surface of the rock, as if it were on wax, she caused a great many characters to be traced.* The sight of these marvels throws everyone into amazement.[3]

At Saint-Martin's suggestion, the French government commissioned a young German professor, Friedrich Eduard Schultz, to go to Van to investigate. At Toprak Kale, a hill about 400 feet high near Van, Schultz discovered, carved upon the smooth wall of an ancient citadel, long cuneiform inscriptions, the Vannic inscriptions. The first dates back to the ninth century BC. Although he could not read cuneiform, Schultz was able to make precise copies to take back with him to Paris. Unfortunately, tragedy overtook him in the mountains of Kurdistan, near

Julamerk, where he and his party, including two Persian non-commissioned army officers, were attacked and murdered by bandits. This event was reported by Major Sir Henry Willock to Captain Harkness, Secretary of the Royal Asiatic Society, London, in 1834, and published in the Society's journal of that year. But Schultz's copies of the Vannic inscriptions reached Paris safely, where they were published in the *Journal asiatique* in 1840.

We now know that the modern town of Van is on the site of Tushpa, the capital of the Kingdom of Urartu (or Ararat). The Urartians were also called Khaldians (often spelt Haldians) or the children of Khaldi, after their god, and the kingdom was a theocracy in which Khaldi was supreme. All work was carried out and wars waged in the name of Khaldi; the king called himself the servant of Khaldi, and it was Khaldi who delivered the armies of Ashur, the corresponding Assyrian god, to the king of Ararat. The inscriptions reveal Urartu as a great and powerful kingdom — indeed, a splendid empire — which had for nearly seven centuries, from *c.* 1300 BC to 600 BC, successfully defied the might of Assyria, prevented its expansion northwards, and for a considerable time dominated Western Asia, including Assyria itself.

It was not for many years after 1840 that systematic excavations at Van were undertaken, for in the years following 1840, the considerable remains of the Assyrian cities of Calah (Gen. X.11) or Kalhu (Nimrud) and Nineveh (Kuyunjik), were being uncovered for France by the Italian archaeologist Paul Emile Botta and the Englishmen Austen Henry Layard and H.C. Rawlinson, Hormuzd Rassam, an Armenian, and others. Although Botta's attempts to open up the mound of Kuyunjik were unsuccessful (he was never convinced, until later in the 1840's when Layard proved him wrong, that Kuyunjik was indeed the site of Nineveh), according to Layard,[4] 'to him is due the honour of having found the first Assyrian monument'. Layard then continues to describe how a peasant informed Botta that he would find all the sculptured stone he was looking for in the mound on which the peasant's own village was built. At first sceptical, Botta later sent an agent with some workmen to investigate:

> After a little opposition from the inhabitants, they were permitted to sink a well in the mound; and at a small distance from the surface they came to the top of a wall which, on digging deeper, they found to be lined with sculptured slabs of

gypsum. M. Botta, on receiving information of this discovery, went at once to the village which was called Khorsabad. Directing a wider trench to be formed, and to be carried in the direction of the wall, he soon found that he had entered a chamber, connected with others and surrounded by slabs of gypsum covered with sculptured representations of battles, sieges, and similar events. His wonder may easily be imagined. A new history had been suddenly opened up to him — the records of an unknown people were before him ... numerous inscriptions accompanying the bas-reliefs, evidently contained the explanation of the events thus recorded in sculpture, and, being in the cuneiform or arrow-headed character, proved that the building belonged to an age preceding the conquests of Alexander; for it is generally admitted that after the subjugation of the west of Asia by the Macedonians, the cuneiform writing ceased to be employed ... M. Botta had discovered an Assyrian edifice, the first probably which had been exposed to the view of man since the fall of the Assyrian empire [at the end of the seventh century BC].

Unfortunately, owing to a fire in ancient times which had seriously damaged the building, the gypsum slabs had been reduced to lime, and they began to disintegrate on being exposed to the air. But the French government, who were financing Botta, quickly sent out the artist, Eugène Flandin, who arrived at Khorsabad just in time to sketch the bas-reliefs, which were thus recorded for posterity. By 1845, Botta had completely uncovered the monuments at Khorsabad, and 'having secured many fine specimens of Assyrian sculpture for his country, he returned to Europe with a rich collection of inscriptions, the most important result of his discovery'. More than 100 rooms had been opened up in the excavated building which we now know was the magnificent palace built by Sargon II, King of Assyria (eighth century BC). Botta could not have known that Khorsabad was by tradition said to be on the site of an ancient city called Saraghoun (Sargon's town) also known as Dur-Sharrukin (Fort of Sargon).

In 1845, Layard himself opened up various mounds around Mosul on the archaeological sites of Nimrud and Kuyunjik.[5] Among the most dramatic of his discoveries at Nimrud were colossal stone sculptures of human-headed, winged lions (or bulls) guarding the entrance to a palace. Layard describes the discovery of these sculptures:

On reaching the ruins, I descended into the new trench, and found the workmen, who had already seen me as I approached, standing near a heap of baskets and cloaks. Whilst Awad [Layard's servant] advanced and asked for a present to celebrate the occasion, the Arabs withdrew the screen they had hastily constructed, and disclosed an enormous human head, sculptured in full out of the alabaster of the country. They had uncovered the upper part of a figure, the remainder of which was still buried in the earth. I saw at once that the head must belong to a winged lion or bull, similar to those of Khorsabad and Persepolis. It was in admirable preservation . . .[6]

Absorbed in uncovering these dramatic monuments, archaeologists seem to have forgotten the promising Vannic inscriptions. But in 1850, after Layard had seen his cargo of sculptures from Kuyunjik safely on its way to England, he began his journey northwards, to the mountainous country of Armenia, away from the malaria-infested lowlands of Mesopotamia. In a half-delirious state of fever he mounted his horse and, accompanied by his Armenian friend and assistant, Hormuzd Rassam, and his servant, he made his way towards Lake Van where he thought there might be more Assyrian antiquities. The route he chose lay through Kurdistan, a wild area which even today is little known to Europeans, and at that time was quite uncharted. Layard and his party made their way through forests, rising towards snow-capped peaks. They rested one night at the headquarters of the very Kurdish chief who had murdered Friedrich Schultz. During his stay at Van, Layard copied 25 cuneiform texts carved on the cliff face of the citadel, besides others he discovered in the vicinity.

Dr E. Hincks was the first to attempt to decipher the inscriptions in 1847. He read two papers on *The Inscriptions of Van* before the Royal Asiatic Society which were published in the Society's journal (vol.IX, pp.387-449). In 1864,

four new ones [decipherments] were published in the Travels of Nerses Sarkisian, a book written in Armenian and published at Venice (nos. 4, 5, 7, 8). Besides these, Sarkisian published four others which had already been copied by Schultz ... Two more were brought before the notice of European scholars by Prof. Friedrich Muller in 1870 (*Bemer-

kungen uber zwei armenische Keilinschriften, Vienna); one of which had been discovered by the Vartabed (Bishop) Mesrob Sempadian, at Tsolagerd near Edchmiadzin, and published in the September number for 1870 of a Journal entitled *Ararat* which appeared at Edchmiadzin. It turns out to be identical with an inscription found at Kästner on the right bank of the Araxes opposite Armavir, and published in the *Mélanges asiatiques* of the Academy of S. Petersburg, vol.v, p.117. Another inscription, unfortunately much mutilated from the neighbourhood of Erzerum, was communicated to M. Lenormant by the Armenian priests of the College Mourat, Paris.[7]

Once the excitement caused by the Mesopotamian discoveries had subsided, attention could be directed to the deciphering of the Vannic inscriptions — those of Schultz in Paris, and Layard's at Oxford. They represented a completely different language from Assyrian. It was Professor M. Stanislas Guyard of Paris who, in 1880, realised that the phrase at the conclusion of many of the Vannic texts represented the imprecatory formula found in the same place in their Assyrian and Achaemenian counterparts, on stelae and other monuments: 'Whosoever damages this inscription, overturns it, destroys it; whosoever does these things for another, let the gods, Khaldi, Teshub and Ardini, wipe him out of the sight of the Sun.' Guyard's discovery enabled A.H. Sayce, Professor of Philology at Oxford, and others gradually, to decipher Layard's copies of the Vannic inscriptions after which it was possible to piece together the history of Urartu.

In 1877, three years before Guyard's discovery, the Trustees of the British Museum commissioned Hormuzd Rassam to carry out excavations at Van on the mound he had discovered and from which he had already extracted some bronze pieces. To that end, the Trustees advised him to apply to the Turkish authorities for a *firman* (or permit) through Layard (by that time Sir Henry, and British Ambassador at Constantinople). At the same time, through Layard's good offices, Rassam was appointed British Vice-Consul at Mosul, which enhanced his prestige in the eyes of the Turks. However, as he could not direct excavations in Mesopotamia (where his work greatly enriched the British Museum collections of Assyrian and Babylonian antiquities) as well as at Van, he entrusted the work to be done in Armenia to the British Consul at Van, Captain E. Clayton, and an American missionary, Dr D. Raynolds, both amateur archaeologists. Under their direction, the mound indicated by Rassam was attacked with picks and shovels, quite indiscriminately, seriously damaging or completely destroying fragile objects — an inevitable outcome in those early days of archaeology. However, some highly decorated bronze shields with cuneiform inscriptions on the rims were brought up, together with bronze ornaments inlaid with gold, bronze animals, human figures carved in ivory, as well as other pieces. Two years later, when Rassam returned to Van, he was obviously disappointed with what were, in fact, the very valuable items that had been unearthed. His reaction is understandable, for this was the infancy of archaeology, particularly because he had experienced with Layard the dramatic finds of the huge sculptures on the Assyrian sites.

Rassam's report described the debris of an ancient building; a good deal of charcoal indicated that it had suffered a great fire. We now know that the stonework of the building Rassam had struck was the temple of the Urartian god, Khaldi[8], founded by King Rusa I (735–714 BC) and completed by the last king of Urartu, Rusa III (610–590 BC). The Medes were responsible for the burning of the temple when they overran Urartu in 590 BC. Rusa I was also the founder of the acropolis on which the temple stood.

The site was left exposed and unguarded. Consequently, between 1880 and 1900, there was a good deal of illicit digging and many valuable objects were stolen and sold to private collectors all over the world. What now seems to us to be a somewhat naïve report from Dr David Raynolds to Dr Samuel Birch of the British Museum is typical perhaps of the manner in which so many pieces of great archaeological and historical value disappeared in those days:

> An Armenian gentleman is possessed of a number of articles which seem to properly belong to some public collection and which he is willing to dispose of, if he can do so advantageously. At his request I have agreed to send a description of them to you, and to one or two other public museums to see if any arrangements can be made regarding them.[9]

In another context, he writes that the 'owner' of certain objects from the site 'has decided not to sell them locally but to take them to Europe'.[10] It was left to Drs W. Belck and C.F. Lehmann-Haupt to reveal in 1908 the true worth of the articles found at Toprak Kale. By that time, much experience had been gained in the science of archaeology and the haphazard diggings of the pioneers had developed into more scientific methods. The stolen pieces were gradually located. However, it was not until 1950 that Dr R.D. Barnett of the British Museum was able to list the material and to review it as a whole. For some of those pieces he was able to reconstruct graphically a sumptuous throne (see Figure 2.1) and stool whose history in itself makes fascinating reading:

Figure 2.1: Divine throne and stool from Van: parts of these magnificent discoveries are exhibited at the British Museum (see Plates 7 and 9)

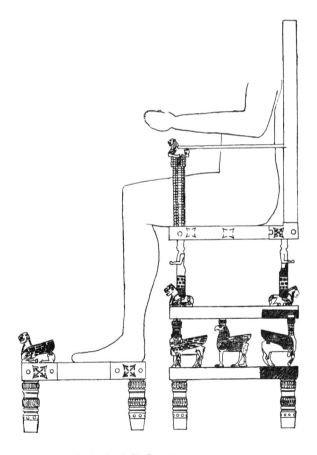

Tentative reconstruction by Dr R.D. Barnett

On August 3rd, 1877, Layard writes to Birch from Therapia telling him that a man (later described as an Armenian) has brought him some Assyrian [sic] bronzes found near Van. 'They appear to me to have formed part of a throne or of a chest. Among them is a human-headed bull, face turned inwards and arms folded across the chest like some that formed portals at Nimrud. The face is wanting and was probably of gold as there are fragments of gold inlaying on other parts of the figure, and a bull with proper horned head. They are of solid bronze and heavy. The fragments consist of pieces of bronze or copper, apparently parts of a panel, and a lion's paw like those found at Nimrud belonging to a throne ...' After some hard bargaining with the Armenian owner lasting over five months, Layard is able to report in December that he has been able to purchase the bronzes through Rassam for the British Museum.[11]

The story continues in the form of a letter dated 10–12 July 1884, and preserved in the Institute of Oriental Studies of the Academy of Science, Moscow. It is in Armenian from an inhabitant of Van and addressed to Professor Kerovp'e Patkamian, Professor of Armenian and Eastern History and Literature at the Lazarist Academy, Moscow. The interested reader is referred to the source from which I quote, for the full story.[12] The following extract is relevant to the above bronzes offered to Layard which, as he writes, appear to have been part of a throne: 'Once there was discovered in these ruins a quantity of magnificent objects, such as an incredible large throne, all covered with cuneiform and gilding, but it is painful to relate that when I returned from Europe I learnt it had been split up and destroyed.'

Among other objects that came to light were a number of ornamental shields and an enormous bronze cauldron with representations of bulls' heads for handles. Archaeologists and historians are indebted to Dr R.D. Barnett, who first drew attention in 1950 to the forgotten discoveries at Van in 1880 by Rassam and his English associates, and to Professor B.B. Piotrovskii of the Hermitage Museum, Leningrad, who directed the excavations at Karmir Blur in Soviet Armenia, for finding the channels through which the discoveries at Van reached the European museums.

Notes

1. Victor Langlois, *Collections des Historiens Anciens et Modernes de l'Arménie* (2 vols). Vol 2: (Paris, 1867); Moses of Khoren, pp. xv-xvi.
2. In Chapter 7, I suggest a connection between this legend and Shamu-ramat, Queen of Assyria 811–809 BC.
3. Langlois, *op. cit.* Robert W. Thomson, *Moses Khorenat's: History of the Armenians. A translation with commentary on literary sources* (Harvard University Press, 1978), pp. 96-101.
4. Austen Henry Layard, *Discoveries at Nineveh* (London, 1851), pp. 3, 48. At the instance of Sir A.H. Layard in 1877, his former assistant, Hormudz Rassam, visited Van and contributed to the collection of Urartian antiquities. In referring to these earlier discoveries of Urartian inscriptions, Sir H. Rawlinson's contribution from the Ruwanduz district must be mentioned.
5. Nimrud (ancient Kalhu; Biblical Calah): one of the four capital cities of Assyria. Kuyunjik: modern site of ancient Nineveh, near Mosul. (The four capital cities of Assyria in succession were: Kalhu, Ashur, Nineveh and Khorsabad, all near modern Mosul.)
6. Layard, *op. cit.*
7. A.H. Sayce, 'The Cuneiform Inscriptions of Van', JRAS XIV, 1882, pp. 380-1.
8. R.D. Barnett, 'Excavations of the British Museum at Toprak Kale', IRAQ XII¹ (1950).
9. Ibid.
10. Ibid.
11. Ibid.
12. R.D. Barnett, IRAQ, XVI¹ (1954).

Additional sources

A.H. Sayce, 'The Cuneiform Inscriptions of Van', JRAS, XIV (1882); XX (1888); XXV (1893); XXVI (1894); XXXIII (1901); XXXVIII (1906).

E. Hinks, JRAS, IX (1848), pp. 387-449.

G.A. Melikishvili, *Urartskie Klinobrazyne Nadpisi* (Moscow, 1960). A collection of Urartian inscriptions, with complete bibliography and history of each inscription.

Stanislas Guyard, J.As, XV (1880), pp. 540-3.

F.E. Schultz, J.As, IX (1840), no. 50, pp. 257-323.

C.F. Lehmann-Haupt, *Armenian Einst und Jetzt* (Berlin, 1910); *Die historische Semiramis und ihre Zeit* (Tubingen, 1910); 'Semiras und Sammuramat', *Klio*, XV, pp. 243-55.

Jean Saint-Martin, *Memoires historiques et geographiques sur l'Armenie* (Paris, 1825).

Diodorus Siculus: Bibliotheca Historica II, 13-14.

3

The Rise of the Kingdom of Urartu

In Chapter 1 the first Hurrian settlements were described as comprising loose chieftainships, in the valleys of the mountainous country south of the Caucasus, between Lakes Van and Urmia. They were probably also found on the northern shores of Lake Van, where later their first capital, Arzashkun, was established. Those independent chieftainships shared not only the same language, but each tribe also worshipped a manifestation of the same god, Khaldi, suited to its needs.[1] It was perhaps c. 1350 BC that the nucleus of the Urartian kingdom was forged by the fusion of a number of these small Hurrian chieftainships, under a now unknown but powerful leader. I offer that tentative date some 75 years before the earliest inscription on which Urartu ('Uruatri') is mentioned, because it would have taken at least two generations before a spirit of common identity could have been imbued in a group of chieftainships, and kept alive by a dynasty of kings powerful enough to confront the might of an Assyrian army. The inscription referred to is that of the Assyrian king, Shalmaneser I (1275-1245 BC), who must have been sufficiently impressed by the strength of the resistance of the Urartian warriors to cause him to record his campaign against them in the first year of his reign, 1275 BC. But as early as the sixteenth or seventeenth century BC, the Babylonians knew of the Armenian highlands as *Urdhu* (probably the contracted form of Urardhu[2]). It is also found in the Qumrum 'Dead Sea' texts as (h)urartu[3]. The Hurrian language can be traced back to about 2400 BC in southwest Asia[4], and Hurrians appear to have been strongly Armenoid in physical type[5]: 'the Van area was certainly inhabited from the Tell Halaf period in the sixth millenium BC, as is shown by the still unpublished finds from Tilki Tepe beside the Citadel at Van'.[6]

The new kingdom of Urartu, which proved to be the last stronghold of the Hurrian race, was situated in the midst of a region with an abundance of mineral and agricultural resources. It might be the 'Gold Land' of the early Sumerians, for there is evidence of a Sumerian presence or influence in the Van area. A magnificent bull, cast in copper and of Sumerian workmanship, dating to *c.* 2300 BC, was discovered in that region; it is now exhibited at the British Museum. The Sumerians obtained at least some of their gold from Armenia, where rich deposits of silver, lead, iron, copper and tin were also found. From the alloy of the last two minerals Ararat produced its famous bronze objects. And the fertile valleys were cultivated for corn, vegetables, fruit and vine yards; cattle and sheep grazed on the lower slopes of the mountains and the region was well known for its fine breed of horses.

In ancient Mesopotamia it would have seemed to be a fabulous and mysterious land, far away to the north, in the fastnesses of impenetrable mountains, like an oriental Valhalla where the Garden of Eden would be found. Genesis II.10 describes its geographical position: 'And the river went out of Eden to water the garden, and from thence it was parted.' One of the tributaries enclosed 'the land of Havilah where there is gold'; another tributary, Hiddekel, 'that is which goeth towards the east of Assyria' — perhaps the River Tigris — 'And the fourth river is Euphrates'. Both the Euphrates and Tigris rise in the mountains of Armenia. The 'land of Havilah' is not known to us, but we do know that gold was found in Armenia.

Archaeologists and philologists have together robbed the Armenians of the tradition dear to their hearts, that the Garden of Eden was in Armenia, by Mount Ararat, and that Noah's ark came to rest on the Armenian Mount Ararat. (Politically speaking, it is now in Turkey, but it will never cease to be an Armenian mountain — it's been that for far too long to change now!) Philologists have translated the Sumerian epic of Gilgamesh and have revealed the origins of the Creation and the Flood stories to be in Mesopotamia; and archaeologists have shown how the Great Flood could have occurred in southern Mesopotamia. A more careful reading of Genesis VIII.4 reveals that the ark came to rest on the mountains (not the Mountain) of Ararat, that is, on the mountains of Urartu; according to Gilgamesh, on the legendary Mount Nisir, south of the Lesser Zab river, which, in the eighth century BC, would have fallen within the boundaries of the Urartian empire and in medieval Armenia, within the great province of Vaspurakan. As the Armenians are the inheritors of Ararat's land and some of its institutions, as well as of partial Hurrian-Urartian racial descent their homeland's claim to be the ark's resting place, to which they attach great traditional value, is still valid.

Urartian territory was at first confined between the banks of the River Arsanias (Murad su) and the northern and eastern shores of Lake Van. Urartian communities were also to be found on the western shore of Lake Urmia, which perhaps derives its name from Urartu. In the last quarter of the ninth century BC, growing Urartian military power encouraged neighbouring countries to ally themselves with Ararat, against Assyria. During the first half of the eighth century BC, Ararat's generals could discuss strategy at the frontiers of an empire stretching from the Caspian Sea to the Mediterranean and River Orontes, and from the River Kura in the north to the southern foothills of the Armenian Alps, and the highlands east and south of Lake Urmia.

Thus, Ararat's political influence over numerous states and extensive territories for a time usurped that of Assyria, but such power was very differently exercised by the two rivals. Whereas Assyria colonised the conquered countries, killing or deporting the original inhabitants of the subject cities, the Urartian monarchs preferred for the most part to federate with, or to champion the cause of, their neighbouring, weaker states against the common enemy. In return, tribute flowed into the coffers of the King. Territorial expansion and military victories also yielded prisoners of war for the slave market (ultimately to be employed in building, agriculture, mining), and control of the commercial routes which was of paramount economic importance.

Shalmaneser I concentrated his military action against the principalities in the northern highlands, together described as the 'Nairi' or Riverlands. The Nairi take the form of an arc touching the highlands to the south and south-east of Lake Van. Shalmaneser's wars there, like those of his successors, degenerated into a series of raids, though one or two were serious and devastating. Assyria was never able to establish garrisons in any part of the Urartian homelands, that is, Armenia (the lands east of the Euphrates) at any time, let alone colonise them. Ararat's powerful kings were to thwart Assyrian ambitions in Armenia and to a serious extent, even in Asia Minor west of the Euphrates, to the very end of Assyria's history.

In the war of 1275 in which Urartu ('Uruatri') is mentioned for the first time, the aggressors were in fact the rulers of eight Urartian districts on the Upper Great Zab river. Urartian territory at that time (1275 BC) might well have had a common frontier with, or even overlapped, the land of Khurri (or Hurri) north-west of Lake Van, which was probably a Mitannian province. Although Shalmaneser's scribes write of rebellion, no evidence is available to show that Urartu had previously been a tributary of Assyria. Indeed, it is difficult to envisage such a situation, for Shalmaneser's immediate predecessors had been fully occupied with wars and intrigues against the Mitanni, Babylonia and the Hittites. The grandiose claims of Assyrian monarchs must, in many instances, be taken with serious reservations. The scribes knew well that flattery could never be too gross for their sour-tempered royal masters. For example, Shalmaneser I boasts of conquering large areas of the Nairi, laying waste some 50 lands, imposing tribute, and carrying off the youth of the conquered peoples to Ashur. Among those kingdoms of the Nairi, 'Uruatri' (Urartu) figures prominently. He alleges that his forces 'climbed up against its mighty mountain fortress' and conquered it and all the other 'fifty-one' lands in no more than three days. These are probably three battles rather than three days.[7] However, the inscription is obviously intended to mislead the reader who takes the written claim as fact. On Shalmaneser's departure, the Nairi principalities resumed their political status quo.

Shalmaneser's successor, Tukulti-Ninurta I (1244–1208 BC), tried to restore Assyrian authority over the small Hurrian states of the Upper Tigris area to which he refers collectively as the land of the Shubari (Shupria). They include Alzi, Purukuzzi and Amadani (in the Diarbakir district). The last two, together with others, formed a coalition under the leadership of the principality of Alzi. However, it seems that the prince of Alzi panicked on the approach of the Assyrians 'and fled to Nairi with members of his family and court, while his leaderless troops took to the hills to save their lives. The resistance of the Alzi having collapsed, Tukulti-Ninurta proceeded to devastate it, sacking 180 towns.'[8]

The possession of the Shubari lands gave Assyria access to rich deposits of copper and command of the routes leading across the Euphrates and Murad su into central and eastern Anatolia. In his own summing-up of the conquered territories, the Assyrian king begins in the south-east, with lands on the eastern side of the

Table 3.1: Synchronous list of Urartian and Assyrian kings

Urartu		Assyria	
		Ashur-ubalit I	1365-1330
		(previous Assyrian rulers were the	
		vassals of the king of Mitanni)	
First reference to Urartu 1275		Shalmaneser I	1275-1245
		Tukulti-Ninurta I	1244-1208
Stems the Mushkian advance but		Tiglath-pileser I	1115-1077
provokes alliances of Nairi		Ashur-bel-kala	1074-1057
chieftains under Urartu		Ashur-rabi II	1001-975
		Ashur-dan II	933-912
		Adad-Nirari II	911-889
		Tukulti-Ninurta II	889-884
Arame — The first *known*		Ashur-nasir-pal II	884-859
Urartian king	858-844	Shalmaneser III	860-824
Lutipri	844-834	Shamshi-Adad V	824-811
Sarduri I	834-828	Adad-nirari III	811-782
Ishpuini the Establisher	828-810	Shalmaneser IV	782-772
Menua, the Conqueror	810-785	Ashur-dan III	772-754
Argishti I	785-753	Ashur-nirari V	754-745
Zenith of Urartian power		Tiglath-pileser III	745-727
Sarduri II	753-735	Shalmaneser V	727-722
Rusa I	735-714	Sargon II	722-705
Argishti II	714-680	Senacherib	705-681
Rusa II	680-639	Esarhaddon	681-668
Sarduri III	639-635	Ashur-bani-pal	668-624
Eriména		Sin-shar-ishkun	
— Armenian dynasty?	635-629	fall of Nineveh	612
Rusa III	629-590	Ashur-ubalit	
	or 629-615	fall of Harran	605
Perhaps Sarduri IV	615-598		
Rusa IV	598-590		

Note: The dates contained on this list, particularly those against the kings of Urartu are approximate. For the latest synchronous list, see R.D. Barnett, 'Urartu', CAH III¹, 1982, chapter 4.

Lesser Zab and ends in the north-west 'as far as the frontier districts of Nairi ...'. But

the Nairi lands by border-raiding or intrigue with dissident elements could imperil Assyria's security. Their rich supplies of metal, cattle and horses were an added incentive to conquest. Their subjection led Tukulti-Ninurta into territory unknown to his predecessors, the mountainous nature of which represented a formidable challenge to the military engineers charged with the task of preparing a passage for troops and chariotry. 'Mighty mountains, a narrow *massif* whose paths no king had known, I traversed in the triumph of my transcendent might, their highlands I widened[?] with bronze axes, their untrodden paths I made broad'. He claims that his conquests extended as far as the shore of the Upper Sea, either Lake Van or Lake Urmia. Forty Nairi kings who opposed him in battle were heavily defeated and taken to Ashur with copper chains round their necks, but were subsequently released to their lands as tributary vassals. In his titulary Tukulti-Ninurta calls himself 'king of the Nairi lands', but neither he nor his successors achieved the permanent subjugation of these mountain peoples and in the course of the following centuries repeated Assyrian attacks led to their unification in the kingdom of Urartu.[9]

Tukulti-Ninurta's greatest military triumph was the defeat and occupation of Babylonia whence he carried off the treasures of the Kassite kings to enrich the temples of his gods (1235 BC). The whole country, down to the Persian Gulf, was occupied and large numbers of its citizens deported to Assyria. He also garrisoned the middle and northern Euphrates, including the important city of Mari, and Arapkha the terminal city of the trade route from Iran. Tukulti-Ninurta could then style himself 'King of Karduniash, King of Sumer and Akkad, King of Sippar and Babylon, King of Tilmun and Meluhha'.[10] The Babylonian wars are the last to be recorded by Tukulti-Ninurta. Twenty-five years later, 'Ashur-nasir-apli, his son, and the nobles of Assyria, rebelled against him and tore him from his throne. In Kar-Tukulti-Ninurta in a house they shut him up and slew him with the sword (1208 BC).[11] There is no doubt that the Assyrian king's violent death was due to a palace revolution provoked partly by military defeats and territorial losses: Babylonia had seceded, and from the recorded prayer to his god, Ashur, it seems that the peoples of the Nairi in the north and the Zagros in the east were in revolt. It is also possible that Tukulti-Ninurta was defeated by the Hittites in his attempts to retain his gains in northern Syria.

The next great name in the Assyrian king lists is that of Tiglath-pileser I (1115–1077 BC). To the north-west, the rich valleys of Alzi and Purukuzzi had been lost to Ashur for some 50 years. They had been occupied by the Mushki, always associated by the Assyrians with Phrygia, though their original homelands were in the area of the Chalybes. Their chiefs were now leading 20,000 of their countrymen down the Tigris valley towards Nineveh, and dominating the countryside west of the Upper Tigris, fomenting revolt. Tiglath-pileser met the horde and defeated it. In the following year (1114 BC) he won back Šubartu and the districts east of the Tigris, along the River Zab. Thus, the power of the Mushki and their allies was broken and the Assyrian king could turn his attention to the north — the Nairi, west of Lake Van.

> Despite abundant geographical detail given in the royal annals the precise route cannot yet be determined. It would seem that the Assyrians marched by Tunube [Turubun] east of the Tigris to the south-west of Lake Van. A coalition of 23 Nairi chiefs was defeated, 120 of their armoured chariots being taken and 60 other tribal groups chased northwards. The decisive battle took place to the north and north-west of Lake Van. At the point farthest north on this expedition, Melazgirt, Tiglath-pileser had an inscribed victory stela set up. Once again hostages were taken and an annual tribute of 12,000 horses and 2000 head of cattle imposed on the conquered tribes ... the rebel stronghold of Milidia [Malatya] was visited and made to produce an annual due payable in lead-lumps ... On these hill frontiers especially the peoples, by nature and location independent, would henceforth be forced to group into larger defensive units.[12]

Ultimately, the dominant kingdom of Urartu was created which would for 500 years sap the strength of Assyria, until it was expunged from the pages of history.

Some of the exploits of Tiglath-pileser I are recorded on the 'broken obelisk' from Nineveh; but it is the campaign of King Ashur-bel-kala (1074–1057 BC) which forms its principal subject. Although that king's name does not appear on the obelisk, the narrative, carved upon it, describing the progress of the Aramaeans from Syria eastwards into 'Uruatri' shows the Assyrian monarch concerned with that event to have been Ashur-bel-kala. Soon after his accession, he had to campaign in 'Uruatri' where the Aramaeans had reached the Tigris north and north-west of Ashur. He expelled them from the vicinity of his capital and himself crossed the Euphrates into Syria. He appears to have reached the Mediterranean.

These Assyrian invasions of the northern riverlands could be interpreted as a continuation of the traditional Assyric–Mitannian struggle. The kingdom of the Hurri–Mitannians (see Prologue) extended into Armenia, probably overlapping parts of Urartian territory. It seems reasonable, therefore, to suggest that after the destruction of their country by Shalmaneser I (*c.* 1275 BC), many members of the Mitannian aristocracy (presumably with their families and large numbers of their Hurrian dependants), perhaps led by their own king, Shattuara II, who escaped from the general holocaust, fled from their homes and joined their Urarto–Hurrian kinsmen to the north of Nisibis-Diarbekir and in the provinces south-east of Lake Van, towards Lake Urmia. This hypothesis is supported by the racial identity, linguistic affinity, geographical proximity and general fear of the common enemy, Assyria. It is also supported by the date, 1275, which is common to the destruction of Mitanni and the first Urarto–Assyrian war recorded in Assyrian annals. The aggressors were the Urartians. It is interesting to speculate on the possibility of the war-like but defeated Mitannian lords inciting the Urartian princes and joining them in an all-out attack upon Assyria. The implications of an Urarto–Mitannian alliance and fusion is a rapid transmission to Urartu of very ancient Mitannian traditions in diplomacy, government administration and social organisation. These had been influenced and shaped during the course of three or four centuries by Mitanni's close relationships with Egypt, the Hittites and the various Syrian seaport city-states, especially with those of Ugarit and Alalakh. The latter were themselves willing commercial servants of Babylonia on the one hand, and the Aegean centres of civilisation, such as Crete and Cyprus, on the other. The Mycenaean seamen and merchant-venturers were unwitting distributors of new ideas and ideals, while enriching themselves by the purchase and profitable sale of the enormous variety of Levantine manufactures and raw materials. The rich advantages of these early interactions of the peoples on the western side of Mesopotamia with Babylonia, Egypt and Crete, would have been slow to reach remote Van and Urmia without the intervention of Mitanni.

Perhaps 150 years after the demise of Mitanni (say, *c.* 1100 BC) Urartu (Ararat or Biaini) the still small Vannic kingdom might have produced a great leader who either by superior military power or diplomacy, welded his own country and those of the Nairi principalities into a powerful bloc, able to match the growing might of Assyria and to vie with her for military supremacy and political prestige. He and his successors called themselves 'King of Biaini'. Other Hurrian kingdoms, such as Isuwa and Hayasa-Azzi (the latter possibly with 'Hayk' or Armenian antecedents[13]) steeped in Hittite and Mitannian traditions, were later to be included in the Urartian hegemony.

With the eclipse of the Hittite and Mitannian kingdoms, and the withdrawal of Egypt from Syria, there remained no power which could effectively prevent Assyrian expansion to the Mediterranean in the west, towards Babylonia in the south and the Taurus in the north. A new and vigorous Assyrian dynasty was founded by Ashur-rabi II (c. 1000 BC), who first reorganised his kingdom, and began extensive public works which were completed at the close of the tenth century by Ashur-dan II (933–912 BC). These works would have been financed by the plunder of neighbouring communities of whom, for a considerable time to come, Assyria became the overlord. Urartu is mentioned by Adad-nirari II (911–889 BC) as one of his defeated enemies, but the battle between the two countries took place on Assyrian soil. The Kingdom of Urartu, already in existence for at least 300 years, then, seems to have been sufficiently confident in its military power to be concerned with adventures so far to the south of its homelands around Lake Van under its unknown tenth century BC king. Indeed, it was Urartu that thwarted Assyrian attempts to advance further into Anatolia; Ararat was the one stumbling-block to absolute Assyrian domination over the whole of the Middle East, which would have been comparable to the much later Persian empire of Darius Hystaspis.

By the end of the reign of Tukulti Ninurta II (889–884 BC), Assyrian power had been firmly established, and his successors over the next 50 years could aspire to the systematic reconquest of the territories of the first Assyrian empire which had gone into a decline in the second millenium BC. This was achieved. Tukulti-Ninurta himself successfully invaded the northern territories, 'like the eagle of heaven', and Assyria then became a more serious threat than ever to the peoples of the Nairi.

It is of considerable interest that the tribute exacted by Assyria from its northern provinces included horses. These were used in regiments of light cavalry, first introduced in Assyria in the ninth century BC, or harnessed to light, two-wheeled chariots. Each chariot carried two warriors — a driver and combatant (with the exception of the king's chariot, in which an additional officer protected the monarch's person with a shield). The horse had become an indispensable unit of Assyrian armaments: 'the Assyrian skill in chariot fighting owed much to Hurrian example, shown by the Middle Assyrian version of a Hurrian treatise on the breaking-in and training of horses for team work.'[14] Horse-breeding was a serious plank of state policy of Urartu, particularly in the Urmia Plain. Horses were harnessed to chariots or used to form cavalry regiments. A regiment of horse-drawn chariots, with the din of galloping, neighing and snorting horses, the combined rumble of the chariot wheels and the shouts and clamour of the soldiers, appearing out of the sun in a cloud of dust, would have been a terrifying experience for those who had to withstand the attack. That tremendous increase in pace and power would be comparable to the armoured divisions of a modern army. The introduction of the motor lorry and armoured units in the latter part of the First World War was largely responsible for British victory in that area. Other engines of war used by Assyria and, in the eighth century by Urartu, included assault ladders and moveable towers, which could be placed against the walls of a beseiged city to enable the attackers to gain a foothold on the battlements while at the same time protecting engineers demolishing the foundations below, and those wielding a great battering ram, with a head of iron to break down the structure of the wall or to shatter the city gates.

Notes

1. A.H. Sayce, 'The Cuneiform Inscriptions of Van', JRAS (1882), p. 412.
2. Ibid., p. 392.
3. R.N. Frye, *The Heritage of Persia* (Weidenfeld and Nicolson, 1965), p. 65.
4. W.F. Albright and T.O. Lambdin, 'The Evidence of Language', CAH I[1]. iv. p. 152.
5. Ibid., p. 153.
6. R.D. Barnett, 'Urartu', CAH III.i. p. 328.
7. J.M. Munn-Rankin, 'Assyrian Military Power 1300–1200 BC', CAH II.ii, pp. 279-80.
8. Ibid., pp. 280, 285, 286, 287, 292; idem, CAH II.ii. p. 111.
9. Ibid.
10. Ibid.
11. Ibid.
12. D.J. Wiseman, 'Assyria and Babylonia 1200-1000 BC', CAH II[2]. v. p. 459.
13. N. Adontz, *Histoire d'Arménie* (Paris, 1946), pp. 41 ff.
14. Munn-Rankin, *op. cit.*, p. 282.

4

Aram (858–844 BC): The First Known King of Urartu

The previous chapters introduced the rise of Urartu from small beginnings, as a principality sometimes helped by and sometimes helping neighbouring Hurrian communities against the common enemy, Assyria. The history of Urartu is documented from 1275 BC. Urartu's wars with Assyria continued under the latter's kings, Tukulti-Ninurta I (*c.* 1230 BC), Tiglath-pileser (*c.* 1060 BC), their successors, and King Ashur-nasir-pal II (884–859 BC), either directly or by way of the Nairi principalities, which were constantly influenced by anti-Assyrian propaganda, probably originating from Urartu. The people of one such principality under a pro-Assyrian, tribute-paying chieftain called Amme-ba'ali, rebelled and slew their treacherous ruler.[1] He was cruelly avenged by his Assyrian royal master. This incident illustrates the constant vigilance to which the Assyrian kings, from the thirteenth century BC onwards, were subjected by the Urartian spirit of independence, ambition and persistent dominance in the mountainous lands north of Nineveh, as well as, most of the time, in the east, towards Lake Urmia and even to the south of that lake. Henceforth Urartians increasingly appear as a threat to Assyrian military ascendancy, rather than as just another mountain people who could be kept in their place by occasional raids.

In the early years of Ashur-nasir-pal's reign there must have been regular frontier skirmishes and forays into enemy territory by one or other of the combatants. Those might be described as a way of life at that time — a practice that persisted for many centuries, in all civilised parts of the world. No self-respecting Assyrian king could allow the war season to go by without insti-gating the traditional 'war games'. Indeed, in the rare absence of opportunities to kill men, the Assyrian king killed lions, as

51

depicted so very well on the fine bas reliefs found at his palace at Kalhu (Nimrud) and now on exhibition at the British Museum.

Ashur-nasir-pal's last major campaign in the distant north took place in 867 BC, when he demonstrated Assyrian military might. Marching through Commagene (Kummuh) he continued northwards as far as Malatia (Milid), then turned south-east to Amid (Diarbekir), where he crucified 3000 men, and then fell upon and captured the provincial capital of Damdamuna, killing 600 in the process. Continuing southwards, through the Kashiari mountains, he returned to his capital, Kalhu or Calah (Nimrud).

Ashur-nasir-pal is careful not to refer to Urartu in his regular annals, and a casual mention of it in one of his standard inscriptions is an inadvertence of the scribe. But we cannot doubt that an expedition which hastily started in September against regions soon to be closed by the snows, was an attempt to check Haldian (Urartian) influence in the north.[2]

He did not reach the Urartian capital, which we can now surmise to have been at that time the city of Arzashkun on the northern coast of Lake Van. All the states in the Nairi territories he overran rebelled and reasserted their independence very soon after his departure. It was a replay of the raids (so-called conquests) of Shalmaneser I, Tukulti-Ninurta I and Tiglath-pileser I whose northernmost tributaries had fallen away 50 years before the arrival of Ashur-nasir-pal II. As to the west, after various military and diplomatic manoeuvres, Ashur-nasir-pal pushed his country's frontiers as far as the Khabur and the junction of that river with the Euphrates, adjoining Syria, or as he himself put it: 'Ashur-nasir-pal, the king whose glory and might are enduring, whose countenance is set towards the desert' — and furthermore, no doubt to everyone's dismay: 'whose heart desireth to extend his protection'.[3] Thus, Ashur-nasir-pal II tried to complete the conquests begun by his father, Tukulti-Ninurta and assimilated into the hegemony of his kingdom the provinces adjoining the Assyrian frontiers to the east, west and north. These campaigns firmly established Assyrian power in those border-lands, where it continued, despite various political convulsions from time to time, for over 200 years.

So far no Urartian king's name has been mentioned, since none has yet come to light dating before the ninth century BC. The first known king is 'Aramu' mentioned on a cuneiform inscription of King Shalmaneser III (860–824 BC), Ashur-nasir-pal's son and successor, found in Balawat, south-east of ancient Nineveh. It appears in the descriptive texts of the repoussé illustrations on bronze strips, showing scenes from Shalmaneser's campaigns in the north. The strips served the dual purpose of decorating as well as reinforcing the enormous double doors of timber in the royal palace. The strips were discovered by Hormuzd Rassam in 1878 and sent to the British Museum, where today a fascinating replica of the doors may be seen. On one of the strips, Shalmaneser describes his northern campaign, in the first year of his reign, briefly as follows:

> I drew near Sugunia, the stronghold of Aramu, the Urartian; I invested the town and captured it; I killed many of his warriors and carried off plunder; I made a pile of heads over against the city; fourteen settlements in its territory I gave to the flames. Then I departed from Sugunia and went down to the Sea of Nairi [Lake Van], where I washed my weapons in the sea and offered a sacrifice to my gods.[4]

The same strip of bronze depicts charioteers and infantry emerging from an Assyrian fort, towards Sugunia, a small fortress town high up on a cliff at the confluence of the tributaries of the Upper Tigris, overlooking an arched bridge, where the Assyrian camp can be seen. The king in a chariot, with others displaying the Assyrian standards, arrives at the gates of the doomed town. Dismounting, and surrounded by his bodyguard, he signals the general assault by firing his arrows against the garrison. Then the sappers, protected by long leather robes, begin to loosen the stones of the city wall, while soldiers place assault ladders against it and break into the town. The besieged Urartians resist with arrows and spears until, with the whole town in flames, they have to submit. The slaughter is merciless and a pyramid of heads is seen, erected outside the town. The prisoners, hands tied behind their backs, and their necks bound to a yoke, are led by a rope, to stand before an official. Surprisingly, all is not over. There are skirmishes between the well-armed, well-shod, well-dressed Assyrians and the stout-hearted and poorly-clad men of Ararat, with their lances and small, round shields, and some of them wearing greaves. The smoking ruins of neighbouring villages, men impaled on stakes fixed in the walls, and severed heads hung on the city gates are seen, and nearby, the Assyrians are carrying away the booty. Then, Shalmaneser strikes camp and leads his troops and cavalry over pathless mountains 'whose peaks point like spears to heaven'. Chariots and baggage are man-handled over them. At last, they descend to the shores of the great Lake Van. Before the eyes of the richly apparelled monarch, sceptre in one hand and wearing a tiara, sacrifices of bulls and rams are made to Ashur, and the weapons are ceremoniously dipped into the salt waters of the lake. The royal effigy is carved on a rock overhanging the lake, after which the enemy returns to Assyria.[5] In that campaign the Urartian king, Aram, was not even so much as sought for an engagement, nor were garrisons established, and tribute could not be exacted. It became a useless, but well-documented, military exercise only, for the interest and instruction of posterity.

Another bronze strip on the Balawat doors illustrates Shalmaneser's last major expedition against Urartu in 849 BC. It has its beginnings in a war against Aram's allies in Hamath and Damascus in Syria. After the submission of those cities, the Assyrian king led a huge army of 120,000 men in an all-out attack on Urartu. The description of the campaign by his scribes is dramatic and detailed enough not to need further explanation or embellishment:

> I departed from Fort Shalmaneser [Til Barsip] and hacked my way with bronze axes through difficult routes and inaccessible mountains that point to heaven like the edge of a dagger. Thus I got my chariots and troops across and came down into the land of Enzite, which is part of Ishua. I conquered the whole extent of Enzite, demolished, destroyed and burnt their cities with fire, and carried off their plunder, their goods, their property beyond count. I made for myself a large royal stele, wrote on it the praise of Ashur, the great lord, my lord, and the power of my might and set it up in the city of Saluria. I departed from Enzite, crossed the river Arzania, and approached the land of Suhme which I demolished, destroyed, and burnt with fire. Then I came down into the land of Dayaeni. The whole extent of Dayaeni I conquered, their cities I demolished, destroyed and burnt with fire, and I seized as plunder their goods, a large quantity of property. I departed from the land of Dayaeni and approached Arzashkun, the royal city of Aramu of the Urartaeans. Aramu of the Urartaeans became afraid when confronted with the terror of my mighty weapons and my fierce battle, he abandoned his city

and climbed mount Adduri. I climbed the mountain in pursuit and fought a terrible battle on the mountain. I slaughtered 3400 of his troops, rained devastation upon them as though I were Adad [god of war], and dyed the mountain with their blood as if it were wool. I took possession of his camp and brought down from the mountain his chariots, his horsemen, his horses, his mules, riding-donkeys, his property, his spoils, his goods in large quantity. To save his life, Arramu climbed to a difficult part of the mountain. With the full force of my manly vigour I trampled on his land like a wild bull and laid his cities in ruins. Arzashkun together with the surrounding cities I demolished, destroyed and burnt with fire. I piled up heaps of heads beside his city gate. Thereon I impaled their young men and young women by the heaps. Then I departed from Arzashkun and climbed the mountain. I made for myself a large royal stele, inscribed on it the praise of Ashur my Lord and the power of my might of which I had given evidence in the land of Urartu, and set it up on Mount Eritia. I departed from Mount Eritia and approached the city of Aramale. The cities there I demolished, destroyed and burnt with fire. On my return I came down to the sea of the Nairi country [Lake Van], I cleansed the fierce weapons of Ashur in the sea and made offerings. I made for myself a royal stele and wrote on it the praise of Ashur, the great lord, my lord, and the nature of my prowess in war together with my achievements in battle. I departed from the sea and approached the land of Gilzani. Asau, king of the land of Gilzani, with his brothers and sons, came out against me. I received from them the royal tribute of broken-in horses, oxen, sheep, wine and seven camels with two humps. I made for myself a large royal stele, wrote on it the praise of Ashur, the great lord, my lord, and the power of my might of which I had given evidence in the land of Nairi, and set it up inside his city in his temple. I departed from the land of Gilzani and approached the city of Hubushkia. The city I surrounded and conquered. I achieved a great victory over them and carried off as plunder, which I brought to my city Ashur, 3000 prisoners and their oxen, sheep, horses, mules and riding donkeys beyond count, I entered the pass of the country of Enzite and emerged from the pass of the country of Kirruri to the east of Arabia.[6]

Shalmaneser claims to have marched as far as the Caspian Sea, which is most improbable. It is more likely that he covered the area between the Mediterranean and Lake Van. He claims to have made 60 kings pay tribute consisting of 12,000 horses and 2000 head of cattle — very little to speak of for 60 kings, and nothing at all, if indeed he marched as far as the Caspian Sea. However, again Shalmaneser could not garrison any part of the country through which he passed, any more than his predecessors or his successors. It is feasible that, after their defeat, the Urartian forces reformed in the inaccessible mountains (perhaps Ala-dagh) and hastened in pursuit of the enemy to attack and harrass him in the little known passes of the wild mountains through which he had to retreat. In the final analysis, Shalmaneser's efforts were in vain. He failed to crush the allies who had given ground but had not been routed. That was a serious set-back for Assyrian arms in the northern territories, while it was an important step for Ararat towards the period when she could take the offensive against Assyria.

When commenting on the reign of Shalmaneser III, something should be said of the famous black obelisk discovered by A.H. Layard at Nimrud (Kalhu; the Biblical Calah) in 1846, one of the most prized treasures of the British Museum. Writing to his Aunt Sara, in November he said:

> But the most remarkable discovery is perhaps that of the black obelisk about seven feet high, which I believe to be one of the most interesting and unique monuments of antiquity. There are in all about 80 figures, all in the finest preservation and capitally drawn. You may conceive with what delight I dug out this splendid monument, and the satisfaction with which I saw it on Christmas Day fairly embarked on the Tigris for Bagdad.

Layard copied its 210 lines of cuneiform and the panels showing the king followed by his attendants, men bearing tribute and leading elephants, camels, wild bulls, lions, stags and various kinds of monkey. The whole of the inscription was roughly translated by H.C. Rawlinson just before the publication of Layard's *Nineveh* in 1849; it was the first translation to be made of the purely Assyrian cuneiform.[7]

Whereas down to Shalmaneser III 'Urartu' seems to have been a shifting region, synonymous with Nairi, south of Lake Van and west of Lake Urmia (spilling over to the south of the Taurus), in Shalmaneser's inscriptions and thereafter it always lies within the region which later became Great Armenia[8] down to the present century within the extensive geographical (though not always the political) region between the Euphrates and the Caspian, and the Caucasus and the Taurus-Hakari mountains.

Under Aram, the boundaries of the Vannic kingdom extended from the Euphrates and beyond it in the west, to Lake Urmia in the east. And in Syria, his influence was felt by the princes of distant Hamath and Damascus. Ararat's southern boundaries were the foothills of the Armenian Alps, and the northern frontiers stretched beyond the western Euphrates (Kara su) and the upper Araxes. The eastern limits were guarded by Musasir, a buffer-state beyond which Hubushkia was in Assyrian territory. The site of Musasir, the holy city of Urartu, 'has now been located with maximum plausibility, at Mudjesir, some 12 miles north of Rowanduz, a little west of Topzawa'.[9]

The political and military problems which Aram successfully overcame have rightly invested him with a reputation of greatness. It was Aram who laid the foundations of Urartian power in Armenia west of the Caspian and east of the Euphrates. He took appropriate action to counter Assyrian attacks upon his country, while in the north, he consolidated his gains. The defence of the north against the incursions of barbarians was a burden shouldered by Ararat for three centuries, not only for her own protection but also by virtue of her role as a powerful buffer-state between them and the cradle of western civilisation comprising the extensive territories of Urartu itself, the western Anatolian states, and Mesopotamia. Moreover, there was the constant danger of revolt from within, since the kingdom of Urartu was a federation of small principalities dominated by the Urartian aristocracy. Such a revolution, indeed, seems to have taken place, for Aram's successor, Sarduri, was a usurper. He was the son of Lutipri, or perhaps Lutipri himself, possibly one of Aram's own ministers.

Notes

1. Sidney Smith, 'Foundations of the Assyrian Empire', CAH III.i. p.13.
2. A.T. Olmstead, *A History of Assyria* (New York, Scribner).
3. Smith, *op. cit.*, p.15.
4. B.B. Piotrovskii, *The Ancient Civilization of Urartu* (Barrie and Rockliff, 1969).

5. Olmstead, *op. cit.*

6. W.G. Lambert, 'Sultan Tepe Tablets', AS, XI (1961), p.143 (paraphrased), part 8.

7. G. Waterfeld, *Layard of Nineveh* (London, John Murray, 1963).

8. Nicolas Adontz, *Histoire d'Arménie* (Paris, 1946).

9. R.D. Barnett, 'Urartu', CAH III[1].i. p.339.

5

Sarduri I (844–828 BC): The First Vannic Inscriptions

Sarduri I, son of Lutipri, claims that Aram became one of the 'kings' of whom he was the overlord.[1] Nothing is yet known of Lutipri, except that, according to the Vannic inscriptions, he was Sarduri's father. Sarduri was the founder of the royal dynasty which endured almost to the end of the Vannic empire (*c.* 590 BC). It was Sarduri who transferred the capital from Arzashkun to Tushpa, on the east coast of Lake Van, on the site of modern Van. The site of the new city was strategically too well situated for its choice to have been fortuitous. A number of facts support the view that the king chose it carefully. Cradled between the deep, alkaline waters of Lake Van and the shadows of the Armenian mountains, it was much less exposed to enemies approaching it along the unimpeded valley of the River Arsanias than the previous capital. Situated further south than the old capital, it was safer from the increasing threat of barbarians pressing on the northern frontiers of the kingdom. Moreover, should enemies from the north or south succeed in reaching and besieging the city, the Urartian fleet in the Sea of Van would ensure the transportation of food to its inhabitants. Because of the soda content of its waters, Lake Van never freezes over in winter and the sheltered fertile soil along its shores escapes the worst rigours of winter. Even the palm tree grows there (though fruitless), as depicted on one of the bronze strips of the Balawat Gates.[2]

Our information on the history of Ararat is derived from Assyrian as well as Urartian cuneiform inscriptions; but the greater part is derived from native monuments. It was Sarduri I who began the inscriptions on the outer wall of the citadel of his new capital, Tushpa. They are the Vannic inscriptions described by Moses of Khoren, noted by Jean Saint-Martin and, with the support of the French governnment, discovered by Fr Schultz.

Those were in the Assyrian tongue, but the records of Sarduri's successors, on stelae found in various parts of the kingdom, though at first bilingual (Assyrian and Urartian), were soon inscribed in Urartian cuneiform only. The bilingual engravings might best be described as the prototype of the much later trilingual inscriptions of Persia's Darius Hystaspis, on the cliff-face at Behistun.

The first lines of Sarduri's description announce the building of the citadel at Tushpa, on the southern and most vulnerable part of the city, with giant blocks of limestone, each measuring up to 6 m long by 1 m wide, stretching out into the lake, as if intended to be a pier or dock. There, the most ancient Urartian structure yet discovered, the 'Sardurburg', at the foot of the west side of the rock on which the citadel was built, protected the local springs which ensured the supply of water to the garrison.[3] On the face of the rock, Sarduri proclaimed:

This is the inscription of Sarduri, son of Lutipri, the great king, King of the world, King of Nairi, the mightiest of all kings. This great captain who knows not fear and whose might subdues all rebels. Sarduri, son of Lutipri, King of Kings, to whom all kings pay tribute; Sarduri speaks: These rocks from Alnium I brought; with them this tower of Tushpa I raised.

The Assyrians would see Sarduri's claim to be 'King of Kings' as a defiant challenge.

King Lutipri seems to have succeeded Aram in 844 BC, for Sarduri, son of Lutipri, is not mentioned until ten years later, in 834, in a report of the Assyrian general Daian-Ashur.[4] Probably too old by then himself, Shalmaneser III sent his general against Urartu. The general's report informs the king that when he led his army across the River Arsanias, 'Sarduri, King of Urartu, confident in the might of his army, came up against me'. Although the Assyrian claims a victory over the King of Urartu, again it was a vain boast, for he left no garrisons and there was no colonisation in any part of the country he had raided. The new capital, Tushpa, proved to be inviolable. It remained a monument of power during the whole history of Ararat, and its citadel wall, with the inscriptions upon it by Sarduri and others, became an extremely valuable historical document. The grandiloquent, trilingual inscription on the rock's southern face, is worth quoting in full:

A great god is Ormuzd, who is the greatest of gods, who has created this earth, who has created that heaven, who has created mankind, who has given happiness to man, who has made Xerxes king, sole king of many kings, sole lord of many. I am Xerxes, the great king, the king of kings, the king of the provinces with many tongues, the king of this great earth far and near, son of king Darius the Achaemenian. Says Xerxes the King: Darius the king, my father, did many works through the protection of Ormuzd, and on this hill he commanded to make his tablet and an image; yet an inscription he did not make. Afterwards I ordered this inscription to be written. May Ormuzd, along with all the gods, protect me and my kingdom and my works.[5]

Sardurburg, and the siting of Tushpa, reflect Sarduri's military astuteness. At this distance in time, one senses political stability in Urartu and a national virility, built upon foundations laid by earlier leaders, culminating in the military and political power of King Sarduri himself. That virility was to radiate outwards from the core of Tushpa, in the form of a great empire, during the reigns of Sarduri's successors. Assyria's repeated aggressions had only emphasised to the Nairi chieftains the need for unity. This they had gradually achieved, over a period of some centuries. Sarduri's government wielded the necessary power and prestige to control the extensive territories which brought economic prosperity to his country in the form of caravans of goods in transit through Urartian lands; while his people began to enjoy the peace, fostering their creative genius which was to flower during the course of the next century and to influence craftsmen and even architects of distant civilisations.

In spite of approximately 50 years of continuous warfare, the limits of the Assyrian empire on the death of Shalmaneser III in 824 did not extend beyond Carchemish on the Euphrates in the west and the Zagros mountains in the east. The 'conquests' in the north, of which Shalmaneser frequently boasts, were all short-lived and not one of the Urartian territories which he overran became part of his empire in any real sense. Although he was more successful in Naharin (northern Syria), his ruinous wars in Palestine, Phoenicia, Cilicia and Babylonia, and the economic hardships suffered by the Assyrian people in consequence, brought about disastrous riots in the cities, with grave political repercussions. One of the royal princes led a rebellion against his father in 827 BC, with the support of many cities, including the great capitals of Ashur and Nineveh. The aged king died in 824, in the midst of that tumult. His heir, Shamshi-Adad V, triumphed over his brother in 821, but only with the assistance of the Babylonian king. For that indispensable help, Shamshi-Adad had to accept the overlordship of Babylon,[6] which implies the payment of tribute. Mighty Assyria had been reduced to a second-rate power. Such is the fate of rulers and countries who seek the aid of powerful 'friends'. Assyria's situation was basically the result of her failure to subdue Urartu and to seize its many potential resources and opportunities for wealth and power. When King Shalmaneser III died in 824 BC, Urartian power was such that Assyria had no alternative but to acknowledge its supremacy in western Asia. Thenceforth, for almost 100 years, Ararat was the most extensive and the most powerful kingdom in that region, comprising the vast territory of the Armenian highlands, Naharin and the Euphrates in the west and the Median principalities on the great caravan routes in the south-east, beyond Lake Urmia.

Notes

1. A.H. Sayce, 'The Kingdom of Van', CAH, III.viii. p.173.
2. A.T. Olmstead, *A History of Assyria* (New York, Scribner).
3. C.A. Burney, 'Urartian Fortresses and Towns in the Van Region', AS, VII (1957).
4. B.B. Piotrovskii, *The Ancient Civilization of Urartu* (Barrie and Rockliff, 1969), p.149.
5. A.H. Sayce, 'The Cuneiform Inscriptions of Van', JRAS, vol.XIV. p.678 (1882). The languages are Babylonian, Persian and 'Protomedic', placed in parallel columns.
6. Sidney Smith, 'The Foundations of the Assyrian Empire', CAH, III.i.

6

Ishpuini the Establisher (828–810 BC) and Menua the Conqueror (810–785 BC)

Sarduri's son and successor was Ishpuini. He reigned jointly with his son, Menua. This information, together with King Ishpuini's titles, are given on a bilingual (Assyrian and Urartian) stele found at Kelishin (south-west Lake Urmia). It reads 'Ishpuini, King of Shura, King of Nairi, Lord of Tushpa; and Menua, his son …'[1] Ishpuini also assumed the title of 'King of Kings', and his prestige and power must have been sufficiently effective for the Assyrians to accept it and to address the king by that title in their diplomatic relations. The prestige of Urartu after the death of Ishpuini was such that all subsequent stelae are in Urartian cuneiform only.

Ararat's military strength must have been superior to that of Assyria. As his titles indicate, Ishpuini established the empire, with his energetic son, Menua, acting as second-in-command. In this context, one is reminded of a similar relationship between Philip and Alexander of Macedon 450 years later, particularly as both Menua and Alexander proved themselves to be outstanding generals in the annals of military history. Ishpuini's titles seem to indicate that his political influence extended as far as northern Syria ('King of Shura'), although this is only a conjecture.[2] In fact, Ishpuini's conquests did not include Syria.

Shura appears to be the earlier form of the name of the principality to the south-west of Lake Van, which later became known as Shupria,[3] and in the Armenian era as Sophene. However, after 810 BC, Menua actually occupied northern Syria, perhaps as far as the River Orontes, where it turns westward to empty into the Mediterranean at the port of Poseidon (modern al-Mina). The Kelishin stele, some 30 miles north-west of Rowanduz, described

Menua's conquests during his father's lifetime. They include the important province of Musasir (west of Lake Urmia), which became and remained a faithful feudatory of Urartu; a valuable region strategically, astride the commercial and military route which follows the valley of the Upper Zab, along which Shalmaneser III had entered Urartu in the time of King Aram. The holy city of Musasir was called Ardini (the 'city of Ardi', a minor god) by its Vannic conquerors,[4] as was the sanctuary of Khaldi where, in his temple, his protection might be sought. Thereafter, the temple was generously endowed by the rulers of Ararat, and housed great quantities of their riches.

By the end of King Ishpuini's reign the southern and eastern frontiers had been secured. Menua's conquests made tributaries of Hubushkia, Mannai and Parsua; Urartu then controlled the caravan routes from central and south-eastern Asia, which, having passed through the Caspian Gate and the Khyber Pass, joined others starting from Elam, and continued towards the Mediterranean and the Black Sea via Armenia and Anatolia, instead of through Assyrian territories. Tribute would then have been collected from the travelling merchants to swell the state revenues.

Menua, who succeeded his father to the throne, proved to be one of the greatest of the powerful Vannic kings. He led a number of campaigns from Gilzan (north of Urmia) to Kirruri on the Upper Zab and penetrated the sources of the Lesser Zab and yet further south as far as the River Diyala. In eight campaigns between 810 and 787,[5] he consolidated his father's gains in Media and Parsua (807 BC) which remained vassals of Urartu, and the whole of that region became a thorn in the side of Assyria for the next 70 years. Dramatic evidence of the conquest of Mannai, at the site of the citadel at Hasanlu, unearthed in 1956–58 by Professor R. Dyson Jr of the University of Pennsylvania,[6] revealed three Urartian soldiers looting a burning building near the citadel. They seem to have been trapped in one of the rooms where they had been overcome by falling walls and burning timber while attempting to make off with a solid gold bowl, measuring approximately 21½ cm in height and 28 cm in diameter. The bowl

> was carried out of the flaming building by one of three men who were on the second floor at the moment it gave way. The leader of the group fell sprawled forward on his face, his arms spread out before him to break his fall, his iron sword with its

handle of gold foil caught beneath his chest. The second man, carrying the gold bowl, fell forward on his right shoulder, his left arm with his gauntlet of bronze buttons flung against the wall, his right arm and the bowl dropped in front of him, his skull crushed in its cap of copper. As he fell his companions following on his left also fell, tripping across the bowl-carriers feet and plunging into the debris.[7]

This bowl is now famous among archaeologists as one of the most interesting examples of religious ceremonial instruments of ancient times. It is known as 'The Golden Bowl of Hasanlu', and is now exhibited at the Tehran Museum. The excavations at Hasanlu strongly suggest a decline in population, after the burning of the citadel by Menua *c.* 800 BC.

Only a year later, having organised the settlement and defence of these early conquests in the south-east, we find Menua in the west, annexing Khattina, Alzi and Shupria. At Palu, on a cliff overlooking the Euphrates, a stele records the annexation of Malatya from Assyria:

By the will of Khaldi, Menua, son of Ishpuini, has gone forth [to war]. He has taken Shebeteria [near Palu], Husana and Supa-ni. He has won the surrounding country of Khattina. This stele, Menua has raised to the honour of Khaldi at Shebeteria [Shupria]. To Khaldi a sanctuary he built at Shebeteria. Sulle is taken, the king of the people of Malatya has submitted to tribute. Through the great Khaldi, Menua, son of Ishpuini, powerful king, great king, King of Biaina, prince of the city of Tushpa, Menua speaks: Whosoever this inscription damages, overturns it, destroys it; whosoever does these things for another, let the gods Khaldi, Teisheba, Shivini, wipe him out of the sight of the Sun.[8]

In the north-west too, by 790 BC, the Urartian frontiers enclosed the land of Dayaeni, when the royal city of Shashilu was captured and its king, Utupurshini, taken prisoner. Beyond the Araxes, Etius was garrisoned and the barbarians between the Araxes and Kura rivers subdued. The conquests of Menua in the north included the land of the Colchians (Kulhai or Qulhi) on whom he imposed heavy tribute, payable in gold, silver and bronze, as well as in horses. That conquest completed the caravan route from the south, via Mannai, through the passes between the two lakes, Urmia and Van, to Erzerum and so to the Black Sea coast, probably ending at the natural harbour where the Milesian Greeks later (757 BC) established a colony, which we know as the great port of Trapezus.

Menua also continued the diplomatic policy of his predecessors: that of establishing coalitions with neighbouring kingdoms, such as Damascus in Syria and Que, Gurgum and Sam'al in Asia Minor, against the common enemy, Assyria. These relationships in Asia Minor later developed into the League of the Northern Nations.

Menua's militia was very powerful by the standards of his time, having permanently under arms 65 chariots, 15,700 infantry and numerous cavalry, which could be increased when necessary. In one of his campaigns, he led 1600 chariots, 9174 horse and 2704 archers.[9] He devoted his energies also to the building of roads wherever the mountainous terrain of his country permitted. The necessarily slow transport and communications were a serious military disadvantage and presented difficulties in the administration of the rapidly expanding empire. This was in contrast to conditions in Assyria where the Mesopotamian steppe made travel relatively easy.

Many canals were constructed by the kings of Ararat, several of them by Menua, some of which are still in use today. The regions through which they flowed became the real granaries of the kingdom. Among these, the canal at Berkri still irrigates the plain on which that city stands, and three other canals bring water to the region around Melaskert (Menuasgert). The most interesting and best known is the Menua canal, later called the Semiramis canal (modern Shamiram su), in the heart of the most ancient part of Armenia called Hayots-Dzor (Valley of the Armenians), east of Lake Van. It started (as it does today) from a generous spring, about a mile from Mzenkert, and after irrigating the gardens of Tushpa, flowed into Lake Van — a total run of some 45 miles, watering an extensive region.[10] One of the 'fourteen inscriptions, most of them near the aqueducts carrying the canal across the side valleys',[11] announce the construction of the canal:

By the will of Khaldi, Menua, son of Ishpuini, has built this canal. This canal is named Menua Canal. Menua the powerful, the great king, King of Biaina, Prince of the city of

Tushpa; Menua speaks in the name of the dread Khaldi: Whosoever damages this inscription, whosoever overturns it, whosoever does such things according to his own desire or in the name of another, Menua warns that the dread god Khaldi, the god Teisheba and the Sun god Shivini will efface him from the sight of the sun.[12]

There are also records of 'storage of water by cisterns ... in this reign. With such works can be associated some of their results, the planting of vineyards, one for the king's daughter, Tariri
a.'[13] The canal flows at the rate of 1500-3000 litres per second, according to the time of the year[14] and is 'as abundant as the Euphrates', a description used by Sargon II's (*c.* 714 BC) scribes. It is also described as 'the queen among canals' as the Euphrates is 'queen among rivers'.[15] Menua has left the greatest number of inscriptions laying claim to the construction of irrigation systems.[16]

It is a strange coincidence that Menua's canal should be called Shamiram waters, for Shamiram (or Shammu-ramat), Queen of Assyria, consort of King Shamshi-Adad, was a contemporary of Menua. But her name is inextricably associated with legend. I have already told how her unrequited love for the legendary Armenian king, Ara the Beautiful, impelled her to make war against Armenia in which he was killed. Grief-stricken, she prayed to the gods to restore him to life. The gods Aralez, the sacred dogs, hear her and licked his corpse back to life.[17] It is interesting that 'Aralez' consists of ar-, the first syallable of the noun *aryun* (blood) and *lez*-, the root of the verb to lick; alternatively, ar-, the root of the verb to take, that is, to take or lick blood.[18] A similar story is told by Plato: Er (Ara?), son of Armenios, is slain in battle but returns to earth after a sojourn in the underworld;[19] while Faustus of Byzantium (V.36) and Pseudo-Agathangelus (Langlois I pp. 197-8) recall the myth of the return to life of Armenian heroes killed in battle, through the intercession of the gods Aralez.[20]

The legend of Ara and Shamiram appears to be a variation of the ancient Babylonian story of Tamuz the Beautiful, beloved of Ishtar and slain by a boar, for whose sake Ishtar descended into Hades to bring the dead god back to the world of the living; just as in Greek mythology, Demeter descended into Hades in the spring, to lead her daughter, Persephone, to the upper world of sunlight and resurgent life. These are different versions of the widespread myth personifying the seasons, in which the lesser gods, goddesses or mortal heroes die in winter and are brought back to the upper world in the spring and the season of the rebirth of life, through the intercession of powerful beings who love them.

Another legend connects Shammu-ramat with an early Babylonian annual festival, the Festival of Sacaea, celebrated down to the Persian period,[21] a five-day period of general feasting, masques and licence, when slaves were made to rule their masters, and a criminal was chosen and given royal privileges until the festivities ended. The masquerading king and his slaves were then put to death. At that festival, so the legend tells, Shammu-ramat, a slave, was put on the royal throne in the palace of Ninus, but at the end of the festive period she contrived to retain the royal office, given to her in a derisory spirit and for a brief period, for the rest of her life.[22] Imagination baulks at the probable fate of her former masters.

According to another tradition, the Assyrian monarch falls in love and marries Shammu-ramat, a beautiful courtesan. She then persuades him to invest her with his kingly powers for five days. On the first day she orders a banquet; on the second day she imprisons her husband (or puts him to death) and thenceforth, continues as sole ruler and queen. But it would be a mistake to dismiss Shamiram merely as a legendary or mythical figure from the point of view of Armenian history without qualification. She was, as Queen of Assyria, a person of great power and influence and, according to tradition, very beautiful; she could conceivably have lived in Armenia for a time, after the death of her husband, King Shamshi-Adad in 811 BC, that is, a year before King Menua's accession to the Vannic throne as sole ruler. Was there a romantic encounter between the proud queen and the great conqueror? We might even speculate about the possibility of Shamiram going to war in Armenia not against the legendary Ara the Beautiful but against Menua's son, Inushpua, the reasons for whose disappearance from the pages of history are not known. Following his father's example, Menua ruled jointly with his own son, Inushpua, as king. However, that association could not have lasted for very long because after 810, but for one brief reference,[23] he is never mentioned again. He might have been killed in battle. Perhaps the handsome youth spurned the advances of Shamiram, by that time, probably a mature lady. Her vanity deeply wounded, the proud queen might well have gone to war against Inushpua and Ararat and — here we can apply the legend of Ara — at the first encounter the young prince is killed. His tragic death is bewailed by the distraught queen. And so Inushpua's personality passes into the world of legend under the guise of Ara the Beautiful.

Of course, historians might raise objections to this proposition, particularly as, after her husband's death, Shammu-ramat became Queen Regent and was burdened with the responsibilities of government. But at that point of Assyrian history, there were no civil disturbances at home; and in foreign parts, under the leadership of Shammu-ramat's husband, Shamshi Adad V, Assyrian power had been re-established. Also, the Queen Regent ruled for only three years, before passing the reins of government to her son, Adad-nirari III in 809 BC.[24]

Menua built a fortress, among others, on the south bank of the River Araxes, on the slopes of Mount Aragats, which he called Menua-hinili,[25] evidently to defend Urartu's northern provinces and to serve as a bridgehead for future campaigns northwards, towards the River Kura. Menua might be described as a great and energetic warlord who could measure his country's strength with Assyria's, on equal terms. He consolidated and almost doubled the extent of the territories he inherited from his father who had himself established the kingdom on solid foundations. The waters of the Semiramis canal (Shamiram-su) which Menua built helped to make a garden city of the capital, Tushpa, where he planted many trees and laid out gardens which bloomed with brilliant, oriental flowers. The construction of that canal would have supported a population of 50,000 in Tushpa.[26] Besides several canals attributed to him, he also built new cities. There were no major fortresses with stone walls in Urartu before the reign of Menua,[27] who seems to have instituted a programme of military and civil works on a grand scale throughout his extensive empire. He is described as the greatest builder of the Urartian royal dynasties. He must have encouraged the development of metallurgy and there must have been a good deal of mining activity to provide the copper, tin, lead, silver and gold for different purposes, as well as iron with which the Urartians were familiar long before they settled in the Van region. The craftsmen of Ararat produced fine bronze objects which were exported to distant lands. Those activities in building, metallurgy, mining and agriculture; the growth of foreign trade and the increase in military power commensurate with King Menua's extensive dominions, are brilliant aspects of the image of the new Vannic empire early in the eighth century BC.

Notes

1. For the full royal titles of the Urartian kings, see Ch. 13, p. 116; and n. 3 below.

2. Nicolas Adontz, *Histoire d'Arménie* (Paris, 1946), p.214. A.H. Sayce (JRAS 1882, p.621) maintains that 'Suras was part of the Kingdom of Van ... possibly it may be the mountainous land of Zihar, where Ursa (Rusa I of Urartu) in 714 BC took refuge' from Sargon of Assyria. Adontz's opinion seems to be more acceptable since Ishpuini might well have had a tenuous domination over northern Syria which, under his son Menua, was actually occupied by Urartu. More modern scholars maintain that Suras designates Shupria.

3. Cyril L. Toumanoff, *Studies in Christian Caucasian History* (Georgetown University Press, 1963). A linguistic interpretation shows the change Shura-Shubartu-Shubria to Shupria (p.51 n.44; p. 321 n.76). See also p.51 n.44 for the royal titles of the kings of Urartu.

4. Boris B. Piotrovskii, *The Ancient Civilization of Urartu* (Barrie and Rockliff, 1969). R.D. Barnett, 'Urartu', CAH, III¹ (1982), p.339: 'the headquarters of the cult of Khaldi were transferred by Ishpuini in his own name and that of his son and grandson Inushpua to the new capital at Van, to take the place of Shivini, the sun god who had previously presided over Tushpa. Possibly as a consequence, it would seem that the name of the city of Musasir was altered to Ardini — 'city of Ardi', a minor god.'

5. Inscription of King Menua, near Mesta (Tash Tepe). A.H. Sayce, JRAS (1882), pp.463-76.

6. R.H. Dyson Jr., 'Expedition I' *Life Magazine*, January 1959, pp.50-60.

7. Ibid., Spring 1959, pp.12-14.

8. Adontz, *op. cit.* pp.153, 216, 239-40, respectively.

9. Ibid.

10. Ibid.

11. Charles A. Burney, 'Urartian Irrigation Works,' AS XXII (1972).

12. Ibid.

13. Ibid.

14. Adontz, *op. cit.*, pp.235, 236, respectively.

15. Ibid.

16. Burney, *op. cit.*

17. A.H. Sayce, 'The Kingdom of Van', CAH, III. iv. pp.184-5.

18. Aralez. This interpretation is discounted by A.H. Sayce, who has a less obvious origin of the noun Aralez to offer, from Babylonian mythology. For that, the reader is referred to JRAS 1882, p.415.

19. Plato, *Republic*, Book X.

20. Sayce, *op. cit.*, pp.184-5.

21. James Frazer, *The Golden Bough*, pp.281-2, 442-3. See also the

historian, Berosus (*c.* 270 BC).

22. D.A. Mackenzie, *Myths of Babylonia and Assyria* (Gresham).

23. That reference is to be seen on a stele at the mosque of Kursun, Van. It is dedicated 'to Khaldi the god: for the [good] life and prosperity and grandeur of Menua and Inuspua' (Adontz, p.159). Barnett CAH III, p.339 n.180): 'a silver libation bowl ... bearing the joint dedication of Ishpuini and his grandson Inushpua ...'. (p. 341): 'the latter is represented first as joint dedicator with his father and grandfather of the *susi*-temple at Tushpa and with his father by three briefer dedications to other deities.'

24. Shammu-ramat's association with Ishtar might have arisen from the word 'Sumat', a dove, a bird which symbolised Ishtar.

25. K.L. Oganesian, *Excavations at Erebuni* (Erevan, 1973).

26. Burney, *op. cit.*

27. Charles A. Burney, 'Urartian Fortresses', AS VII, 1957.

7

Argishti I (785–753 BC) and the Zenith of Urartian Military Power

Argishti, son of Menua, continued his father's policy of expansion for political, economic or military reasons. He recorded 14 campaigns on Sarduri's Rock at Van, including those which confirmed his sovereignty over the vast territories from the northern province of Etius, towards the River Kura, down to the principality of Mannai in the south. His inscription testifies:

> I prayed to the powers mighty who have given me the land of Etius and the land of the Minni. On approaching the land of Minni, the populations I carried away, the cities I burnt; their plunder for a spoil I acquired; the men and women, the boys and girls I carried off. I slew and took prisoner many thousands of men. I carried off horses, camels, oxen, sheep. On departing out of the lands of Assyria, the land of Algas,[1] 6471 of its men partly I slew, partly alive I took; also, 286 horses, 2251 oxen, and 8205 sheep I took. To Khaldi and to the powers mighty I prayed, who have given the land of Minni and other lands towards Minni, as a gift to the family of Argishti, son of Menua. The land of Minni as the satrapy of the son of Argishti I established.[2]

Thus, in the south-east, Urartian hold on the important state of Mannai as well as perhaps that of Parsua (which was attacked in Menua's time), was strengthened[3] — regions which straddled the caravan route leading to the heart of Urartu and therefore of the utmost economic and military importance.

The armies of Ararat penetrated into the homelands of Assyria no more than 25 miles from Nineveh, as testified on the fragment of an inscription found at Dehuk.[4] Argishti claims that in the fifth year of his reign, he 'annexed Ashur's cities[5] and in the sixth year of his reign he took into captivity the army of Ashur'.[6] North-west of Lake Van he overran Dayaeni, taking 28,519 prisoners and carrying off 4426 horses, 10,478 head of cattle and 73,770 goats as well as large quantities of gold, silver and bronze. Yet further towards the Pontic lands, south of the Chalybes, he records the plunder and destruction of the palaces and cities of Zuas:

> The people of the three countries, Bias, Khusas and Didis, I despoiled. The soldiers with fire I burnt; 15,181 children, 2734 men, 10,504 women, 4426 horses, 10,478 oxen, 73,500 sheep, I carried away. The people of the two kings I destroyed. Governors and law-givers I set up. The king of Diaves [Diauehi] and his son I carried away. I changed his name [thus erasing his identity] and he to Argishti brought 41 manehs of gold, 37 manehs of silver, 1000 manehs of bronze, 1000 war magazines, 300 oxen and 1000 sheep. And he my laws took. In the land of King Diaus, I set up impost and tribute gold, bronze, oxen, sheep and war magazines ...'[7]

In the west, attempts by Assyria to expel Urartu from Malatya failed utterly. It was the Assyrians who were driven beyond the southern boundaries of the Nairi, and the all-important mountain passes fell to Urartu. In Syria, Argishiti added Khatarika and Arpad to his empire and retained the Mediterranean port of Poseidon (Al Mina) as an important outlet for his country's exports to the Aegean and the west.

The Urartian armies went abroad again and again and returned with prisoners and spoils, the livestock and the tribute paid by vassal princes in 'pure gold, silver, bronze'. Thus, according to Argishti's inscriptions at Van, known as the 'Chronicle of Horhor'[8] did 'Khaldi fight Ashur and deliver him to Argishti'. According to the chronicle, the king's forces subdued Assyrian power everywhere. Much of this wealth, and slave power provided by the prisoners of war, was used to extend the fortifications of Van's citadel and make Tushpa a garden city, with vine and corn and dairy produce which that fertile region yields (thanks partly to Menua's canal). At the same time, defensive towns and citadels in strategic positions north of the River Araxes, in Etius,[9] were established against the ever-present menace of the barbarians of the northern steppe lands — the Cimmerians and Scythians — pressing against the Urartian frontiers in increasing strength. Thus the River Kura marked the northern frontiers of the Urartian empire. West of the modern city of Erevan, Argishti constructed and fortified the city of Argishti-hinili, the site of the much later city of Armavir. Built on the western border of the plain of Ararat and ringed on the western and southern sides by the Armenian Alps, and partly moated by the River Araxes, Argishti-hinili presents a formidable barrier to any foe from the north aspiring to invade Urartu. In common with some other great Urartian fortresses, the fortifications of Argishti-hinili comprise a base of huge basalt blocks, laid without mortar, which carried enormous, crenellated walls of unbaked bricks. The inscriptions at Argishti-hinili reveal the city's economic and administrative regulations and record its foundation, when the vines were planted and gardens laid out. A bronze helmet belonging to King Argishti was found. Chased decorations and a short inscription dedicated it to 'Khaldi, my Lord'. An inscribed tablet revealed the construction of Erebuni, a powerful citadel of primary importance, on the hill of Arin Bert (Castle of Blood) on the Plain of Ararat at the southern edge of modern Erevan. (The modern name, Erevan, suggests an historical continuity from ancient Erebuni.) The site of Erebuni was identified in 1950 by the Armenian archaeologist and architect, Professor K.L. Oganesian, from inscriptions found scattered amidst the ancient fortifications.[10] The tablet states that 'Argishti, son of Menua, built this strong fort to the glory of Khaldi' and that he called it Erebuni, 'to fortify the land of Biaina and to terrify the king's enemies. Argishti says: The land was a desert, before the great works I accomplished upon it.'[11]

When I visited Armenia in August 1968, the last stages of excavations, which had begun 18 years earlier, were about to reveal the whole of the ancient city and citadel. Vigorous preparations were in progress for the celebrations in September of the 2750th anniversary of the city's foundation. In plan, the site was a huge, triangular stronghold, enclosed within powerful ramparts whose daunting strength consisted of outer, central and inner walls.[12] These became evident to me as I climbed the high earth mound of the citadel. Three walls built of massive blocks of basalt rise defiantly one beyond the other, in stages, up the side of the hill. At the time of its construction, Erebuni was in size and importance second only to the capital, Tushpa. It was a fortress city, with a considerable garrison, which was also the king's residence in the north.[13] The excavations have revealed the royal assembly hall, boasting 60 columns, a huge audience hall, with adjoining living quarters, dormitories and storerooms. In the centre of the fortress, there were many buildings including a temple, with heavy basalt walls, dedicated to Khaldi, and a palace, the complex of buildings together comprising a self-contained unit, well prepared for a long siege.

The walls of the palace and the temple were decorated with beautiful frescoes in brilliant colours, which had fallen over, fortunately on their faces, thus preserving them through centuries against erosion and damage. Two pieces, one of them in an almost perfect state of preservation and the other restored, were exhibited at the Armenian State Historical Museum at Erevan when I was there. The representations are of religious or mythical subjects: gods, trees-of-life, bulls, lions. These, together with the many excellent collections of bronze shields, helmets, quivers, bowls and various figurines, stand witness to the flowering of Urartian civilisation at the time of Argishti I, in the eighth century BC. Erebuni was among the most important of a chain of defensive fortresses constructed in the north, even as far west as modern Kars and Erzerum. It survived the destruction of Urartu in the sixth century BC, and became the capital of the Achae-menian satrapy of Armenia. Archaeological finds dating to the fifth century BC, such as silver rhytons and Milesian coins, show Erebuni straddling the historical periods of the most Ancient East and the classical period,[14] a rare continuity of cultural traditions in that region.

Further evidence of the building activities of Argishti (and Menua) was unearthed in the first months of 1960 by Turkish archaeologists. A well-preserved temple, with cuneiform inscrip-tions on its walls, was brought to light at Aznavur, near Patnos, about 30 miles north of Lake Van, in a palace two miles to the east of Girik Tepe, which seemed to have been destroyed by fire. The bodies of 40 richly apparelled court ladies were found, who must have been trapped in the building during the fire.[15] (See pp. 121-2 for some details of construction.)[16]

Argishti's reign witnessed the complete humiliation of Assyria. Her military prestige was utterly destroyed. She lost control of the trade routes from northern Iran, and in the west, she forfeited the great Syrian lands as well as the valuable territories north and west of Carchemish.[17] These areas were garrisoned and adminis-tered by her rival, Urartu; Assyria had therefore lost the rich metal trade of Asia Minor. Another serious consequence to

Assyria of her military misfortunes, was the loss to Ararat of areas in Anatolia which used to provide her with horses for her military forces, and their forfeiture had serious adverse effects on her military efficiency. The trade routes to and from Asia Minor had also come under the control of Van. These economic disasters following upon Vannic victories, caused general disruption and distress in the Assyrian polity, which led to revolution in Syria and revolt in various cities in Assyria itself. Ararat now stood as the premier power in Western Asia.

Notes

1. Perhaps Alki-Algani to the south of Lake Van.
2. A.H. Sayce, 'The Cuneiform Inscriptions of Van', JRAS (1882), pp. 602-5, 615-16.
3. A.H. Sayce, 'The Kingdom of Van', CAH, III.ii.
4. N. Adontz, *Histoire d'Arménie* (Paris, 1946), pp. 91-2, 186.
5. A.T. Olmstead, *A History of Assyria* (Scribner, New York).
6. Ibid.
7. Sayce, 'The Cuneiform Inscriptions of Van', *loc. cit.*; Adontz, *op. cit.*, pp. 167-8.
8. B.B. Piotrovskii, *The Ancient Civilization of Urartu* (Barrie and Rockliff, 1969).
9. Ibid.
10. K.L. Oganesian, *The Wall Paintings of Erebuni* (Erevan, 1973).
11. Ibid.
12. Ibid.
13. Ibid.
14. Ibid.
15. Ibid.; C.A. Burney and G.F.J. Lawson, 'Measured Plans of Urartian Fortresses', AS.X, 1960; 'A First Season of Excavations at the Urartian Citadel of Kayalidere, AS.XVI, 1966.
16. Argishti also built four canals to bring water to an arid stretch of the Araxes valley, where he had founded two fortresses at Argishti-hinili (Armavir Blur). Vineyards and orchards were planted on previously desert land.
17. Sidney Smith, 'The Foundations of the Assyrian Empire', CAH, III.v.

8

Sarduri II (753–735 BC): The Golden Age of Vannic Power

The reign of Sarduri II, King of Kings, son of mighty Argishti, marks the apogee of Urartian power. In 1912, I.A. Orbeli, the Armenian archaeologist, explored Urartian sites, and at Van discovered inscriptions of Sarduri II, from which the following are two extracts:[1] 'Sarduri speaks: I went to the country of Mannai, I conquered the country, I burnt the towns, pillaged the countryside and exiled the population to Biaina. In the same year, my troops went to the country of Eriahini [or Eriach in Transcaucasia, north of Mount Ararat] conquering the country, setting fire to the towns, pillaging the countryside.' Claims of conquests such as this appear repeatedly: 'The same year, for the third time, I went to Eriahini, fired the cities, pillaged the countryside and exiled the population to Biaina. I built forts at Eriahini and annexed the country. The god Khaldi I glorified. Sarduri speaks: I made prisoners: 6436 men I took, 15,553 women. In all I led [away from their country] 21,989 people, some I have killed, others I have taken alive. 1613 horses, 115 camels, 16,529 head of cattle, 37,685 sheep [I have taken].'

Another 500-line text describes with pride his conquest of the rest of Commagene and Urartu's complete triumph over Assyria in Mannai. Between Isoglu and Kumu-han on the left bank of the Euphrates, an inscription gives details of Sarduri's conquest and occupation of Malatya. The Vannic texts furnish us with a complete list of Milidian kings from the time of Menua of Urartu to Sarduri II. The contemporary of Sarduri II was Khila-ruada II (whom Sarduri must have rendered tributary before the year 743 BC) and his successor, King Sulumal. Like so many other Urartian inscriptions, this too is damaged. It dramatically describes the manner in which, after offering a prayer to the mighty god Khaldi, King Sarduri successfully invaded the country of Malatya, capturing 108 cities, numerous palaces, fortresses and villages. He plunders and burns the cities, 'digs up' and razes palaces, and carries away booty consisting of great quantities of gold, silver and vessels of bronze. He imposes tribute on the wealthy aristocracy and transports 50 of them — 'fifty mighty men' — to Biaina as hostages. He proclaims that he carried away the inhabitants and 'removed' the boys and the unmarried girls, probably taking many of them into exile to his capital, Tushpa. King Khila-ruada of Malatya is himself transported to the capital of his conqueror. Sarduri humiliates him by 'changing his name', thus relegating him to anonymity and oblivion — a king's final degradation.[2]

Another inscription carved by King Sarduri's scribes on the face of the Rock at Van, describes his two invasions of Colchis in 750–748 and between 744–741 BC, respectively: 'Khaldi's own chariot drove out; he descended on the land of Qulhi and on the land of Abiliande; he forced them [the countries] down before Sardur, the Argistide.'[3] Qulhi is the ancient name for Colchis, situated on the south-east coast of the Black Sea; yet Urartu is not credited with a sea-port there (see Adontz, p.203). At the end of the first campaign Sarduri led the Colchian king and his people as prisoners to Biaina. The same pattern was repeated in Sarduri's second campaign when his army captured and sacked the Colchian royal city of Ildamusha,[4] leading the prisoners into exile. He states that he raised a special iron stele to celebrate these victorious campaigns. This appears to be the first reference to iron in Urartian inscriptions. It is extraordinary that Urartu, by far the most powerful state in eastern and central Anatolia, and its king, Lord of Colchis, seems not to have secured a port on the Black Sea coast. Much as it is tempting to presume that he did so, there is no evidence so far to support such an assumption. Sarduri had, in fact, important trading relationships with the Colchians, a maritime people. That area was first opened up to Urartu by King Menua. I believe that Ararat did have a Black Sea port and that archaeologists will eventually discover the site of one, perhaps at Phasis, situated on the south bank of the river of the same name (Sebastopolis).

For over 80 years from the death of Shalmaneser III to 743 BC, the ascendency of Van over Assyria was secure. That period could be described as the Golden Age of Vannic power, when Assyria was continuously confined to the left bank of the southern Euphrates. Parsua and Mannai to the east of Assyria and Hubushkia and Carchemish in the north-west were occupied by Urartian troops. Even the territories of Babylon in the valley of the Diyala fell to Urartu. The Nairi lands were inaccessible to and safe from such military power as was left to Assyria, and indeed the arms of the northern empire pressed hard against the very gates of Assyria's magnificent city of Nineveh. This alone must have been a bitter memory for future Assyrian rulers. Khatarika and Arpad in Syria, Que, Gurgum and Sam'al in southern and central Anatolia and, most important of all, the key city of Carchemish, commanding the crossing of the Euphrates, had all become subjects and adherents of Ararat. At that time, Sarduri could muster a powerful force of 37,011 foot and 3600 horse with provisions for them in the form of 21,357 head of cattle and 35,467 sheep; and huge quantities of corn, butter and wine. His scribes list a reserve of bows and arrows, 49,990 pickaxes and mattocks and much copper; and 336 slaves[5] — presumably for the personal use of the king himself.

During that century, the trade caravans from Iran and the Far East must have travelled through Urartu as a matter of course, and Biaina also controlled the metal trade and the general commerce of Syria and Asia Minor. The metal mines of the Taurus were made to yield their wealth, and tribute was gathered from regions as far away as the Araxes and Kura in the north and the Orontes and the Diyala in the south. Moreover, since the foundation of the Milesian colony of Trapezus (Trabizond) in 757 BC, and the establishment of other Greek colonies along the Pontic coast, Greek merchants were procuring for sale in their own cities as well as for export, the many products of Urartu — iron, gold, silver, bronze, works of art, furniture, flax, wool, wax and timber. The wealth thus acquired went to enrich the temples, particularly that at the holy city of Musasir, to build roads and canals, and to furnish the palaces of the wealthy with beautiful and useful products of artists and craftsmen.

The consequences to Assyria of Vannic victories and the severing of communications with Cappadocia and the West, were serious indeed. Apart from the loss of extensive tracts of land and the wealth of the western and eastern provinces, economic and political disorganisation overwhelmed her. The misery of the society generally, lacking its life-blood of raw materials, and markets for its manufactured goods, exploded in insurrections and riots everywhere. The ancient city of Ashur, with other cities, declared its independence of Kalhu, the capital, and during the ensuing most bloody revolution which broke out in Kalhu itself, resulting from the general foment, the king and the whole of the royal family were put to the sword. Thus ended a royal dynasty of Assyria (745 BC) which had endured for over two centuries, leaving Assyria in a state of disorder and poverty, confined within narrow frontiers.[6]

A usurper now mounted the Assyrian throne, the first of a succession of great kings who ruled Assyria during the course of the next 100 years. His name was Pul (2 Kings XV.19; 1 Chron. V.26), but he assumed a former monarch's name and called himself Tiglath-pileser III. He appears to have been one of those rare military commanders who are able to seize the initiative in a difficult situation and successfully retrieve a failing cause. Having suppressed all the revolts in various parts of his kingdom and reorganised the army, one of Tiglath-pileser's first campaigns (743 BC) was concerned with the conquest of Syria, within Urartu's sphere of influence, in order to secure Assyria's trade with the Mediterranean countries and to control the north–south artery of commerce. The Assyrians laid siege to Arpad, in northern Syria, and thus provoked war with Van.

Tiglath-pileser had disciplined his army into a new and efficient fighting machine — a single unified force matched against Urartu's heterogeneous armies. Confronted with this new power, Sarduri had to retire northwards where, at a decisive battle at Arpad, he was utterly defeated. He and the remainder of his army fled over the Euphrates, which marked the western boundary of the Vannic kingdom. One of Ararat's vassals who had joined forces with Sarduri against Assyria, was Sulumal, King of Melitene. Sulumal's son, Tarkhu-nazi, last king of Melitene, suffered the savage vengeance of Assyria's King Sargon II in 712, when his kingdom was attacked, his capital Til-Garimu (Togarmah) destroyed, an Assyrian governor placed over the district, and he himself, together with 5000 of his subjects, led away captive to Assyria.

In 736, Tiglath-pileser marched against Urartu's homelands, and again defeated Sarduri. The latter retired into the impregnable fortress of Tushpa. The Assyrian could then only express his chagrin by putting up a statue of himself outside the citadel, which he could not take, and destroying the city of Tushpa; after which he retired to his own country.

Although Urartu was thus defeated, she was by no means

conquered. In spite of her losses west of the Euphrates, she continued to exercise a powerful influence over the chieftains and kings in those countries. Her very considerable remaining possessions, from the Euphrates to the Caspian Sea and to the eastern side of Lake Urmia, and from the land of the Colchis to Mannai and Parsua, still constituted an extensive and powerful empire, which continued, as ever, to be a very serious menace to Assyrian security.

Notes

1. N. Adontz, *Histoire d'Arménie* (Paris, 1946), pp. 173-4; B.B. Piotrovskii, *The Ancient Civilisation of Urartu* (Barrie and Rockliff, 1969), p. 20.
2. A.H. Sayce, 'The Cuneiform Inscriptions of Van', JRAS 1882.
3. F.W. Koenig, *Handbuch der Chaldischen Inschriften*, p. 120. Also, Sayce, CAH III. p. 176: 'Sarduri could exact tribute from the tribes beyond the Araxes.'
4. Adontz, *op. cit.* p. 203: 'A l'ouest Sarduri dut affronter le peuple Qulhi qui apparait pour la première fois a l'horizon de l'Empire. Les Qulhi sont les Colches, le peuple pontique bien connu.'
5. Ibid.
6. Sydney Smith, 'The Foundations of the Assyrian Empire', CAH III.v.

Further sources

N. Marr and J. Orbeli, *Archaeological Expedition to Van* (Petersburg, 1922; in Russian). Quoted by A.H. Sayce in his bibliography to 'The Kingdom of Van', CAH III. viii. p. 717; 'A sumptuous account of the excavations under the wall of the citadel of Van where Professor Marr discovered a rock temple of Sarduri II with inscriptions of the highest importance both historically and linguistically. The book contains photographs and copies of them with translations and commentary by Prof. Marr.'

G.A. Melikishvili, *Cuneiform Inscriptions of Urartu* (Moscow, 1980; in Russian).

9

Rusa I (735–714 BC): Urarto-Assyrian Balance of Power Upset

Tiglath-pileser departed from Urartu leaving a trail of destruction behind him. According to the reports of Assyrian agents in Urartu at the time, a number of Urartian princes and chieftains took advantage of the disorganised state of the country and rose in rebellion against their defeated king, Sarduri. It was the eldest of Sarduri's eight sons,[1] Uedipri, who seized the throne and then not only subdued his rebellious subjects, but also won their support for his various campaigns, which restored to Urartu a number of the provinces so recently lost to Assyria by his father.[2] He thus re-established Urartian power in the west. Uedipri assumed the name 'Rusa' (the Assyrians call him 'Ursa'). The Assyrian scribes describe his statue in the temple of Khaldi at Musasir, bearing the inscription: 'With my two horses and driver, my hands have seized the Kingdom of Ararat.'

In the light of the events which followed Tiglath-pileser's retreat, this boast seems to be justified. He overcame the insurgents at home and restored Urartian military power or influence abroad. Having won the crown, put down the rebels, reconquered many of Ararat's former provinces, and generally reorganised his kingdom, the energetic Rusa turned his attention to the north, beyond the Araxes, where Urartu was being increasingly beset by the barbaric Cimmerians and Scythians. He led an army to the Sevan region and there followed a war in which, according to the inscription found on a rock along the coast of Lake Sevan, he subdued 23 princes,[3] between present-day Erevan and remote Tiflis, in a single year. It appears that these rulers would have supported the barbarians. The pressure of the northern wildmen was very serious at this time and Rusa must have found it hard to contain them beyond the Kura. Indeed, there were already settlements of Cimmerians west of the Euphrates (perhaps paying tribute to Rusa), probably in contact with other Cimmerians in the north-east, who were to play an important role in 714 BC as unwitting allies of Assyria.

At the same time, Ararat was under pressure from Iranian tribes, from the steppes of Russia. Some of these tribes, those of Zikirtu and Andia in particular, had already settled in regions east and south of Lake Urmia, close to other Iranian states, such as Media and Parsua, and indigenous peoples such as Mannai to the south of the lake. Here Rusa attempted to implement the traditional Urartian policy of forming federations of neighbouring countries with common interests, such as those of the early Nairi chieftainships which had become part of the nucleus of the Urartian kingdom itself, and the later Northern Federation, organised by King Menua in the west. Rusa's own attempt to create a single buffer-state in the south, composed of the Iranian kingdoms and indigenous states, was unsuccessful, however, although he was able to secure a military alliance with some of them against an ever-threatening Assyria. Among his new Iranian allies he could count on King Metatti of Zikirtu, King Tilusina of Andia and King Deioces of the infant Median state. This is the Deioces, ruling the principality around the later city of Ecbatana (modern Hamadan), whose descendant of the same name, is credited by Herodotus (I.96, 102) as the founder of the Median royal dynasty, which was to destroy mighty Assyria in 612 BC. Rusa, then, incited Metatti of Zikirtu to intrigue with a revolutionary faction in Mannai, paying tribute to Assyria, to revolt against its pro-Assyrian king, Aza. A palace revolution was fomented in which the king was murdered and his brother, Ullusunu, who favoured Urartu, was placed upon the throne. As an expression of his gratitude, the new ruler gave Rusa 22 frontier districts as well as a promise of his allegiance. King Sargon of Assyria was quick to put down the Mannaian revolt, forcing Ullusunu to pay tribute, flaying alive the pro-Urartian king of Uishdish (a country along the eastern side of Lake Urmia), who had assisted Metatti of Zikirtu in inciting trouble in Mannai,[4] and deporting Deioces of Media to Syria. In 715 Assyria attacked Parsua, but the continued prestige of Urartu was such that when she went to Parsua's assistance, Ullusunu of Mannai dared to support Urartu. As an additional defensive buffer-state, as well as a spring-board whence he might himself attack Assyria, Rusa reconquered the ancient Urarto-Hurrian province of Musasir or

Ardini, a small mountain kingdom, west of Lake Urmia, a religious centre, with a temple and a palace. A bilingual stele found at Topzaüe,[5] near one of the eastern passes,[6] is inscribed by Rusa:

> Urzana I established as ruler of Ardini. I took Urzana by the hand and set him upon the high throne of the kings of Ardini. He led me into the temple. For fifteen days sacrifices he offered, in the presence of his gods and in my presence. Urzana and his men took the oath of loyalty to me. Urzana gave me his warriors and all his war chariots.[7] In obedience to Khaldi, my Lord, I went to the mountains of Assyria, into the land of Lullu [Akkad, in the heart of Assyrian Mesopotamia[8]] and did a great slaughter of the men of Ashur, the enemy of Khaldi.

These events probably took place in the reign of King Sargon's predecessor, Shalmaneser IV.[9]

In the final analysis, however, Rusa was unable to create an Iranian buffer-state; otherwise, the history of the following century might have been quite different. But he seems to have made a mutually beneficial trade agreement with the Iranians, with special reference to the transit of goods from Elam, India and perhaps China, through Urartian territory. The caravans from Elam and India then passed through Urartu to a Black Sea or a Mediterranean port, and Assyria was deprived of the dues she extracted from merchants travelling through her territories, Urartu being the beneficiary. These goods, together with Ararat's own famous bronzes, were widely distributed throughout the Mediterranean lands. Articles with marked Urartian characteristics have been found in Greece and even as far west as Etruria in Italy, and France.

Here, then, is a catalogue of events unfavourable to Assyria and of serious concern to Sargon, which can be attributed directly to Rusa's activities. The diversion of east–west trade through Urartu; Rusa's self-appointed role as kingmaker in Mannai; Urartu's occupation of Mannai — Mannai with its rich grains 'as numberless as the stars of heaven'; Rusa's part in the fomentation of trouble by Metatti of Zikirtu between Mannai and other Iranian states on the one hand, and Assyria on the other. But trouble was also brewing in Syria where Rusa had revived Urartian influence. To the north of that country, the Kingdom of

Phrygia was allied to Urartu, and Rusa had contrived to rouse anti-Assyrian movements in other neighbouring countries. These resulted in frequent border clashes between the northern and southern empires. In 717 BC, King Araras of Carchemish (who seems to have accepted Rusa's suzerainty) was plotting against Sargon with the central Anatolian states of Que, Gurgum, Milid, Kumukh and part of Tabal. It was the 'man [the king] of Urartu', together with 'Mita of the Mushki' (Midas of Phrygia), who encouraged these subversive movements against Assyria.

Rusa's provocative policy in supporting the Iranian states, and his apparently aggressive activities against Assyria, might be interpreted as attempts in the first instance to divert from himself to his Assyrian foe the wild and war-like energies of the new Iranian kingdoms and secondly to intimidate the Assyrian monarch in his attempts to mobilise his forces for a major attack against Ararat. For 20 years from his own accession to the throne in 735, and for the first seven years of Sargon's reign, Rusa successfully implemented this policy. However, in 715 BC, Sargon was able to mount an attack against a recalcitrant Carchemish, the key city guarding the passage across the Euphrates, which he occupied. He pressed northwards, reached Tabal and thus forced a wedge between Urartu and her ally Phrygia.

With his western frontiers secure, Sargon could turn his undivided attention to Urartu and her Iranian allies. In July 714 BC, he led his forces out of Kalhu for the purpose of crushing, once and for all, Zikirtu and Andia, two of the most troublesome of the Iranian states. Sargon's own account of his campaign is paraphrased as follows: His infantry and cavalry flew like eagles over the Lower and Upper Zab rivers and they cut their way with mighty bronze axes up densely forested[10] and pathless mountains, with deep, dark gorges where the sun never penetrated; while the baggage train of camels and asses leapt like wild ibex[11] over crags and rocks. Thus having crossed six mountain passes touching the clouds and negotiated two major rivers in flood and 26 times crossed the Buia in its wanderings,[12] and having overcome numerous other physical obstacles, Sargon led his troops, his cavalry, archers, spearsmen, pioneers and a convoy of laden asses and camels into Mannai, where he received the abject submission of Ullusunu, who diplomatically forgot his obligations to his benefactors, Rusa of Urartu and Metatti of Zikirtu.

A repose as the guest of his servant Ullusunu implies festivities for Sargon, much eating drinking and merry making, as recorded by his scribes. Having rested, the Assyrians departed. When they appeared on the frontier of Zikirtu, King Metatti dispersed his people into the safety of the mountains and himself led his army westwards, out of his country, to support his ally King Rusa in the defence of Urartu, on whose power hung the independence of his own country. As to King Rusa himself, threatened by Sargon's movements, he ordered his own troops to the 'Mountains of Assyria' to reinforce the garrison of his province of Uishdish,[13] on the eastern side of Lake Urmia, where Metatti had led his own troops. Sargon's spies, under the direction of the crown prince, Sennacherib, quickly reported this movement. They also reported the rebellion of Rusa's governor of the fortress city of Uasi (south-west of Lake Van)[14] as well as the revolt of one of Rusa's generals in Tushpa, the capital itself, and how the Urartian monarch suppressed them. He captured the seditious general and 20 of his officers, executing at the same time 100 soldiers who had taken part in the mutiny.[15] Sennacherib also informed his father of Rusa's war against an invading horde of Cimmerians who had crossed the Caucasus mountains. That invasion of 714 BC is mentioned in the Assyrian royal correspondence from the archives of Kalhu and Nineveh. In response to the urgent calls of his northern command, Rusa led a strong contingent of his troops out of Tushpa, heading north to meet the Cimmerians. This manoeuvre Sargon derided as 'Rusa leading his troops in flight'.[16]

Although Rusa was defeated by the Cimmerians, he was able to divert them to the east and to the west and they did not overrun his own kingdom. No less than nine of his generals were killed in that fierce battle. Small, peaceful groups of Cimmerians were allowed to settle in Urartu after the war, and later used as mercenaries in the Urartian army. Sargon seized this opportunity to strike at harassed Ararat. His recorded invective against Rusa emphasises his respect for the power of his rival:

> Ursa, that mountain dweller from a race of murderers, who knows not the meaning of law, whose lips speak words of war and injustice, who obeys not the mighty words of Shamash and has each year rejected his rules. He has multiplied the weight of his sins by raising a great army, by daring to form it in battle array in the strong mountain of Uaush (in Uishdish) with his allies of Zikirtu and Andia and all the chieftains of the mountain peoples.[17]

Sargon turned back from Zikirtu towards Uishdish and fell upon the depleted forces of Rusa in the gorges of Mount Uaush and routed the allies 'amidst rivers of blood and corpses without number'. The country now lay wide open to Assyrian depredations, and Sargon's triumphant and destructive march northwards. Up the eastern side of Lake Urmia he advanced, destroying all before him — fortresses, villages, towns; and laying waste the fertile fields. He reached the city of Ulhu, to the north of the lake, a centre of farming and horse rearing. The city had been built on arid land but Rusa had brought water in abundance by a system of canals, and the land was replete with fruit and corn and trees, as well as pasturage for the spirited stallions found in their stalls by the Assyrians. The stone city walls were razed and the palace demolished 'like an earthern pot'.[18] The hidden pits of barley were found and their contents carried off, the wine skins were slit open and the enormous, 100-gallon *pithoi* of wine[19] were smashed and the wine flowed out and was soaked up into the hot earth. Thousands of mighty axes broke up walls, houses, furniture and property of every kind. Trees were felled, and not a stone left unturned, not a stalk of grain allowed to stand amidst the ruin that was once a city, once a field rich with grain, once a meadow on which fine horses had grazed. The hamlets that surrounded the once beautiful city, were burnt to ashes.[20] The canals were blocked up and the waterlogged land turned into a swamp.[21]

We are given an insight into Assyrian morals when we realise that it is the Assyrian scribes, not their enemies, who at the behest of their master, give these terrible details, and more, with malicious delight. Nor did Urartian construction skills go unnoticed either by the scribes or the Assyrian army technicians. For a modern archaeologist suggests the possibility that today's qanat system of conveying water in Mesopotamia may be attributed 'to the Urartian prototype, seen by Sargon II at Ulhu on his eighth campaign [714 BC] and subsequently introduced into Assyria'.[22]

Having rounded the northern coast of Lake Urmia, Sargon's troops marched towards the north of Lake Van, passing close by Tushpa. Sargon did not venture to attack that powerful bastion. Nor, having crossed the 7000-foot Mount Uizuku and its neighbouring mountain of cypresses, did he attack the northern strongholds of Argishtiuna and Qallania, solidly set in the folds of the mountains, where they gleamed like stars.[23] South-west of

Lake Van, the mighty walls of Uasis (modern Bitlis) marked the frontiers of the Urartian homelands. Sargon took and destroyed the city, but the citadel defied his arrogance. That stronghold, together with the other fortresses he had failed to take, remained a threat in his rear. Thus did he enter his tribute-paying Hubushkia, whose king humbly paid Sargon his annual due.

To the east of Hubushkia lay the holy mountain kingdom of Musasir, whose king Urzana was Rusa's faithful ally. It was the oldest religious centre of Urartu, situated some 18 miles north of Rowanduz, to the west of Lake Urmia; its temples were endowed by generations of Urartian kings. The Assyrians called it the City of Ardini, the Sun god. The most important reference to the temple is to be found in Sargon's history of his campaign against Musasir although the main part of our knowledge is culled from Urartian inscriptions. King Urzana, by not sending tribute to Sargon, by not acknowledging his suzerainty, by not sending messengers with gifts and friendly and loyal greeting, was in every way defying the proud Assyrian conqueror. In fact it was because of Urzana's revolt that Sargon turned eastwards, allegedly 'to punish that barbarous highlander'.[24] He could have waited to chastise a small king of Urzana's calibre in his own good time, but Sargon was well aware of his own dangerous situation in enemy territory. Although Rusa had been defeated by the Cimmerians as well as by the Assyrians, he was still free and at the head of forces, however weak, which, in those dark, mountainous regions, were at all times dogging the steps of the Assyrians. Sargon decided to throw dust in the eyes of his enemy and carry out his determination to destroy Musasir and Urzana. He ordered the whole of his infantry and baggage train to continue south, homewards. If Rusa was indeed in pursuit, that manoeuvre would put him on a false track. Also, Urzana's spies would report the apparent retreat of the enemy and they might not realise that Sargon himself, at the head of an elite bodyguard of 1000 horsemen was moving east, on Musasir. Too late to organise any sort of resistance, Urzana fled from his panic-stricken city. Sargon's horsemen spread like locusts over the country outside the city and with terrifying war cries like thunder, assaulted the walls and broke into the city.

Seated on the throne in the palace, Sargon received the homage and submission of the people and made Urzana's family prisoner. He entered the temple of Khaldi, god of Biaina, ransacked and burnt it and carried away the effigy of the god and all its fabulous treasures, as well as the enormous pile of sparkling wealth of the palace, in all amounting to 333,500 objects, together with a great part of the population, to Assyria. Details of some of the loot are given in Chapter 16 on the art of Urartu. But briefly, the hoard included over a ton of gold, over 9 tons of silver, 109 tons of bronze ingots,[25] jewellery, a variety of gems, ceremonial vessels and weapons of war, made of gold and silver, and all kinds of rare articles contrived by the secret skills of Urartian craftsmen. However, like his predecessors who had invaded Urartu, Sargon, too, was unable to garrison Musasir or any other part of Urartian territory. He would undoubtedly have wished to stay in Musasir, particularly as it abutted on the infant Iranian states which could be seriously influenced in their political attitudes by a powerful neighbour.

And what happened to King Rusa? According to Assyrian records 'When Ursa [Rusa], king of Urartu, heard that Musasir had been destroyed and his god Haldi carried away, then with his own hand, with the iron dagger which hung at his side, he put an end to his life.'[26] A modern scholar, however, writes of the death of Rusa from wounds he received during his war with the Cimmerians.[27]

There are various version of the above events, the most usual of which follows closely Sargon's own colourful story of a Rusa who, on being defeated, fled to Tushpa where he committed suicide by falling upon his sword. But as I have already suggested, the details of the campaigns of Assyrian monarchs given by their obsequious scribes must be taken with reservations, for scribes wishing to retain their position in the royal service (or even their heads on their shoulders) would have found it prudent to flatter their royal (and often savage) masters. On analysing the situation carefully, a modern historian holds the view that too much has been made of Sargon's success in this instance. It brings out Sargon's character and illustrates the impressive height of Ararat's civilisation, but ultimately the expedition it records was not of great political significance and did not yield lasting results to Assyria.[28]

Indeed, according to recent research,

In 713 BC, Assyrian eponym lists indicate that Sargon returned to Musasir the statue of the god [and perhaps other booty] which he had taken the year before. How much of this action was prompted by religious feelings, and how much by continuing fear of Urartian counterattacks is uncertain, but some of the intelligence reports sent to Sargon, which indicate tension on the Urartian border, may refer to this period. One letter from Urzana, the king of Musasir, to a high official in Assyria, bluntly asserts his freedom to allow the Urartians to sacrifice in his city, and his independence of Assyria.[29]

Summing up the salient points in this chapter, we see that Rusa seized the throne of Biaina in 735 BC at a time of increasing Cimmerian pressure against the northern frontiers of the empire. Dangers from the infant Iranian states in the east and the south had to be dealt with diplomatically and with circumspection, and measures had to be taken to guard the country against the perpetual threat of a powerful Assyria. Themselves beset by the Scythians further north, the Cimmerians broke through the Urartian defence lines, caused Rusa to abandon his war with Sargon, and enabled the latter to win an easy victory. But Sargon's invasion, described by his sycophantic scribes in such flattering detail, did not develop beyond a large-scale raid, thanks to some extent to the rebellion against him of Ararat's vassal, King Urzana, and the threat of an offensive by Rusa (or his generals) who was probably able to reform his army in the north, after his encounter with the Cimmerians.

However, the destruction wrought by Sargon briefly impaired Ararat's function as a powerful buffer-state and at that moment she was unable to contain the wild Cimmerian and Scythian horsemen in the north beyond the limits of the River Araxes. They poured down the eastern and western sides of her frontiers, though not through her own territory, to destroy ancient kingdoms and establish new ones. In the final analysis, Sargon should have regretted his lack of foresight in not making common cause with Rusa against the barbarians. For, apart from the serious political consequences beyond the frontiers of Ararat, which militated against Assyria, Sargon forged the links in the chain of events which ultimately led to his own death, at the battle in Tabal against the Cimmerians in 705 BC.

Sargon's invasion is, as we have seen, extensively and minutely documented, but its long-term effects are much exaggerated, for propaganda purposes. In less than a year, under Rusa's successor, Urartu had recovered. It resumed its aggressive policy as a military priority, especially on its eastern frontiers and asserted its status as a powerful kingdom which was to be placated.

Rusa's public works included the construction of an even stronger citadel than the then existing one at Tushpa, with the temple (unfinished until Rusa III's reign, 100 years later) and an acropolis. He rebuilt, beautified and made a garden city of Tushpa 5 kilometres from the old city which had been destroyed by Tilgath-pileser III. As the new city was at a higher level than the Shamiram canal, he built a canal fed by the waters of Lake Keshish, to bring water into the new city.[30] Sargon's scribes sing their admiration of the public works undertaken by Rusa who had 'cut canals and caused waters to run abundantly as the River Euphrates; constructed channels and waterways to irrigate the fields and to transform arid land into flowering gardens, where the raisin and the fruit fall from the trees as rain falls from the very heavens'. In other parts of his kingdom, he had built great dams and walls to control the gushing, life-giving waters. There were huge granaries, rich vineyards and magnificent forests, and in the long valleys the renowned Urartian horse was bred. He added two fortresses to the defence system of the north, in the vicintity of Lake Sevan. On a high crag west of the lake, he built Khaldi's fortress and inscribed a dedication in stone: 'This mighty fortress, the gates of my god Khaldi, I constructed ...'. On the south side of the lake, Rusa built the powerful fortress of Teisheba, dedicated to the god of war of that name 'to demonstrate the power of Biaina and to cow her enemies'. He also built a fortress at Melaskert, the entrance of which has a rounded roof,[31] the prototype of the rock-cut tombs with rounded roofs, of the Pontic kings.[32]

Notes

1. A.H. Sayce, 'The Kingdom of Van', CAH, III. ii. p. 178. Adontz argues that Uedipri was not Sarduri's son, although a member of another branch of the royal family (pp. 178, 189, 191-3).

2. Sayce, *op. cit.*, iii. p. 178; Sydney Smith, 'Foundations of the Assyrian Empire', CAH, III. v; *idem*, 'The Supremacy of Assyria', CAH, III. iii.

3. B.B. Piotrovskii, *The Ancient Civilisation of Urartu* (Barrie and Rockliff, 1969).

4. N. Adontz, *Histoire d'Arménie* (Paris, 1946).

5. Ibid.

6. A.T. Olmstead, *History of Assyria* (New York, Scribner).

7. Piotrovskii, *op. cit.*

8. Olmstead, *op. cit.*

9. Adontz, *op. cit.*
10. Olmstead, *op. cit.*
11. Ibid.
12. Ibid.
13. Sydney Smith, 'The Supremacy of Assyria', CAH III. iii. p. 52.
14. Piotrovskii, *op. cit.*
15. Ibid.
16. Adontz, *op. cit.*
17. Olmstead, *op. cit.*
18. Ibid.
19. Ibid.
20. Ibid.
21. Piotrovskii, *op. cit.*
22. Charles A. Burney, 'Urartian Irrigation Works', AS XXII (1972).
23. Olmstead, *op. cit.*
24. Adontz, *op. cit.*
25. Piotrovskii, *op. cit.*
26. Ibid.
27. Adontz, *op. cit.*
28. Olmstead, *op. cit.*
29. David Frankel, *The Ancient Kingdom of Urartu* (British Museum, 1979); R.D. Barrett, 'Urartu', CAH, III (1982), p. 356.
30. Adontz, *op. cit.*
31. Piotrovskii, *op. cit.*
32. Sayce, *op. cit.*, iv. p.185.

Further sources

H.W.F. Saggs, IRAQ, XXV. pp.145-54. On Sargon's War against Rusa I: Goetze, *op. cit.*, pp. 124-30.

10

Argishti II (714–680 BC): Urartian Military Recovery

King Sargon's own records show that after Rusa's defeat, Ararat continued to enjoy a considerable part of its former prestige. The northern empire was still the champion of the small central and southern Anatolian states and still a serious political and military menace to Assyria. So low had Assyrian prestige fallen that the King of Commagene preferred to pay tribute to Argishti, son of Rusa, than submit to Assyria. Sargon's governor at Amidi, Upahir-bel, speaks of peace to the Urartian monarch in the most obsequious terms, and argues that he has been inoffensive to his neighbours, so why does the king attack the Assyrian city of Harda (near modern Diarbekir)?[1] This from the servant of one who claimed to have reduced hundreds of Urartian cities to rubble. Far from accepting these conciliatory overtures from his traditional enemy, Argishti is ready to 'saddle his horse' to seek revenge on the borders of Amidi.[2] In other words, Urartu now takes the initiative in matters of war and peace, while Assyria is reduced to defending her territories.

A message from crown prince Sennacherib to his father, Sargon, states that one of the Assyrian governors had been threatened with arrest by Ararat's generals in Kumani; he begs for immediate reinforcements. There is also a report of a quarrel over a quantity of timber the Assyrians were not allowed to take away (intended for the building of Sargon's palace at Dur Sharukin).[3] The supply of those timbers were part of the peace treaty, after Sargon's campaign in 714, while the Assyrians agreed to return the effigy of the god, Khaldi, to Musasir.[4] Argishti also takes an aggressive attitude along the eastern Tigris. Another Assyrian official, Ashur-risua, received a report that Argishti's men had captured the spies he had sent to Tushpa; and that there had been a rebellion there, which Argishti had suppressed, putting to death many of the insurgents.[5]

Sargon did not take any action against the provocations of Urartu. Here then, is a picture of two monarchs, the one asserting his arrogance after his father's defeat in the field, and the other taking up an attitude of diplomatic prudence. On the other hand, when Sargon attacked Commagene, Argishti did not go to her aid; Ararat had to conserve her strength for her wars with the northern barbarians. Of incidental interest, and as an illustration of Urartian skills in wielding weapons of war, we are informed that 'Argishti, son of Rusa, fired an arrow 950 cubits (about 500 metres)'.[6]

In 708 BC, according to a report from the Assyrian officer, Ashur-risua, Argishti was collecting a great army. Although the Assyrian rightly guessed that it was in preparation for an attack upon his own country[7], it was in fact used for the purpose of waging war on the Cimmerians who were once again threatening the northern provinces of the Vannic empire. The battle between the Urartians and Cimmerians took place in the following spring. Argishti faced the full brunt of the savage hordes and was defeated, but on Cimmerian territory. The barbarians were unable to press their advantage however, for they had spent their energies in the great battle itself, and Urartian territory remained intact although Ararat sustained heavy losses.[8] This information, given by Assyrian intelligence officers, is gathered from a letter of Sennacherib to his father. Urartu's preoccupation with the Cimmerians would be enough to account for Assyrian military supremacy at this time.

Warned of the advancing Cimmerians after the defeat of Argishti, Sargon prepared to confront them on Assyria's northwestern frontiers. They had been diverted by Ararat southwestwards into Anatolia, where it was the turn of Midas, King of Phrygia, to come into conflict with them. Midas succeeded in repulsing them, but they continued their impetuous charge towards Assyrian territory. Sargon gave battle to a Cimmerian force which must have been considerably weakened by the great battle with Urartu, its confrontation with Phrygian troops and by a long trek from the north through hostile and mountainous country. The Assyrio-Cimmerian battle took place in Tabal, and although the Assyrian forces prevailed, Sargon himself was killed (705 BC). The Cimmerian hordes then dispersed.

The last years of Sargon's reign are not well documented.

After his death, an abortive palace revolution took place, led by the brothers of the crown prince, in an attempt to wrest the throne from him. On succeeding to the throne, Sennacherib inherited the struggles of Assyria, not only with its powerful southern neighbour Babylonia, but also with Syria and Palestine, and he himself made preparations for an invasion of Egypt. It seems, therefore, that after the Cimmerian ravages, the exhausted northern kingdoms had ceased to be troublesome, and the Cimmerians themselves, had temporarily dispersed. Around the year 695 occurred two events of interest to later Armenian history. The first of these is concerned with the Phrygian king Gurdi, probably the son of Midas (of the golden touch) who in Sargon's time had repulsed the Cimmerians, and the grandson of Gordios. Sennacherib went to war against him in Tabal, but he was not very successful. There was no decisive battle; Gurdi contrived to avoid an encounter and the Assyrian expedition degenerated into a raid. It was probably this Gurdi who conducted into Tabal that part of the Phrygian community from whom, according to Herodotus (VIII. 73) the Armenians are descended.

The second event is told in the Old Testament, according to which Sennacherib was murdered by two of his sons, Adramelech and Sharezer, while he was praying in the temple. The patricides fled to Urartu, or probably more precisely, to the principality of Shupria: 'And it came to pass, as he [Sennacherib] was worshipping in the house of Nisroch his god, that Adramelech and Sharezer his sons smote him with the sword; and they escaped into the land of Armenia' (II Kings XIX. 37). Moses of Khoren in his *History*, founded the Armenian tradition that one of the two fugitives fathered the Armenian princely dynasties of Artsruni and Gnuni. At that time, Assyria and Urartu still had a common frontier, but it consisted of the high mountains of Kurdistan between upper Mesopotamia in the south and the basin of Lake Van in the north, which ensured peace between he two enemies. An interesting document describes how Senacherib built a great aqueduct, raised on walls and arches, to carry water from Mount Tas (modern Mount Bavian), on the Urartian frontier, to Nineveh. That inscription proves that at this time the southern frontier of Urartu was a mere 50 kilometres from Nineveh. In the east, Mannai was an Assyrian tributary. The proximity of the Urartian forces to Assyria, had created a mutinous spirit even among some of Sargon's troops, who had seen the destruction of their homes and the death of their kin by the command of the very man for whom they were forced to fight.[9]

In 1938 an Urartian stronghold was discovered at Altin Tepe (Golden Hill), near Erzincan. It had remained unharmed after Urartu had been overrun by barbarians and conquerors early in the sixth century BC. Here stood the citadel of an Urartian prince whose overlord would have been King Argishti II (714–680 BC).

Altin Tepe was a formidable citadel, guarding Urartu's western frontiers. Its walls enclosed a palace and temple and storerooms, as well as a large audience hall. The walls of the latter were decorated by brightly coloured murals of which fragments still remain. Many examples of work of a high standard in bronze, iron, gold, silver, ivory, stone and wood have been unearthed inside the citadel and cemetery. The tombs in the cemetery simulate miniature houses which, archaeologists suggest, are probably the burial places of the wealthy aristocracy. The entrance to each house was secured by an enormous stone block weighing several tons, to discourage theft and the disturbance of the owner's last resting place. Here also an ancient tomb was accidentally discovered containing some treasure, now exhibited at the National Museum, Ankara. Yet another tomb was discovered in 1958 which prompted the Turkish government's Department of Antiquities and Museums to sponsor excavations. Most of the tombs contained a coffin with the remains sometimes of a single person or those of a man and a woman, both dressed in rich garments with their personal possessions near by. Among articles of a decorative or ornamental nature the tombs were furnished with chairs and tables, standing on bronze legs, with representations of lion's paws and the hooves of cattle; and large cauldrons on tripods with handle mounts depicting bull's heads. In one of the tombs, there was even a war chariot complete with all the paraphernalia of horse trappings — harnesses, bits and belts.[10]

In contrast to the adornments of the persons of the defunct rich, the bodies of the less privileged members of the Urartian community were cremated. Dr R.D. Barnett of the British Museum, London, reports:

The burning [cremation] was done there [southern Caucasus] in the absence of forests, with fuel of dung-bricks. ... Bodies were burnt clothed, wearing ornaments e.g. beads which were found in urns, though weapons and bracelets were put in the burial after burning ... . That cremation was probably a normal burial custom of the Urartians, as Kuftin said, is again shown by its occurrence in a small group of tombs similar to those of Igdyr recently discovered at Nor Aresh, a village on the outskirts of Erevan and reported only in an Armenian periodical. Here three cremation burials containing Urartian metal ornamental equipment were recently found and recorded.[11]

The situation at Altin Tepe dominates two east-west mountain passes, astride the communications between central and western Urartu. Thus, the citadel had to be in constant state of preparedness against possible attack by an enemy and the storerooms are tangible evidence of this military necessity. As in other Urartian fortresses, at Altin Tepe also, large urns stand in rows, and the cuneiform inscription upon each indicates its contents: wheat, barley, sesame, beans, oils or wine. The royal cellars at Tushpa alone had a storage space for over 50,000 gallons of wine, while the jars in Teishebaini in Transcaucasia had a total capacity of some 40,000 gallons.

Although Altin Tepe was only a provincial city, it had a palace and therefore a viceroy or governor. Some of its public buildings were much more impressive than those in the capital cities of its powerful western neighbours. Of particular interest in this respect is the great audience hall which was 130 ft long and 75 ft wide, with 18 columns supporting a flat roof. The 9-foot thick walls were completely covered with intricate murals. The great halls (or *apadana*) of the ancient Achaemenid royal palaces appear to be reproductions of this great hall at Altin Tepe. This is similar to a hall uncovered at Erebuni, a city which, unlike others in its vicinity, survived beyond the Achaemenian period.

Notes

1. N. Adontz, *Histoire d' Arménie* (Paris, 1946), p. 120.
2. Ibid., p. 119.
3. Piotrovskii, *The Ancient Civilization of Urartu* (Barrie and Rockliff, 1969), Civi, p. 125. Piotrovskii, p. 159 describes Urartian skill in archery: 'Argishti, son of Rusa, fired an arrow from this spot, in front of the grove called Gilurani, as far as the garden belonging to Ishpilini, son of Batu: 950 cubits' [about 500 metres].
4. R.D. Barrett, 'Urartu', CAH III (1982), p. 356.

5. Olmstead, *History of Assyria* (New York, Scribner).

6. Ibid.

7. Adontz, *op. cit.*, pp. 125-8; Cyril Toumanoff, *Studies in Christian Caucasian History* (Georgetown University Press, 1963), p. 199.

8. Adontz, *op. cit.*

9. Olmstead, *op. cit.*

10. R.D. Barnett and N. Gökce 'The Find of Urartian Bronzes at Altin Tepe', *AS* III, 1953; Piotrovskii, *The Ancient Civilization of Urartu*, pp. 127-8.

11. R.D. Barnett, 'Excavations of A.S. Uvarov in 1870 at Armavir Blur', AS XIII (1963), quoting *Nor Areshi Uratian Kilumarium: Teghekagir* (the Academy of Science of the Armenian SSR, Erevan; in Armenian), vol. X (1958), pp. 63-84.

11

Rusa II (680–639 BC): Urartu and Assyria at Peace

The inscriptions of Rusa II, son of Argishti, testify to the re-establishment of Urartian power. One of these, found near Melaskert, refers to the occupation of Alzi,[1] in the west. Altin Tepe, near Erzincan, was still one of Ararat's north-western bastions. On another inscription, found at Adilcevas, on the northern side of Lake Van, Rusa claims to have invaded Phrygia and other regions west of the Euphrates, thus ensuring his control of the trade routes leading to the Mediterranean.[2] A letter from a Mannaean prince to his workmen, carrying out building operations for Rusa in Van, shows that Urartian authority again extended over the important Mannaean state.[3] At this time, the movements of the wild, horse-riding nomadic Cimmerians and Scythians had important effects upon the peoples of Anatolia, including Urartu, as well as on the Iranian peoples, and others especially Mannai, and consequently upon Assyria also. Herodotus (IV. 12) descibes how the Cimmerians and Scythians crashed southwards through the Caucasus:

> It appears that the Cimmerians, when they fled into Asia [through the Caucasus] to escape the Scyths, made a settlement in the peninsula where the Greek city of Sinope was afterwards built. The Scyths, it is plain, pursued them, and missing their road, poured into Media. For the Cimmerians kept the line which led along the sea-shore, but the Scythians, in their pursuit held the Cascasus upon their right, thus proceeding inland and falling upon Media.

It is suggested, then, that there were Cimmerian hordes on the southern coast of the Black Sea, whence they raided southwards into Phrygia and ultimately destroyed that kingdom (*c.*675 BC). In the time of Rusa II, they settled for a considerable period in the region of Lake Van, it seems as allies of Rusa, for the Assyrian king, Esarhaddon, expresses his fears of the Urarto-Cimmerian alliance (*c.*678) in his prayers to his god, Shamash: Would they (the allies) occupy the buffer-state of Shupria?[4] In 670 the Cimmerians attacked Assyria but they were repulsed. Their energies unquenched, in 652 their chief Tugdame (the Lygdamis of Herodotus) led them against Lydia and in the ensuing battle in which they captured and sacked Sardis, Gyges, the Lydian king, was killed. Subsequently, Tugdame himself was killed in Cilicia and the Cimmerians eventually settled in north-eastern Cappadocia, in a region later known as Lesser Armenia. In Armenian, Cimmerians are called 'Gamirk' and Cappadocia is called 'Gamir', which supports the proposal that they settled in Cappadocia.

As to the Scythians, they burst upon the Iranian states east of Urartu and occupied for a time some parts even of so powerful a state as Mannai. Their incursions into Urartu itself seem to have been softened by Rusa's diplomacy, and friendly relations were maintained. This is shown by various Scythian objects found in the important northern Urartian fortress of Teishebaini,[5] built by Rusa II. When, however, the Scyths attacked Hubushkia, on the frontiers of Assyria, Esarhaddon defeated them. But it was not a guileless victory, for the Assyrians had sown the seeds of ill-faith and division within the Scythian ranks before the battle. It is said that the Assyrian monarch then prudently agreed to give one of his daughters in marriage to Bartatua (the Protothyes of Herodotus, I. 103), perhaps the greatest of the Scythian chiefs. According to a romantic legend, the dowry of the princess included the fabulous Treasure of Ziwiye (found in 1947 in Kurdistan, buried in a metal bath,[6] part of which is now exhibited at the British Museum). After this alliance with the Assyrians, in 673 BC, Bartatua, most probably at the instigation of Esarhaddon, led his horde into Armenia and killed and usurped the power of another Scythian chief, Ishpaka,[7] who was presumably on friendly terms with Urartu. This constituted an indirect Assyrian attack upon Urartu.

In 672 BC, Esarhaddon attacked Shupria, razed the capital, Uppume, and reduced it to a colony, deporting large numbers of the population. But he refrained from carrying his war into the territories of Urartu proper. On the contrary, he made a peace gesture to Rusa by returning to Urartu some of Rusa's subjects who seem to have taken refuge in Shupria from the justice of their own country. A similar demonstration of war occurred when Urartian army officers led a Cimmerian contingent and fell upon Shupria. But the Assyrians were alert and the attack failed. They cut off the Urartian commander's head and sent it to Nineveh.[8] However, the Assyrians realised the foolishness of open warfare with Urartu at a time when the restless nomads and savage warriors were seething around them, and the quarrel was patched up diplomatically, by assuming that the dead Urartian commander was only an irresponsible village chief who had been justly executed. And that was the end of the matter, and the last encounter ever to take place between the two kingdoms.[9] At last they had realised their common danger and had the wisdom not to start a war which could only favour the horse-riding Indo-Europeans: Cimmerians pouring down through the central pass of Darial, and the Medes already established along the northern side of Elam, the latter a powerful buffer state on the eastern flank of Assyria.

The energetic and cruel Ashurbanipal had been reigning since 669 and his wars were widespread and successful. In particular, he destroyed the ancient state of Elam, an effective military power between the Medes and Assyrians, and with the same blow he helped his own empire towards its final destruction, for he had opened the floodgates of future Median invasions which would expunge Assyria from the pages of history.

After the destruction of Elam in 654 BC, Urartian ambassadors appear at the Assyrian court to congratulate Ashurbanipal on his victory. On a relief from the palace at Nineveh, they are depicted watching the execution of the Elamite prisoners and, according to Dr R.D. Barnett (in a verbal comment), they are being implicated in the victim's guilt. Nevertheless, these embassies could be regarded only as expressions of courtesies as from one soverign state to another, not as the attempts of a weak kingdom to placate a stronger neighbour, particularly as at that time (towards the end of Rusa's reign), it is doubtful if any part of Urartu's borders was contiguous to those of Assyria. Ashurbanipal's scribes record: 'Rusa, King of Urartu, was overcome by my majesty. Then he sent his princes to Arbela to bring me greetings.'[10] Such boastfulness, given the political and geographical situation between the two countries at that time, might well be interpreted by the modern reader only as an empty echo of the traditional arrogance of Assyrian monarchs.

Rusa II was the builder of the gigantic fortress of Teishebaini on the mound of Karmir Blur, near Erevan. The dramatic discovery of that citadel in 1939 was the climax of much research by Russian and Armenian archaeologists, after the decipherment of the Urartian cuneiform by Guyard and Sayce in the 1880s. At that time, a search began for likely sites of Urartian buildings. The archaeologists were assisted by cuneiform inscriptions on rocks, stelae and stones of ancient buildings scattered over the plain of Ararat, near Lake Sevan, north of Erevan. After many disappointments and the intervention of the First World War, they were rewarded in 1939 by the sensational discovery of Teishebaini on Karmir Blur. There was no doubt about the respective identities of the fortress and its builder, for in 1936 an inscription on a rock, which led to the systematic excavations of the site, read: 'Rusa Argishti-hini' — Rusa, son of Argishti, that is, Rusa II (680–639 BC). An archaeological expedition was organised under the auspices of the Hermitage Museum, Leningrad, which in due course yielded finds of paramount importance. The work was interrupted by the outbreak of the Second World War.

At the end of the war, a committee comprising members of the Academy of Science of the Armenian SSR and the Hermitage Museum, under the direction of Professor B.B. Piotrovskii, resumed the work so auspiciously initiated in 1939, on the site of what we now know to be Teishebaini (or Teshebani, the city of the god of war, Tesheba) on Karmir Blur. During the initial investigations, a fortunate downpour of rain revealed the hidden top of the brick walls of the ancient, buried city, which remained moist while the earth around them dried quickly. The plan of the whole of the buried city thus became visible and the archaeologists were able to dig with speed and accuracy. It became apparent that the ancient city had fallen into ruin only gradually and over a long period. The main building appeared to be a government house, and the city proved to be the capital of the Urartian Transcaucasian provinces. A bronze belt and bronze bolt, with rings at its extremities, were found. Both articles were inscribed in cuneiform: 'Rusa Argishtihini, fortress of the city of Teishebaini'. Thus, the date of the citadel was established. It was built by Rusa II in the first half of the seventh century BC. It was called the citadel of Tesheba, after the god of war, and an ivory statuette of the god was found on the site in 1941. Rusa III must have completed the construction of the city, palace and citadel of

Teishebaini at Karmir Blur. The site of the city and citadel together measure over 100 acres, the Urartian governor's residence, an enormous palace of 120 rooms spreading over some 10 acres, with many turrets and towers, occupying the whole of the hill. The bases of these towers (the towers themselves have fallen long ago) are to be seen on the top of the gigantic walls of the citadel. Constructed of huge basalt blocks, they appear as strong and defiant today as they were when placed in position by the original Urartian masons. The palace was constructed of stone, with timber columns supporting the roof, while the ceilings of the lofty rooms were also made of timber. It was the residence of the king or viceroy.

The Urartians had a highly developed agricultural technique. A stele found in the ruins of the medieval church of Zwartnots, near Erevan, is inscribed: 'Rusa Argishtihini speaks: In the valleys of Kuturlini there was no cultivated land. By the command of the god Khaldi, I have planted these vineyards, I have sown the fields with corn and I have laid out all the orchards, and surrounded the whole with towns.'[11] These agricultural enterprises were achieved by the building of canals some of which are still in use today. The canal serving Teishebaini is fed by the river Ildaruni and emerges into the surrounding fields from a tunnel bored through the solid basalt rock at the foot of Teishebaini's city wall; another proof of the engineering skill and craftmanship of the Urartians. The above inscription concludes: 'Rusa Argishtihini speaks: He who destroys this stele, he who profanes it, he who steals it, he who buries it in the earth, he who throws it into the water, he who proclaims: "It is I who carried out these works", and who replaces his own in place of my name, whether he be from the country of Biaina or from enemy country, may Khaldi, Tesheba, Ardini and all the gods destroy him, his seed and his posterity.'[12]

Many objects were found in Teishebaini belonging to a succession of Urartian kings — Menua, Argishti I, Sarduri II and Rusa II. The royal treasures were transferred from lesser strongholds such as Erebuni and Argishtihinili to Teishebaini when that great fortress, dedicated to the god Tesheba, was completed. A list given by Professor B.B. Piotrovskii includes 'Fourteen large decorative bronze shields with dedicatory inscriptions of Argishti I, Sarduri II and Rusa I around their rims; twenty pointed bronze helmets, with reliefs on the front of each; eighteen bronze quivers with representations of chariots and horses, like those on the shields' all belonging to one or other of the above Urartian monarchs. The storeroom of Teishebaini contained wheat, barley, millet and sesame in earthenware urns (*pithoi*), and the remains of these are exhibited at the Armenian State Historical Museum, Erevan. From the barley they brewed beer in vats; one of these was found with a covering of straw and branches, full of barley, showing signs of fermentation.

Piotrovskii describes his impression of the palace when the debris of earth and stones had been cleared away: 'There was an atmosphere of desolation in the palace. There were wasp's nests and skeletons of mice, and in one of the jars the skeletons of a mouse and cat were found. The cat it seems chased the mouse into the jar and both found themselves trapped because of its depth. When the dust of centuries had been removed, the warehouses gave the impression of having only recently been occupied. Jars full of corn, bowls, lamps of clay, iron knives — all tidily laid out. And no one had lived there for over 2500 years.'[13]

In 1966 excavations were carried out by an English expedition under Professor Seton Lloyd, assisted by Mr C.A. Burney, at the Urartian citadel of Kayalidere, on the top of a hill on the right bank of River Murat in the upper Euphrates, where it turns southwards towards the plain of Mush. Inscriptions show that it was built by Rusa II. It commands the junction of two important routes one of which was used by the earlier Assyrian invaders, and it was feared that it might be used again. It was strategically situated not only against possible invasions from the south, but also against nomadic invaders from the northern steppes. Excavations suggest that agricultural and animal husbandry were carried on perhaps more efficiently than they are today in the region. The Urartians were breeders as well as riders of horses, and their flocks of sheep and herds of cattle represented the main sources of their livelihood. The climate is bitterly cold in winter, and for that reason it would have been cut off in the period of the Vannic kingdom both from friend and foe; that is to say, it would have been safe from attack and at the same time isolated from the central administration.

As in Teishebaini on Karmir Blur, in the citadel at Kayalidere too, numerous very large jars for food storage were found, but unlike Teishebaini, where supplies were laid in against the possibility of seige, at Kayalidere the food stores were kept against the rigours of winter. On this site, rock-hewn tombs, which had been robbed in antiquity, were also found. There was a temple built astride the cliff-top fortifications and constructed of huge basalt and granite blocks. A great many bronze and iron objects were found including military equipment, such as bronze shields and quivers for arrows, bronze ornaments from furniture, and among some of the pieces in the last category there were some extremely well-preserved metal fittings of chairs, stools and tables.

One of the most important finds at Kayalidere is a solid bronze couchant lion, approximately 6½ inches long and 4½ inches high, in quite perfect condition. It is of the highest order of Urartian bronze casting. This is, according to Dr Mauritz van Loon, a typical Urartian lion of the type exemplified by the bronze candelabrum from Toprak Kale, with an inscription of Rusa II. Many other pieces of great interest were found, including bronze belt fragments with lion-hunting scenes of delicate workmanship and outstanding merit. The fortress seemed to have been robbed. There had been a fire which had destroyed it and articles which have been found there must have been hidden in the building or buried for recovery in the future. The objects found at this site, which are of considerable value, would have been made in the eighth century BC[14].

Rusa II also completed the extension of the city of Tushpa, started by his father, on the hill of modern Toprak Kale. He called it the City of Rusa — Rusa-hinili. It extended from the crag of Van, to his palace on the mountain ridge. An artifical lake provided water for the new canals which irrigated the fields, vineyards and gardens. A new waterway also served the old city of Tushpa.[15] The water supply of the city was assured by subterranean aqueducts[16].

The foregoing account of the reigns of Argishti II and Rusa II describes and illustrates Urartian power fully restored, relative to that of Assyria. This balance of power did not change even in the time of Rusa II, whose contemporary was the notoriously cruel and war-like Ashurbanipal. The construction by Rusa II of the massive fortress of Teishebaini and other strongholds in Transcaucasia, as well as in central Urartu, stand witness to a long period of security and economic stability. After the reign of Rusa II, Urartian political power began to decline. That serious factor appears to coincide with the decline of royal authority. As proposed in Chapter 1, the rulers of Armenia 'had to possess more than average organising ability and considerable aptitude in the art of diplomacy to control' their independent-spirited chieftains and, in the troubled times to come, the heterogeneous population of their country.

Notes

1. A.H. Sayce, 'The Kingdom of Van', CAH III. iii. p. 182.
2. B.B. Piotrovskii *The Ancient Civilization of Urartu* (London, 1969),
3. Sayce, *op. cit.*
4. Piotrovskii. *op. cit.*
5. Ibid.
6. R.D. Barnett, 'The Treasure of Ziwiye', IRAQ XVIII^2, 1956.
7. Sidney Smith, 'Senacherib and Esarhaddon', CAH III. iv, and 'The Age of Ashurbanipal', CAH III.
8. A.T. Olmstead, *A History of Assyria* (New York, Scribner).
9. Ibid.
10. Piotrovskii, *op. cit.* Ref. 10: Although Piotrovskii dates the end of Elam in 654 BC, Sidney Smith ('Ashurbanipal and the Fall of Assyria', CAH III. ii) gives the approximate date of 651 as the beginning of the war and the fall of Elam (*c.* 642–39 BC).
11. Ibid.
12. Ibid.
13. B.B. Piotrovskii, 'L'Orient Ancien Illustré', vol. VIII (Paris, 1955).
14. Seton Lloyd and Charles Burney, 'A First Season of Excavations of the Urartian Citadel of Kayalidere', AS XVI, 1966.
15. Piotrovskii, *op. cit.*
16. D.A. Mackenzie, *Myths of Babylonia and Assyria* (London Gresham).

12

The Last Kings of Urartu

	Tentative dates
Ashur-bani-pal,	
(King of Assyria)	668-626
Sarduri III	639-635
Erimena	635-629
Rusa III	629-615
	or
	629-590
Sarduri IV	614- after 608
	(perhaps 598)
Rusa IV (Piotrovskii)	598-590

The chronology of the reigns of the last kings of Urartu is still in dispute among scholars. The list above, down to Sarduri IV, was compiled by archaeologists after the discovery of inscribed tablets at Karmir Blur in the 1960s.[1] Professor Piotrovskii's chronology of the last rulers differs from the above. He quotes the inscription on a seal, found at Karmir Blur, stating: 'This is the seal of the palace of Rusa, son of Rusa.'[2] Rusa IV would then be the successor of Rusa III. He proposes that Sarduri IV should follow Sarduri III. His chronology would then read as follows: Sarduri III, Sarduri IV, Erimena, Rusa III, Rusa IV. Another Karmir Blur tablet mentions 'Sarduri son of Sarduri'.[3] Professor A.H. Sayce mentions yet another Sarduri to whom a memorial was discovered on the southern shores of Lake Sevan.[4] He calls himself 'the son of Rapis'. Was he the successor of Sarduri III? The kingdom of Urartu was probably destroyed in 590 BC. I give below my reason for fixing it so precisely.

Sarduri III's contemporary on the Assyrian throne was the

notoriously cruel but scholarly King Ashurbanipal, who appears to have held Urartu in high respect. There was peace between the two countries at this time. The Assyrian king proudly records that Sarduri's 'royal fathers' had allied themselves with his own 'royal fathers', thus confirming Sarduri's direct descent from the ancient royal house of Biaina; he acknowledges at the same time Sarduri's own 'fraternal' greetings and gifts.[5] There is also evidence of Urartian ambassadors at the court of Ashurbanipal who represented, in the words of the Assyrian scribe, 'the great king inhabiting the city of Tushpa', and there might have been complementary ambassadors of the Assyrian monarch at Sarduri's court. However, while Urartu's monarch sent King Ashurbanipal greetings and gifts, he remained at the same time on friendly terms with the formidable Scythians; which reflects the diplomatic skills of Sarduri. Yet, even when thus provoked, the Assyrian king only expresses annoyance, impotently, in a hymn composed by himself, addressed to his god Ashur: 'The Urartians also, that proud mountain people, carry on intrigues with the Umman-Manda [the nomads], the perfidious foe, and are constantly committing great abominations against thee.'[6] Little is known of Sarduri III's reign. Buildings erected during his reign include the fortress of Chavushtepe (S.E. Lake Van), excavated by archaeologist Erzen. He brought to light walls and towers, a temple and sundry domestic buildings, fragments of wall paintings and a bronze plaque showing horsemen and chariots.[7]

Between the reigns of Sarduri III and Sarduri IV, Rusa III ruled for 14 years. It is certain that he was the son of King Erimena, who is known to us from a bronze shield, ornamented with two rows of lions, discovered by Hormuzd Rassam, the Armenian assistant and successor of Sir Henry Layard, at Toprak Kale in 1880, now at the British Museum. An inscription around its rim reads: 'For Khaldi, the mighty, the lord, this shield Rusa, son of Erimena, has dedicated ... Belonging to Rusa, son of Erimena, the strong king, the king inhabiting the city of Tushpa.' Dr R.D. Barnett suggests, and he is supported by other scholars, the possibility of Erimena meaning Armenian: therefore, 'Rusa, son of the Armenian'. Thus, it appears that Erimena established an Armenian royal dynasty. 'Rusa, son of Erimena', also appears in a brief inscription recording the construction of a granary, found at Argishtihinili, in Transcaucasia.[8]

Armenians had been infiltrating Urartu, in increasing

numbers, since the appearance of the Phrygians in *c*.1150 BC, to the west of the Euphrates; and before them, from Hayasa-Azzi-Alzi. Sarduri IV's brief reign seems to indicate that Erimena might well have unsurped the Urartian throne after a palace revolution with the support of the many Armenians who must have been living in Urartu at that time.

However, there is little or no information on Erimena or Sarduri IV, whereas there are inscriptions at Van, and objects have been found there, as well as at Armavir (Argishti-hinili), perpetuating the memory of Rusa III, including the shield described above, winged bulls with human heads, libation bowls, friezes and, above all, part of the model of a palace. The last item, now exhibited at the British Museum, is unique evidence of the architectural style of that period (described in Chapter 13). Also, inscriptions on bronze pieces discovered at Toprak Kale, record that Rusa III ordered the restoration and construction of buildings in the garden-city of Tushpa, and that he completed the construction of the Temple of Khaldi at Tushpa, founded nearly a century earlier, by Rusa I. Such peacetime activities indicate that Rusa was not expecting any serious onslaught by his enemies upon his empire, for by the standards of those days, Urartu was still an empire comprising an area of some 200,000 square miles, reaching from the River Kura to the southern or more probably the northern foothills of the Taurus, and from the Euphrates in the west to the Caspian sea in the east. There must have been an atmosphere of tranquillity in Tushpa and in Biaina as a whole, a tranquillity which the high priest of Khaldi might well have interpreted as portentous of the tempest which was soon to destroy Khaldi's empire for ever.

But the king could not have foreseen those happenings; on the contrary, he must have been perfectly confident in the strength and ability of his armies to withstand the usual frontier skirmishings and the wars of the annual 'war season'. He could not have foreseen, nor did his spies inform him of the Scythian hordes gathering in the north, or of the ambitions of Cyaxares, king of the Medes, in the south. For 200 years these Indo-European people had been growing in numbers within small kingdoms and principalities along the eastern periphery of Urartu and Assyria. We have seen how Mannai, Parsua, Zikirtu and Andia, and other Iranian states were involved in Urarto-Assyrian politics and wars. We might recall also a Median prince, Deioces, who was deported to Syria by Sargon. His descendant of the same name proclaimed himself the first king of the Medes (*c.*708–655 BC) and consolidated his people into a nation within and around the capital city of Ecbatana, which he built (Herodotus I. 96, 101).

He was succeeded by his ambitious son Phraortes (655–633), who led his newly organised armies against Parsua (Persia) and occupied that country (Herodotus I. 102). Then he turned his attention to Assyria. There were no barriers between himself and what must have seemed to the Medes a fabulously wealthy country whose people luxuriated in the great cities between the banks of the rivers Euphrates and Tigris. The power of the buffer-state of Elam on the eastern flank of Assyria had been broken by Ashurbanipal and there was nothing to stop a Median army from advancing to the very frontiers of Assyria. However, Phraortes was killed in battle and Assyria was given a respite.

Cyaxares, a worthy son of Phraortes, succeeded to the throne of the now powerful Median kingdom. Herodotus (I. 103) writes: 'Of him it is reported that he was still more warlike than any of his ancestors, and that he was the first who gave organisation to an Asiatic army, dividing the troops into companies, and forming distinct bodies of the spearmen, the archers, and the cavalry, who before his time had been mingled in one mass, and confused together.'

On the southern side of Assyria, Babylon's king, Nabopolassar, had succeeded in breaking away from Assyrian domination and in declaring his country's independence by a demonstration of his military forces. He attacked Assyria, but when he was confronted not only by Assyria but also by its allies, Egypt and a horde of Scythians, he prudently retreated. While the Assyrian army was thus engaged, Cyaxares besieged and occupied the ancient Assyrian city of Ashur in 614 BC, and took the opportunity to conclude, from his position of strength, an alliance with Babylon's Nabopolassar. The Scythians who were supporting Assyria, tempted by the rich promises of Cyaxares, defected from their allies and joined the Medes. The joint forces of the Medes, Babylonians and Scythians defeated the Assyrians, laid siege to Nineveh in 612 and in the same year took it by storm. The Assyrian king, Sin-shar-ishkun, (the legendary king Sardanapalus) perished in the conflagration which destroyed his palace and treasures, his family, his concubines and servants. Then, like locusts invading a field of fat harvest, not only the invaders but the rulers themselves together with their own people of Nineveh looted and carried off its fabulous wealth, destroyed what they could not take away and, of all the city's great marvels and glories, left nothing but a ruined mound. And the prophet Nahum sang: 'Woe to the bloody city! It is all full of lies and rapine and a multitude of the whoredoms of the well-favoured harlot that selleth nations through her whoredoms. O king of Assyria, thy nobles lie in the dust; thy people is scattered upon the mountains; all that hear of thy ruin shall clap their hands over thee; for upon whom hath not thy wickedness passed continually?' (Nahum III).

Ashur-uballit, successor of Sin-shar-ishkun, fled to Harran, the administrative centre of Assyria's former western provinces, and prepared to defend there the vestiges of the empire. He hoped to receive help from his ally, Pharaoh Necho of Egypt (who would not wish to see Babylon, a neighbouring country, too powerful), while Nabopolassar of Babylon awaited the arrival of his allies the Medes and Scythians, before attacking the Assyrians. But the Egyptians were held up in their progress towards Harran by Josiah who, in spite of Necho's conciliatory messages, would not allow him to pass through his territory. There was a pitched battle at Megiddo (Armageddon) in which Josiah was killed and the Judeans slaughtered (2 Chron. XXXV 20-4). Pharaoh Necho could then continue in haste towards Harran. In 610 Nabopolassar attacked Harran. Ashur-uballit, fearful of being besieged and preferring to fight in the open, led his men out of the city to battle. The Babylonians seized the opportunity to charge into Harran, which they devasted. But suddenly it was the Babylonians who found themselves besieged in their turn, for the Egyptians had arrived, joined forces with the Assyrians, and invested Harran. This Assyrio-Egyptian triumph was short-lived however, for the long-awaited Median army appeared and relieved the hard-pressed Babylonians, who then emerged from their perilous situation and joining their allies in a final assault, crushed and destroyed Assyria for ever. The date of 607 BC, after the fall of the key city of Carchemish, is given for this final curtain on Assyrian history.

According to the above chronology, then Sarduri IV would have witnessed the fall of Nineveh in 612, two years after his accession to the throne. It is even possible, though there is as yet no evidence for the proposal, that he assisted the Medians and the Babylonians in the destruction of his country's traditional enemy. Once Assyria had been disposed of, the Babylonians consolidated their gains and became the real heirs of the Assyrian empire. Babylonian chroniclers give details, on two tablets, of expeditions against Urartu between 609 and 605. One of them refers to an attack on the Urartian town of Urashtu in 609 of which the outcome is unknown, and the other refers to Nabopolassar's expedition into the mountains around Bit-Hanunia, 'in the land of Urartu'.[8] This shows that Urartu was very much in existence after 608 and down to 594 BC, during the reign of King Zedekiah of Judea, when the prophet Jeremiah called upon the assistance of Urartu (Ararat), Mannai (Minni) and the Scythians (Ashkenaz) against the Babylonians (Jeremiah Ll. 27). In fact, the Babylonian crown prince, Nebuchadrezzar, defeated the Judean forces at Jerusalem in 587 and deported thousands of leading men and craftsmen to Babylon. It is possible that the last king of Urartu's reign ended at about the same time or a little earlier. They are years of confusion and tremendous political and ethnic upheavals.

The relationship between the barbarians, especially the Scythians, and the government of Urartu in the Transcaucasian provinces was mainly a friendly one, and according to texts of Ashurbanipal, the Urartian alliance with the barbarians was a constant and very serious menace to Assyria. Indeed, if it were not for Scythian support of the Medes against Assyria in 612 BC, Assyria would not have succumbed on that occasion. It is possible that apart from the rewards offered to the Scythians by Cyaxares in return for their defection from Assyria, Urartu might also have exerted her influence on them to join the Medes against her ancient enemy.

However, once Cyaxares had established himself as master of northern Mesopotamia, he cast a covetous eye towards western Anatolia and Lydia, and in 590 BC, the Medes marched westwards. The final battle (585 BC) between Cyaxares and Alyates, King of Lydia took place on the banks of the River Halys (Kizil Irmak), and in order to reach that position the Medes had to overrun and destroy Urartu, which lay astride their route.

In these harassing circumstances, when Urartu's military resources were already fully engaged, Teishebaini (or Teshebani, the city of the god of war, Tesheba) the Transcaucasian capital, was attacked by the Scythians, for since the destruction of Assyria, the Urarto-Scythian alliance had gradually broken down. The Scythians laid seige to the city; the inhabitants ran out of food and suffered great privations. A bombardment of burning missiles set the palace alight, and the citadel, where the besieged had taken refuge, was then taken by storm. A bloody massacre followed, the palace was ransacked and the temple of Tesheba was pillaged. A great quantity of treasure was looted by the enemy and those who had survived the onslaught were taken into slavery.[9] The manner in which the last king of Biaina died is not known; he might have been killed while leading the defence of Teishebaini.

Although a great deal of treasure was carried away by the invaders, large quantities of objects remained to be found by modern archaeologists — gold, silver, bronze and ivory articles; helmets, shields, quivers, vessels, cups, chalices, goblets, seals. Inscriptions upon them indicate their owners: Menua, Argishti, Sarduri and Rusa. All these articles, made at different periods, had been brought to Teishebaini from lesser strongholds by the Urartian sovereigns when the city became the capital of the Transcaucasian provinces.

Thus, after three centuries, the northern gates of the ancient kingdom were shattered, offering the barbarians an entrance through which they could swarm down into the lands of Biaina. They did so and established themselves in an eastern province of what was soon to become (if not already) the Kingdom of Armenia. The region in Armenia where the Scythians are supposed to have settled is called Sakashen of the province of Uti-k'-Oten, of which the main city is Ganjak (east of Lake Sevan). This settlement, if true, might have first taken place according to Dr Nicholas Adontz, in *c.* 680 BC when Rusa II reduced 28 chieftainships around Lake Sevan. But the Scythians remained separate and did not influence the Armenians. They have distinctive features and this is evident today in the town of Nukha in Azerbaijan, the eastern neighbour of Armenia but formerly Armenian territory.[10]

Before its destruction, Teishebaini was already declining into decadence. Urartian power was crumbling; tribute from vassal states came irregularly; since the conquest and occupation of Elam by the Assyrian king Ashurbanipal, the caravans from the east, which brought much wealth and prestige, no longer passed through Urartu, which in itself would be a serious economic setback. The controversial date of these events is given by some scholars as 585 BC. The drama of the destruction of Ararat might be heightened by associating the end of an empire with the eclipse of the sun, which took place in 585 BC, as predicted for the first time in history of science, by Thales of Miletus. The year 585 was also the fifth year of the war between the Medes and the Lydians and the eclipse was the reason for a peace treaty between the terrified belligerents. It is, therefore, possible to fix 590 BC as the year when the Medes overran Urartu and ended the reign of its last king, before their five-year war with the Lydians. There is no doubt that the kingdom of Ararat was still in existence in the year 594 BC, for it was in that year (i.e. in the fourth year of Judea's king Zedekiah's reign) that Jeremiah called against Babylon the nations of the north — Ararat, Minni (Mannai) and Ashkenaz (Scythians) (Jer. Ll. 27). The final deportation of the Judeans took place in 587–586 BC and it is dramatically described in the Old Testament (Jer. LII.).

It seems possible that since the evidence referring to King Sarduri IV has been found at Karmir Blur, while Rusa III appears to be mainly associated with Toprak Kale, that in the last years of the Urartian kingdom, when it might have been fragmented by the invasions of Scythians and Medes, there were two kings ruling at the same time: Sarduri in the north, leading the defenders of Teishebaini against the Scythians, and Rusa in the south fighting against the Medes and the Armenians. It was during that military and ethnic chaos that the Armenian government must have asserted itself in part or parts of Urartu, when the Urartian aristocracy, perhaps under a native leader by the name of Rusa IV,[11] fought a rearguard action against Medes, Armenians and Scythians and eventually settled in the mountainous region on the Upper Araxes. The members of the Armenian royal dynasty, established by King Erimena, would have probably identified themselves with their Urartian subjects; Rusa IV, Sarduri IV or Rusa III being the last of that dynasty. It is unlikely, therefore, that there was a continuity of rulers from the Urartian to the Armenian kingdom which followed.

Armenia is mentioned among the satrapies (governorships) of Persia's King Darius the Great (522–485 BC), in the famous trilingual inscriptions (Old Persian, Elamite and Babylonian) upon the cliff face at Bisitun (Behistun, northern Persia). There Darius describes the organisation of his empire into 20 satrapies, of which Armenia is the 13th and Urartu within the 18th. However, before him, Hecataeus of Miletus was the first to mention 'Armenoi', c.525 BC, which leaves a gap of a mere 60 years between the end of the kingdom of Van and the first historical evidence of the existence of the state of Armenia. During that period, and the previous generations of infiltrations, conquests and consolidation, the Armenians would properly be described as the ruling aristrocracy of those territories (and eventually of the whole of the ancient Kingdom of Urartu), where they imposed their language upon those Urartians who chose to stay (and according to recent findings, there was a large proportion of the population who did so), and even Armenised Urartian names.

Those of the Urartians who fled continued to live in the highlands of the upper Araxes. They are referred to by Xenophon (*c*.400 BC) as Khaldians. He describes them (Anabasis V. 5) as a free and brave people, 'who were not subjects of the King and were exceedingly formidable'. The name persists, and as late as AD 1404, when the Castilian ambassador accredited to the court of Trebizond, Don Ruy Gonzales de Clavijo, wrote of his travels from Trebizond to Erzincan. On the third day out, he describes his journey through the snowy mountains of the 'province of Chaldia', where all caravans pay toll. The territory formed part of the empire of the Grand Comneni. The name Chaldia survived until the early part of the nineteenth century in the diocese of the Greek Orthodox Church, with the capital, Kumush-Khaneh, on the road from Trebizond to Baipurt.

Notes

1. I.N. Diakonov, Urartskie pi'sma i documenty, akademia nauk SSSR (Inst. Arkeologii, Moskva/Leningrad). Quoted by Guitty Azarpay, *Urartian Arts and Artifacts* (University of California Press, Berkeley, 1968). R.D. Barnett, 'Urartu', CAH III¹, 1982, ch. 4.
2. B. B. Piotrovskii, *The Ancient Civilisation of Urartu* (London, 1969).
3. Ibid.
4. A.H. Sayce, 'The Kingdom of Van', CAH III. iii. p. 183.
5. Nicholas Adontz, *Histoire d'Arménie* (Paris, 1946).
6. Piotrovskii, *op. cit.*
7. Ibid.
8. Ibid., p. 195.
9. B.B. Piotrovskii, *L'Orient Ancien Illustré*, VIII (Paris, 1955); Seton Lloyd, *Early Highland Peoples of Anatolia* (Thames and Hudson, London, 1967).
10. Adontz, *op. cit.*, p. 309.
11. Piotrovskii, *op. cit.*

13

Political Organisation:
Towns and Buildings

The Kingdom of Urartu appears to have been governed by a feudal monarchy. The king, ruling from Tushpa, styled himself 'Erili Erilaue',[1] King of Kings. The full royal titles were: Mighty King; Great King; King of All; King of Kings; King of [the land of] Biainili; Ruler of the City of Tushpa. The members of the aristocracy, who governed the provinces, derived their powers and privileges from him. In most cases, it seems reasonable to suppose, they had inherited their estates from their forefathers, the original Hurrian chieftains of the territories between Lakes Van and Urmia, and northwards, beyond Lake Van, where they had enjoyed the benefits of uninterrupted development since the Middle Bronze Age (c.1900 BC).[2] The various dependencies of the kingdom paid tribute in gold, silver and agricultural products, particularly in corn wherever it was cultivated.

There appear to have been three broad categories of territories owing allegiance directly, and voluntarily, to the king at Tushpa:[3] (1) Urartu proper, with the capital cities of Tushpa and Arzashkun and the adjacent provinces, each one under a governor; (2) territories which had been organised as provinces directly under the central authority, but most of which had retained their basic independence, merely paying tribute to the Great King; (3) independent kingdoms and principalities which were voluntarily bound to Urartu for reasons of political, military or economic advantage. These regions together comprised 15 provinces, none of which could be said to have been acquired by force. It was in these provinces that Urartian institutions and their general culture developed. A fourth category would consist of the conquered territories, some 64 principalities in the Plain of Ayrarat, together constituting one of the 15 great provinces of ancient Armenia. There was, in addition, the extensive Sevan region and the country of Qulhi (Colchis), where Urartu had a Black Sea port, though there are no records as yet to support this claim.

Before Urartian dominance, the greater part of the Armenian plateau was broken up and ruled by many chieftains of whom the strongest gave himself the title of king. The Vannic kings proved to be the most powerful and they succeeded in defeating them one by one and uniting their territories under their own ruler (hence their title 'Erili Erilaue'), eventually sharing with them the wealth and glory of their empire. They were hard taskmasters. They devasted towns and villages carried away whole populations and large herds of cattle, thus ruining the social and economic life-pattern of the principalities and breaking their resistance. Argishti I and Sarduri II deported during the combined periods of their reigns (eighth century BC) over half a million people and brought away the bulk of the herds belonging to the territories they occupied. They enslaved their kings before finally annexing their lands to Urartu. After a prolonged struggle, the kings of Urartu succeeded in making themselves masters of the whole Armenian plateau and establishing their own administrative system. By the time of Rusa I that ambition had been attained.[4] On the Assyrian frontiers in the south, there were 12 states, which together made up the two great provinces of Arzanen and Sophene, extending as far as the right bank of the River Tigris, to the confluence of the Botan tributary. To the east and west of Lake Urmia, Urartu possessed several Iranian districts and, above all, the important state of Mannai.[5] Thus, there were regions in and around Mannai in the south-east, and in and around Malatya in the south-west, which were often within the Urartian hegemony. The importance of those two regions can hardly be exaggerated because of their proximity to — indeed their common frontiers with — the great predator, Assyria. Urartu would go to their defence, while they, on their part, constituted very important allies and buffer-states. Musasir fell outside the Urartian homelands; it was a feudatory state, owing alliegance to Tushpa.

Many of the Urartian towns were built on and around high hills, each chosen for its strategic situation.[6] A citadel or acropolis on the highest point of the hill, its walls rising sheer from the hillside, made them practically impregnable.[7] The dwellings of the people were often carved out of the cliff face[8,9] but at several fortresses there are traces of a lower town, outside the walls, built in the shadow of the acropolis.[10] Around Lake Van, the most easily obtainable stones are basalt and limestone, enormous blocks of which, laid without mortar, were used for the construction of fortresses and palaces. 'Every natural approach to Lake Van was guarded by at least one fortress, and every fortress was built in a naturally defensible situation, often on a hill or spur with precipitous cliffs. The roads to Van itself, from all sides, were guarded by castles and fortress-towns constituting a ring of strongholds. All Urartian settlements of any size were wholly or partly fortified.'[11] The thickness of the defensive walls was 10-14 feet, consisting of large blocks on the inner and outer sides which enclosed stones and rubble between them. The towers and buttresses at regular intervals along the fortress walls relieved the wall face and they were carried up to a projecting cornice, often decorated with open work composed of bricks laid diagonally and capped with stepped battlements.[12]

The town's main building, palace or citadel, might be very large, measuring as much as eighty metres in either direction; its basement would consist entirely of magazines — of the seventy magazines beneath the citadel of Karmir Blur seven were for wine and contained 360 huge clay vessels holding in all more than 350,000 litres! — with the living rooms above, approached by a ramp or staircase; and the building might have three or more storeys. Doorways were sometimes flat-topped sometimes arched; the roofs and flat ceilings were supported by columns — one large room at Arin–berd (Erebuni) had no less than thirty columns.[13]

A columned hall, similar to that at Arin-berd, was discovered at Altin Tepe, near Erzincan. These were probably the proto-types of columned halls (*apadana*) (see Figure 13.1) of Achaemenid architecture whose walls, as in the Urartian examples, served as 'curtains' rather than bearers. The Islamic *aiwan* has inherited similar architectural characteristics. Archaeologists are supported in their descriptions of the likely original appearance of Urartian fortresses by a unique bronze model, of a castle wall, with crenellations, complete with a battlemented turret. It also shows doors and windows, features which are never available in surviving remains.[14] It is exhibited at the British Museum. The fragment of a similar turret, in ivory, was discovered at Karmir Blur.[15] Such models were often carried as tribute[16] to conquerors,

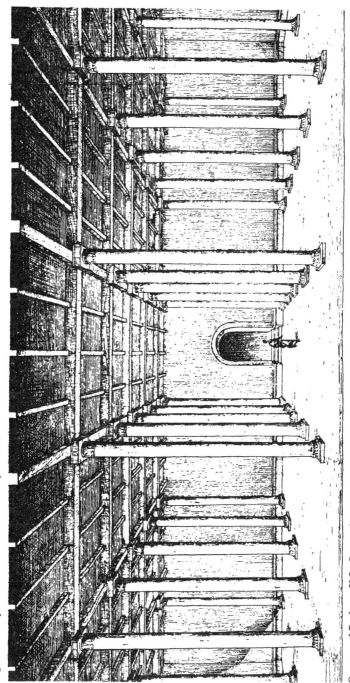

Figure 13.1: Apadana or multi-columned hall, Erebuni

Courtesy of Professor K.L. Organesian.

symbolising the fall of the city. The entrance to a fortress was so disguised as to make it very difficult for the enemy to locate it. The Van citadel has an internal staircase, tunnelled through the solid rock, with windows at intervals along its length, the bottom end of which, at ground level, is the entrance to the fortress. It is only just large enough to admit one man. The cyclopean style of architecture (large blocks of stone laid without mortar), frequently used by the Urartians for their public buildings, would have been even more austere if it were not softened and even beautified by the employment of decorative motifs. A broad platform in front of the temple at Toprak Kale was composed of light and dark basalt slabs, inlaid with concentric rings of alternating black and white limestone and marble mosaic a style of decoration which Persian architects adopted for the palaces at Pasargadae at a later period.[17] That decorative scheme was also evidently used in the temple at Musasir.[18] Fragments of marble frieze with an incised design of cattle were also brought to light at Toprak Kale.[19] However, the Urartians seemed to have used frescoes for decorating the interiors of their public buildings. At Erebuni, both in the temple and the palace, there were elaborate paintings all round the walls of the main halls, 'in red and dark blue on a white ground'[20] in successive tiers (starting from the upper part of the wall) of multi-starred circles, pelmets, stepped battlements, figures of kneeling bulls and rams (or bulls and lions), ending with a band of repeated pattern of a sacred tree with a deity holding a basket and fruit, on each side of it. That decorative scheme (and other such patterns at Erebuni) was reconstructed by Professor K.L. Oganesian, the Armenian archaeologist who discovered Erebuni and directed excavations at the site, using as his model a large piece of wall plaster with the designs described, which had fallen on its face and had thus been preserved through 2700 years. Certain aspects of those designs have Assyrian affinities (see Figure 16.5, p. 178).

Urartian contributions to architectural planning include the pitched roof and triangular pediment, exemplified in the design of the temple at Musasir, as depicted in relief by Sargon's artists in his palace at Khorsabad (see Plate 4). It is built on a podium and has a collonaded front, supporting the gabled and tiled roof.[21] It is the most ancient of its kind yet discovered.[22] The facade of that temple inspired both the Greek and the Achaemenid architects.[23] There is a similarity between the rock-hewn tombs at Karmir Blur and those of the Achaemenid monarchs in Persia, of which the sixth-century tomb of King Cyrus at Pasargadae is an example.[24] It has a double sloping roof, similar to that of the Musasir temple. Buildings with sloping roofs dating to the eighth century BC have been found in Phrygia, at Pazarli and Gordion, but they were most probably built in accordance with the earlier Urartian models. Similar buildings have been discovered at Sardis (seventh century).[25] Thus, their development may be traced westwards to their stylistic apogee in classical Greece.

Urartian town planning seems to have been very advanced. Zernaki Tepe, high above to the north-west of Ercish in the Van region, is laid out on a regular quadratic grid,[26, 27] recalling, strangely, Moses of Khoren's description of the city supposed to have been built by the legendary Queen Shamiram in Armenia: 'Each district of the city was separated from its neighbour by a broad street.'[28] The grid plan was about 18 metres square, with a 5 metre-wide street, the main thoroughfare being 7 metres wide. There are no traces of gateways, as the remaining stone walls are too low. All the houses were uniform in size and built at the same time, but building operations appear to have been abandoned at an early stage, as indicated by the walls which stand only one course high.[29] It is possible that the grid system of streets to be found in the fourth-century remains of Ionian cities of Asia Minor was influenced by Urartu.[30] Zernaki Tepe appears to have been left unfinished, but it does supply evidence of an advanced form of Urartian town planning which is amazingly modern in conception. However, the enemy could by-pass these towns and fortresses and pillage and burn the surrounding countryside and the unprotected villages. That he was able to do so in the heart of hostile country with such ease, as in the case of the raids of Shalmaneser III, Tiglath-pileser III and Sargon II, might be due to the small population of Urartu relative to the immense areas controlled by its powerful monarchs.[31]

Another example of Urartian town planning is that of the fortress of Aznavur (Patnos, about 25 miles north of Lake Van):

It comprises a large lower enclosure and a fortified citadel or keep, on a hilltop about 900 feet above. The best preserved and most prominent feature of the site is the enclosure wall, which is 3.70 to 3.90 m thick and built in the usual Urartian manner, with large stones along each face and rather smaller stones or rubble in the middle: the hard stone used (andesite?) is not found in the immediate vicinity. The towers, built at more or less uniform intervals of about 20 m along the enclosure wall, are approximately square, though their dimensions vary from about 8.00 to about 8.80 m, and some are rectangular rather than square: they have a clear face on all four sides, suggesting that they were built as self-contained units of masonary within the wall. Very probably the towers were built of stone up to a greater height than the wall, which may have resembled Karmir-Blur, in having a stone footing not more than two or three courses high, surmounted by mud brick. Some of the towers are filled fairly solidly with rough stones, but others are filled with rubble and earth: all, however, have large stones along all four faces. There is nowhere any conclusive evidence of a gateway, although it might possibly have been at the north end of that stretch of the wall which runs almost due north-south, where the corner was cut off by a short length of wall now badly destroyed; but this is quite uncertain, and since the wall is nowhere preserved more than two courses high, the gateway could have been at any point.[32]

This, as suggested by Professor Seton Lloyd (quoted by Mr Charles Burney[33]), might mark the position of a cistern or reservoir 'so placed as to take the fullest advantage of the catchment-area. This theory explains how so waterless a site could be chosen for so large a stronghold.'[34]

The great fortress city of Argishti-hinili (Armavir), on the River Araxes to the south-west of Erebuni, in the 'land of Aza', was founded by Argishti I (785–753 BC). A formula of dedication, discovered on the foundation stones of a number of major cities, including Erebuni, Teishebaini and Adilcevaz, was also found in Argishti-hinili (henceforth Armavir). That city was built in the valley of the River Araxes, perhaps the most fertile region of Urartu, which might almost be described as the kingdom's granary. There was also much stock-breeding in the area. As in other large cities, at Armavir citadel, too, there were granaries and *pithoi* of wines, oils, and foodstuffs, set deep into the earth for maximum protection in times of war, invaders' first objective usually being the food magazines. The contents of each *pithos* were recorded in cuneiform or pictograms on the container. Here, as in many other parts of Urartu, canals were built wherever needed. As in the case of most major undertakings in the ancient world, great, imposing buildings — palaces, temples or fortified cities — were ostensibly built to glorify the gods, but in reality to perpetuate the memory of the builder, the king. The population of Armavir would have been about 30,000, which compares with Tushpa's 50,000, according to Burney.

Notes

1. A.H. Sayce, 'The Cuneiform Inscriptions of Van', JRAS, 1882.
2. C.A. Burney, 'Urartian Fortresses and Towns in the Van Region', AS VII, 1957.
3. Adontz, *Histoire d'Arménie* (Paris, 1946), pp. 203, 211, 212
4. Ibid.
5. Ibid.
6. Ibid.
7. Burney, *op. cit.*
8. Adontz, *op. cit.*
9. Ibid.
10. Burney, *op. cit.*
11. Ibid.
12. Ibid.
13. L. Woolley, *Mesopotamia and the Middle East* (Methuen, 1961).
14. Seton Lloyd, *Early Highland Peoples of Anatolia* (Thames and Hudson, 1967).
15. B.B. Piotrovskii, *The Art of Urartu* (Evelyn Adams and Mackay, 1967).
16 R.D. Barnett, 'British Museum Excavations at Toprak Kale', IRAQ XIII¹, 1950.
17. R.D. Barnett, IRAQ XVII¹, 1954.
18. Woolley, *op. cit.*, pp. 167-8.
19. Ibid.
20. Ibid.
21. Ibid.
22. Piotrovskii, *op. cit.*
23. Ibid.
24. Lloyd, *op. cit.*
25. Woolley, *op. cit.*
26. Burney, *op. cit.*
27. Leo Oppenheim, *Ancient Mesopotamia.* Quoting D. Stanislawski, 'The Origin and Spread of the Grid-pattern', *Geog. Review* 36 (1946) pp. 103-20.
28. Moses of Khoren, *History of Armenia* (R.W. Thomson) I. 16 (Harvard University Press, 1978).
29. Burney, *op. cit.*
30. Oppenheim, *op. cit.*
31. Burney, *op. cit.*
32. C.A. Burney and G.R.J. Lawson, 'Measured Plans or Urartian Fortresses', AS X, 1960, p. 192.
33. Ibid.
34. Ibid.

14

Trade and Commerce

Information on the economic structure of Urartu is scarce. But even fewer facts are available on Urartian trade and commerce, business transactions and methods of payment. Where information is not to be found from native sources, it seems that (within reasonable limits) some of the known methods of trading and commercial transactions of neighbouring countries (themselves inheritors of the earliest traditions of Babylonia) might be applied to Urartu. A number of examples given below from Mesopotamia and Syria might well have had Urartian parallels, especially as the earlier commercial institutions would have developed very considerably by the time Urartu appeared on the historical scene, early in the thirteenth century BC, as a confederacy of principalities culminating in a powerful kingdom and extensive empire in the eighth century BC. Thus, they must be relevant in the Urartian context whose kings manifestly realised the economic importance of protecting the trade routes and encouraging the development of agriculture and the industry of their country. The merchants of so advanced a civilisation as Urartu must surely have acquired the trading and commercial skills of their immediate southern neighbours.

Indeed, such skills must have been demonstrated by nascent Urartu's western neighbours, the early Assyrian trading stations (or *Karum*) at Kultepe (Kanesh) and other districts in central Anatolia, whose purpose was to export and import goods to and from their Mesopotamian homelands. Their successors, the Hittites, who infiltrated the Kanesh territories, must surely have absorbed, understood and adopted the trading practices of the Assyrians (heirs of the even more ancient Babylonian experience), before expelling them. Later, in the fifteenth and fourteenth centuries BC, the Mitanni, who colonised and traded with such ancient establishments as Alalakh and Ugarit, themselves past masters of sophisticated commercial practice, could not have failed to learn from the south and transmit to the north, the hoary and complex Babylonian knowledge. I am aware that some scholars disdain to accept such a practical and natural process of learning and adoption of the skills of older civilisations by neighbouring newcomers. They insist upon documentary evidence from the newcomers' own sources, before crediting them with trading and commercial practices such as those I have offered. But of course, mine is an interim response to a difficult problem, and one must hope for more direct evidence from Urartian sources in the future.

Trade Routes and Transport

The wealth of any civilised country has never depended entirely on plunder, although fabulous fortunes from colonial sources have enriched powerful nations down to our own day. From the earliest times, trade and commerce have been carried on, and of course foreign trade, both in goods and services, has always been of paramount importance. It is a favourable balance of payments (the excess value of exports over imports of goods and services) which increases the wealth of a country. This principle, wholly true today, must have been just as true in ancient times. The transportation of goods from place to place, apart from the administration and control of extensive territories, implies a system of roads and posthouses for travellers (and the king's messengers), consisting mainly of companies of merchants carrying their wares on beasts of burden to distant places. The construction of good roads became imperative soon after the city-states of Sumer had given way to the Akkadian king Sargon's empire (*c.* 2371–2316 BC). King Shulgi of Ur (*c.*2060 BC) proclaims in a hymn that he widened and straightened the highways of his kingdom, and that he covered the return journey Ur–Nippur, a total distance of some 200 miles, in a single day![1] However exaggerated that claim might be, it still indicates the existence of a good road between the two cities and the recognition of their importance. Other such roads must have connected various cities to give cohesion to the first kingdoms and empires.

By the eighth century BC, there was much caravan traffic all over the ancient world. Caravans of camels and oxen, onegars and donkeys, and perhaps also yaks in Central Asia, laden with the textiles and embroideries of Elam and Media; lapis lazuli from Afghanistan; perfumes and dyes from the Far East, made their ponderous way towards the Mediterranean and Black Sea ports, whence they might have been shipped to Egypt, Cyprus, Crete and the Mediterranean lands generally. Dromedaries were known from very early times in Arabia (c. 3000 BC). They were used by Mesopotamian armies (c. 900 BC). The Persians, after the sixth century BC, discovered their use for crossing the Syrian desert, a shortcut to the Mediterranean. The Persian Royal Road from Susa to Sardis and the Mediterranean, some 2000 miles long, was probably constructed over existing irregular roads and paths, to which the Persian engineers gave uniformity throughout its length. Merchant travellers in Anatolia (including the Urartians, certainly after the ninth century BC), could use not only the long east-west valleys and the great north-south rivers, but from the Pontic ports they could also sail to the Danube estuary which opened up to them the heart of barbaric Europe and the tin mines of Bohemia; while the Russian rivers emptying into the Black and Azov Seas invited northward adventures. The seas, especially the eastern Mediterranean, were infested by pirates. (Homer considered piracy to be more honourable than trading. In short, he categorises aristocratic piracy with war for plunder and loot — true in his time and true today, with a few exceptions.)

It might also be reasonable to suggest that a certain amount of advantageous trading by barter might have taken place between the 'civilised' adventurers and the nomadic 'savages' of the southern Russian steppes. Similar contacts might have been made in early times, at first overland, through the passes of the Caucasus: the wheel came (c. 3000 BC) via those passes to Anatolia and Mesopotamia; the Hurrian, 'Hittite', Iranian, Scythian and Cimmerian invaders of the Near East appeared from the passes of the Caucasus. There might, therefore, have been a growing flow of western Asiatic merchant-venturers in the opposite direction, northwards, into the steppe lands on the northern side of the Black Sea, where the great Russian rivers — the Don, Bug, Dniester, Dnieper — flow out into the Azov–Black Seas; and later, mapping the sea routes to those outlets from the southern Pontic ports would have been an adjunct to good business practice.

From the northern foothills of the Caucasus, one could also travel eastwards along the Russian steppes to Central Asia and the Far East. Some fragments of silk found at Toprak Kale[2] are the earliest yet known in the West, and are evidence of a link between Urartu and remote China in the eighth century BC. It is unlikely that it was a direct connection. There are no records before about 200 BC, when the Han Dynasty was founded, of the transportation of silk from China to the West. At that time, even in China itself, where it was a secret industry, silk was so highly regarded that it was used as a means of exchange.[3] It was hoarded as one might hoard gold. Lengths of silk (instead of ounces of gold) were used as standards of value; and soon, silk served also as a means of payment for China's imports. In the times of the Han emperors, unending lines of lumbering beasts of burden, accompanied by their drivers and riders, merchants and their assistants and a variety of camp followers for safety or gain — altogether an enormous army of men and women — trudged across the vast spaces of Central Asia, many dying from fatigue, killed by bandits or accident, their skeletons marking the great trail; the survivors carried their bales of silk from Ch'ang-an (Sera Metropolis) along the shores of Lop Nor, the edge of the Gobi desert and through the oasis of Takla-Makan, to the caravan-serais of Khotan and Kashgar. And so over the unmapped passes of the icy Pamirs to Merv or Shahrud, by the south-eastern tip of the Caspian Sea, having escaped, unlike some of their fellows, the perils of robber Huns, the burning heat of the deserts, and the crumbling paths along daunting precipices, to deliver silks to the Roman world. The journey was long and hazardous at all times; it would have been particularly so in that remote period when Urartu was at the height of its power (*c.* 750 BC). There is no evidence of such organised enterprise until well after 200 BC. It seems more likely that silk reached Urartu through the nomadic, horse-riding Scythians, whose territories stretched from the western end — southern Russian — of the great belt of the Asiatic steppe, eastwards to the frontiers of China. They mingled with the Mongol peoples and there must have been a good deal of trading between them.

The caravans from the East emerged from the Caspian Gate or from Iran and proceeded either through Mesopotamia or Anatolia, that is either through Assyrian or Urartian territory, to reach Mediterranean lands. There is evidence that Urartu maintained commercial relationships from the Mediterranean to

India. The military power that dominated the kingdom of Mannai, to the south of Lake Urmia, also dictated the direction in which the caravans were to travel, and the economic welfare of the country controlling that trade would be assured. When Assyria controlled Mannai, traffic travelled through Rowanduz to Nineveh and so to the Mediterranean ports of Syria and Palestine. When Urartu occupied Mannai, or when she could exercise military or diplomatic pressure upon her, the caravans travelled northwards, west of Lake Urmia, to Lake Van and Tushpa, Melaskert, Erzerum and so to the Milesian colony of Trapezus (Trebizond), Sinope and other southern ports of the Black Sea, whence ships sailed to the Hellespont and the Mediterranean. Thus, customs dues, tolls and other forms of revenue directly or indirectly fell into the treasury of the country through which thousands of merchants, their servants and their goods passed.

The westward route from Urartian cities, via Carchemish, could lead to the Urartian port of Poseidon (Al Mina) at the mouth of the Orontes in Syria, whence ships carried Urartian, Iranian and central Anatolian cargo to the Aegean centres of civilisation, such as Samos, Cyprus, Crete, Rhodes, Egypt, Greece and Etruria. It seems very reasonable, and there is some evidence to suppose that in the eighth century, down to 743 BC, when Poseidon was an Urartian port, the products of Ararat, such as bronze cauldrons with ornamental handle mounts, tripods with animal feet, stands, votive shields, furniture or its bronze accessories (e.g. the feet of a throne), and other goods already mentioned above, including some military equipment, were shipped from Poseidon. At an exhibition (March 1980) at the British Museum, London, of items of archaeological and historical interest found in Cyprus, there was a 'Bronze conical helmet decorated with a winged sun disc between curving lines of the (Cypriot) Archaic period 750–650 BC from Palaepaphos at Mavrommatis' (*Imported from Urartu.* Cyprus Museum Nicosia 1965/62). There would also have been a demand for Ararat's many mineral products, such as gold, silver, iron, obsidian. Urartian timber was in great demand. A sepulchral inscription dating from the fifteenth century BC, states that hardwood was carried from Armenia to Egypt (via Mitanni) for chariot construction.

Another route from Urartu to the West, particularly to the Ionian cities, followed the long east–west valleys, across central Anatolia and Phrygia; from Melaskert to Mush, Erzincan, Sivas, and the north side of Lake Tuz, to Smyrna, Ephesus and Miletus. Evidence supports the view that Ararat was using that route to the West, particularly after 743 BC when victorious Assyria occupied northern Syria, and the port of Poseidon was no longer available to Urartu. After 680 BC when the Cimmerians had invaded central and western Anatolia and blocked the passage to the West; and Urartian political power and prestige had declined, Ararat must have once again depended largely upon the Pontic outlets for her communications with the West. Although there is yet no evidence that Urartu had a Black Sea port of its own, it is incredible that it did not. It was by far the most powerful state at the south-eastern end of the Black Sea, and even if the mountainous nature of the country in the vicinity is taken into account, its long-standing road-building technology would have overcome such barriers in the pursuit of such an important adjunct to commercial enterprise as a seaport, particularly one on a sea which had an outlet to the Mediterranean and also received the flow of great rivers from the heart of Europe and the north (cf. p. 78 and Ch. 8 n.4 above). And could not the Choruh river, which flows through Chalybes into the Black Sea, have been regularly used?

The north-south trade arteries were to be found at the eastern and western extremities of the Urartian and Assyrian empires, where the important junctions of the caravan routes and the most accessible mountain passes were situated. The southern frontiers of the Urartian empire were to be found along the River Diyala. Reference has already been made to the approaches to Assyria and Urartu from the East. In the West, northern Syria was a terminus of several trade routes. The prosperity of Assyria largely depended upon its complete control of the route across the Khabur-Balikh rivers, northwards up to the Taurus and into Cappadocia, westwards to the sea. Beyond Carchemish, the valley of the Euphrates carried the trade between central and eastern Anatolia on the one side and Syria, Palestine and Egypt on the other; the latter assisted by the valleys of the Rivers Orontes and Jordan. It was precisely in those eastern and western regions that the conflict between the two contestants for the indispensable trade of Asia expressed itself in almost ceaseless warfare. They fought for the approaches to the mountain passes, be they rivers, valleys or mountain roads; they intrigued to dominate the rulers of, or to colonise key towns and countries, such as Carchemish and Rowanduz, Phrygia and Syria, Mannai and Hubushkia, all of which were at junctions of caravan routes, where tolls were levied on carriers of goods in transit. The long wars between the two empires represent a bitter struggle for the capture of no less than the commerce of Asia — and for survival.

The Economy

In the early alluvial civilisations of Mesopotamia, the standard of value by which wages could be paid and every commodity purchased might well have been corn, since it possesses most of the attributes essential to a common medium of exchange: it is easily divisible into minute units, is fairly easily transportable, is desired by all, since it is a staple food, does not perish too readily and so might be kept in storage for a moderate length of time. There were cylindrical containers in Sumer whose capacity could be estimated, for by the third millenium BC, the Sumerians had discovered the ratio of the circumference of a circle to its diameter. Much later on, Urartu's palace seneschals also stored their stocks of grain, wine and oil in huge earthenware jars, the capacities of which could be measured on the Sumerian principle. Hundreds of large, earthenware *pithoi* (jars or urns) came to light in a cellar at the archaeological site of Karmir Blur near Erevan and elsewhere, some with remains of grape pips[4] (now exhibited at the State Historical Museum of Armenia at Erevan), all arranged in orderly rows, each with a cuneiform inscription indicating its capacity.

> The *pithos* inscriptions all come from a 'store-house' complex of two rooms which lay on a terrace at the northern side of the citadel [at Altin Tepe near Erzincan]. Sixty large jars were sunk into the floor of the eastern magazine and at least eleven more in the other room, so far only partially excavated. Such facilities, which were a usual feature of every Urartian citadel, must have served as central depots for storage and redistribution of the agricultural produce of the administrative regions. Judging from the evidence of the royal inscriptions, and other sources, it would seem that wine was the usual commodity stored in the jars ... The *pithoi*, themselves are of the normal Urartian type, as known from many sites, with a thick, angular lip and several plastic bands around the body. The fabric is a coarse and gritty red, containing large white inclusions and

having a smooth, polished outer surface. At nearly all Urartian sites, some accounting system was used to record the contents of the individual vessels in *aqarqi* and *terust*, the basic units of Urartian liquid measure.[5]

Accounting methods were commonplace for recording details of stocks held in warehouses, as those found at Karmir Blur. Other accounting documents must have existed, of which one unskilled scribe's example, with spelling mistakes, has survived[6].

We get an entirely different impression from the letters addressed to the viceroy of Teishebaini (Karmir Blur) by the Urartian kings and high officials in the capital. They are well written, in a handsome cuneiform script. ... These letters deal with the redistribution of land, the return of a runaway slave girl, the collection of tribute, the movement of people or animals, or problems of inheritance. ... Another series of records, written on papyrus [as opposed to the clay tablets described above] are evident in reliefs from the Assyrian palaces showing the counting up of plunder. Unfortunately, our only evidence at Teishebaini of documents written on papyrus is a flat bitumen *bulla* which has been used to seal such a scroll.[7]

The prosperity of Ararat was based on agriculture. Other countries paid tribute to Urartu in the form of cattle and sheep, never in cereals. When in 714 BC Sargon of Assyria invaded Urartu he found great stocks of grain everywhere. In the frontier province of Uisdis and in every major centre, there were, according to his scribes, many capacious storage magazines, each containing large quantities of grain.[8] We are informed that he distributed generous quantities of grain to his troops. But his jealousy, envy and arrogance were such that he turned that part of the flowering country into a desert, just as if a great natural catastrophe had devasted it. Urartian monarchs never mention cereals among the items of tribute paid to them and the loot carried away by them from countries they themselves overran. That supports the view that they had such an abundance of corn in their own country that it was not worth burdening themselves with additional stocks of cereals. It was much easier to drive live-stock to their homelands. They never write of destroying harvests or plantations.

Economic expansion became possible when the surplus product of the great landowners was collected for accumulation in the royal granaries, and ultimately distributed throughout the country in the form of wages paid to labour for services in war and peace; when minerals of the state-owned mines and quarries were extracted, refined and cast for the equipment of armies, and the manufacture of war machines, for the building of fortresses and temples, for the construction of roads and reservoirs and the cutting of canals for irrigating the land and increasing the product of each acre. The increasing number of large estates in successive periods, is a measure of the economic expansion of the state.[9]

Such an increase might presuppose a greater surplus product which supported more nobles who in their turn patronised a greater number of merchants, craftsmen, clerks, scribes, teachers and others. We know that in Nineveh, in the seventh century BC, the middle class enjoyed a high measure of freedom, and the merchants within it had a wide market, comprising mainly people of their own class and that of the increasing members of the nobility, who themselves supported an army of slaves and a variety of dependants. In Urartu, the merchant middle class must have been in fullest flow of wealth during the eighth century BC, when Van was at the height of its military and political power. At that time, too, there must have been in Urartu, a number of social classes who were independent of any patronage save that of the state. There were scribes and an army of literate civil servants (clerks and their assistants) who recorded the accounts and the state economic transactions; the legal hierarchy, ranging from the lowest rungs of the professional ladder to the judge himself on the topmost rung; not least, there were the priests, whose ranks swelled as an increasing number of young men were attracted to the sumptuously furnished temples. Many of these temples might have been endowed by the king, as in the case of the temple of Khaldi at Musasir and probably also that of Tesheba or Teshub, god of war, at Teishebaini (or Teshebani), Karmir Blur. All these persons, representing the merchants themselves and their families, the civil service and the temple, together with many soldiers on leave, created a new and substantial home market for consumer goods, including exotic foodstuffs, clothing and a variety of decorative and practical articles.

Only a substantial population could supply the necessary labour force for the construction of the extensive public works, such as canals, roads and the exploitation of quarries and mines, which became necessary for economic, military and political purposes, and were undertaken by the Urartian kings, from Menua onwards. A population of about 50,000 is suggested by Charles Burney for the larger cities of Urartu.[10] Ararat had grown from a collection of village communities to a federation of cities and citizens, while government under the powerful kings was wealthy enough to employ and pay for the labour force necessary for its manifold purposes. Those labourers, though slaves, had to be fed. Half the surplus product of the farmer (that is to say, the noble landowner) was distributed in due course among the labourers for their sustenance; the remainder was claimed by the king for accumulation in the royal granaries. The construction of canals under the direction of successive Urartian monarchs has already been mentioned. Some of them represented quite remarkable engineering feats, even supposing that modern machinery and modern techniques had been available at that time. Burney writes of Urartian canals, reservoirs, dams and cisterns, and he gives reasons for their construction:

1. Shortage of water due to: (a) an influx of population when a city was first founded or (b) growth of population when a city was rebuilt on a larger scale. The construction of the Menua canal would have made a population of fifty thousand in Van itself, the city and its garden suburbs, a conservative estimate. Since the population in the nineteenth century AD exceeds that figure, there is no need to suggest a smaller population in the Urartian capital. [In fact, the Van population might have been a good deal larger; the population of the most ancient cities of Ur and Babylon numbered a few hundred thousands.] 2. Political reason: a ruling dynasty could have no surer means of security than by the construction and maintenance of canals to bring water to the fields and gardens, to ensure an improved and reliable variety and quantity of food. Urartu was densely populated in its more fertile areas.[11]

Since Ararat was situated astride the commercial highways between East and West and between the north-south routes at its extremities, it was bound to receive information about social and economic changes and innovations and, in particular, on new modes of husbandry, throughout the ancient world. For example, that a given vine stock might produce different varieties of grapes when planted under different climatic conditions or altitudes; that selective breeding of cattle could produce better strains; and animals from other lands might be introduced (such as the camel) for employment in Urartu. According to T.S. Khachaturian:

> Cuneiform inscriptions show that Urartians had discovered advanced methods of animal husbandry. King Argishti I (785–753 BC), in an inscription, informs us that after one of his campaigns, he transported from conquered lands in Eriach (Transcaucasia, north of Mount Ararat) to Biaini, 10,000 head of cattle. Unfortunately, we are unable to describe now with any certainty the methods used in animal husbandry by the Urartians because of the haphazard manner in which early archaeologists excavated the foothills of the mountains of Aragadz, when they did not pay sufficient attention to bones of animals they found there.[12]

The kingdom of Urartu was sufficiently secure from invasions to encourage experiments among the great landowners who would have realised sooner or later the economic advantage of better strains of stock and higher productivity of the land. The latter was enhanced by the extensive network of canals for the irrigation of the land, the introduction of improved seeds and the application of iron tools or implements; for example the use of an iron ploughshare, instead of the original wooden one, which could dig deep into the soil. A large variety of iron weapons and tools have been excavated at Karmir Blur.[13] The carbonised remains of wheat, barley, millet and sesame, as well as the grain-grinding quern which were found in the store rooms of Teishebaini, stand witness to the advanced agricultural methods used by Urartian farmers.[14]

There must have been much sheep rearing, as the manufacture of woollen garments had been common in the Near East from very early times. Woollen (and some linen) 'garments were worn in Syria and furniture was upholstered in wool. Bolts of woollen cloth are listed by weight and dimensions and both dyed cloth and sewn garments were important commodities in commerce and figure prominently in the dowry lists and in inventories of tribute.'[15] Although this quotation refers to transactions and events in fifteenth-century Syria, its application to Urartu in the eighth century BC is not difficult. With Ararat's frontiers stretching into northern Syria itself, commanding easy and safe caravan routes, Urartian merchants would have certainly carried their 'dyed vestments of linen and their scarlet textiles of Ararat and Kurkhi'[16] to all parts of their empire and exported them to Syria and the eastern Mediterranean cities and islands. From Sargon's narration of the capture of Musasir, we are informed of the 'costly woollen fabrics, dyed in many colours', manufactured in Urartu. There were, according to Professor Boris Piotrovskii, 'weaving shops [or factories] in Teishebaini'.[17]

Since Urartu has so often been cited when at the peak of its power, it might be as well to recall that it was first mentioned by Assyria far back in 1275 BC, when it already appears as a principality (or even perhaps as a kingdom) powerful enough to confront Assyria. Ararat was largely a federation of Hurrian principalities which would almost certainly have had dealings with Hurrian Mitanni, in neighbouring northern Mesopotamia and Assyria-on-northern-Tigris:

> a tablet from Ugarit [15th century BC] lists merchants, some with Hurrian names, dealing in bulk consignments of purple-dyed wool. Purple was the colour of royal raiment, the robes of nobles and the hangings of palaces. Garments of purple stuff and purple shoes were among the items of clothing sent by king Tushratta [of Mitanni] for the trousseau of his daughter, and purple cloth and robes were sent as tribute by the king of Ugarit to the king and dignitaries of the Hittite court. A cheap vegetable subtitute for red-purple dye was obtained from madder[18]

— a herbaceous climbing plant found and cultivated in hill districts, such as Caria in south-west Asia Minor and in most parts of Anatolia, including Armenia.

Dr Georges Roux[19] describes how the 'inhabitants of Iraq exploited their native bitumen, a related ['parent'] substance, which they obtained from seepages [of petroleum] in various parts of the country' especially from a site between Hit and Ramadi on the Middle Euphrates. At that time (*c.*2000 BC), in architecture bitumen was used as mortar for brickwork, water-proofing linings in bathrooms and drainage; in sculpture and inlay (mosaic) work, in boat-building for caulking boats; as fuel; and as a drug. From time to time they exported it, probably in return for the products which were not available in Mesopotamia: metal ores, hard stones, good timber, which are all to be found in Armenia and easily accessible via the two great rivers. Copper, generally believed to have been first discovered in northwest Iran or in the Caucasus, 'was perhaps first obtained from Armenia or Azerbaijan (Urartu)'; tin from Iran, Caucasus, even Afganistan; silver from the Taurus; gold from Armenia, and from deposits scattered between Egypt and India; semi-precious and hard stones from Iran; black diorite from Oman (or Magan), used by sculptors in the third dynasty of Ur (2113–2006 BC).

Trade and Means of Payment

Gudea, the governor of Lagash (*c.*2200 BC), could purchase his imports either by barter or against payment of precious metals. It is recorded that he imported gold dust from Armenia.[20] At that time and for perhaps another 1000 years, Anatolia and particularly Armenia, where deposits of gold, silver, copper, tin and later iron were to be found, was the metal market whence Mesopotamia obtained much of its metal wealth.[21]

> At the mound of Metsamor, west of Erevan, a metallurgical centre, dated to the 20th–13th centuries BC, was discovered [in 1966]. The mound itself goes back to ·the 3rd millenium BC, but the installations for the refinement of copper and cassiterite (tin) ores and numerous blast furnaces for the production of tin-bronze may go back to the Late Bronze Age (*c.*1500 BC). Tin was probably mined in the alluvial deposits of Paleo-araks [my hyphen] at the foot of Mt Aragats, a little to the north of Erevan (see 'Alagoz'), where the presence of tin, gold and silver has been confirmed by a recent [1966] geological survey .... The expansion of Hittite New Kingdom power eastwards in the reigns of Tuthaliyas III, Shuppiluliuma and Mursilis in the 14th century seems to have brought the kingdom of Azzi-Hayasa at least under nominal Hittite control. This state (Azzi-Hayasa) seems to have extended eastwards from the bend in the Euphrates near Kemah through the plains of Erzincan, Tercan, Erzerum, and quite possibly down to the Araxes valley near Erevan. Not only did the main east–west route to Iran and Transcaucasia run through this state, but Metsamor and the tin deposits of Paleo-araks may have belonged to it. There is thus a possibility that Hittite control of

this region may have been partly motivated by economics, i.e. control of an important tin source.

In the 13th century, however, the Hittite historical sources dry up, as they do for western Anatolia. The new establishment at Metsamor [in eastern Armenia], and the rise of a wealthy local dynasty, whose rulers were buried with carts and chariots in the cemetery of Lechashen on the shores of Lake Sevan, might be interpreted as a revival of local autonomy and prosperity after the Hittite interlude ... Metsamor seems to have flourished until Urartian rule was established in these parts. In general the 13th (or 14th)–10th centuries see the rise of important metalworking cultures in Transcaucasia and N.W. Iran (where this period is already called 'Early Iron Age') connected with the appearance of the Medes.

There is therefore a possibility that the Hittites during the 14th century might have had access to tin from Transcaucasia (Azzi-Hayasa), but it would be unrealistic to assume that they had the Ararat plain under firm military control! As tin was a necessity for the war effort they could well have been seeking to establish control over the alternative route, nearer home and much more easily accessible, the one that led from Europe along the southern shore and the sea of Marmara.[22]

It was, in fact, Dr Koriun Meguerdichian who discovered the Medzamor metallurgical factory, the oldest in the world, in Soviet Armenia. As Mr Mellaart states it was built nearly 5000 years ago.

Vases and objects of all the common metals have been found: knives, spearheads, arrowheads, clasps, rings, bracelets, etc. The foundry had a series of vats, hollowed out of rock, in which ore was crushed, pounded, washed, refined, and enriched until pure metal was obtained. Twenty-five furnaces have been uncovered, but more than two hundred are thought to be still buried. Medzamor was an industrial centre of the period derisively called the Neolithic. Imported ore was treated there, and the finished products were distributed among the peoples of the Near East. Craftsmen worked with copper, bronze, lead, zinc, iron, gold, tin, arsenic, antimony, manganese. *And also steel!* Steel tweezers, slender and still shiny, have been found. They are a little more recent — they date from only three thousand years ago! Fourteen varieties of bronze were smelted in the plant and used for different purposes. These discoveries have been verified by scientific organizations in the Soviet union, the United States, France, Britain and Germany. ... The metal-working people of Medzamor had a three-storey astronomical observatory in the shape of a triangle whose apex pointed towards the south, where stars are most numerous.[23]

Glass was also manufactured at Medzamor, where the necessary ingredients, such as zinc and manganese were available.[24]

The metal units were measured by weight. This marks a transition from a natural economy, in which agricultural products were used as a means of exchange, to a money economy in which a metallic medium was used as a universal means of exchange for goods and services. At first in the more substantial transactions only, and later on (*c.*800 BC) in Syria and Assyria (and probably also in Urartu) in all transactions, bars of silver were used as means of payment. To forestall the cupidity of some owners of those bars and to obviate falsification of weights and the debasement of the metal, the Syrian and Assyrian kings guaranteed both weight and purity of metal by having each bar stamped.[25] As early as the third millenium BC, silver in various forms (e.g. ingots) was weighed and stamped to guarantee a standard minimum percentage of silver.[26] Although bars of Urartian origin with the royal stamp have not yet come to light, they might well do so during future excavations. Professor Boris Piotrovskii, who supervised the excavations at Karmir Blur, mentions part of a gold ingot (unstamped) weighing 14.85 g, found wrapped in a rag and buried in a mound on the floor of one of the rooms in the fortress of Teishebaini at Karmir Blur.[27] Goods were bought and sold in precise quantities. In the Sargonid period (after 722 BC) 'bronze lions furnished the exact weights used in Assyrian metrology. Previously, the Assyrians used the heavy mana (about 1 kg)[28] while Babylonia and Syria preferred the light or Carchemish mana (about 500 g)'. The increase of trade stimulated the universal use of money in the form of scarce metals, the most valuable not always necessarily being gold but sometimes an even scarcer metal — iron. In the Near East generally, Anatolian iron was a precious commodity in the second millenium BC. 'At Ugarit, it cost double the price of silver, and objects of iron are scarcer than those of gold.'[29] In time, however, the discovery of increasing deposits of iron re-established silver and gold as the standards of universally accepted means of exchange.

The home trade in Mesopotomia was at first limited to the demand of the royal and aristocratic houses and the temples. Throughout the Bronze Age, (down to *c.*1200 BC) the middle class remained completely subordinate to the monarchy and the priesthood who controlled the metal trade. The comparative scarcity of copper and tin (the constituents of bronze) made this easy for the rulers. The self-contained guilds of craftsmen — smiths, carpenters, masons, jewellers and potters — were permanently attached to their masters. Their purpose was to supply their employers' and their own personal needs, and like the peasants on the land, they too changed their masters only when the estate on which they worked changed its owner.[30] In short, they were serfs and craftsmen, as within a feudal system. They were necessarily bound to their masters who alone had the means to obtain the raw materials, without which their skills were useless. Their enforced immobility was a very important factor which helped the development of their respective technologies. One of the reasons for the slow progress of the European barbarians was their ease of movement and their seeming reluctance to live in towns. Furthermore, the development of one technology often relies upon that of another, and the close proximity of craftsmen in an urban situation in the Near East made the interchange of ideas possible. This must have been the case in Urartu. The craftsmen in metal, the metallurgists, soon became a group apart. The complicated processes involved in metal casting made them specialists, and the secrets of their craft were transmitted from father to son. In such circumstances it is not difficult to imagine a 'mystery' ceremonial in which the son, after a long apprenticeship, is initiated into the more advanced techniques or 'mysteries' of the craft.[31] This was probably the tradition which produced the highly skilled eighth-century Urartian metallurgists who influenced certain aspects of European art.

Urartian imported goods might conceivably have included lapis lazuli from Afghanistan, spices from India, embroideries of Elam, ivory from the south and east, amber from Scandinavia, silk from China (via the Scythians), and from Syria, edible and other oils and fats, some of them used as bases for the cosmetic industry: 'Nefertiti must have been the Queen of Egypt to whom the Queen of Ugarit sent a present of a pot of Balm'.[32] In many instances, imports would include, besides goods actually purchased from other lands, the tribute from colonies, dependencies and conquered countries generally. These might be classed as invisible exports, together with payments made by foreign merchants to Urartian businessmen for their services in various forms, such as transport, the hire of beasts of burden, innkeepers tariffs, warehousing, dock charges, state dues and other charges incidental to the transit of goods through Urartian territories. Plunder, a substantial item, might be classified as an 'invisible' export since it is value in kind, acquired without payment in any form. The kings of Ararat themselves brought to their country enormous quantities of booty from invaded and conquered territories, displacing the populations of some cities and replacing them with those of others in order to minimise the possibility of rebellion, as was the way of conquerors of those days and for centuries to come. But that policy also postulates only minimal loyalty of such cities to the Great Kings, their masters in time of war, when they were likely to capitulate to the enemy only after a short siege. A more constructive view of the distressing practice of shifting such large numbers from their homes to distant cities, is that commercial and cultural developments, which might have otherwise remained localised, were much more quickly diffused over extensive areas. With the spoils of war, the monarchs of Urartu furnished and adorned their palaces and temples, and in course of time, some of the accumulated wealth thus acquired and from the products of their land, filtered down the social scale, to the advantage of their people. Prisoners of war swelled the labour force, many of whom worked with their new iron tools on the land, in the quarries and the mines; for the construction of canals, roads, temples, palaces and fortresses and new cities. Craftsmen produced the various necessities and luxuries for the great households of the wealthy.

As to visible exports, Armenia's mineral wealth was coveted by neighbouring powers from the earliest times. Gudea's imports of Armenian gold dust have already been mentioned. Somewhat earlier, before Gudea, King Sargon of Akkad boasts of reaching the 'mountains of silver (the Taurus Range) and his son, Manishtusu, gloried in the conquest of lands amidst the 'silver mountains' beyond the Lower Sea, perhaps Lake Urmia (the Upper Sea being Lake Van) whence he carried off quantities of silver from the mines and the beautiful and very hard mineral, diorite (the latter was probably from Elam). It is understood, of course, that like these earlier invasions of Sumer-Akkad, the later

Assyrian attacks on Urartu had economic as well as political motives. Among other minerals already mentioned, there were also important deposits of iron in Armenia, which would be exported, as demand for it increased at the same time as tin, copper and obsidian. Also, from the earliest times, the indigenous Armenian vine produced a fine wine which was exported to Mesopotamia for the royal tables of Sumer and Babylonia. Viticulture was a widely cultivated branch of horticulture. Exports of manufactured goods would include, besides the 'scarlet textiles of Ararat', the famous bronzes of Urartu which had extensive markets abroad, even to the distant shores of Etruria in western Italy.

There must have been an astonishing amount of business acumen and financial skills in those remote times, among the internationally-minded community of guilds of merchants and individuals. Such mercantile organisations were centred in the *Karum* the nearest ancient counterpart, perhaps of today's market or exchange say, in the City of London, such as the Produce Market or the Metal and Wool Exchanges, where merchants and financiers of like interests have their offices; except, of course that the *Karum* traded in every variety of goods, as the turnover would not be comparable to the mammoth transactions in specialised areas of the modern business world. Members of the modern Stock Exchange are familiar with the motto: 'My Word is my Bond'. So, too, in the second millenium BC, members of the *Karum*, situated outside the walls of Ur, had to behave like 'sons of gentlemen — *mar awilum*'[33] and to obey the laws of King Hammurabi (1802–1750 BC) to honour their contracts, signed and witnessed in the presence of the effigy of Shamash, god of oaths and of justice. The *Karum* is particularly associated with foreign trade and might be likened to the entirely self-contained, non-political, nineteenth-century British (and other Western European) trading stations in various parts of the world. Such was, for example, the *Karum* at Sipar, and the better known *Karum* at Kanesh (near modern Kayseri, central Turkey) whence the Assyrian resident merchants exported to their country Anatolian minerals, and imported the much sought-after Assyrian textiles, loaded upon the backs of a train of hardy Cappadocian donkeys. The *Karum* was also a tribunal where disputes could be settled and judgment passed on the validity of a creditor's claims. It could act as a broker for loans against securities and also fix prices at suitable rates.[34] Business correspondence in cuneiform, accounts and contracts on baked clay tablets stand witness to the profitable trade that was thus carried on by the Assyrian merchants of *c.* 2000 BC.

The rulers of Urartu would have been able to pay for their imports, as has been implied above, in precious metals, which might have included iron, since this was a scarce commodity at one stage. The process of producing good quality iron in quantity, seems to have been developed by certain Hurrian tribes in eastern Anatolia — that is, the geographical region commonly referred to as Armenia, which was preceded by Urartu. In the fourteenth century BC, the smelting of iron became a monopoly of the Hittites,[35] who seem to have possessed, by right of conquest from Hurrian Mitanni, iron-smelting centres in a region called Kissuwadna, somewhat to the west of the Euphrates, in southern Anatolia, adjoining Armenia. In the Iron Age (after 1200 BC; Urartu is mentioned for the first time in 1275 BC), the increasingly expanding use of iron gave the peasantry some of the important advantages of progress, such as cheap iron tools which made the small producers less dependent on state monopolies and the resources of the great estates they served. The enterprising farmer could now, and for his own practically independent benefit, use the new iron ploughshare, and sturdy iron tools for reclaiming wasteland. A large variety of iron weapons and tools have been excavated at Toprak Kale,[36] as well as at Karmir Blur. Industry also benefited from much more efficient and versatile tools. Vehicles and ships, made with iron components, could also offer a more reliable, faster and cheaper means of transport and communications.

At last, in the first quarter of the first millenium BC, increasingly sophisticated methods of iron working had made metal a cheap commodity. While 'during the eighteenth century BC, in the time of Hammurabi, a shekel of silver would buy 120 to 150 shekels of copper or perhaps 14½ shekels of tin (in Asia Minor at this date it would purchase 40 shekels of iron)', in the eighth century BC, at the zenith of Urartian power, the silver shekel could buy as much as 225 shekels of iron.[37] Also, as a result of the use of more efficient tools in mining and manufacture (iron, instead of copper tools), the price of copper had dropped from 150-180 to one of silver.[38] After 1200 BC, iron brought some aspects of the advantages of technology within the reach of ordinary folk, particularly the peasantry. They could produce, with their metal tools, more from the land by breaking the ground easily, draining and irrigating the fields and felling trees.

In the towns, too, various utensils as well as more efficiently constructed vehicles were available at less cost. Agricultural products, construction of sundry equipment, communications and transport were thus substantially reduced in price.

Plunder from the wars, the manufactures of craftsmen and artisans and the services of slaves provided the new merchant class of Urartu with the means of profit-making. In speaking of profit, we assume a money economy, though not yet 'coin' money — specie. Although it is usually early sixth-century Lydia which is credited with the invention of coinage, it appears that King Sennacherib of Assyria (704–681 BC) minted copper coins: 'I built clay moulds, poured bronze into each and made their figures perfect as in the casting of half-shekel pieces.'[39] There is no evidence of similar Urartian specie, nor, of any other country with state coinage apart from Assyria, before the Lydians. But it seems to me that such a convenient means of payment would have very quickly spread, and in the future, archaeologists may find evidence of imitators of Sennacherib's innovation; or even perhaps preceding Sennacherib in the invention of coined money.

Until that idea was widely practised, the value of precious (that is, scarce) metals commanded sufficient confidence to be used as means of exchange for the purchase of every conceivable commodity. The development of such an economy based on coined money would be greatly desirable because of enemy raids. We have seen how Assyria attacked and ravaged Urartu on a number of occasions. There was a constant threat of such raids throughout Urartian history, and the safety of the land depended entirely on the military might and the character of its kings. The danger was always present, and in such circumstances the rapid spread of a money economy would be desirable, since money is more portable than any other unit of exchange; it can be hidden or carried away easily by the fleeing owners. In a state with a money economy, production for the consumer market tends to become a daily affair.

The introduction of money in the form of metal (replacing barter), even if not coined, and the consequent rate of its circulation, must have caused erratic price fluctuations, and producers, in their role as consumers of raw materials, must have found it difficult to keep their prices steady. In Mesopotamia, the price of the staple food, barley, rose steadily throughout the Bronze Age (which merged into the Iron Age *c.*1200 BC). A *gur* of barley cost a shekel of silver at the end of the third millenium BC, two shekels in the first half of the second millenium, and well over three shekels in the last quarter of second millenium BC.[40] In modern idiom, these price rises would be described as the effects of inflation.

The traders who brought the merchandise from the East, certainly did not return to their homelands empty-handed; for where there is export, there must also be import of goods. (Examples of exotic goods from distant countries have already been given.) Transportation of goods over difficult terrain was overcome, as I have illustrated in describing the enormously long and dangerous journey from China to the West. But the hazard of gangs of bandits had to be minimised. In Syria, Khatti and Mesopotamia, the safe passage of caravans over mountain passes and the steppes of northern Mesopotamia was guaranteed by the parent state of the travelling merchants by reciprocal treaty with their 'brother' kings with whom they traded, since the king had a direct financial interest in their safety. The merchants handling the wares were government agents, acting for the king. Restitution was made to the wife of a merchant who had been killed while engaged on the king's business, and fines and other forms of punishment were imposed upon malefactors. Nevertheless, highwaymen abounded and the merchants' personal safety often depended more on the great retinue of fellow merchants and their servants in the caravan — a daunting sight to would-be marauders — than perhaps on the prestige of the great king in his distant capital, in whose service they travelled.

Of course, the safest method of transferring the titles to precious metals was through quasi-banking institutions, comparable to the modern letter of credit. Credit and credit-at-interest had been known in Mesopotamia from very early times, even before Hammurabi (*c.* 1790–1750 BC), when temples served also as community banks. Hammurabi laid down 20 per cent interest on loans of silver and 33⅓ per cent on barley.[41] A merchant could avoid the risk of carrying silver or gold overland by disposing of his goods, *en route* to a given destination, at a trading post controlled by an accredited agent. The agent would hand the merchant a receipt on a clay tablet for the value of the goods, in shekels, which would be negotiable at a later date and place.[42] In modern terminology, the agent would draw a bill in favour of the merchant which would be honoured in cash (perhaps bars of silver, before coinage appeared) at the end of his outward journey, with which he would buy goods for sale in his home market. Such 'bills' or tablets were always payable on demand.

The laws of Hammurabi provide for merchants' loans to 'gentlemen' (*awilum*) on security of agricultural land; loans of travelling traders in cash or goods primarily obtained on security of real estate. They show how the fertile fields of Mesopotamia were in fact the very base of Babylonian financial structure and business enterprise. Astute men who could gamble on a future bumper crop of barley would invest and risk their capital in anticipation of rich returns; while the adventurous merchant would buy cheaply in the producing country to sell at immense profit in distant places where his goods were scarce and demand for them high. The sophisticated financial transactions involving loans made at interest to those needing capital seem quite astonishing. They were essential to what seems to have been the quite complex financial, commercial and trading activities of those remote times, 3000-4000 years ago. Would not those economic institutions and customs, which must have been widespread by 1400 BC, have filtered down to the Urartians in even more developed forms?

By the late sixth/early fifth century BC, banking had become an indispensable institution of the commercial world of Babylonia, and the names of Babylonian private bankers, such as the Egibi and Murashu families have come down to us.[43] Thus, the fundamental aspects of the economic and mercantile institutions, as we know them today, were to be found in Mesopotamia, Anatolia and the Levant by the end of the sixth century BC — the exchange of goods (in foreign trade), a universally acceptable currency, the service offered by various mercantile establishments in the forms of transport, warehousing, distribution and banking. There was usury in its worst forms; that is, lending to people in distress at exhorbitant rates of interest, as, for example, practised by the Murashu of Nippur (*c.*450 BC), who charged 40-50 per cent interest.[44] However, such abuses were, in many instances, eliminated by state regulations. It is interesting that the Jews, with whom we have learnt to associate usury, were the very people who deplored it, as they saw it practised by some Babylonians. (Exod. XXII. 25; Lev. XXV. 36; Deut. XXIII. 19; Neh. V. 10; Ezek. XVIII. 8,13,17; XXII. 12). From its crude beginnings, usury, with its unsavoury connotations, developed into forms of money lending, at acceptable rates of interest, before appearing in its modern, respectable form as the lynchpin of banking and investment, on which western society now thrives and without which it would collapse. The ancients were quite as eager to associate themselves with activities closest to Mammon as are most of our contemporaries.

Notes

1. C.J. Gadd, 'Babylonia *c.*2120–1800 BC', CAH, I^2.i. p. 606.
2. R.D. Barnett, 'British Museum Excavations at Toprak Kale', IRAQ, XII (1950); XVI (1952).
3. I. Boulnois, *The Silk Road* (George Allen and Unwin, 1966).
4. B.B. Piotrovskii, *The Ancient Civilization of Urartu* (Barrie and Rockliff, 1969).
5. Jeffrey J. Klein, 'Urartian Hieroglyphic Inscriptions from Altin Tepe', AS XXIV (1974).
6. Piotrovskii, *op. cit.*
7. Ibid.
8. Ibid.
9. Gordon Childe, *What Happened in History* (Max Parrish, 1960).
10. Charles Burney, 'Urartian Irrigation Works', AS XXII (1972).
11. Ibid.
12. T.S. Kachaturian, *The Material Culture of Ancient Artig* (in Russian and Armenian) (Erevan, 1963).
13. Piotrovskii, *op. cit.*
14. Ibid.
15. Margaret S. Drower, 'Syria', CAH, II^1.viii. p. 510.
16. A.H. Sayce, 'The Kingdom of Van', CAH, III.iii.
17. Piotrovskii, *op. cit.*
18. Drower, *op. cit.*, pp. 510-11.
19. Georges Roux, *Iraq* (Pelican, 1980), pp. 29-30.
20. G.J. Gadd, 'The Dynasty of Agade and the Gutian Invasion', CAH, I^2.v. p. 460.
21. James Mellaart, 'Anatolia *c.* 4000–2300 BC', CAH, I^2.ii. p. 370.
22. James Mellaart, 'Anatolian Trade and Geography Late Bronze Age', AS XVIII (1968), p. 200-1.
23. Robert Charroux, *Lost Worlds* (Fontana and Collins, London).
24. R.D. Barnett, 'Urartu', CAH, III^1.iii. p. 328.
25. Childe, *op. cit.*
26. Joan Oates, *Babylon* (Thames and Hudson, 1979).
27. B.B. Piotrovskii, *The Art of Urartu* (Evelyn Adams and Mackay, 1967).
28. A.T. Olmstead, *A History of Assyria* (Charles Scribner's Sons, New York).
29. Drower, *op. cit.*, p. 514.
30. Nicholas Adontz, *Histoire d'Arménie* (Paris, 1946).
31. Childe, *op. cit.*
32. Margaret S. Drower. 'Ugarit', CAH, II.i. p. 134.

33. Oates, *op. cit.*; Jacquetta Hawkes, *The First Great Civilizations* (Pelican Books, 1977).

34. Seton Lloyd, *Early Highland Peoples* (Thames & Hudson, 1967).

35. Oates, *op. cit.*; O.R. Gurney, *The Hittites* (Penguin, 1976).

36. Barnett, *op. cit.*

37. Childe, *op. cit.*

38. Ibid.

39. Oates, *op. cit.*

40. Childe, *op. cit.*

41. W.H.F. Saggs, *The Greatness That Was Babylon* (Sidgwick & Jackson, 1962).

42. Oates, *op. cit.*; Hawkes, *op. cit.*

43. Oates, *op. cit.*

44. G. Cardascia, *Les Archives des Murashu* (Paris, 1951). Quoted by Georges Roux, *Ancient Iraq* (Penguin, 1950); Hawkes, *op. cit.*

Further sources

R.D. Barnett, *Oriental Influences on Archaic Greece. The Aegean and the Near East*, ed. S. Winberg.

J.M. Birmingham, 'Overland route Across Anatolia 8th and 7th centuries BC', AS XI, 1961.

J.G. Macqueen, 'Geography and History of Asia Minor in the 2nd mill BC', AS XVIII, 1968.

James Mellaart 'Anatolian Trade with Europe and Anatolian Geog. and Culture Provinces — Late Bronze Age', AS XVIII, 1968.

L. Casson, *Travel in the Ancient World* (London, 1974).

E.D. Phillips, *The Royal Hordes* (Thames and Hudson, 1963).

15

Religion of Urartu

The Urartians and their contemporaries cannot be credited with conceptions of religion with which we are familiar — self-denial, self-effacement, spiritual purity and the renunciation of worldly goods and pleasures. These are the intellectual and emotional products of long centuries of philosophical thought expressed in the Hindu scriptures, the Old and the New Testaments, and argued in Europe by the Greek philosophers and their successors. Yet it would be unwise to adopt too superior a stance in religious matters *vis-à-vis* the first civilisations, for very little appears to have changed in popular religious attitudes since the earliest times. Polytheism persists with present-day Christians as much as it did with the ancients. Christians worship God and His Son, and the latter's Mother; and most practising Christians worship a host of saints, many of whom are individually invested with the power to protect or are responsible for one or other aspects of our lives. The ceremony of the sacrament at High Mass and Holy Communion is as ancient as our palaeolithic ancestors, except that we carry out its rituals of partaking of Christ's flesh and blood symbolically, whereas our more ignorant, and therefore more fearful forbears actually ate the flesh and drank the blood of particularly brave or especially endowed enemy prisoners, having first ritualistically killed them. That cannibalistic ritual was perpetrated by many peoples in the sincere belief that they would, by eating his flesh and drinking his blood, acquire something of their victim's quasi-divine power and glory.

The root of religion is fear — fear of the Unknown, which becomes a Mystery. That Mystery is then symbolised and finally venerated and adored. Sargon of Assyria describes himself as a king who is fearful of the gods and attentive to their commands, while portraying Ursa (or Rusa) of Urartu as 'the king of murderous mountain-dwellers, who heeds not his religious obligations'.[1] The piety of the Urartian monarchs is demonstrated by their generous endowments to the sanctuaries of their gods. The best example of such a sanctuary is the temple of Khaldi at Musasir which overflowed with examples of royal treasure. Man worships that which he cannot comprehend. There are those who emphasise and emulate the frightfulness of their god while others symbolise him in a variety of artforms as a benevolent deity; a propiatory measure expecting its own reward, and indeed reaping valuable psychological benefits. That warmer conception of gods, comparable to a child's idea of its parents, tends to soften some aspects of religious institutions and social mores. But the Good would be incomprehensible without a knowledge of Evil. The Good god is invoked to protect his suppli-cants from his Evil counterpart which Judaeo-Christian tradition personifies as Satan. This subject has been discussed exhaustively by Plato and others. Plato attempts to define the Good by equating it with Justice, Truth and Beauty; they in turn have to be defined. Such philosophical discussions however are well beyond the scope of this work.

The primitive idea of a deity is that of a powerful being who can provide or withhold the necessities and the luxuries of life: success in business, good fortune in war and love, and the general welfare of one's family; one who can invoke the proper sequence of the seasons, each with its characteristics of sun and snow, of wind and rain, which enrich the earth and bring prosperity to mankind.

The one person able to provide all these material essentials was the Great King who was (in a number of the ancient civilis-ations) also god-incarnate, from whom all things good and evil flowed. The king was the warrior of Khaldi. It was Khaldi who led the Urartian armies, vanquished the enemy and finally allowed his servant, the king, to reap the fruits of victory. The annals stand witness: 'Khaldi set forth'; 'his forces gave battle'; 'Khaldi is powerful'; Khaldi leads'. Khaldi is therefore credited with military success. In peacetime, it was in the name of Khaldi that all public works — the building of cities, palaces, canals, fortresses — were undertaken. Is not the British Queen 'Defender of the Faith'? Is not the monarchy (any monarchy) closely associated with the Church or Temple? Does not the most ancient, as well as modern, protocol require the High Priest, that is, the spiritual head of the Temple or Church, to follow, in a procession, the monarch, and precede the temporal head, or prime minister, even though the latter might be the most powerful individual in matters secular?

The conqueror acquired not only fresh territories, ruled over not only a defeated king and his people, but the conqueror-god also became supreme over the corresponding enemy-god. Thus, if the Urartian king prevailed over the Assyrian monarch, Khaldi at the same time prevailed over Ashur, and Ashur took a place below Khaldi in the hierarchy of the gods. The effigies of the defeated gods were carried off by the conquerors and installed in their own capital cities — the final humiliation and profound demoralisation of the defeated king and his people. Thus, according to the Louvre Text 'when Ursa (Rusa) King of Urartu, heard that Musasir had been destroyed *and his god Khaldi carried away*, then with his own hand, with the iron dagger which hung at his side, he put an end to his life.'[2]

The gods had to be propitiated, and ritualistic ceremonies were at last organised into forms of prayer, and the religious ceremonies of the temples were directed by the priesthood, as delegates of the kingly high-priest. Those ancient ceremonies must have consisted substantially of magical elements, developed mainly from primitive sympathetic magic. One aspect of the principles on which sympathetic magic is purported to operate is to be found in Sumerian mythology where the name of a subject was regarded mystically to be the same as the subject itself. Hence the gods had merely to utter the name of a subject in order to create it. If, then, a magician knew the name of a subject, he also had power over it, for by knowing its name, he also, in theory, knew its nature. (The implications of the foregoing are interesting and far-reaching, but beyond the scope of the present essay.[3,4]) The Assyrians had a list of terms to designate the different sorts of prayers and sacrifices.

In Urartian, the verbs 'to sacrifice', 'to make offerings' are known, and the victims were goats, sheep, cattle and other animals.[5] King Ishpuini, together with his joint ruler and son, Menua, inscribed a long list of religious offerings on that precious rock at Meher Tur, about 2 miles from Van. It shows a list of sacrifices and offerings respectively to each of their greater and lesser deities, particularly to the numerous family of Khaldi, a tradition perpetuated from the times before the small chieftain-ships, each with its own distinct version of Khaldi, were unified into the Kingdom of Urartu. The Assyrians (and probably also the Urartians) sacrificed birds, and offered to their gods bread and wine and other foods and drinks, showing their understanding of the fact that gods, like men, must recoup their energies.[6]

The mysteries of the afterlife invoked fears which curbed the savage instincts to which we are all heirs. Immortality was understood essentially as a continuation of earthly life. The wealthy defunct were often buried fully clothed, adorned with their jewels and fineries, and provided in their graves with every necessity, as if for their daily life on earth, including their wives and slaves, their war-chariots and weapons, their fineries and furniture.

Urartu was a theocracy and the king represented Khaldi, the supreme god of Biaina. He was the native god of the people, depicted as a man standing on a lion or a bull, symbolising physical courage, power and fecundity. The people believed themselves to be his children. He had sanctuaries in numerous places within the kingdom.[7] As in the case of many other religions, that of Urartu also seems to have had a trinity, Khaldi, Teisheba and Shivini, who frequently appear on inscriptions, particularly as the vengeful gods in the imprecatory formula to be found at the end of inscriptions. Khaldi, the father god, was a warrior in whose name the king went to war, prayed to him for victory and gave an account of his conquests. On the celebrated stele at Meher Tur, his name appears no less than 19 times.[8] His wife in Urartu proper, was Arubani, but in Musasir (the holy city called Ardini) he had another wife with the Iranian name of Bagmastu. Next in the hierarchy of the gods came Teisheba, the god of storms and thunder, widely worshipped in Asia Minor, Syria and Mesopotamia, under the Hurrian name Teshub. The Assyrian counterpart of Teisheba was Adad.[9] He is shown standing on a lion or bull (see Figure 16.1) grasping a fistful of thunderbolts. Huba (or Khuba) was his wife, corresponding to the very ancient Hurrian goddess Khepa in north Syrian texts, in which King Abbael I of Aleppo (*c.*1740 BC) records how she supported him in one of his campaigns.[10] The name of the Hurrian goddess was appended to those of the two Mitannian princesses, Gilu-Khepa and Tadu-Khepa who married the Pharaohs Amunhotep III and Amunhotep IV (Akhenaten) respectively. The city of Teishebaini at Karmir Blur was dedicated by Rusa II to Khepa's husband the thunder-god Teisheba.[11]

The third Urartian god, in order of importance, was the sun-god Shivini, depicted kneeling and holding up a winged solar disc which symbolised him, recalling the Iranian god, Mitra, who has the sun behind his shoulders. The corresponding Assyrian sun-god was Shamash.[12]

The correlation of the gods of the two countries is revealed by the Urartian use of ideograms of Adad and Shamash to designate Teisheba and Shivini, respectively.[13] Anthropomorphic birds, such as the handle mount found at Alishar in 1851, are sometimes set against the sun disc of Shivini of Urartu. Such female figurines probably represented Shivini's consort, Tushpues,[14] who is shown as the third in the pantheon of goddesses in the inscriptions at Meher Tur. Tushpa, the Urartian capital, was her city. Thus, a number of important Urartian cities were named after native gods or goddesses.

By implication, Shivini, with his benevolent goddess-wife, might be described as a good deity, as were Aten, the Sun-god of the highly civilised Pharaoh, Akhenaten (fourteenth century BC) and the much later Persian Zoroastrian Ahura-Mazda. In contrast, the sun disc of the Assyrian Ashur represented a frightful and cruel god to whom human sacrifice was made.[15] To his solar symbol was added the warrior with his bow and arrow.[16] Although this in itself need not be significant, it seems to be so in the case of Assyria because of her self-confessed barbarities. The great gods of Ararat were warrior-gods and the temples of Khaldi and Teisheba were respectively known as the House of Weapons, decorated with many cult weapons, but Urartu is not, like Assyria, known for cruelties and sadistic aberrations. Does not the character of a god reflect that of its worshippers? Yet, although man might reflect the morals of his gods, and he would wish his gods to be righteous and good gods, he could not escape the evil man who might confront him at any time in his daily life. So, there had to be wicked gods as well as good ones. For the extent or magnitude of the Good can only be measured against that of the Bad. Good alone is an ethical but meaningless abstraction. Enormous quantities of weapons were stored in Ararat's temples. At Musasir, Sargon's scribes counted '25,212 bronze shields, 1514 bronze javelins and 305,412 swords', among other items of arms made of precious metals for ceremonial purposes: 'One large sword, a weapon worn at his waist, to the making of which went 26 minas and 3 su (about 30 lb) of gold; 96 silver javelins; ... silver bows and silver spears, inlaid with gold and mounted; 12 heavy shields, the bosses of which are made in the form of the heads of monsters, lions and wild bulls ...; 33 silver chariots.'[17] The precious belongings of Khaldi's spouse, Bagmastu, are also listed by Sargon: 'one gold signet ring with a seal for certifying the decrees of Bagmastu, wife of Haldi, inlaid with precious stones; 9 fabrics for the clothing of his godhead, embroidered with golden discs; 1 bed of ivory; 1 silver couch for the repose of his godhead, framed in gold and decorated with stone. ... 14 various stones for the ornament of the divinity, precious stones belonging to Haldi and Bagmastu his spouse.'[18] In Teishebaini at Karmir Blur, the inscription on a foundation stone, part of which was found in 1936 and the remainder in 1962, records that sacred weapons were brought to that city-fortress and deposited at the gates of Khaldi's temple. Great quantities of military equipment were kept at Karmir Blur, many of them made of iron. A find of particular interest was a hoard of scale armour in iron and bronze, together with the button of a fine piece of that armour, indicating that it was the property of King Argishti I.[19] Many other pieces of war-like material were found belonging to Urartian kings, in many instances having an inscription upon each, dedicating it to Khaldi:

> Three silver medallions were also found on Karmir Blur, one with a representation of a sacrifice to Haldi, another with a figure of the goddess Arubani and the third with the symbol of the god Shivini (a winged solar disc). An interesting feature is that on the medallions with the figures of Haldi and his spouse the heads of the two divinities are on a small round gold disc soldered on to the medallion. Figures of the three principal Urartian gods were also found on bronze belts; and near a sacrificial altar in a wine-store were discovered some clay figurines of fish divinities, similar to the corresponding Assyrian deities and to figures found in the Urartian fortress at Adilcevaz. In another store-room was a painted pottery statuette of a scorpion god.[20]

Thus, there appears to have been a well-established, important tradition of dedicating precious materials and weapons of war to the gods Khaldi, Teisheba and Shivini, to propitiate them and to associate them closely with priest and temple, king and palace as well as with the ordinary people who looked to their priest-king for protection against human enemies and evil spirits.

The Tree of Life, that universal symbol of faith and super-
stition, not unmixed with truth, was often incorporated in
Urartian decorative motifs. Among primitive peoples and the
ancient civilisations, a tree was believed to possess a life comparable to sentient life: there were male and female trees, who, in the
spring, were married to one another by their owners; there were
spirits which resided in trees and they could be invoked for good
or evil; the soul of the dead could animate trees:

> When a tree comes to be viewed, no longer as a body of the
> tree-spirit, but simply as its abode which it can quit at
> pleasure, an important advance has been made in religious
> thought. Animism is passing into polytheism. In other words,
> instead of regarding each tree as a living and conscious being,
> man now sees in it merely a lifeless, inert mass, tenanted for a
> longer or shorter time by a supernatural being who, as he can
> pass freely from tree to tree, thereby enjoys a certain right of
> possession or lordship over the trees, and, ceasing to be a tree-
> soul, becomes a forest god. As soon as the tree-spirit is thus in
> a measure disengaged from each particular tree, he begins to
> change his shape and assume the body of a man, in virtue of a
> general tendency of early thought to clothe all abstract
> spiritual beings in concrete human form.[21]

Urartian religious attitudes seem to have been very liberal. In
their pantheon the chief gods and their consorts are followed by
foreign gods and goddesses (including nature gods, such as the
moon, earth and water) which are listed on that priceless
document, the stele at Meher Tur, together with a very infor-
mative list of offerings, some in the form of sacrifices to be made
to them. By thus providing a place to foreign gods and goddesses
within their own pantheon of divinities, the Urartian monarchs
not only confirmed the annexation of their respective countries,
but at the same time promoted the political stability and the
social cohesion of their government. An outstanding example of
that liberal attitude is demonstrated by their acceptance of
Khaldi's wife at Musasir, the native Iranian goddess, Bagmastu,
betrothed to Khaldi by the priests and people of Musasir, when
that city and province were brought within the Urartian hegemony by Kings Ishpuini and Menua. At Tushpa, the Babylonian
goddess, Ishtar, the mother-goddess and the embodiment of the
reproductive energies of nature, was worshipped in her own

right. She was called Sari and, in course of time, she appears in the legends of Indo-European Armenia in the guise of Semiramis or Shamiram.[22] It is possible that the Indo-Aryan gods, Indra (with his thunderbolt) and Varuna, were also worshipped by the Urartian aristocracy, if not by the common people, for it is possible that they were the kinsmen of the Mitannian rulers who worshipped those gods. It is also possible that the worship of Indra and Varuna had penetrated into other parts of Anatolia, including the Hittite lands, during the heyday of Mitannian political power.[23]

The Babylonian moon-god, Sin, is the Urartian Sielardi,[24] and Nicolas Adontz[25] proposes that 'Sielardi' is derived from 'Siela', woman or sister, and 'Ardi', sun. He points out that in the East, since the most ancient times, the moon has been venerated as the sister of the sun. Another god, Sardi, recalls Sarduri or Sardauri. The town of Sardauri, it seems, derives its name either from King Sarduri or the god Sardi.[26] The Urartian kings appear to have been selective about the foreign gods they adopted. Although Argishti I, Sarduri II and Rusa I all made considerable conquests in the north, particularly in the Sevan region, the respective gods of those peoples do not appear among the foreign pantheons of Urartu. Those northern countries were still in a barbaric state and the Urartian monarchs disdained their gods. On the contrary, they introduced their own gods into those regions. Thus, Rusa constructed a temple to Teisheba and installed that god's effigy in it, in the Sevan area, amidst 23 principalities he had subdued.[27]

The offerings to the gods always included libations of wine, particularly as the vine is an indigenous plant in Armenia. Sargon's text at the Louvre lists the appropriate implements for use in ceremonies involving libations of wine, including '3 heavy brazen cauldrons, each with a capacity of 50 measures of water, and 1 large cauldron of 80 measures, with a large brazen ladle, which the kings of Urartu filled with sacrificial wine when sacrifices were made to Haldi'.[28] Among the king's quasi-religious obligations was his privilege to plant the vine, which was supposed to possess magical properties. Libations of wine frequently constituted an essential part of any important state or religious ceremony, of which one was the king's coronation. On that occasion, the first minister of state had the prerogative of placing the crown upon the king's brow, and he was, by tradition, the custodian of the crown. The Armenian conquerors adopted this Urartian tradition, and the Armenian *t'akatir* (Keeper of the Crown) had the sacred duty to guard the crown and to place it on his sovereign's head at his coronation.

Notes

1. N. Adontz, *Histoire d'Arménie* (Paris, 1946).
2. B.B. Piotrovskii, *The Ancient Civilisation of Urartu* (Barrie and Rockliff, 1969).
3. Gordon Childe, *What Happened in History* (Max Parish, 1960).
4. James Frazer, *The Golden Bough* (Macmillan).
5. Adontz, *op. cit.*
6. Ibid.
7. Ibid.
8. Ibid.
9. Ibid.
10. J.R. Kupper, 'Northern Mesopotamia and Syria', CAH, II¹. ix. p. 41.
11. Margaret S. Drower, 'Syria 1550–1400 BC', CAH, II¹.i. p. 419.
12. Percy Gardener, *Coins of the Greek and Scythian Kings of Bactria and India.* Quoted by H.R. Hall, *The Ancient History of the Near East* (Methuen, 1963).
13. Adontz, *op. cit.*
14. Piotrovskii, *op. cit.*
15. Sidney Smith, 'The Age of Ashurbanipal', CAH, III.i.
16. D.A. Mackenzie, *Myths of Babylonia and Assyria* (Cassell).
17. Piotrovskii, *op. cit.*
18. Ibid.
19. Ibid.
20. Ibid.
21. Frazer, *op. cit.*
22. A.H. Sayce, 'The Kingdom of Van', CAH, III.iv. p. 183.
23. H.R. Hall, *The Ancient History of the Near East* (Methuen, 1963).
24. Sayce, *op. cit.*, p. 184.
25. Adontz, *op. cit.*
26. Ibid.
27. Ibid.
28. Piotrovskii, *op. cit.*

16

Art of Urartu

The civilising influence of Ararat was widespread. It reached even such distant peoples (geographically and chronologically) as the Etruscans, the Greeks and the Achaemenid Persians. The nomadic Scythians and Cimmerians and the semi-civilised Iranian states no doubt regarded the Urartian officials and army officers as the representatives of one of the most highly civilised countries; and as prisoners of war, slaves or as soldiers serving in the armies of Ararat, they witnessed the luxurious life led by the aristocracy and the relatively high standard of living of the people in the great Urartian cities and fortresses such as Tushpa, Erebuni, Argishti-hinili and Teishebaini.

The abundant deposits of iron, copper, tin, lead and silver in Armenia were generally employed in the service of various manufactures. Weapons of war and certain agricultural implements, especially ploughshares, were made of iron, and it was with iron tools that the Urartians excavated their homes out of the mountain rock face,[1] a kind of dwelling to be found frequently in Asia Minor even today. The rock-hewn fortresses were also fashioned with iron tools. It was not until Sargon's reign (722–705 BC) that iron replaced bronze extensively in Assyria, the change probably being due to Sargon's invasion deep into Urartian territory where he must have seen the advantages of the use of iron over bronze, especially for weapons of war.[2]

Bronze was much applied to domestic implements and to works of art, the latter being especially important in the export trade. Our still very imperfect knowledge of the early history of Urartu cannot answer the question as to the length of time it took the Urartian metalworkers to reach the height of technical skill demonstrated by their bronze products during the eighth century

BC. It is interesting to set the problem within the context of known facts.

First, the two metals, the alloy of which produces bronze (92 per cent copper: 8 per cent tin), were found together in Armenia and northern Syria, and not in Mesopotamia.[3] Therefore the discovery of bronze-casting might well have first occurred near the sources of those metals; that is, in Armenia and northern Syria. From about 2500 BC, experiments with alloys of bronze and lead showed that the addition of 5–10 per cent lead to bronze alters its properties when molten, yet it does not impair its strength as a metal for the manufacture of tools and weapons. The advantage of adding lead to copper and tin is that the alloy becomes much less viscous at low temperatures and pours more freely into moulds of fine and intricate patterns.[4]

Secondly, the Urartians, who appear as members of the greater Hurrian community in Armenia well before 2000 BC, might reasonably be associated with the earliest bronze-casting communities in Asia Minor.

Thirdly, we know that Sumerian interests in the third millenium BC ranged over wide areas of the ancient world and there are indications of their presence in Armenia. A splendid copper bison of superb Sumerian workmanship, depicting one of the three main species in ancient Babylonia, now extinct,[5] was found near Lake Van, dated *c.* 2300 BC (see Plate 1), and 'a remarkable cylinder seal of late provincial Sumerian style from Goek Tepe, near Urmia'[6], stand witness to a close relationship between the natives of Armenia and the colonists of Sumer-Akkad, each exercising some influence upon the other. The wealthy cities in southern Mesopotamia might well have imported their metals from Armenia or Syria, an easy journey down-river, for the use of their metallurgists and craftsmen, as well as for commercial distribution.

The invention of the bellows towards the end of the third millenium BC considerably increased productivity. Also, larger castings became possible, since greater quantities of metal could be melted at the same time. A Mesopotamian inscription dated *c.* 2000 BC asks for two large goatskins for the making of bellows for a bronze-founder.[7] By 1500 BC, Elam could cast the large statue of Napir-asu, now exhibited at the Louvre, Paris.[8] Although the known comparable life-size Urartian statues and groups of figures are of much later date, the eighth century BC, the process of achieving a high standard in the casting of such large and complex pieces must have taken a very long time, probably some centuries. In the temple of Musasir, Sargon found, among other large bronze castings, a bronze life-size statue of Argishti I, weighing 60 talents (about 1.8 tons). But such large metal objects (bronze, gold or silver) were broken up on the spot and melted down for recasting, as depicted on a relief from Sargon's palace at Khorsabad; soldiers are seen breaking up such large pieces with axes.[9] They were too large to carry away.

The Louvre Text[10] also mentions a number of large bronze objects, some of which appear as decorations on the façade of the temple represented in the relief in Sargon's palace. These include '3 brazen cauldrons, each with a capacity of 50 measures of water, and 1 large cauldron of a capacity of 80 measures, with a large brazen handle, which the kings of Urartu filled with sacrificial wine when sacrifices were made to Haldi.' In a later passage the Louvre text enumerates some large pieces of brass (or rather, bronze sculpture which stood in the temple — examples of Urartian monumental art, about which otherwise we know nothing: '4 brazen statues of tall door-keepers, guardians of the temple door, and 4 supports which, together with the seat (pedestal), are of cast brass; 1 statue in an attitude of prayer, a representation of Sarduri, son [father] of Ishpuini, king of Urartu, and his seat of cast brass; 1 bull and 1 cow with its calf, cast by Sarduri, son [father] of Ishpuini, who caused to be melted down [?] the brass of the temple of Haldi; 1 figure of Argishti, king of Urartu, crowned with the stellate tiara of divinity, with his right hand raised in blessing, together with its receptacle, of a weight of 60 talents [about 1 ton 16 cwt] of brass; 1 figure of Ursa (Rusa) with his two horses and his driver's horse, with their seat (pedestal), cast in brass, on which can be read the king's boast, 'With my two horses and my charioteer, my hands conquered the kingdom of Urartu.'

Some of these pieces of sculpture can be seen in the relief from Sargon's palace. On each side of the entrance to the temple stand two of the four statues of 'tall door-keepers', and to the right of the entrance is the cow with its calf 'cast by Sarduri, son of Ishpuini'; there is no sign of the bull mentioned in the Louvre Text. At the base of the platform, apparently on either side of the steps, are two huge cauldrons supported on tripods. Two similar cauldrons were found in the excavations of the fortress of Teishebaini (Karmir-Blur), the cauldrons themselves being wrought from brass sheet and the rims cast in bronze.[11]

Of large pieces of statuary, only the six fragments of a relief sculpture carved in basalt of the god Teisheba have come down to us from the first half of the seventh century BC. He stands on a bull, facing to the left towards two triple spearheads and the figure is about 3.5 m high. The fragments were discovered as part of the walls of the medieval castle at Adilcevaz, on the northern coast of Lake Van (see Figure 16.1).

Five of the fragments belong to this figure, but the sixth shows that there was another figure, looking towards the first and likewise facing a triple spearhead. Behind the righthand figure stands a single triple spearhead, rather taller and more slender than those in the middle, and perhaps fixed on some solid base, only part of which remains. The god or king wears an elaborately decorated garment, probably woven of wool: the pattern, perhaps in gold brocade, is repetitive, with a wide border, edged with a fringe and band of 'herring-bone' pattern. The second figure wears a garment ornamented with the same pattern, but worn differently: the outer cloak or robe falls straight down, showing the kilt over the forward leg. The bull seems to wear a rug on its back, with two large tassels; the lines down the shoulder probably represent five straps.[12]

Further evidence of large-scale Urartian sculpture in stone was found by German archaeologists in 1898. It was the headless, upper part of a badly damaged statue of (probably) an early Urartian king. Another section of the same part of the statue was thrown up by an explosion. These portions, without head or lower limbs, measure 1.2 m and the whole piece must have been life-size. The suggestion that it represented a king is supported by 'wavy hair, falling over the back and shoulder, as well as a narrow beard. The hands are laid on the chest, the right holding a club or a whip with a forked tip, and the left, probably a bow and some arrows. A long sword is represented on the left side; it is in a scabbard which hangs from a belt and has three lines in relief along its length.'[13] Another example of large stone statues is that of King Sarduri, found by the Assyrians in the temple of Musasir.

Those scholars who hold the view that Urartian artists and craftsmen (in particular the bronze workers) were influenced

Figure 16.1: God standing on bull: artist's impression of the reconstructed stone relief found at Adikevag (Lake Van)

Arakel Patrik, Costumes Arméniens, Erevan

mainly by Assyria, base their opinion primarily on the evidence of seventh-century BC, Urartian pieces found in Assyria, during Urartu's decline.[14] Considering Assyria's immense importance as an extensive market for all classes of goods, it would have been commercial suicide for Urartu if its craftsmen had not, as sensible businessmen, offered their nearest and biggest customer, Assyria, just the styles that would best stimulate trade — styles to conform with Assyrian taste. Nevertheless, it must be said that the Vannic monarchs and their people must have adopted some aspects of Assyrian culture (for Assyria was heir to the culture of Sumer and Babylon) but only as additions to their own Hurrian civilisation, developed through centuries of Hittite, Mitannian and Mediterranean influence.

The resemblance found between Urartian art on the one hand and Cretan and Etruscan art on the other, may be due either to the influence of exported items on native craftsmen, or to fugitive Urartian master-craftsmen who in the seventh and sixth centuries BC fled from the barbarian invasions of their country, to Mediterranean lands and settled, among other places, in Crete and Etruria.[15] Resemblance of style might also be due to metalwork schools operating under the supervision of Urartian craftsmen who had, for personal reasons, travelled to the various centres and settled at places where examples of Urartian or pseudo-Urartian craft have been found — Gordion, Rhodes, Crete, Delphi, Corinth, Athens, Etruria. 'Their [the Urartians'] culture is western, with only minor traces of Assyrian influence. They influenced archaic Greek art in their turn and had peculiar relations to the Etruscans. They were also called Chalybes, probably from the name of the steel which they were the first to produce.'[16]

In fact, much of Urartian work is unique. Its eclectic character has given it the stamp of originality, since it does not resemble the work of its mentors. But some of the finest pieces are to be found in foreign countries. At the zenith of her military power (*c.* 800–743 BC) Ararat occupied the Mediterranean port of Posiedon (Al Mina), at the mouth of the River Orontes, whence its bronze articles (among other goods), despatched from Tushpa and elsewhere, through Carchemish, were shipped via Rhodes or Samos, Corinth and Delphi; or Cyprus and Crete to Italy; or overland, via Phrygia and the Ionian cities on the coast, to Samos and Greece. The alternative route to the west was by way of the long and dangerous voyage via the Greek colonists' Black Sea ports (assuming that, in the absence of evidence to the contrary, Urartu did not possess a Black Sea port of its own), the most important being Trapezus (Trebizond), established by the Milesian colonists in 756 BC. That route was perhaps frequently used by the Elamite and Indian merchants, accompanying their wares, in transit through Urartian territories, to the Levantine markets, or selling them to the Greeks on the coastal towns of the Black Sea, for shipment to their homelands on the west coast of Asia Minor. It was probably also used by the Urartians much more frequently in the seventh century when the Cimmerian depredations of central and western Anatolia made peaceful trading and the transit of goods through those parts impracticable.

The Urartian bronzes that were shipped abroad were copied extensively by the smiths of the importing countries. Those commercial relationships helped to mould the art even of Classical Greece.[17] In this context, the great ceremonial bronze cauldrons, with representations of animal or human heads around the rim (described as handle mounts or *protomoi*) are of primary importance. The handsomely cast *protomoi* are artistic expressions in their own right. They were probably exported to be fitted to cauldrons made in the importing country. Nothing like those stands and tripods in bronze had ever been produced anywhere else, although terracotta bowls on terracotta stands, as depicted in Sargon's palace at Khorsabad, were in use.[18]

The universal admiration of the art of classical Greece has, during the past 50 years, been extended to the works of art of ancient Mesopotamia, such as those found in the royal tombs of Ur (*c.* 2600 BC) as well as to the much later Iranian contributions. It is only in recent years that even archaeologists have been able to study and assess the significance of Urartu finds, of which many pieces are of great artistic and historical merit.

An eminent scholar, Leonard Woolley, suggests that 'the most original and the most fruitful contribution to art was made by the metal-workers of Urartu' (*Mesopotamia and the Middle East*, London 1961).

The flowering of Urartian art coincided with the period of Urartu's military greatness in the eighth century BC when the Urartian empire included central and eastern Anatolia, and extensive provinces in Syria, and northern Mesopotamia. In 743 BC Urartu suffered a military setback and the serious territorial losses to Assyria included Syria, with its Mediterranean port of

Posiedon (modern Al Mina), at the mouth of the River Orontes, an important outlet for Urartu's exports. A much more serious defeat was sustained in 714 BC when King Sargon of Assyria invaded Urartu, laid waste the land, and pillaged the cities. His troops overwhelmed the holy city of Musasir, west of Lake Urmia, and ransacked its temple, the treasure house of generations of Urartian kings. Sargon and his officers were astonished at the enormous quantity and superb workmanship of the articles they found there, consisting of over 330,000 objects made of gold, silver and precious stones; as well as ivories and bronzes, and rare textiles and embroideries.

Among that great hoard, there were life-size statues and even whole groups of figures made of bronze. This type of bronze-casting presents special technical difficulties which could only have been mastered by the Urartian craftsmen through an accumulation of experiences, handed down by successive generations of schools; a period probably representing several centuries. The development of skills in metalwork would have been encouraged in Armenia as the region is rich in minerals, including copper and tin, the constituents of bronze.

Although it is true that at first Urartu borrowed heavily from Assyrian styles as well as from the artforms of its Hittite and Hurrian neighbours, by the middle of the eighth century BC the Urartian craftsmen had developed their own particular styles. Urartian art was eclectic, a synthesis of the arts of many peoples, yet it was unique and it reached a very high level of competence. But some of Urartu's finest bronzes are to be found in foreign countries, exported during the eighth century BC from Anatolian ports, including those of the Black Sea, as well as from the port of Poseidon, via Rhodes and Corinth or via Cyprus and Crete to Greece and even as far as Etruria in Italy and eastern France.

This is supported by reference to one important category (among others) of Urartian exports: bronze cauldrons. Embellished by handle mounts (*protomoi*) and decorative figurines, which give them an impression of lavish wealth, they are placed either on intricately embossed bases or on tripods standing on representations of animal feet. Such cauldrons in bronze had never been produced anywhere else before.[19] Their individuality established their Urartian origin.

The cauldron discovered in the Tomba Barberini at Praenesta (modern Palestrina), Italy, is one of the finest examples of bronze art from antiquity. Made of hammered sheets of bronze, it has lion and griffin *protomes* (see Plate 5) which are themselves beautiful pieces of casting and typical of the best Urartian art. On the Assyrian reliefs at Khorsabad, Sargon's troops are depicted bearing away similar cauldrons and stands from the Urartian temple of Musasir in 713 BC. As in Urartu, so in Etruria such cauldrons must have had some important ritual use, reflecting the religious beliefs of the Etrurian aristocracy. It is in this context that the elaborate decorations of the stand and the fine animal figurines must be considered, particularly as this factor supports the view that the Barberini cauldron is an Urartian product.

Depicted on the stand in repoussé, are winged, human-headed lions (to ward off evil spirits) confronting each other on either side of a sacred tree. The engraved triangular decoration at the base of the siren's neck, a particularly Urartian feature, and the knob on the king's horned head-dress, should be noted. Metal stands such as this were quite unknown in Italy before the appearance of the Urartian model in the eighth century BC.

The date of the Barberini, Bernardini and other Urartian cauldrons found in Italy, including that discovered at Vetulonia, is controversial. I adhere to the view that they belong to the eighth century BC, rather than the seventh century. The seventh century was a time of decline in Urartian art and political power. The important trade route of Poseidon–Cyprus–Crete–Etruria could only have been operating during the Urartian occupation of northern Syria down to 743 BC when Assyria defeated Urartu and occupied Syria. Furthermore, Poseidon was not only the outlet for Urartian bronzes made in Van but also for those made by Urartian metalworkers who might have established themselves in Syria. Poseidon in 743 BC might have been the embarkation port of fugitive, emigrating Urartian craftsmen who seem to have established schools of metalworkers in Cyprus and Crete as well as, perhaps, in Greece and Etruria. The southern and western Anatolian ports were probably accessible to Urartian exports, and fugitive craftsmen, until Urartu's crushing defeat in 713 BC, and perhaps for some years later. It is suggested that Urartian cauldrons found in Etruria should be dated to the last half of the eighth century and that they must have been in use for several generations before they were finally deposited into the tombs after which they were named. The tombs themselves — the Barberini and the Bernardini — are dated to the seventh century, and it seems to be mainly this factor that has influenced those scholars who place the Urartian bronzes found there, in the seventh century BC. Other factors which support the view that the Barberini cauldron is of Urartian origin are the similarity of the siren's features on the stand to that of a king of Tabal in the Taurus, depicted on a relief at Ivriz; and the religious significance of certain parts of the whole design which are comparable to similar designs on Asiatic monuments, such as the round knob on the top of the horned head-dress which is frequently also found on reliefs depicting the Western Asiatic storm god, Teshub.

The decorations on the Barberini stand recall the Urartian human-headed winged lion and the faceless winged bull, (see Plate 9) called *lamassu*. Both are believed to be decorative parts of a magnificent throne. Those *lamassu*, like the gigantic Assyrian ones, embody in one fantastic creature the most powerful attributes of man and beast. In these examples we see the face and torso of a man or woman, the feet and body of a lion or a bull, and the feathers and wings of a mythical and mysterious creature, a griffin.

The griffin heads which decorate the rim of the Barberini cauldron, described as handle mounts or *protomoi*, are additional examples illustrating Urartian influence in the Aegean, Etruria and Greece.[20] Almost identical griffin heads have come to light in those regions. Even in the sixth century BC, when Etruscan metal-smiths were producing magnificent objects with relief decorations influenced by Greek art, Urartian techniques were still used. A winged human figure, with the head of a griffin, in white and black ivory, found at Van, emphasises the Urartian stylistic origins of these mythical bird representations (see Plate 11). Note especially the stylized lock of hair down the neck — a typical Urartian form.

Those *protomoi*, with or without cauldrons, were probably also shipped from the Milesian colonial Black Sea port of Trapezus (modern Trebizond) founded in the year 757 BC, in the heart of the Colchis. At that time, Urartu was at the zenith of her power when she controlled the important trade route passing through the kingdom of Mannai (the Biblical Minni), on the south-western coastal strip of Lake Urmia. The road, having passed through the narrow corridor between the lake and the Kurdish mountains, reached Transcaucasia by way of the valley of the Araxes river. The caravans from India, Elam and Iran then unloaded their cargo of spices, lapis lazuli and embroideries at Trapezus, for shipment to the Aegean world, along with the

Urartian exports comprising, besides its famous bronzes, precious metals — gold and silver, copper and iron — craftwork and textiles as well as, perhaps, some of her abundant crops of wheat, barley, rye, millet, sesame and flax. Even certain items of 'palace' furniture might be included among Urartu's exports.

A cauldron with lion handle mounts, similar in design to those on the Barberini bowl, was found in the Tomba Regolini Galassi, Cerveteri. It is an excellent example of local imitations in which the Etruscan craftsman has reproduced the original Urartian design. The five lion *protomoi* are in hammered bronze. A close examination of the *protomoi* shows an amateurish finish. The hard angles at the folds of the muzzle and of the nostrils; of the eyebrows and the ears, are treated in a non-Asiatic fashion and the workmanship is inferior. These roughly finished aspects of the lion's features are emphasised when they are compared, for example, to the bronze lion from a sumptuous throne discovered at Van. The handle mounts are obviously copies of the Urartian model, made by a local smith (see Plate 7). The cauldron is dated to the second half of the seventh century BC.

On another cauldron from the Tomba Regolini Galassi (see Plate 6), the elongated necks of the six snarling lion handle mounts have an exact parallel in an Urartian *protome* found at Karmir Blur (Armenia) in 1957. It has an inscription in two lines round the collar which reads: '[Belonging to king] Sarduri, son of Argishti'. It is exhibited at the Armenian State Historical Museum, Erevan. Its position on a cauldron could only have been the same as those of the *protomoi* on the cauldron found in the Tomba Regolini Galassi. This, like the Barberini cauldron, must be of Urartian workmanship. A fine Urartian recumbent lion in bronze discovered at Kayalidere has the typical Urartian snarling muzzle.

A cauldron found in the royal burial mound of the Phrygian king, Gordius (*c.* 750 BC) with handle mounts of anthropomorphic birds, consisting of two male (with beards) and two female heads is designed in a characteristically Urartian fashion. This is one of three large cauldrons found, among the other articles, in the Phrygian royal tomb. They demonstrate that in the eighth century BC Urartian influence extended to the west, well beyond Syria and central Anatolia, and that Urartu would have had access to the southern and western ports of Anatolia.

A human-headed *protome*, discovered at Gordion, is very similar to the handle mounts of the Gordion cauldron. The geometric or triangular pattern at the base of the neck and on the chest is a typical Urartian design, already noted on the figures on the stand of the Barberini cauldron. There is an almost identical *protome* from Vetulonia (Italy) (see Plate 8) and another from Ptoion (Greece), both with the same type of triangular decoration at the base of the neck which betrays their Urartian origin or influence, apart from the strong similarity of their features.

A particularly sumptuous cauldron was discovered at Vetulonia, Italy. It has, in addition to six griffin *protomoi*, similar to those on the Barberini cauldron, two bearded siren handle mounts with lifting rings. Each of the griffin heads has the two curled tresses which are characteristic of Urartian griffins. The siren figures on the lifting rings, with their curious hat, may be compared to a bronze Urartian figure to be seen on the reliefs from Tell Halaf, northern Syria. These Urartian cauldrons must have been imported into Greece and Etruria as objects essential for rituals performed by the priests of those countries. Indeed, they must have travelled even as far as St Colombe, France, where an Urartian type, bronze cauldron with griffin protomoi, on an elaborate tripod was found (see Figure 16.2).

Figure 16.2: Cauldron on tripod, fifth century from Côte d'Or: obviously copy of earlier seventh century Urartian workmanship, compare with Plate 7.

Courtesy of Professor J.M. Cook.

A handle mount found near Alishar, and acquired by the Hermitage Museum in 1851, was the first such figurine that came to light. It is a winged woman's head and has quite large and distinct Urartian triangular patterns on the chest. The female-headed version of bird figurines, such as this one, often seen as *protomoi* of cult cauldrons, are sometimes set against a disc, corresponding to the Urartian sun-gold, Shivini. The female *protome* then, when represented with a disc, might well portray Shivini's consort, Tushpuea.

A particularly large anthropomorphic bird, with a 33 cm wingspan, was found at Van. It is of the highest quality and has a variety of decorative chased patterns upon it. The handle mounts have loops through which the lifting rings were passed. Such winged figures have been unearthed at Van, Alishar, Rhodes, Delphi, Olympia, Vetulonia and Praenesta, and they were frequently copied by Greek craftsmen. Thus, Urartian handle mounts are widely dispersed and their great artistic variety expresses the individual genius of each of their makers. It is possible to identify handle mounts which were attached to cauldrons by the Urartian craftsmen, and those which were exported separately and later attached to cauldrons by metalworkers of the importing countries. The former fit closely over the edges of the cauldron and are obviously made to fit the particular vessel to which they are attached. It is suggested that examples found in Asia are Urartian and that most of the Aegean ones are copies of the Vannic originals made by Greek craftsmen.

Two bull's heads, clearly the handle mounts of a cauldron similar to that from Altin Tepe, were found at Van (see Plate 10) and are now exhibited at the British Museum. Two other almost identical ones from Van are respectively to be seen at Baltimore, USA in Walter's Art Gallery and in Sir William Burrell's collection of antiquities in Glasgow. Another magnificent bull's head from Van, probably a handle mount, is also to be found at the British Museum, and one at the Louvre, Paris. Other *protomoi* in the form of bull's heads are dispersed among various museums and private collections.

Like the cauldrons from the Etruscan tombs, to which reference has already been made, a bronze cauldron found at Altin Tepe, near Erzincan, with bulls' head *protomoi*, ranks among the largest surviving vessels from antiquity. It provides important additional evidence for the view that the cauldrons with human, lion, griffin or bulls' heads attached to them or made for that purpose, found at Gordion, in the Aegean islands, in Greece and in Etruria are all of Urartian origin; for this class of object appears to have been a characteristically Urartian device. The bull's head handle mounts around the rim of the Altin Tepe cauldron are fine pieces of cast and chased metalwork. Each one is brazed onto a bird-shaped plate at right-angles, which in its turn is riveted to the rim of the cauldron with four rivets. The cauldron is mounted upon an iron tripod, standing on artistically modelled bulls' feet. In the Bernardini tomb a smaller bronze cauldron and tripod stand with bulls' feet, of Urartian type, were found, comparable to the Altin Tepe example. At Cerveteri, a bronze tripod was discovered, certainly of Urartian type, having winged sirens with bulls' heads.

The bulls' feet on which the Altin Tepe tripod stands, recall those of the magnificent candelabrum found at Van, although the latter are more elaborate, showing the bulls' feet emerging from the mouths of lions, a zoomorphic juncture restricted to the Urartians and the later Etruscans. That candelabrum is among the most beautiful works of art in antiquity (see Figure 16.3). A

Figure 16.3: Bronze candelabrum from Van: reconstructed, height 136.5 cm

Museum für Kunst und Gewerbe, Hamburg

four-line cuneiform inscription on its shaft mentions the name of King Rusa of Urartu, thus establishing its undoubted Urartian workmanship. Another bronze candelabrum, with feet similar in concept to those of the candelabrum just described, is certainly in the Urartian style, if not necessarily in workmanship. It is much more elaborate, but less elegant, than Rusa's candelabrum.

Much of Urartian art was formalised as befitted its mainly decorative purpose. Its precise proportions may be adapted equally on a monumental or a miniature scale. But the stylised shapes of animals and the decoration of their bodies are rich with ornamentation of an individual character which can always be recognised as Urartian. The influence of Urartian artists, craftsmen and architects on an international scale is of considerable significance:

> Today it has come to be realised that the high accomplishment and far reaching significance of Urartian culture has in the past been consistently underrated, simply because its remains have been insufficently explored. Urartu is now being presented to us as a nation — and in its time a very great nation — whose history and even identity seem to have been completely expunged from the records of human memory for two-and-a-half thousand years. Yet, today, everything about it — its characteristics, political and economic history and its art — constitute one of the most intriguing problems in Near Eastern archaeology. (Seton Lloyd, *Early Highland Peoples of Anatolia*, Thames & Hudson, 1967)

And finally, on the subject of ceremonial cauldrons, the bronze one, mentioned above, discovered at St Colombe, Côte d'Or is of fascinating interest, because its design and motifs are close variations of the finds in Italy and Anatolia. Furthermore, its tripod stand, mounted on representations of bulls' feet, is easily comparable to that of the great Urartian cauldron found at Altin Tepe, near Erzinean. This further confirms Urartian influence on Western European metalwork.

In support of possible immigration into Etruria of Urartian master-craftsmen, their families and apprentices and others, I quote the following extract from Dr G.A. Wainwright, *The Teresh, the Etruscans and Asia Minor* (AS IX, 1959, p. 209):

> It is this very part of Asia Minor, Armenia and the north-east

that Sir Gavin De Beer finds the high percentage of the blood-group A which differentiates the present inhabitants of Central Italy from other Italians. Moreover, within this Italian A-group area there is a smaller one almost exactly covering Etruria where there is a high proportion of B-group of the same value as that of the inhabitants of Anatolia. This characteristic, therefore, did not come to Etruria in the 13th and 12th centuries with the Teresh from Lydia, but in the 8th and 7th centuries with the influx of what we know as 'Etruscan' and of the Urartian bronzes. It must have been not only an intrusion of some art influence but also of a large movement of population to have altered the blood.

(Sir Gavin de Beer in *Revue des Arts* (1955), p. 146. Unfortunately he does not specify which part of Anatolia.)

We have seen how after Hormuzd Rasam's departure from Van a great deal of illicit excavation and much looting took place. During the course of many years, the stolen items came to light one by one either in private collections or museums in various parts of the world. Some of these pieces seem to be parts of a sumptuous throne and stool which might have been used by the king in his dual role of monarch and high priest. Such items of decorative furniture and their artistic embellishments are classified as 'palace art'. The bronze figurines on the state throne and those embossed on the shields of the Urartian monarchs may be enlarged graphically or physically without causing any deterioration from the appearance of the original. For the artists of Ararat in accordance with the custom of Middle Eastern craftsmen of ancient times, followed certain rules of proportion and used stereotyped patterns.[21] From these rediscovered items, Dr R.D. Barnett of the Western Asiatic Antiquites Department, British Museum, was able to offer a graphic reconstruction of the throne and stool, and perhaps in the future a complete model might successfully be produced. For the pieces that are left to us 'are the still striking remains of one of the most splendid monuments of ancient metallurgy to survive in our time'.[22]

Some of the main figurines referred to above are human-headed, winged bulls and lions; and recumbent lions and griffins with birds' claws. The wings of the human-headed beasts and those of the griffin have traces of gold leaf in their recesses. The face of the human-headed bull (in the British Museum) was made of stone but is now missing (see Plate 9). A similar statuette

(Hermitage Museum) but with the body of a winged lion has an intact face of stone. The winged griffin has inlaid eyes and eyebrows and traces of gold leaf, while a snarling, recumbent lion, also with traces of gold leaf, sits on an openwork column, inlaid in parts with coloured enamel (British Museum).[23] These brief descriptions of a few of the figurines are intended as no more than an introduction to what was probably an elaborate and sumptuous throne and stool of which they seem to be parts, illustrating the supreme status and might of an Urartian King of Kings, who was also the high-priest of Khaldi.

Other notable examples of bronze craftsmanship at the British Museum are four royal shields from Van (see Plate 2). Two of the shields have the names of their respective owners chased upon their rims in cuneiform: 'Rusa Erimenahini' (Rusa son of Erimena) and 'Rusa Argistihini' (Rusa son of Argishti). A number of other royal

Figure 16.4: Bronze royal shield, belonging to King Sarduri II: reconstructed

Armenian State Historical Museum

173

shields belonging to Argishti I, Sarduri II and Rusa I came to light at Karmir Blur (see Figure 16.4). Some of the shields have repoussé representations of lions and bulls in two (British Museum) and three (Armenian State Historical Museum, Erevan) concentric bands.[24] The dedicatory inscription with the king's name is along the rim. The embossed animal representations are so arranged as to appear always in an upright position, when the shield is correctly held (see Plate 3). This is 'a peculiarity recurring on Cretan shields of the Archaic Period'.[25] The more elaborate and richly decorated royal shields, were intended for ceremonial purposes. Those hanging on the façade of the temple at Musasir, for example, were made of gold and silver, with animal head bosses, as depicted on the reliefs in Sargon's palace at Khorsabad. Manifestly, then, there must have been a great deal of activity in the manufacture of bronze objects, not only for the royal palaces but also for those of the aristocracy; for the temples of Khaldi, Tesheba and Ardini; for the armed forces, shields, helmets, arrowheads; and for export.

Gold and silver were also much used in the services of the arts. Excavations at Van have brought to light the figure of a fertility goddess and her female adorer engraved upon a gold medallion, 6.5 cm in diameter, 'the peculiarities of which have left their mark on archaic Greek, especially Ionic art'.[26] In a large earthenware jar, two pots of silverware were discovered. The most interesting item found in one of the pots was a small silver box with a double lid, containing some kind of powder. The analyst's report on it indicates that it was used in the goldsmith's and silversmith's craft for drawing black lines. That particular aspect of the jeweller's art is now called 'Toula', after the Russian city whence it came to Western Europe. The city of Toula itself probably received it from the Caucasus where the ancient Vannic art had continued. There were also ivory statues of which one, a nude female figure, had traces of blue colouring in the eye-sockets, 'plainly suggesting that the Urartians were a blue-eyed race',[27] as well as a golden bolt, shaped like a hand with a winged dragon design engraved upon it. There is 'no doubt that oriental art directly influenced the Aegean and Etrurian, which, as early as 700 BC, was probably importing bronzes from Urartu'.[28] The temples must have been lavishly furnished and decorated with precious stones, metals and rare materials. At the temple of Khaldi at Musasir, for example, the bed of Khaldi and his consort Bagmastu, was made of ivory, having a mattress of silver, encrusted with precious stones. When the Assyrian troops looted that temple, they were astonished at the enormous quantity, over 333,000 pieces, and superb workmanship of the metalwork they found there. Khaldi's temple at Musasir was probably built by King Menua and furnished by him and his successors lavishly, as befitted the temple of the supreme god. The attack on and the destruction of the temple are depicted on a frieze on the walls of Sargon's palace at Khorsabad (see Plate 4). It shows the Assyrians taking away the booty. Two scribes, supervised by an official, are seen recording, on a large clay tablet, each item as it is carried off. The articles in metal are carefully weighed before being consigned to Khorsabad.

As well as listing the magnificent haul, the table carries a description of Sargon's campaign. It is now exhibited at the Louvre. The following is a paraphrased list of the loot:

The temple of Khaldi, the god of Biaina, contained gold and silver, precious woods and stones, ivory and rich furniture, numberless vessels of gold and silver, including the silver cup of Rusa with cover, cups from the land of Tabal, and silver censers from the same country. There were bronze and iron objects of all kinds and sizes, and dyed vestments of linen, including the scarlet textiles of Ararat and Kurkhi. The temple treasury included talents of gold, of silver and of copper, a great sword of gold as well as lances, bows and arrows of silver inlaid with gold, chariots of silver and 293 silver cups, the workmanship of Assyria, Ararat and Kurkhi, daggers of ivory and hardwood set in gold, ivory tables and baskets for holding flowers and many ivory wands. The flame-red shields of gold were hung three on either side of the temple door which was bolted with a golden bar, moulded in the form of a winged dragon, seated on a human hand, and locked by two golden keys that were fashioned in the likeness of protecting goddesses with the Hittite tiara on their heads. There were 12 silver shields adorned with heads of lions and wild oxen and the gold ring which confirmed the commands of Bagmastu, the spouse of Khaldi and special goddess of Musasir, and the ivory bed with silver mattress on which the divine pair were believed to lie. There were also images of the Vannic kings and a great bowl of bronze capable of holding 80 measures of water, with its great bronze cover, which the kings of Ararat filled with wine for libations when they offered sacrifices to Khaldi.[29] The façade of the temple at Musasir is depicted with votive shields of electrum (a mixture of gold and silver), hanging above the entrance, and with cauldrons for cult ceremonies, on each side of it, a custom which Urartians had in common with Minoans.[30]

In 1947 some peasants in Ziwiye, a village near Sakkis in Persian Kurdistan, discovered a Scythian royal tomb below the walls of a Mannean fortress, containing a rich treasure hoard which is now known as the Treasure of Ziwiye. Many articles in the collection appear to be linked with Scythian art, as represented, for example, in the gold facings of dagger sheaths discovered at Kelermes and Melgunov on the River Kuban in Scythian *kurgans* or barrows, in embossed gold plate with strikingly Scythian features, and a network of decorative format 'corresponds to Urartian taste as manifest in bronze belts (and other articles) found in Armenia'.[31] 'It is now no longer possible to study the relationship between the Scythian and the various countries of the Ancient East without taking into account of the Karmir Blur-Teishebaini material.'[32] Many of the articles are of Urartian design and workmanship. For example, a number of pectorals show the adoption of ornamental breast-plates by Scythians from Urartians, while they were in Transcaucasia. Such pectorals are unique Urartian ornaments and are never found in Assyrian or Babylonian art.

Dr R.D. Barnett recalls a romantic legend in which a part of that treasure represented the dowry of the Assyrian princess who married the Scythian warrior, Bartatua.

Much of the gold work of Ziwiye is also made in the Urartian tradition of metal-working. A gold bracelet consisting of two pairs of lions cubs' head facing each other in the middle of the bracelet and two adult lions' heads, one of which is removable to facilitate the wearing of the bracelet, depicts their peculiarly gabled foreheads which are similar to that of the lion from Toprak Kale. Their curved necks recall the bronze handle mount of a cauldron — a lion's head on a curved neck — found at Karmir Blur, bearing the inscribed name of King Sarduri II.[33] This tomb confirmed the findings of Professor Boris Piotrovskii, the Russian archaeologist who led the first expedition to Karmir Blur. He noted that the arts and cultural development of the nomadic Scythians were greatly influenced by the civilised Urartians who were universally acknowledged to be masters of the arts and the metal industry.

There is also evidence of the influence of Urartu on other forms of Persian art, architecture, as well as on the writing and even on the state protocol and traditions of administration. Only in Urartian texts, for example, are royal inscriptions divided into sentences each one beginning with the formula: 'Saith (e.g. Menua) and king ...' and that formula was borrowed by the Achaemenid monarchs. The manner in which Rusa I claims to have won his kingdom is emulated by Darius the Great, quoted by Herodotus (III. 88): 'And now when his [Darius'] power was established firmly throughout all the kingdoms, the first thing that he did was to set up a carving in stone [at Behistun] which showed a man mounted upon a horse, with an inscription in these words following: "Darius, son of Hystaspes, by aid of his good horse [here followed the horse's name] and of his good groom, Aebaras, got himself the Persians".' A similar statue with golden horses, dedicated to a god by the owner, a Bactrian nobleman, imitating Rusa, was found among the Oxus Treasure, a mixed collection of artworks, said to have been found in 1877 on the site of a temple on a tributary of the Oxus river in Turkestan. Thus, Urartian influence is evident even in such a distant culture as that represented by the Oxus Treasure.

As to graphic art in Urartu, the finds at Karmir Blur, Altin Tepe, Aznavur and Erebuni have shown wall painting to have been an integral part of monumental architecture (see Figure 16.5). The site of Erebuni had been almost completely cleared of its 2750 years' burial when I was there in 1968, the year in which the city's foundation by King Argishti I was celebrated. Under the direction of Professor K.L. Oganesian, systematic excavations, over a period of 18 years, had revealed the huge triangular plan of the stronghold, with its outer, central and inner ramparts. Besides lesser buildings, the remains of the king's palace and the temple of Khaldi, were brought to light. They were richly decorated with some 2000 square metres of wall paintings, integral parts of the buildings, to give credence to their respective monarchical and religious functions. These impressive murals are witness to the high artistic attainments of the Urartian painters. The geometric, vegetable, animal and human motifs have been reconstructed from the many large fragments of decorated plaster. They reveal religious themes, such as processions of gods, sacred animals and trees of life; and secular motifs of scenes from hunting, cattle breeding and agriculture.[34]

The most elaborate wall paintings were many-tiered, each tier somehow related to the others.

They were basically executed in three colours: red and dark

Figure 16.5: Palace wall decoration: reconstructed

K.L. Organesian, Arin-Berd, Erevan

blue on a white ground. On the upper part of the wall, on the projecting cornice, there were circles containing many-rayed stars. Lower down there was a row of alternate red and dark blue pelmettes — a characteristic Assyrian pattern — and below them a band made up of stepped battlements, which also occur commonly in Assyrian paintings. Below these three ornamental bands there was a narrow frieze containing figures of bulls and rams, and below again, in the fifth band, there was a painting of sacred trees with gods standing on either side of them. The shape of the trees recalls the one which is found on the helmets of Argishti and Sarduri but they are rendered much more schematically. Dark blue paint was used for the outline, for the stem, and for the branches, which end in circular fruits. The figures of the gods also recall those on the helmets. They have neither beards nor wings, and they hold fruit and baskets in their hands.[35]

Much of the most characteristic Urartian pottery was found at Toprak Kale by Dr C.F. Lehmann-Haupt in the 1890s, consisting of carinated bowls and one-handled jugs in a brilliant polished red. A significant contribution to our knowledge of pottery has been made by the enormous number of jugs, many of them unbroken, found in the citadel of Karmir Blur (cf Plate 12). Some large jars of a common character for storing wine, oil and corn, have been brought to light at Toprak Kale, Karmir Blur and elsewhere. Their appearance and design are perpetuated in the Armenian pottery of today. Some are said to be similar to the Greek Samian ware (possibly through Phrygian influence), which has also been found at the Hittite site of Khattusha, Boghaz Koy. There is yet much pottery in Armenia, bearing cuneiform inscriptions indicating the nature of the contents, to be classified. At Karmir Blur, 400 jars were discovered, their capacity varying between 17½ and 26 gallons.

While it is difficult to estimate precisely where Ararat's culture originated, there is no doubt that the Vannic conquerors spread their rich heritage among the less civilised peoples on the periphery of their empire as well as inspiring certain aspects of Aegean art and architecture, including those of classical Greece. The art of Urartu has proved to be more varied than earlier scholars thought.

Notes

1. A.H. Sayce, 'The Kingdom of Van,' CAH, III[1]. iv. p. 185.
2. Ibid., p. 186.
3. Margaret S. Drower, 'Syria *c.* 1550–1400 BC', CAH, II[1]; James Mellaart, 'Anatolian Trade, Geography and Culture', AS, XVIII (1968); C.J. Gadd, 'Babylonia *c.* 2120–1800 BC', CAH, I[2].
4. Henry Hodges, *Technology in the Ancient World* (Allen Lane, 1970)
5. C.F. Lehmann-Haupt, 'Urartu', *Encylopaedia Britannica* 14th rev. edn.
6. R.D. Barnett, 'British Museum Excavations at Toprak Kale', IRAQ, XII[1], 1950.
7. Hodges, *op. cit.*
8. Barnett, *op. cit.*
9. B.B. Piotrovskii, *The Art of Urartu*, (Evelyn Adams and Mackay, 1967); idem, *The Ancient Civilisation of Urartu* (Barrie and Rockliff, 1969).
10. The Louvre Text: A large clay tablet exhibited at the Louvre Paris, was engraved by Sargon's scribe. It is addressed to the god Ashur and gives an account of Sargon's Urartian campaign in 714 BC.
11. Piotrovskii, *The Art of Urartu*; A.H. Sayce, 'The Kingdom of Van', *CAH* III.iii.
12. C.A. Burney and G.R.S. Lawson, 'Urartian Reliefs at Adilcevaz on Lake Van', AS, VIII, 1958.
13. Piotrovskii, *op. cit.*, p. 62. The German archaeologists referred to in the text were C.F. Lehmann-Haupt and W. Belk.
14. Leonard Woolley, *The Art of Mesopotamia* (Methuen).
15. Barnett, *op. cit.*
16. Lehmann-Haupt, *op. cit.*
17. Woolley, *op. cit.*
18. K.R. Maxwell-Hyslop, 'Urartian Bronzes in Etruscan Tombs', IRAQ, XVIII[2], 1956.
19. Ibid.
20. Lehmann-Haupt, *op. cit.*
21. Piotrovskii, *op. cit.*
22. R.D. Barnett, 'British Museum Excavations'; Addenda IRAQ, XVI[1], 1954.
23. Piotrovskii, *op. cit.*
24. Ibid.
25. Lehmann-Haupt, *op. cit.*
26. Ibid.
27. Barnett, *op. cit.*, IRAQ, XII[1] 1950.
28. M.E. Mellowan, *25 Years of Mesopotamian Discovery.*
29. B.B. Piotrovskii, A.H. Sayce and others.
30. Lehmann-Haupt, *op. cit.*
31. K. Jettmar, *Art of the Steppes* (Methuen, 1967) pp. 31, 220.
32. Piotrovskii, *The Ancient Civilisation of Urartu*, p. 176.
33. R.D. Barnett, 'The Treasure of Ziwiye', IRAQ, XVIII[2], 1956; 'Urartu', CAH, III[1], 1982; E. Porada, *Ancient Iraq* (Methuen, 1962). The authenticity of the Ziwiye Treasure has been questioned. But that is the specialists' battleground. See article in *The Sunday Times*, 7 May 1978.
34. K.L. Oganesian, *The Wall Paintings of Erebuni* (Erevan, 1973).
35. Piotrovskii, *op. cit.*, pp. 78-9.

Further Sources

R.D. Barnett and N. Gokce, 'Urartian Bronzes from Erzincan', AS III, 1953.

R.D. Barnett, *Ancient Ivories and the Middle East. Oriental Influences on Archaic Greece. The Aegean and the Near East.* ed. S. Weinberg.

For ancient technology, see also:

R.J. Forbes, *Studies in Ancient Technology* (Leiden, 1964).

M.N. van Loon, *Urartian Art* (Istanbul, 1966).

P. Amandry *The Aegean and the Near East*, ed. Sweinberg, XXIV-XXXII.

17

Military Equipment: Costume

The earliest illustrations of Urartian dress and military equipment are depicted as reliefs on the broad bronze strips which at the same time decorate and reinforce the Balawat Gates. The dresses reach down to the ankles of the wearer and they are gathered at the waist by a belt. They are short-sleeved and have a pattern around the hemline. Warriors and even naked prisoners of war wear crested helmets, and the former carry small, round shields, recalling Phrygian shields and the later Armenian ones, described by Xenophon. The repoussé figures on the bronze strips are armed with spears and bows, with arrows in a quiver. Their dress and equipment resembled those of other peoples in Anatolia. 'The Vannic dress was that of a cold climate. The people wore buskins which reached half-way up their legs, tunics and possibly drawers, and the soldiers protected their heads with helmets, many of which had crests like the helmets of the Greeks or the Hittites of Carchemish.' Thus, the Urartian fashion differed markedly from that of the Assyrian warriors, as indeed it must, for apart from the greater proximity to Urartu of its western neighbours, the climate of low-lying Assyrian Mesopotamia is very different from that of the cold country of Armenia.

The ambassadors of Rusa II at Ashurbanipal's court are shod with high laced boots. Some clay beakers, unearthed at Karmir Blur, are made in the shape of such boots. They are exhibited at the Armenian State Historical Museum, Erevan. The envoys wear hats of soft felt, with tassels, which recall the Armenian hats depicted on reliefs commissioned by Xerxes at Persepolis.

The following describes the illustrations shown in this chapter, with some details of the garments worn by the people of Ararat.

The bronze helmet of King Argishti I, found at Kamir Blur, now exhibited at the Armenian Historical Museum Erevan, is similar in shape to that shown in illustration 4, but is highly decorated. On each side of the front of the helmet, as if spurting vertically out of the temples of the wearer, four fountains fall towards the centre of the helmet, over a Tree of Life, on either side of which stands a winged priest. Below this top band, there are two others which in turn show five groups of two winged priests, one on each side of the Tree of Life. The back of the helmet is decorated with two bands, each with representations of chariots and their occupants, drawn by horses.

(1)

(1) Detail from Argishti's helmet. A chariot, drawn by two richly caparisoned horses, with its occupants, a beardless, youthful driver and an older, bearded officer. The driver holds a spear in his right hand and the reins in his left hand. The officer extends his hand in a gesture of command. His lance stands at the back of the chariot; near the top of it can be seen some kind of ribbon, probably a sort of flag or a means to identify the owner and the troops under his command.

(2)

(2) Urartian mountain soldier. He wears a bronze helmet, protective body clothing and greaves on his legs. He carries a small, round shield and a spear. (The character of the shield seems to have persisted for over 1000 years from the Hittites down to the Persian period (*c.* 400 BC), when it is described by Xenophon and Herodotus as 'a small round shield').

(3)

(3) A soldier, armed as (2) above, wearing a knee-length dress with belt round the waist from which hangs a sword.

(4)

(4) Bronze helmet of Urartian soldier from Karmir Blur (Armenian

State Historical Museum). The trident-like design on the front is, according to some scholars, a symbol of the god of War, Teisheba.

(5)

(5) Statuette of King Urzana of Musasir standing between two subdued ostriches. This royal representation, having perhaps the same significance as a coat-of-arms, might also be applied to the Urartian monarchs, since in ancient times, in many cases, kings were also chief priests of the temple, and they are associated with wings and winged creatures. (This is said to be an Assyrian tradition.) On his head he wears a closely fitting hat; his ceremonial robe is gathered at the waist by a wide belt, possibly decorated by brocade work, and by three rows of fringes. This costume could be taken as an example of Urartian royal robes.

(6)

(6) Gold medallion with representation of enthroned queen or goddess. She wears a decorated covering over her head, which also covers her back, and its length reaches below her knees; and a short-sleeved jacket. Below this, she wears a tunic with a wide, fringed hem. Round her waist is a wide, bejewelled belt, while around her wrists there are bangles. Opposite her stands a lady-in-waiting or votary, wearing similarly decorated garments but with a head covering, the length of which falls short of that of the queen.

(7)

(7) Detail from a winged statuette from Van to show probable hair-style of high-born ladies of Urartu.

(8)

(8) Rare example of an Urartian mountain-dweller who wears a heavy-looking coat which opens outwards near the hem to reveal

a fringed skirt. The coat from waist downwards is also fringed. He wears pointed, high boots, typical of those worn by mountain-dwellers.

(9)

(9) Statuette of Teisheba, god of war. Bronze. Karmir Blur (British Museum, London). The god wears a bell-shaped crown upon his head, on the top of which a horizontal hole has been devised so that the statuette might be hung on the wall of its votary's home. He has a pair of horns, representing power and wisdom. Over the short-sleeved ceremonial dress, he wears a decorated, possibly brocaded, coat, hanging over one shoulder only, and fringed around all the edges, the hem as well as the wide sash falling from left shoulder to right hip. This describes a garment also worn by high-placed personages both in Urartu and Assyria. In his hands Teisheba holds symbols of power.

(10)

(10) Details from Argishti's helmet. Winged temple-priest with hat having extension at back which might unfold to cover the nape of the neck. He has curled hair, falling down to his shoulders. He wears a wide-sleeved, fringed coat over a tunic; the sleeve is so wide that when he raises his fore-arm, it falls back to reveal the narrow sleeve of his undergarment.

(11)

(11) Royal attendant. Bronze statuette from Toprak Kale, Van (British Museum, London). The main features of the dress are similar to those of Teisheba (10). His curled hair falls in thick profusion onto his shoulders. He is beardless, which is a reason for the belief that he is a palace official. A wide sash is thrown over his left shoulder, which might indicate his status. In his right hand he carries a fan to signify the high office of a royal functionary.

(12)

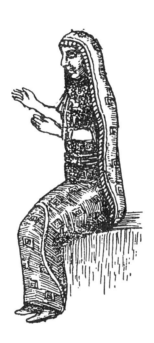

(12) Goddess of fertility or, specifically, goddess of fruit-culture, called Bagrartu, who might possibly have evolved and given place to the later Armenian fertility goddess, Anahit. The dress of this statuette gives a more complete picture of the dress of an Urartian high-born lady than can be seen from the representations on the gold medallion (6 above). Bronze. From Van (Armenian State Historical Museum, Erevan).

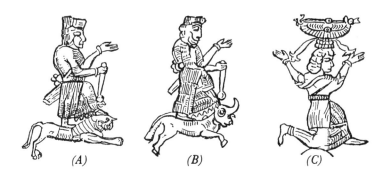

(A) *(B)* *(C)*

A, B, C. Three gods from Karmir Blur. A: Khaldi standing on lion. B: Teisheba standing on bull. C: Goddess Shivini wearing on her head a representation of the Sun, recalling Egyptian winged goddess. The clothing worn by these deities is presumed to be similar to those worn by the highest dignitaries of the land.

(D)

(E)

(F)

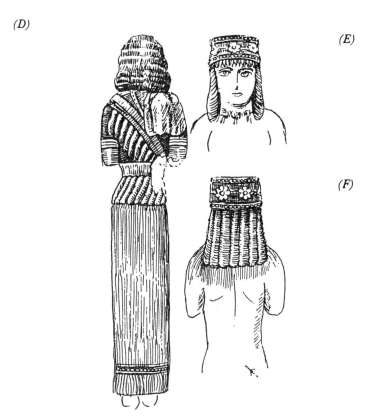

D, E, F. Two ebony statuettes from Toprak Kale, Van, representing Urartian womanhood. D: Curled hair falls upon shoulders. Belted skirt decorated with wide fringe at hem. Sash from left shoulder to right hip signifying her office. E, F: Detail of head from another ebony statuette from Toprak Kale, Van. Hat decorated with floral patterns. The front of the hat (E) is fringed with representations of small leaves, while the lady's curled hair fringes her face, and at the back of her head (F), it falls as low as to touch her shoulder blades. She wears a necklace.

See page 161 for a description and illustration of a sculpture of the god Teisheba or Teshub standing on a bull. It is suggested that the garments were probably made of wool. Indeed, fragments of woollen clothing were found at Teishebaini and woollen clothing seems to have been much used, particularly by the wealthy.

Some Sources

Arakel Patrik *Armenian Costumes from the Most Ancient Times Down to Our Own Days* (Erevan, 1967).

B.B. Piotrovskii, *The Ancient Civilization of Urartu*.

B.B. Piotrovskii, *The Kingdom of Van and its Art — URARTU* (Evelyn Adams and Mackay, 1967).

A.H. Sayce, 'The Kingdom of Van', CAH, III. iv.

18

Ararat and Assyria: A Brief Review

The Assyrian king, Shalmaneser I (1276–1257 BC) refers to 'Uruatri' as one of the Nairi kingdoms he overran during his campaign in the thirteenth century. The fact that he mentions Urartu to the exclusion of any other of the Nairi states must be a measure of its relative importance. Urartu, then, must have been in existence, at least as a small state, yet powerful enough to cause Assyria some trouble, in the fourteenth century BC, and long before that time, as an infant principality growing to maturity. The Babylonian chroniclers in the sixteenth century BC, refer to the Armenian highlands as URDHU (URARDHU). However, it is not until the reign of Shalmaneser III in the ninth century that the name of an Urartian king, 'Aramu', is recorded. During that period, no less than four centuries, the political character of the country had changed, for the powerful Urarto-Hurrian princes ruling the regions around Lake Van and the western side of Lake Urmia since the Late Bronze Age, had united the Nairi chieftainships into a federation under their leadership.

Warned by the manner in which Shalmaneser III took and sacked the strategically-exposed capital, Arzashkun, Arame's successor, Sarduri, chose another and better-protected site for a new capital, Tushpa, on the eastern shore of Lake Van, where the Armenian mountains are practically impregnable from the south, but for the valley of the Great Zab. Sarduri built fortifications on the upper reaches of that river, where it pierces the Taurus chain, and so closed the gap. Situated between the Great Zab river and the Zagros Mountains, was the small but important kingdom of Musasir, which early in the recorded history of Urartu, became its vassal. Further south, the kingdom of Mannai, the perpetual Urarto-Assyrian bone of contention, was invaded and occupied by King Menua, thus securing the last gate to the defences of the south-eastern arteries into Ararat. It was Menua also who grasped the political significance of federating under Urartu the many weak, independent kinglets in the valley of the Euphrates: Malatya, Commagene (Kummuh), Marash (Gurgum), Carchemish, Sinjerli (Sam'al) and others around the periphery of his kingdom. Alone each an easy prey to Assyria, they constituted a powerful unit when federated. Menua had then the military and strategic resources which enabled him to enter Syria and occupy the port of Poseidon. All this was achieved in a matter of approximately one hundred years, between the reigns of King Aram (880–844 BC) and King Menua (810–785 BC). Assyria was thus encircled all along the north and the two sides of her domains. And the bitter struggle between the two powers continued for the dominance of the Fertile Crescent in the west and the Valley of the River Zab and the kingdom of Mannai and the small Iranian states in the east.

Some Assyriologists appear to put too much confidence in the overstatements of Assyrian monarchs. One would think from Sargon's braggings, for example, that he broke the power of Ararat for ever, after his campaign of 714 BC against King Rusa I. Indeed, some writers state, without any qualification, that Ararat never recovered from that blow. That is demonstrably inaccurate for it is quite plain from the confidential reports sent by the Assyrian espionage to their king, that Rusa's successor, Argishti II, was not only in control of the military situation, but that the initiative for war operations was in his hands, not Sargon's. It was Assyria that feared an Urartian offensive. Subsequently, in 708 BC, Argishti demonstrated his military power by preventing the Cimmerian hordes from overrunning his kingdom.

Assyrian military power, undoubtedly of the first order, tends, none the less, to be overstated. Her dominions in the north-east, for example, did not go beyond Lake Urmia, as we are sometimes asked to believe, since 'the Sea of the Rising Sun' of which Assyrian scribes write, would most likely be Lake Urmia, not the Caspian Sea. Again, on reading of the Assyrian attacks on Urartu one receives a false impression of a kingdom at the mercy of its traditional enemy. We are informed of the manner in which the Assyrian armies invaded Urartu a number of times, marching right into the heart of the land and devastating town and country, leaving nothing but blood and ashes in their wake. Indeed, while reading the history of that remote period and place, time tends to be so telescoped that the Assyrian invasions of Urartu seem to be much more frequent and permanent than they were in fact. How many times did Ashur invade the land of Khaldi? Five times during the course of over three hundred years, all of them raids, not conquests, for Assyrian garrisons were never established in Urartu. These raids, then took place in the following order: once by Ashur-nasir-pal II in the ninth century, while Ararat was still an infant state, and twice by Shalmaneser III, also in the ninth century. Then there was a period of one hundred years in which Ararat not merely raided but conquered and garrisoned Assyrian vassal states, such as Gilzan and Hubushkia in the east, and Arpad and Hamath in the west, and Mannai and Parsua in the south-east, and even attacked strongholds of metropolitan Assyria, notably the great city of Nineveh itself. In consequence of these extensive conquests, Urartu appropriated the trade from east to west and the commerce between Egypt–Palestine which travelled via Syria to Anatolia — the trade and the destinies of peoples who were geographically much more accessible to Assyria than to Urartu.

Under Tiglath-pileser III, Assyria's situation was considerably ameliorated. He reorganised the Assyrian army, drove Ararat out of his metropolitan territories and recaptured some of Assyria's former western tributaries, and in 736, he attacked and overran Urartu itself. But he could not garrison the country and soon he had to retire, leaving Ararat's prestige among the tribute-paying states intact, and making no difference to the territories directly under its control, bounded by the Euphrates in the west, Urmia and the Caspian in the east, the River Kura in the north and Mannai and Parsua in the south-east. Very soon after 736, under Rusa I, a number of the provinces west of the Euphrates reverted to Urartu. Sargon's raid in 714, 22 years later, was more serious, for he struck when Urartu was already harassed by the Cimmerians who threatened to overrun its northern provinces and even, perhaps, the whole country, and at a time of rebellion in its capital. It took Sargon several years of preparation and this sort of strategy to deal his blow. Even so, Ararat was far from subdued. It remained a powerful and extensive empire; it continued to champion the weaker states on its borders, and to be a serious menace to Assyria to the very end, ultimately surviving its rival. Thus, Ararat's imperial status was equal to that of Assyria and certainly superior to its rival in the century between 836–736 BC.

Some scholars also tend to idealise Assyria. It is true that Assyria transmitted Babylonian culture to posterity through her conquests, eastwards beyond the Zagros Mountains, subjecting a host of primitive societies; westwards beyond the Euphrates bearing down her savage yoke upon Syria and Palestine. Assyria's role in this respect is comparable to that of the Romans who transmitted Greek civilisation, from which they themselves benefited, to their western colonies. But the means adopted by Assyria for that conveyance of Babylonian civilisation reflect precisely her notorious savagery. It was achieved substantially by the wholesale deportation of Babylonians, her very own kith and kin, from their cities, including some from the capital itself, to Syria and elsewhere.[1] The few members of the Samaritan community surviving today at the foot of Mount Gerizim, stand witness to the transplantation of their ancestors from the cities of Babylonia.[2] The Assyrians completely lacked the most important attribute of civilisation: a respect for life in general and human life in particular. Far from attempting to conceal their savagery, they arrogantly boast of ravaging enemy lands 'like a wild bull and an enraged dog', and describe with malicious pleasure the horrors committed in enemy territory: the destruction of cities, the burning to ashes of pastures and forest lands and poisoning them with salt, to make them barren for years to come; the massacre of whole populations, the burying alive of youths and maidens, the mutilations inflicted on the bodies of their victims, and such aberrations as cutting off hands, fingers, ears, flaying alive men and women and stretching their skins on the walls of their cities, the construction of pyramids of skulls of their slaughtered victims and lining around them stakes on which impaled men and women died.

Urartu's contribution to civilisation was to thwart the penetration into Asia Minor of Assyrian frightfulness. Ararat, too, was influenced by Babylonian civilisation, but by no means wholly so. As a member of the great Hurrian community, Urartu was the recipient of Egyptian, Cretan and Hittite civilisation, largely through its neighbour and kin, the Khurri-Mitanians. From those legacies she forged a cultural metamorphosis which she transmitted not only to the peoples inhabiting the peripheral lands of her empire, such as the Iranians and the Scythians; the Phrygians and the people of the Colchis, but especially to the peoples of the Aegean lands, including those of Classical Greece,

Etruria in Italy and, indirectly, western Europe, e.g. France (see Chapter 16).

Assyria was destroyed in spite of the fact that she never ceased to be aware of the importance of keeping up with the changing methods of warfare and the development of military equipment and organisation.[3] Ironically Tiglath-pileser III, who did just that and succeeded in re-establishing Assyrian military might, suffered from the megalomania which seems to afflict all conquerors, expressing itself in unquenchable desire for territorial expansion, invariably the harbinger of ultimate disaster. He threw diplomacy to the winds and, stretching his military strength to its limits, attacked in turn Babylon, Elam and Egypt, each one of them potentially or in fact, as great a military power as Assyria herself. [4] He ignored the lesson learnt by his ninth century predecessors in Syria. At that time, in 853 BC, Shalmaneser's aggression in Qarqar inspired a hasty coalition of the Syrian states which checked the Assyrian advance, while in Armenia, the tighter federation of the Nairi principalities with the kingdom of Urartu[5], closed the gates of Asia Minor against Assyria forever. Tiglath-pileser's aggressions, particularly that against Babylonia, proved to be a fatal self-inflicted wound. It set in motion a series of events which a little over a century later annihilated his country. So thorough was that destruction that only 200 years later when Xenophon passed by the ruins of Nineveh, he had no idea what they represented nor, indeed, had he ever heard of Assyria. Assyria's attempt gradually to enslave Babylonia, caused a great insurrection in 694–689[6], which led to the installation of Esarhaddon in the capital as viceroy. Thenceforth, sinking their mutual antipathy, Babylonian nomads, citizens and tribesmen fused themselves into a new nation which could neither forget nor forgive, and which could never rest until it had brought its oppressor to the ground.[7] They witnessed the destruction of Elam by Ashur-banipal and the rise of the Iranian Medes under Cyaxares. The Babylonian leader-king, Nabopolassar, seized the opportunity of an alliance with Cyaxares and within sixteen years of the destruction of Elam, Assyria herself was crushed into oblivion.

Ararat was the bastion of the ancient Anatolian civilisations. For three hundred years she held back the tide of the northern barbarians. At the same time, particularly in the last decades of the eighth century BC, she succeeded by astute diplomatic manoeuvres, in maintaining friendly relations with the Medes on the south-eastern extremeties of her empire, while confining mighty Assyria to the lands beyond the southern passes of the Taurus range of mountains.

In the year 590 BC, over 22 years after its rival, the Vannic kingdom also expired while fighting invaders of its territories from all sides. From the north the Scythian horseman poured down through the eastern Caucasian Derbent Pass, into the fertile valleys of Ararat; and from the south Cyaxares led his Medians across Urartu on his way to the River Halys to wage war on the Lydian king, Alyattes, while the Armenians broke in from the west and must have been opposed or joined by other Armenians already well established in Urartu.

Notes

1.-7. Arnold Toynbee, *A Study of History.* Abridgement by D.C. Somervell (Oxford University Press, 1960).

Part Two:
The Kingdom of Armenia

19

Introduction

Armenia emerged immediately after the demise of Urartu (*c.* 590 BC). She inherited many characteristics of Urartu's very ancient civilisation which had been closely associated with Assyria–Babylonia in the south and the Mitannian–Egyptian–Hittite cultures in the west, through Hayasa and Phrygia; the former with its long political, economic and social connections with the Hittite empire, and the latter as the occupants of its territories. Indeed, there seems to be evidence of Armenian presence in a number of places within the Urartian empire long before its collapse (cf. Chapter 20 and references made on the subject in the text of my histories in this work.)

The earliest references to Armenia were made by Hecataeus of Miletus (*c.* 525 BC), Darius the Great in his celebrated inscriptions at Behistun (*c.* 520 BC), Herodotus (*c.* 450 BC), Xenophon (*c.* 400 BC) and later classical writers. Armenia has no known historian before the Christian era. The fourth and fifth centuries produced some authoritative Armenian historians who recorded mainly accurate accounts of their own contemporary events. Only Moses of Khoren (Movses Khorenats'i), sometimes described as the Herodotus of the Armenians, attempted a comprehensive history, starting from the earliest legendary heroes down to his own time, perhaps the fifth century. Much of what he wrote has been criticised as inaccurate, but having said that, it must be acknowledged that his narratives are probably often used by historians as basis for further research and study. Professor C.J.F. Dowsett, in his *Historians of the Middle East* (1962), concisely states the Armenian position in the world of historiography in the early Middle Ages:

Historiography is a principal genre in Armenian literature, which is not the case with the literature of the much greater powers of India and Persia. Indeed, when one considers that Armenia's geographical position afforded its inhabitants a close-up view of major world events such as the fall of Sasanid Persia, the rise of the Arabs, the Seljuq conquests and the invasion of Timūr, one may perhaps be glad that the affairs of this world were thought worthy of record by the writers of Armenia. The facts contained in their pages are thus often of first importance; their interpretation was however frequently impaired by the prejudices of a people too closely and usually too painfully involved in the political convulsions of the world around them to be wholly objective ... historical writing in Armenia Major was primarily confined in the hands of the clergy, with the exception of Faustus Biwzandatzi who appears to have been a layman.

The following are some of the scholarly clergy who have left us with records of their times:

Katholicos John of Draskhanakert
Archbishop Stephen Orbelian
Bishops Sebēos and Ukhtanēs
Vardapet Eliseus ⎫
Lazarus of Pharp ⎪
Vardan Areweltzi ⎬ monks
Kirakos of Gandja ⎭

Until the invention of the Armenian alphabet early in the fifth century, the learned Armenian clergy were conversant with Greek and Syriac. The literacy of the clergy contrasted sharply with the other sections of Armenians, including the aristocracy who were mostly illiterate. Movses Khorenatzi bitterly complains of this ignorance among prominent members of his countrymen. The historical literature of Armenia is particularly important since by it we are, in many cases, enabled to complete and correct the information furnished by Byzantine historians.

In this part of my work I have endeavoured to show ancient and medieval Armenian history not, as seems customarily to be the case, as that of a tribute-paying or colonial province of Persia, Macedonia, Parthia or Rome, but as a country with a continuous and largely independent history, albeit ruled by kings whose forebears were Persian or Parthian princes. In European history, too, it is not at all unusual to find kings of foreign dynasties ruling another country either concurrently with their own kingdoms or as true kings of the land of their adoption, with its own quite independent domestic and foreign policies.

The reason for the inclusion of some of the legendary kings of Armenia in the following chapter, must be explained. In an article which appeared in the Journal of the Society for Armenian Studies, 1985, and later, in the same year, in an extended version of the same article, as an 'Occasional Paper' published by the same organisation, I attempted to substantiate the existence of some of those kings, I hope, persuasively. The article is too specialised, and unsuitable, for inclusion in this work. Yet I am concerned that the names of those kings — legendary or not — should remain in the memory of Armenians in the diaspora; they constitute part of the traditions and the early historical ethos of the nation. I, therefore, dismembered my article and merely mentioned them by name and the most basic aspects of my findings in favour of their possible historical legitimacy. May I refer those who wish to know more of this subject to my Occasional Paper? (*Some Legendary Kings of Armenia, Can They be Linked to Authentic History?* (Society for Armenian Studies Occasional Paper No. 5, Glassboro State College).) The first historically accepted ruler of Armenia was Hydarnes III *c.* 427 BC.

Table 19.1: Proper names

European (Greek) spelling for reference purposes	Eastern Armenian spelling	Phonetic spelling
Orontes	Ervand	Yervant
Artaxias	Artashes	Ardashes
Artaxata	Artashat	Ardashad
Zariadris	Zareh	Zareh
Arsaces	Arshak	Arshag
Tigranes	Tigran	Dikran
Artavasdes	Artavasd	Ardavast
Tiridates	Trdat	D(e)rtad (e as in 'her')
Tigranes V	Tiran	Diran

Note: Greek or Graecofied names have a suffix to the name (the nominative) as in Socrat(es), Artistotel(es), Archemid(es). So, Tigran(es), Aršac(es), Artavasd(es).

20

Early History

Hayk means Armenians in the native tongue. Hayk, the eponym of the mythical founder of the Armenian people, is said to have been the son of Togarmah (T'orkom in Armenian), grandson of Japhet, son of Noah (Gen. X. 1-3). That is the legendary version of the nation's roots. However, the two names — Hayk and T'orkom (Togarmah) — each in its own right, possibly represents the nucleus of the Armenian nation, with the people and civilisation of Urartu superimposed upon and absorbed by it.

Hayk (Armenians), Haay (Armenian), Haya-stan (Armenia): these names together appear to originate from the name of the ancient kingdom of Hayasa (c. 1400 BC), situated on the eastern frontiers of the Hittite empire. Hayasa is closely associated with the principalities of Azzi and (possibly) Alzi or Alshe, on its southern borders, which seem to have been absorbed into Hayasa's political hegemony.[1] Hence 'Hayasa' infers Hayasa-Azzi and perhaps Alzi, too. Its eastern boundaries might have reached as far as Ararat.[2] Southwards, the joint kingdom straddled the western Euphrates (Kara su).

Togarmah, the main city of Tabal, was on the western side of the Euphrates (Firat su), opposite Urartu and its dependencies. It was in that region of Tabal-Togarmah that the Armenians seem to have first settled. They appear to have been a tribe within the Phrygian community which crossed the Bosphorous into Asia during the tumultuous times of great ethnic movements and political change towards the end of the thirteenth century BC. They must have witnessed the destruction of the Hittite empire; indeed, they probably took part in it, and occupied its lands. Other theories have been suggested as to the original appearance of the Armenians in the land which bears their name, but this one seems to be historically the most acceptable.³ Togarmah is possibly the Biblical name for Armenia. There appears to have been an ancient, pre-historic, Armenian kingdom in that region, ruled by a royal house, referred to by Ezekiel (XXXVIII.6) as 'the House of Togarmah'.

The section of the Phrygian community which would most likely have dominated Hayasa, were the Armenian tribe, since their territory within Phrygia seems to have been contiguous with Hayasa's south-western borders. That Armeno-Phrygian territory overlapping into Hayasa-Azzi much later became known as Lesser Armenia. Thenceforth, perhaps from the eleventh century BC, when the people of the eponymous Armenos (who had led the Armeno-Phrygian tribe from Thessaly (Strabo, XI.xiv.12), and that of Hayasa had probably merged. They appear to have infiltrated, gradually and continuously the Urartian territories.⁴ There are place names (Aramili, Armarili, Urmenu-hini, Arme), which inspire curiosity as being of possible Armenian origin. The first two are associated with King Aram(e), the first known king of Urartu (858–844 BC) who appears in Armenian legends and has been discussed by scholars at some length. His true identity as an *Armenian* king may be established by a future scholar. He was deposed in 844 BC by Sarduri, who founded a royal house of Urartu which continued unbroken for over two centuries.

In 714 BC, when King Rusa I of Urartu was harassed at the same time by a palace revolution, assaults of Cimmerian hordes from the north and an invasion, on a major scale, from the south-east by Assyria, the Armenians could have seized the province of Shupria (or part of it), to the west of Lake Van, near Urmenu-hini and Arme, not too distant from the homeland of the Armeno-Phrygians and Hayasa-Azzi. Shupria, whose princes dissociated themselves from Urartu and Assyria, sometimes appeared as an independent state, without the protection of the might of Assyria or Urartu, and therefore vulnerable to an unexpected invasion. It was, in fact, independent during the reign of Esarhaddon (705–681). The Armenian *coup* in 714 BC might well have been led by a chieftain whose might and prestige is testified by his name — the Giant (Armenian, *Hskan*), thus establishing the first Armenian state. Moses of Khoren (sometimes described as the Herodotus of the Armenians and known as Movses Khorenatsi) has preserved in his king list (I.22) the name Skayordi or, phonetically spelt, *Hsgai-vorti*, Son of the Giant. Before the advent of Skayordi, long lists of Armenian rulers are to be found in Moses and in the

Primary History of Armenia, which might reflect the names of dynastic chieftains in Armenian enclaves within the Urartian empire. It would have been Skayordi, successor to the Armenian chieftainship or principality in Shupria, who sheltered Adramelech and Sharezer (murderers of their father, King Sennacherib of Assyria (705–681 BC) when 'they escaped into the land of Armenia' (2 Kings 19.37).[5]

After the destruction of the Assyrian empire by the Medes and their allies in 612 BC, Urartu was invaded from the north by large hordes of Scythians. The powerful fortress of Karmir Blur (near modern Erevan), was destroyed by them and their allies, the Medes, and northern Urartu was overrun. It appears that at the same time, the Armenians, taking advantage of the general turmoil — Medes and Babylonians, Assyrians, Scythians, Cimmerians and Phrygians, all preoccupied with invasion or defence — struck eastwards from Hayasa-Azzi and settled in the valleys of the mountainous country of the River Araxes, while others invading Shupria had become, perhaps, masters of the whole province. As described above Shupria must already have had substantial numbers of Armenians, since the first invasion under Hskan and his predecessors, 100 years earlier. Over a considerable period of time, the Armenians, and the greatly weakened Urartians in their extensive territories, appear to have intermarried and merged, the Urartians adopting the Aryan Armenian language and the Armenians appropriating the wealth as well as certain aspects of Urartian social and political institutions.

Thus Urartian history is part of Armenian history, in the same sense that the history of the ancient Britons is part of English history, and that of the Gauls is part of French history. Armenians can legitimately claim, through Urartu, an historical continuity of some 4000 years; their history is among those of the most ancient peoples in the world.

The demise of Urartu (*c.* 590 BC) marks the beginning of historical Armenia, in the time of Cyaxares the Mede (d. 584), who had become master of northern Mesopotamia and Anatolia as far west as the River Halys and eastwards, along the right bank of the River Araxes to his own homelands of Media and Atropatene; presumably ruling also the Armenian settlers north of Shupria and in Media. Shupria seems to have become, after a brief period of Median rule, a Babylonian colony under King Nabopolassar, ally of Cyaxares.[6]

Kings Paroyr and Hratcheay

According to Moses of Khoren (I.22), Paroyr, son of Skayordi, was crowned King of Armenia (Shupria) by Varbakes (viceroy of Cyaxares) in 612, for his assistance in the war against Assyria and the destruction of Nineveh. That implies the succession of three known Armenian rulers in Shupria: Hskan, Skayordi and Paroyr.[5] Then, Nabopolassar, King of Babylon (625–605 BC), appears to have colonised Shupria, whose ruler at that time would have been Hratcheay, son of Paroyr. During Hratcheay's reign, Nabopolassar died and was succeeded by his son, Nebuchadnezzar II (605–562 BC). Armenia, under Hratcheay, seems to have been involved in Babylonia's war against Judea (*c.* 586 BC).[7] In Khorenatsi's king list (I.22), Hratcheay is followed by Kings P'arnavaz, Pachoych and Kornak. Cyaxares, the Mede was succeeded by his son, Astyages (*c.* 584–559). The Median dynasty was overthrown by Cyrus the Great (559–530), the first Achaemenid king of Persia.

P'aros

Cyrus was killed waging war against the Scythians on the northern bank of the Araxes. His eldest son, Cambyses, succeeded him as King of Persia. On his deathbed, Cyrus appointed his second son, Bardiya, full brother of Cambyses, to be viceroy of Armenia, Media and Cadusia.[8] Cambyses was killed in Syria, on his way back from Egypt. Bardiya (Bardes or Vardes) succeeded him and reigned for eight months. He was murdered in a palace revolution by 'The Seven', that is Darius Hystaspis (who seized the throne), Hydarnes I and five others. Bardia-Bardes-Vardes appears to be none other than Khorenatsi's P'aros-Phardos-(V)Bardes-Bardiya.[9]

Haykak

On the death of P'aros-Bardiya, a certain Haykak, whose name is next on the list of Khorenatsi (I.22), seized power in Armenia and led the Armenians in the widespread revolution which had broken out throughout the Persian empire on Bardiya's murder and Darius's usurpation of the Persian throne. At first successful, he was finally defeated and killed (*c*.520 BC).[10]

Under Darius I Hystaspis, the empire was divided for administrative purposes into 20 satrapies[11] (Herod., III. 90-4). The 13th was Armenia, that is, Western Armenia, with its heartland in Shupria. The 18th and the 10th must have had many enclaves of Armenians who had settled in the valleys on both sides of the Araxes, the southern side being mainly Media, the 10th satrapy. An Urartian province, south of the Chalybes (Xenophon's Khaldians and Herodotus's Alarodians and Matienni (Mitanni?)), as well as a settlement of Scythians, were included in the 18th satrapy, besides the several enclaves of Armenians already suggested, overlapping the Araxes and in communication with other enclaves of Armenians in the 10th satrapy, Media.

Armog

Armog is probably the Graecofied (nominative) Artoch(mes), in command of the Armenians and Phrygians in Xerxes's armies (Herod., VII.73) and probably the successor of Haykak, satrap of Western Armenia.[12] He was the brother-in-law of Xerxes (486–465 BC), taking part in the second Persian invasion of Greece in 480 BC. Their dress was modelled on the Iranian, as depicted on the walls at Persepolis, but their head-covering comprised a hat with three horn-like projections, and flaps and streamers which fell over the neck. This, incidentally, is part of a relief showing Armenian gifts to the Persian king, a special breed of horse for which Armenia has always been renowned, and a beautiful vase whose two handles were carved as winged griffins; the gifts led and carried respectively by two attendants.

Ampak

Ampak (or Ambag) was perhaps satrap of Western Armenia after Pachoych and Kornak, about whom there seems to be no information, apart from Khorenatsi's *obiter dictum*. He might be equated with Xenophon's Emba(s) (*Cyrop.* V.3.38), who assisted with his Armenian forces the rebel Cyrus the Younger, against Cyrus' brother, King Artaxerxes II. He would have been slaughtered with the rest of Cyrus' leaders, by the Persian loyalists in 401 BC.[13] The Western Armenian satrapy was then given to a Persian nobleman, Tiribazus, who was highly regarded at the Persian court, a favourite of the Great King.

Eastern Armenia

The succession of viceroys and satraps in Western Armenia, were coincidental with developments in Eastern Armenia, Darius' 10th and 18th satrapies. Cyaxares the Mede invaded Urartu from the east and what later became the 10th satrapy (Media) must have been under his own direct rule. He was followed by his son, Astyages. We know that Cyrus the Great, too, was directly involved in that area because he crossed the Araxes, invaded Scythian territory and was killed in the resulting battle with the Scythians (530 BC) (Herod. I.214). He was succeeded by his son, Cambyses. Then Darius Hystaspis seized the throne and divided his empire into 20 satrapies, to facilitate its administration. He describes the manner in which he achieved this on the smooth face of a high cliff at Behistun or Bisitun in Kermanshah. Much of that fascinating document has been reproduced by Herodotus (III.90-4). It is possible that Hydarnes I (one of 'The Seven') was in overall command of 'Eastern Armenia', i.e. the regions which a little later became the 10th (Media) and the 18th (Alarodii, Matieni and Saspeiri) satrapies. A frail reason for such a suggestion is that his grandson, Hydarnes III (*c.* 430–424 BC) was actually viceroy of Eastern Armenia. The latter was probably preceded by Hydarnes II. A more substantial reason comes from evidence recently found on Persepolis tablets, showing Hydarnes I as governor of Media (that is, the southern half of eastern Armenia) from 521 to 499 BC. His successor seems to have been a certain Tigranes the Achaemenid[14] who was in command (which implies that he was satrap) of the Medians in Darius' invasion of Greece in 490 BC. Perhaps he led Median and Armenian contingents out of Media, while Hydranes was in charge of the 'Immortals'. He must have survived that first war for he held the same office again in Xerxes' invasion in 480 (Herod., VII.62), when he was killed. It is probable that this Tigranes is the name that Khorenatsi confuses with Tigranes the Great (first century BC), in his king list (I.22). He fits in very well chronologically (but not regionally) as the successor of Haykak. If so, Ervand-Orontes (a common Achaemenid aristocratic name, nothing to do with Orontes son of Artasyras), would, indeed, have been 'short-lived' as stated in the list (I. 22), if he had succeeded Hydarnes in 499 and died before 490, when Tigranes became satrap. There is a gap of about 50 years between 480 and 430, in which Hydarnes II (of whom very little is known) might have ruled Armenia.

Notes

1. Nicolas Adontz, *Histoire d'Arménie* (Paris, 1946), p. 275; E.V. Gulbekian, *The Significance of the Narrative Describing the Traditional Origin of the Armenians* (Le Museon, Louvain, 1973).

2. James Mellaart, 'Anatolian Trade and Geography, Late Bronze Age', AS XVIII, 1968.

3. Robert Graves, *Greek Myths* II, pp. 247-8, 'one of them [Jason's companions], Armenus, a Thessalian from Lake Boebe, settled in Armenia, and gave his name to the entire country. This view they justify by pointing to the monuments in honour of Jason, erected at the Caspian Gate; and that the Armenians wear the ancient Thessalian dress' (Strabo, xi. 14.12 and xi.13.10; Herodotus, VII.73; Eudoxus, quoted by Stephanus of Byzantium, *Ethnica*).

4. Movses Khorenatsi (Moses of Khoren), I.12-15, trans. Robert W. Thomson (Harvard University, 1978, pp. 92-6). See also Index and his valuable notes and references; Cyril L. Toumanoff, *Studies in Christian Caucasian History* (Georgetown University Press, 1963), pp. 55 n. 49, p. 75 n. 84.

5. M. Chahin, *Some Legendary Kings of Armenia, Can They Be Linked to Authentic History?* (Society for Armenian Studies, Occasional Papers No. 5, Glassboro State College, Dept of History.

6. Ibid.

7. Ibid.

8. Xenophon, *Cyropaedia*, VIII.7, quotes the dying Cyrus: 'You, Tanaoxares (Bardiya-Smerdis), I appoint you to be satrap of Medes, Armenians, and Cadusians'; also, Adontz, *op. cit.*, p. 353; Chahin, *op. cit.*

9. Chahin, *Some Legendary Kings.*

10. Ibid.

11. G.B. Gray and M. Cary, 'The Reign of Darius', CAH IV.iv. p. 195, for a list of the satrapies, with map, showing their geographical positions.

12. Khorenatsi, *op. cit.*, I.32; Sebeos trans. *Primary Hist. of Armenia* (Thomson, p. 362); Toumanoff, *op. cit.*, p. 296.

13. Chahin, *Some Legendary Kings.*

14. See D.M. Lewis, *Sparta and Persia* (1977), 83-5, quoted by J.M. Cook, *The Persian Empire* (London 1983), p. 170 and n.6, p. 257.

21

The Royal House of Ervand (the Orontids)

Hydarnes III was succeeded by his son, Terituchmes. His daughter, Stateira, married the Persian Great King, Artaxerxes II (404–358). Their daughter, Rhodogune, was given in marriage to Ervand (Orontes-Oroandes), son of Artasyras, the 'King's Eye', sometimes called 'Orontes the Bactrian', because of his princely, Bactrian parentage. For important services rendered to the king, Ervand-Orontes was not only given the hand of the king's daughter, but was also elevated to the satrapy of Eastern Armenia. In fact he would have been more of a viceroy, since he was himself of royal blood and had also married into the Persian royal family. Armenian tradition recognises him under the name 'Ervand'.

His domains lay over the entire basin of the western Tigris and probably also that of the Arsanias and the eastern Euphrates (Murad su). This area must be distinguished from Western Armenia which appears to have been a district north of Mush and the River Teleboas (the upper regions of the eastern Euphrates), where Xenophon (*Anabasis*, IV.4) met its governor (or satrap) Tiribazus, who is described by Xenophon as 'a personal friend of the king [Artaxerxes II] and when he was present, no one else had the right to assist the King in mounting his horse' (IV.3).[1]

The satrap's was often an hereditary office. If not he, then his son usually associated himself with the people he ruled. A satrap sometimes successfully defied the Great King in the distant Persian capital, and ruled, in all but name, as king. Such seems to have been the Armenian experience. Ervand and Tiribazus took part in the triumph of Artaxerxes II against Athens, when that city (and its allies) was subjected to the shameful 'King's

Figure 21.1: The Hydarnid-Orontid-Achaemenid Connection

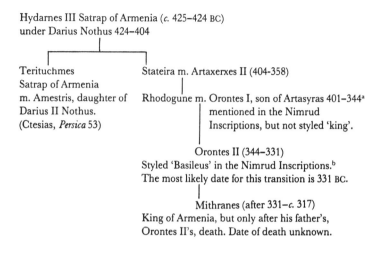

Hydarnes III Satrap of Armenia (*c.* 425–424 BC)
under Darius Nothus 424–404

Terituchmes
Satrap of Armenia
m. Amestris, daughter of
Darius II Nothus.
(Ctesias, *Persica* 53)

Stateira m. Artaxerxes II (404-358)

Rhodogune m. Orontes I, son of Artasyras 401–344[a]
mentioned in the Nimrud
Inscriptions, but not styled 'king'.

Orontes II (344–331)
Styled 'Basileus' in the Nimrud Inscriptions.[b]
The most likely date for this transition is 331 BC.

Mithranes (after 331–*c.* 317)
King of Armenia, but only after his father's,
Orontes II's, death. Date of death unknown.

a. Toumanoff, pp. 287-8.
b. Nimrud Dağ: Mountain in central Turkey, 2100 metres high, on top of which a tumulus was built by Antiochus I of Commagene (64–51 BC), to accommodate marble statues of gods and heroes, seated upon great thrones, guarding the royal necropolis. Inscriptions discovered there show the Orontids to be, indeed, a branch of the Achaemenids, and Antiochus himself, a scion of the Orontid line. (Toumanoff, p. 278, Index, s.v., 'Nimrud Dağ').

Peace' in 386 BC (when Persia dictated terms to Greece, 'liberated' the Ionian cities from Athens and Sparta, and, in short, succeeded where Darius and Xerxes had failed — with no calamitous results on later European history!).

In 366 Ervand, who was hereditary satrap of Armenia, rose up [against Artaxerxes] together with Mausolos of Caria and other Greek cities, and most of the coast people from Syria to Lydia.[2] Ervand-Orontes, however defected from the alliance. He was rewarded by the king with Mysia and the coast. 'By 360 or 359 the revolt was over and between December 359 and March 358 Artaxerxes died in peace. He introduced Asiatic polytheism into Zoroastrianism, raising temples to the important [Armenian] nature-goddess, Ana'itis in the chief cities of his empire.'[3]

Artaxerxes III Ochus (358–338) diagnosed the cause of his father's troubles. It was the satraps' self-arrogated right to wage private wars. In 356 he ordered the disbandment of their armies. All but two satraps obeyed: Artabazus of Hellespontine Phrygia and Ervand of Armenia. Artaxerxes' unsuccessful attempt to invade Egypt was the signal of renewed satrapal risings. Ervand, as ruler of Mysia and much of western Asia Minor, including Pergamon, had in the past supplied the Athenian navy with corn. He was honoured and fêted at Athens. He minted his own gold coins in the Greek cities of the coast. In *c.* 355 BC he allied himself with Athens and led a second satrapal revolt. However, the king appears to have isolated Ervand by joining forces with Thebes (Greece) and perhaps with Macedon also. In the event, Ervand appears to have returned Pergamon to the king (*c.* 350 BC) and, having been forgiven, retired to his estates in Mysia, an old grandee of Great Armenia. Thus, for half a century, under Ervand-Orontes I, Armenia, with it colonies of Pergamon and Mysia, played an independent and important role on the international political stage.

A précis of Ervand's reign should highlight the fact that while his predecessors were true Persians and absolutely faithful to the Great King, Ervand, who came from Bactria, and was indeed described as 'the Bactrian', could have had no such loyalties, although some writers believe that he had Hydarnid antecedents (Strabo, XI.xiv.15). He was connected to the Persian royal Achaemenids only through his marriage to the king's daughter. He could, and did, therefore give rein to his independent spirit; his ambitions nearly carried him to the imperial throne. An hereditary viceroy or satrap would sooner or later identify himself with the people over whom he ruled. He therefore usually behaved first in his own and secondly (fortuitously) in that of the interests of his people, rather than his overlord's, the king.

There are many examples of such a situation everywhere in the world, including (perhaps, particularly) in Western European history. Ervand I is a good example of the amibitious, adventurous ruler who was, however, also a diplomat; a man who knew when to keep faith to the letter and when to find excellent reasons and arguments for behaving otherwise than might have been expected, when his personal interests were at stake. In 401, Ervand was ruler of Eastern Armenia, at the time when Tiribazus was satrap of Western Armenia. During Persia's wars against Cyprus and its mainland Greek allies (381 BC), Ervand caused the disgrace of Tiribazus and so was vested with the sole command of all the Persian forces, in which, of course, there would surely have been two Armenian contingents, representing Eastern and Western Armenia respectively. He was also rewarded (deservedly or not is irrelevant — he was *rewarded*) with the viceroyalty of Mysia and Pergamon, and, presumably, he took over the satrapy of Western Armenia from Tiribazus. During the reign of Artaxerxes III Ochus, Ervand led a second satrapal revolt. He seemed to be aiming at the Persian Imperial throne. But when the king outmanoeuvred the rebels, he defected, was forgiven, and allowed to retain his immense viceroyalty, with the exception of Pergamon. He might be described as something of an adventurer, with a certain élan, a powerful and proud personality, with astute diplomatic skills that could confront the immensely powerful Great King. All of which nearly carried him to the throne of the Achaemenid empire. His prestige, leadership, authority and achievements in the affairs of Persia and his adopted country, Armenia, distinguish him for the appellation of Ervand the Great. He paved the way for the complete independence of Armenia under his successor, his son, Ervand II who ended his reign as King of the whole of Armenia (Eastern and Western).

Codomannus (344–336 BC)

About the year 344, Artaxerxes 'made war upon the Cardusii, in the course of which one Codomannus engaged with the enemy chieftain that offered himself in single combat, and having killed his antagonist, regained the victory for his fellow soldiers, as well as the glory which they had almost lost. For this honourable service, Codomannus was made governor of Armenia' (Justin X.3). Presumably he succeeded Ervand the Great when the latter retired in 344, which coincided with the Carducii war, resulting in the elevation of Codomannus whose family had Achaemenid antecedents. In 366, the short reign of the Persian king Arses ended, when he was murdered by the son of Tiribazus. Codomannus was called to the Persian throne as Darius III, the last of the Achaemenids, who fell at the Battle of Gaugamela against Alexander the Great in 331 BC.

Ervand-Orontes II (336–c.325 BC)

When Codomannus left Armenia, Ervand II, son of Ervand I inherited the satrapy of Armenia. At the Battle of Gaugamela, he commanded the Armenian contingent (now his countrymen) on the right wing of the Persian host, in the forefront of the battle formation. He appears to have survived the war. On his return to his capital, Armavir (in the Plain of the Araxes, on the site of the ancient Urartian city, Argishti-hinili), he abandoned the fiction of satrap and declared himself King of Armenia, promulgating in fact the true status of the Orontid dynasty. He is described as *Basileus* on the inscriptions on the monumental, marble statuary guarding the royal necropolis of Antiochus of Comagene, on the top of Mount Nimrud (Nimrud Dağ) in central Anatolia.[4] His successors continued as independent kings, and were internationally recognised as such, with only very brief interruptions, down to the time of Antiochus the Great (223–187 BC) of the Syro-Macedonian House of Seleucus.

Armenia's Wealth

Xenophon (*Anabasis* IV.4,5) describes Armenia's agricultural wealth:

Most of the houses were built like fortresses and there were plenty of provisions: they had all kinds of goods, foods — meat, corn, old wines with delicious bouquet, raisins and all sorts of vegetables. ... A lot of ointment was found in this place and they used it instead of olive oil. It was made of hog's lard, sesame, bitter almonds and turpentine. A perfumed oil, too, made from the same ingredients, was found here. ... there were goats, sheep, cows and poultry. There was also wheat, barley, beans and barley-wine in great bowls. The actual grains of barley floated on top of bowls, level with the brim, and in the bowls there were reeds of various sizes and without joints in them. When one was thirsty, one was meant to take a reed and suck the wine into one's mouth. It was a very strong wine, unless one mixed it with water, it was a very pleasant drink. Everywhere he found them [his soldiers] feasting and merry-making, and they would invariably refuse to let him go before they had given him something for breakfast. In every

215

single case they would have on the same table lamb, kid, pork, veal and chicken, and a number of loaves, both wheat and barley.

While Strabo (XI.xiv.9) writes:

There are mines of gold in the H(S)yspiritis, near Caballa. Alexander sent Menon to the mines with a body of soldiers, but he was strangled by the inhabitants of the country. There are also other mines, and also a mine of Sandyx as it is called, to which is given the name of Armenian colour, it resembles the Calche. This country is so well adapted, being nothing inferior in this respect to Media, for breeding horses, that the race of Neaean horses, which the kings of Persia used, is found here also ... Artavasdes [first century BC] when he accompanied Antony in his invasion of Media, exhibited, besides other bodies of cavalry, 6000 horses covered with complete armour drawn up in array.

Mithranes (*c.* 325–317 BC)

King Ervand II was followed by his son Mithranes. Although Mithranes went to Armenia ostensibly as Alexander's satrap, as a reward for supporting him in his Persian campaigns, in fact Mithranes succeeded his father as King of Armenia after the latter's death; he did not depose him.[5] The circumstances in which Mithranes succeeded to the throne, made such tribute as he was expected to send to Alexander's treasury very tenuous. Armenia was geographically too inaccessible for the tribute to be enforced. (See above, Strabo's account of Menon's attempt to collect Armenian gold.) The claim that Mithranes sustained his royal status is supported by the appearance in 323 of a highly placed Macedonian usurper, Neoptolemus, who could not retain his position; he departed after only a year on the Armenian throne. Mithranes resumed his rule as King of Armenia until his death in *c.*317 BC.[6]

Ervand-Orontes III (*c.* 317–260 BC)

Ervand II's son, Ervand III, does not appear on the Nimrud Dağ inscriptions. He is, however, mentioned by Diodorus (31.19) as

'King'. He appears to have been much involved in an alliance with the King of Cappadocia, against that country's Macedonian (Seleucid) strategos (governor). The Armenian king must therefore have been in control of the large province of Sophene, very nearly covering the ancient site of Shupria, close to Cappadocia, and therefore having an interest in Cappadocia's independence from the powerful Syro-Macedonian Seleucids. In fact, Ervand's fears were realised. Not only Cappadocia, but Armenia, too, fell[7] to Seleucus I (312–230 BC), however tenuously. Armenia had to pay Syria tribute, although it might have been only a nominal one (Toumanoff, pp. 289-90). Nevertheless their *stema* shows all the Orontids, from Ervand II to Ervand IV (*c*.212–*c*.200 BC) were styled kings, even those who were from time to time tributaries of the House of Seleucus.

Samus, Arsames, Xerxes (*c*. 260–*c*.212 BC)

Seleucid power over Armenia was intermittent and tenuous. King Samus, successor of Ervand III (*c*.260 BC) gave refuge to the King of Bithynia who had fled from his Macedonian masters. It is possible that Samus was the founder of the important city of Samosata in Commagene. Another city in Commagene, Arsameia, was founded by King Arsames, son of Samus (after 260– before 228 BC). Arsames ultimately lost his throne to Seleucus II,

Figure 21.2

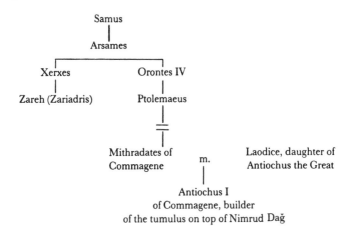

217

after a struggle provoked by the Armenian, who chose to shelter the brother of Seleucus, viceroy of Asia Minor. Although Arsames was worsted, it is a comment on Armenian political and military power that it could defy the Seleucids, whose empire stretched from the Mediterranean to India and Central Asia.

Xerxes, son of Arsames (*c*.228–*c*.212 BC) was besieged in his capital, Arsamasota, by Antiochus the Great, because he would not pay his dead father's tribute. These Armenian kings appear to have had two capital cities — Armavir in the north, and another residence in the south-west. The latter would have been important because it adjoined the territories of the House of Seleucus, the greatest military power in western Asia at that time. Xerxes submitted to Antiochus and peace was symbolised by his marriage to the Macedonian's sister. However, when his wife discovered that he was plotting against her brother, she decided to betray him; and, to put an end to the embarrassing situation, she murdered him.

The connection between these Armenian Orontid kings and Commagene was evidently very close. So much so that Armenia might well have occupied part of that extensive principality. This theory is supported by the presence of two large cities in Commagene — Samosata and Arsameia — built respectively by two successive Armenian kings. Furthermore, it was Ptolemaeus, the grandson of Arsames and perhaps the nephew of Xerxes, who founded the royal dynasty of Commagene (*c*.163 BC). Antiochus I of Commagene (*c*.64 BC), was a member of that House. He is now best known from the great burial mound which he built on the summit of Nimrud Dağ, embellished by gigantic marble statues of seated gods and heroes. Inscriptions discovered there opened up an important era of early Armenian history since Ervand-Orontes I; showing also the Armenian-Achaemenid origin of Antiochus of Commagene himself.[8]

Ervand-Orontes IV (*c*. 212–*c*.200 BC)

Ervand IV was the last Orontid king of Armenia. He may have been the brother of Xerxes. Another brother, Ervaz-Mithras, was the high priest of the temples of the Sun and the Moon at Armavir. These temples and the statues of the Armenian king's brother (as its high priest) indicate that Hellenism had penetrated far into Armenia. A Greek inscription from the high priest, Ervaz, is addressed to his brother, the king; another refers to the king's death. Ervand IV transferred his capital from Armavir which had been built by his forefathers on the River Araxes, to another site, near the confluence of the River Akhurian (Arpa Çay) and Araxes. He named it Ervandashat-Orontosata, after himself, and all the royal treasure was brought to it from the old capital. A new religious centre, Bagaran, was established nearby, to which all the idols were transferred. Ervandashat was a strongly fortified city, with high walls. The rivers constituted natural moats. The flourishing cities of Armavir, Ervandashat and other cities on the Plain of Ayrarat, built during the Orontid period, indicate that Armenia had been transformed from a purely agricultural economy, to one which had strong commercial and trading interests, as in the Urartian period.

Armenia was situated on one of the important crossroads of Eurasia, and the peace that prevailed, practically without interruption for some 500 years, down to the close of the Christian era, must have encouraged the pursuit of commercial and cultural activities. (For the many highways passing through Armenia, see Chapter 14 on Trade and Commerce.)

Notes

1. See also W.W. Tarn, 'Persia from Xerxes to Alexander', CAH VI. i. p. 12. Xenophon meets Tiribazus, satrap of 'Western Armenia', north of the river Tolebaos (Murad su), which Tarn describes as Darius's 13th satrapy, 'Armenia proper', while Orontes is satrap of 'Eastern Armenia', Darius's 18th satrapy. (CAH VI, map 1).

2. Ibid., pp. 20-1.

3. Ibid., p. 22.

4. Tarn, 'The Heritage of Alexander', CAH VI. ii. p. 464; Toumanoff, *Studies in Christian Caucasian History* (Georgetown University Press, 1963) p. 289.

5. The usual manner of recording the appearance of Mithranes in Armenia is that of Alexander's satrap after the Battle of Gaugamela. I have shown how tenuous that interpretation is. Some writers even assume that Orontes II was killed in battle while supporting the Persian king, and that is presented as an example of Armenia's chronic tragedy of factions, of father against son, brother against brother, and sometimes fighting with the enemy against their homeland. But were not such divisions common in European history? By isolating such Armenian examples, as though they were unique, the injurious impression of an alien and constantly divided people is perpetuated.

6. Tarn, *op. cit.*, p. 466: 'Perdicas then detached Alexander's armour-

bearer Neoptolemus of the Epirot House to attempt the conquest of Armenia' (which was unsuccessful).

7. C.L. Toumanoff, *Studies in Christian Caucasian History* (Georgetown University Press, 1963), p. 449. To hold the Orontid monarchy at all, Seleucus I (312–280 BC) had to have the alliance of the ambitious Iberian Royal House of the first Pharnabazids. Thus the Armenian kings were briefly — for about 50 years down to the end of Antiochus I's reign (280–261 BC) — obliged to pay at least a nominal tribute to the House of Seleucus. In Toumanoff's words: 'The Iberian alliance ... was needed by the Seleucids in order to hold the Orontid monarchy within a pincer movement.' His overlordship is described as tenuous (pp. 289-90).

8. Toumanoff, *op. cit.* pp. 281-3, 292.

22

The Royal House of Artashes (the Artaxiads)

Artashes-Artaxias and Zareh-Zariadris

A successful revolt against Ervand IV by two princes of his own royal house, Artashes and Zareh, probably instigated by Antiochus the Great (223–187 BC), in accordance with a policy of divide and rule, destroyed Ervand. Under the aegis of Antiochus, two Syrio-Macedonian tribute-paying provinces appeared in Armenia: Greater Armenia,[1] the lands east of the Euphrates (Firat) almost to the Caspian under Artashes, and the province of Sophene under Zareh, both *strategi* of Antiochus. Three Aramaic stelae discovered near Lake Sevan, record the fact that Zareh was the father of Artashes and that they were Orontids.[2]

In accordance with the nature of conquerors, Antiochus, though already master of all Asia, from the Mediterranean to the Indus and the Oxus, crossed into Europe and occupied Macedon. In Greece, he met Hannibal fleeing from the Romans after his defeat at Zama (202 BC) and the destruction of Carthage. In a turmoil of humiliation and hatred for his terrible enemies, Hannibal induced Antiochus to make a stand against the Romans and strike a blow for ancient Greece. Unfortunately for Antiochus and his empire, and ultimately for the whole of Asia, he was signally defeated at Thermopylae and again decisively at Magnesia (190 BC), somewhat to the east of Smyrna. The Romans carried off 1300 elephants' tusks. For over 150 years before that time, elephants had been an important element in warfare, particularly in Asia (Hannibal had used them in Europe). They would open battle meeting forehead to forehead, while pikemen struck from their towers, till one beast or the other turned its flank and was gored. Antiochus's scythed chariots became useless when their horses were shot down.

The Peace of Apamea (188 BC) divested Antiochus of all his possessions in Anatolia forever. Artashes then scized the Armenian throne at Ervandashat and declared himself King of Greater Armenia (188–159 BC), thus establishing the Third Monarchy of Armenia,[3] the Artaxiad. Its territories included all but Sophene of the entire kingdom. Zareh, on his part, declared himself King of Sophene, and his expansionist policy took his armies into the lands of Acilisene and beyond the Arsanias and even across the Euphrates into the traditional territories of Armenia Minor, toward the River Halys into Cataonia (Strabo, XI.xiv.5).

Artashes, on the other hand, marched south to occupy the ancient Urartian homelands between the Caspian Sea and Lake Urmia (Atropatene-Media (Strabo, XI.xiv.5)). The Armenian frontiers in the east then marched with the steppes of central Asia. His new boundaries would have encroached upon those of the Seleucid colonial territories. Furthermore, Artashes and Zareh jointly wrested from the Iberians 'the land along the side of Mount Paryadres and Cholarzene and Gogarene' (Strabo, XI.xiv.5). Thus, the two Armenias (i.e. Great Armenia) sometimes overlapped. 'Consequent on this near-unification, was the growing linguistic homogeneity of the country.'[4] Strabo (XI.xiv.5) emphasises this common use of the Armenian language throughout the length and breadth of Great Armenia ruled by the two kings: 'The Armenian language, of Indo-European origin, which had been carried from Hayasa to the east side of the Euphrates by Gurdi's Phrygian-speaking followers, whose own name for themselves was 'Hayk' — had become the common language of the heterogeneous population of Armenia Major only as a consequence of the political unification of all these people under the Artaxiad Crown.'[5] And, it appears, that Zareh cooperated with his son Artashes in this and other respects, as described above. Possibly, the seeds of the Armenian *permanent* claim to the royal title of *King of Kings* and assumed by Tigranes the Great and his successors, were sown during the Artaxias/Zariadris period. The title claimed sovereignty over Albania and Iberia. 'The cosmocracy of the Armenian Monarch hinged on the claim to control the entire Caucasian peoples. Armenian historical writings of the Christian phase tend to treat, especially Albania and Iberia, as dependencies of Armenia.'[6]

There is an interesting tradition founded on the accounts given by Plutarch (Lucullus 32.3) and Strabo (XI.xiv.6) that *c.*185 BC, Hannibal, the Carthaginian, while still fleeing from his implacable enemies the Romans, sought and received hospitality at the Armenian court, and that he expressed his gratitude to his royal host by planning and supervising the building of the city of Artashat (Artaxata) on the River Araxes. It was a magnificient city and Strabo (XI.xiv.4-6) writes of it and its beautiful surroundings with admiration. There must have been celebrations to mark the integration of the new city into the national ethos. Statues of the national divinities, particularly that of Anahit (Aphrodite, goddess of love and procreation), were transferred from Bagaran to Artashat thus giving the new city not only the status of the political but also that of the religious capital of Armenia, and no doubt, there must have been a suitable temple to house the statue of Anahit, to which pilgrims might travel.

While Artashat was being built, Armenia was according to Khorenatsi (II.50, 85) invaded by the Alans (the forbears of those who crossed into France and Spain, with fire and sword in AD 405–408).[7] Artashes defeated them, pursued them beyond the River Kura and, at the same time, took prisoner the Alan chief's son and heir. Nor would he return him to his father, in spite of the chief's pleas. Part of an epic celebrating that victory is perpetuated in a collection of poems, known as *Songs of Koght'en*, in which the chief's beautiful daughter, Sat'enik, steps forward to the river bank and begs Artashes to release her brother:

O brave Artashes, conqueror of valiant Alani,
Hear the plea of a princess:
Return my brother to the king, his father.
'Tis unworthy of heroes to enslave their prisoners,
Forever perpetuating
The enmity 'twixt Great Armenia and the Alani.

The undeniable wisdom of those words from the lips of the beautiful Sat'enik, confirmed the decision the king had already made:

Brave Artashes rode his spirited steed,
Like a winged eagle leapt across the stream.
Then from his saddle unleashed he a cord,
Bejewelled with rings flashing in the sun.
Then casting his belt round her lithe waist,
    Upon his strong horse bore her to his camp.

There was love and reconciliation; and inevitably the king's marriage to the princess:

> For Artashes, the gallant groom,
> Showers of gold brightened the land;
> Pearls rained from smiling heaven
> For Sat'enik, the comely bride.

In the year 170 BC, Antiochus IV (175–164 BC) caused a revolt of the Jews, now known as the Maccabees Wars, because they would not accept his self-styled title of Theos Epiphanes (God Manifest), although it was not at all unusual for kings traditionally to assume such a title. But the Jews were the children of Jehovah and were monotheists. He was unable to subdue them. That setback was followed by another degradation: in 168 BC, he was ignominiously humiliated by the Roman consul, Caius Popitius Laenas, at Eleusis near Alexandria. Before he was allowed to depart, he had to submit to the arrogant consul and tacitly to acknowledge that his Syrio-Macedonian empire was thenceforth a client-state of Rome. But he had already lost control of large tracts of territory in the east, to the Parthian satraps of Bactria who seized the ancient Achaemenid throne in 171 BC. On his return to his capital in Syria, Antiochus unleashed his rage by breaking the terms of the Treaty of Apamea and invading Armenia, in defiance of Rome. His unprovoked and surprise attack in 165 BC, when Artashes had been king for 23 years, was successful. However, Artashes simply bought him off his territories. The following year, Antiochus died.[8]

Artashes reigned for another five years over a vast, independent realm, which had continued to prosper under his rule, as it had under his Orontid predecessors. He died in 159 BC, after a long reign of 30 years. He seems to have had philosophical propensities, for on his deathbed he is said to have expressed his view of the ephemeral nature of life's struggles. With his dying breath, we are told (Khorenatsi, II.13), he murmured: 'Woe that my glories are of the past!' — 'Avakh paratzes antsavorin!'

Artavasd-Artavasdes I (159–95 BC)

The momentum of Artashes' vigorous rule carried the kingdom down to his grandson, Artavasdes I (henceforth, Artavasd), a contemporary of the Parthian king, Mithradates II (123–87 BC). The Parthians from Khurasan, at first satraps of Bactria, were the successors of the Macedonians, east of the Euphrates. Arsaces I (*c.*247 BC), who claimed descent from the Achaemenid Artaxerxes II, was the founder of the royal house of Arsacids, while the Parthian empire was founded by Mithradates I (177–138 BC), who seized the throne of his Persian ancestors from the Syrio-Macedonian king, Antiochus IV (*c.*171 BC). It is to the credit of both the Parthians and the Seleucids that they realised their mutual interest in keeping trade routes between east and west open; and they carried out this policy.

Since part of that trade and commerce might well have affected Armenia's wealth, perhaps a passing reference ought to be made to the business relations which were opened up by Mithradates of Parthia with the Han Emperor of China. And so, the caravans from China, in increasing numbrs, were joined *en route* by those from Central Asia and India, bringing their wares and carrying them through Parthia and Mesopotamia (or Armenia and Asia Minor) to the Seleucids and the Mediter-ranean — a route which was later to be identified as the Silk Route.

In 92 BC Mithradates sent an ambassador — or a kind of trade delegation — to Sulla, who was at that time on the Euphrates in Asia Minor and so, for a time, Parthia became an entrepôt between East and West. He drew his western frontier at the Euphrates, facing Seleucid (soon to be Armenian) Syria. Thus, in spite of political rivalries, and even wars, between Parthia–Syria–Armenia, by common consent, trade between East and West continued, uninterrupted, unmolested, to the benefit of all concerned. It was the Romans who destroyed that sensible arrangement between Syria and Parthia, when they thirsted for the possession of Parthia after they had expelled Armenia from Syria and Mesopotamia. They were to regret their greed, which could not stop, as it should have, on the western side of the Euphrates, if they were to be in Asia at all.

Tigran-Tigranes the Great (95-55 BC)

As a result of a defeat in a war with the Parthians, King Artavasd I of Armenia had to give them his son, Tigranes (Tigran, hence-forth) as hostage. On Artavasd's death in 95 BC, Tigran was released in return for Armenian territories (seized by Artashes from Parthia) comprising 70 valleys in Atropatene. Little did the Parthians realise the energy they had released in the person of Tigran the Great (95–55 BC). 'When he acquired power, he recovered these valleys, and devastated the country of the Parthians, the territory about Ninus (Nineveh), and that about Arbela. He subjected to his authority the Atropatenians, and the Gordyaeans; by force of arms he obtained possession also of the rest of Mesopotamia and, after crossing the Euphrates, of Syria and Phoenicia' (Strabo, XI.xiv.16). He also seized Adiabene and Nisibis. Thus, his southern frontier reached beyond Singara. More importantly, he united his kingdom to the ancient and extensive province of Sophene, by plucking it from its king, Ervand V (Orontes–Artanes) of the House of Zareh (Zariadris).

Tigran realised the economic importance of opening up trade with Babylonia. To this end, he established friendly relations with the Skenite Arabs, through whose territories (avoiding politically unfriendly towns) trade and commerce could be conducted with Babylonia via the Mesopotamian desert, skirting Carrhae, across the River Balikh and so reaching the Euphrates opposite Bambyce, to the north-east of Antioch. The Artaxiades had welded the Armenian people into a single nation by encouraging the use of the Armenian language, as a common — indeed, national — language, throughout their extensive domains. Tigran inherited that basically essential advantage. When he married Cleopatra, the thirteen-year-old daughter of Mithradates of Pontus, he let him retain Lesser Armenia, adjoining Pontus[9] thus strengthening his political and military potential. In 88 BC, Tigran and Mithradates together defeated the Romans under Manlius Maltinus and Aquilius, when the latter went into Asia as consular legate in the Mithradatic war, under the overall command of Sulla. Lucullus, too, had arrived on the scene in that year as Sulla's quaestor, but when Sulla departed in 84, Lucullus remained until 80; a useful qualifying experience for his Asiatic command later.

The defeat of the Romans is attributed by Cicero to the 'fear that had fallen upon those peoples [the Asiatics]' through whose territories the Romans had marched. Cicero's allegation is supported by Justin (XXXVIII.iii.): 'Having put them to flight, he [Tigran] was received with great joy by the cities [in Cappadocia] in which he found a great quantity of gold and silver and vast warlike stores, laid up by the care of the former princes.

Taking possession of these, he remitted the cities all sorts of debts, public and private, and granted them immunity from tribute for five years.'

This illustrates the generous spirit of the Armenian king, who is commonly portrayed by his European biographers as an arrogant barbarian who, according to Plutarch (Everyman's II, *Lucullus*, p. 219) was 'insolent and overbearing and had risen from a small and inconsiderable beginning'. This is pure rhetoric, because Armenia was neither small nor inconsiderable when Tigran came into his inheritance in 95 BC. So hated were the Romans that when Aquilius fled to Mytilene, its inhabitants handed him over to Mithradates who put him to death by pouring molten gold down his throat.

In Syria, after Antiochus IV Epiphanes, the last of the Seleucids with any credence was Antiochus VIII Grypus (125–96 BC),[10] who was murdered by his general, Heracleon. Anarchy then prevailed throughout the country. It was so serious, that the people were prepared, for the sake of peace and stability, to have a foreign ruler who had no commitments either to Rome or to the Ptolemies of Egypt. They invited Tigran to rule their country. This was by no means without precedent. As is well known, Attalus of Pergamum bequeathed his kingdom to Rome (133 BC). The kings of Cyrenaica (96 BC) and later Bithynia (74 BC) also willed their respective kingdoms to Rome.

After the kings and kingdom of Syria had been exhausted by intermitting wars, occasioned by mutual animosities of brothers, and by some succeeding to the quarrels of their father, the people began to look for relief from foreign parts, and to think of choosing a king from among the sovereigns of other nations. Some therefore advised that they should take Mithridates of Pontus, others Ptolemy of Egypt, but it being considered that Mithridates was engaged in war with the Romans, and that Ptolemy had always been an enemy to Syria, the thoughts of all were directed to Tigranes, king of Armenia, who, in addition to the strength of his own kingdom, was supported by an alliance with Parthia and by a matrimonial connection with Mithridates. Tigranes, accordingly, was invited to the throne of Syria ... where he reigned for eighteen years (83–69 BC) (Justin XL.1)[11]

This account of Tigran's presence in Syria seriously differs from that of other classical writers (mentors of modern scholars) who disdainfully describe a 'barbarian' invading a weaker country beyond his borders (as if no 'civilised' country — Rome, for example — would do such a thing!). In fact, there is no evidence that Tigran, in accordance with the traditions set by his predecessors, had any ambitions south of the Taurus. Armenia was 'a great kingdom whose geographical territory next to Parthia is of greater extent than any other Kingdom' (Justin, XLII.ii), a rich land; agriculture, stock-breeding and mining of almost every mineral being available within its own borders. There was no need to crave for the deserts of Syria or the marshlands of Mesopotamia. However, once in Syria (83 BC), Tigran became embroiled in the politics and the wars of Palestine and Mesopotamia. Queen Alexandra ruled Palestine. Josephus (*Wars*, I.v.3; *Antiq.* XIII.xvi.4) writes: 'She was a sagacious woman ... she increased the army the one half, and procured a great body of foreign troops, till her own nation became not only very powerful at home, but terrible also to foreign potentates.' She marched north and 'got possession of Damascus'. In these circumstances, any responsible ruler of Syria would have marched south in order to outflank Damascus; which Tigran did, by taking the great port of Ptolemais (Acre) in Phoenicia and by successfully besieging the Seleucid eastern capital, Seleucia-on-Tigris, taking prisoner Queen Selene Cleopatra, who had fled from the Seleucid western capital, Antioch, and executing her (Strabo, XVI.ii.3).

Josephus goes on to report that Queen Alexandra 'prevailed with Tigranes, with many valuable presents, as also ambassadors ... by agreements and presents, to go away. ... He commended them [the ambassadors] for the respects they paid him at so great a distance, and gave them good hopes of his favour.' It suited Tigran to accede to Alexandra's plea, for messengers had informed him 'of those domestic tumults which happened upon Lucullus's expedition into Armenia'. Lucullus, at war with Mithradates of Pontus, father-in-law of Tigran, was pursuing him towards Armenia. In the meantime, in Tigran's absence, Syria was being ruled by his viceroy, Bagatades, who appears to have been the earliest known member of the illustrious Bagratid family who gave kings both to Armenia and Georgia in the Middle Ages.[12] Between 83 and 69 BC, Tigran the Great, King of Kings, was the most powerful potentate in the whole of Western Asia. Plutarch (ibid., p. 219) is derogatory and practically caricatures

Tigran who had 'many kings waiting on him, but four he always carried with him as servants and guards'. This shows Plutarch's or his informant's lack of knowledge as to the status and protocol of the 'kings', particularly the 'four he always carried with him'. The 'four' were in fact Tigran's counsellers, companions and bodyguard, who, as princes or dynastic 'kings' in their own right, ruled four marches of Great Armenia (Great Armenia comprehended Major and Minor Armenia together). They and their respective armies, castles and estates, situated in strategic positions of the country, together and separately constituted the first line of defence of the realm — four viceroyalties. Strabo (XI.iv.4) 'They fight on foot and on horseback, both in light and heavy armour. (The horses, too, are protected by armour). They use javelins and bows and wear breastplates, shields, and coverings'; (XI.xiv.12) 'They have a passion for riding and take good care of their horses.'

At the height of Tigran's power, the great city of Tigranakert (Tigranocerta) was built, somewhat to the east of modern Diarbekir, on the River Tigris and along the ancient Persian Royal Road. The precise site of the city is not known. Tacitus (*Annals* XV.5: '37 [Roman] miles [north–east] from Nisibis'. But this is questioned by modern writers. It was possibly on the site of modern Siirt. It was not only strategically well situated, and within easy reach of the king, when he was in the central and southern parts of his empire, but also, as Appian (*Mithra.* XII.84) writes, it was built as a powerful stronghold, with walls rising to a height of 50 cubits and so thick that warehouses and stables were built into them. In accordance with the then current Hellenistic custom, Tigranakert, too, boasted a theatre where Greek plays were performed. Outside the ramparts, a magnificent palace arose, surrounded by parks and gardens, and the city generally attracted and welcomed Greek scholars. Plutarch (*Crassus*, p. 224) describes it as 'a rich and beautiful city where every common man and every man of rank studied to adorn it'. Hellenistic influence was strong in Armenia (although Alexander the Great or his Macedonian successors did not conquer it) and the Greek language was extensively used, especially by members of the aristocracy. Greek literature was familiar to them and Greek plays were performed in the more important cities of Armenia.

Leaving Bagatades as viceroy of Syria, Tigran hastened to his northern capital, Artashat (Artaxata), to give shelter to the fugitive Mithradates and, if necessary, to confront the Roman legions under Lucullus. Mithradates reached Armenia in 72 BC. If the Roman ambassador, Appius Claudius, did indeed visit Antioch, in order to threaten Tigran, and to demand the delivery of Mithradates, the Great King himself could not have been there. It is unlikely that Claudius travelled to the distant Armenian capital, Artashat (Artaxata). Claudius's interview must then have been with the Armenian viceroy, Bagatades in Antioch. The arrogant praetor was sent away with offers of diplomatic gifts, but nothing else. Thus, Armenia could defy Rome by sheltering the King of Pontus and by dismissing a Roman ambassador empty-handed, from Antioch.

Lucullus had not achieved any marked conquests, and his soldiers were becoming restive — they wanted the loot of conquered cities, as indeed their masters, the rapacious Romans, did, in Asia (and in Rome) with its accumulated wealth of 3000 years. He decided to attack and take Tigranakert. Plutarch unwittingly confirms how feared and unpopular the Romans were, when he lists (*Lucullus* p. 224) the small independent principalities and chieftainships who willingly came to join the Armenian forces in the battle about to take place against the Romans: 'Gordyenians, Medes and Adiabenians; Arabians from the sea beyond Babylon; and from the Caspian Sea, the Albanians and the Iberians their neighbours, and not a few of the free people without kings, living about the [river] Araxes (in the northeastern lands within and adjoining Armenia).' Plutarch continues that Tigranes then 'marched on with all his army, lamenting, *as it is said*, that he should fight with Lucullus alone and not with all the Roman generals together' — a most unlikely attitude when he had gone to the trouble of enlisting the support of so many peoples, obviously aware of the military strength of Rome. He even appealed for help to the kings of Parthia and Commagene; they did not respond. Again, we are misled by Plutarch as to the enormous numbers in Tigran's army, according 'as *Lucullus* wrote to the Senate' (ibid., p. 224). Plutarch and Appian (*Mithr.* 84) (taking Lucullus's own figures as their source) show an Armenian total force of well over a quarter of a million infantry and cavalry, against the Romans' 20,000 foot and horse. Memnon of Heraclea Pontica (55) reduces the Armenian force down to the more reasonable figure of 60,000. Such seems to have been the extent of the opposing forces at the Battle of Tigranakert, *if, indeed, it ever took place.* On the approach of the Romans,

Tigran is said to have abandoned his treasures and his concubines in the city, entrusting its defence to its governor, in order to return to the shelter of the Armenian mountains to muster his army. Lucullus then laid siege to Tigranakert, but his investing army was so small that an Armenian force dispatched by Tigran, entered the city and brought away not only his women but *a part* of the royal treasure.

There are some incredible statements here. Why, on the approach of Lucullus, should Tigran have abandoned the city so readily? There could have been no lack of confidence; he had already demonstrated his military power at the battle against Aquilius in 88 BC. How did he contrive to return to the heart of Tigranakert to collect his harem; but only part of his royal treasure — why not the whole? How could the palace and his household have remained intact if Romans or traitors had broken in and stolen the remainder of his treasure? It all seems to add up to a dubious narrative, one part not supporting the other. As to Tigran's alleged comment, when he saw Lucullus's legions: 'Too large for an embassy and too small for an army', it seems to me to be a most unlikely, frivolous witticism at such a critical moment. It sounds much more like the invention of Lucullus's companion, flatterer and chronicler, the poet Archias.[13] There are no original records, other than the biased ones from the camp of the Roman Imperator, which tell the true state of affairs of those times in Armenia and in the Armenian dominions. Finally, at the end of the battle: Plutarch (ibid., p. 227) says 'It is stated that above one hundred thousand [Armenian] foot were lost and that of the horse very few escaped. Of the Romans, one hundred [!] were wounded and *five* killed'.

The following account of the war, which is contrary to the conventional sources and much more likely to be the truth, is given by Cicero in a speech (*Pro Lege Manilia,* IX, 23)[14] in support of the Consul Manilia (66 BC) proposing a law granting to Pompeius the command of the war against Tigran and Mithradates, which was being pursued unsuccessfully by Lucullus. Cicero was among the prominent Roman critics of his ambitions and adventures in Asia, which he rightly foresaw as boding ill for Rome. It was because of these adventures that Armenian affairs were to clog Rome's movements there for centuries to come. Cicero, praetor for the year 66 BC, speaking in the Forum, at the Assembly of the People in Rome, told the true story, for it was a very recent one, and he had had no active part in it, having had the details from reports at first hand, during the course of Lucullus's campaign:

> Mithradates meanwhile, a panic-stricken fugitive, found welcome with Tigranes, King of Armenia, who comforted his despair, raised his drooping spirits and restored his ruined fortunes. [cf. Plutarch, ibid., II, p. 220.] On the arrival of Lucullus and his troops in Armenia, yet other nations rose against our general; for fear had fallen upon those peoples when Rome had never intended to attack in war or even to disturb: besides which, a strong and fanatical belief had become general among the barbarous nations, that our army had been directed to those regions in order to loot a very wealthy and *much-venerated temple*. In this way many great peoples were roused to action by a new feeling of terror and alarm. Our own army, moreover, despite their capture of *a city* from the kingdom of Tigranes and their successes in battle, began to feel the extreme remoteness of their position and to long for home.[15]

It seems that everyone of any consequence realised that Lucullus was being over-bold in his attempt to reach Armenia, where he would find Mithradates being fêted by his son-in-law. René Grousset writes: 'Mithridate faisait un peut figure client de Tigran' (*Histoire d'Arménie*, p. 85). Even Plutarch, who is usually biased against 'barbarians', writes: 'He [Lucullus] seemed to be making reckless attack, and one admitted on no saving calculation, upon warlike nations, countless thousands of horsemen, and a boundless region surrounded by deep rivers and mountains covered with perpetual snow' (p. 22).

In fact, having recovered his energies and ascertained the military state of his own remaining loyal members of the aristocracy, Mithradates was able, in the middle of the year 70 BC, to give chase to Lucullus. In those circumstances, the Imperator could not possibly have made his way across the Euphrates as well as the western bend of the Tigris if he were to reach Tigranakert, invest it and take it (69 BC), as is alleged by most of his classical biographers, who have become the sources for modern writers of the history of that period. What I believe really happened is as described by Cicero above. He took — or rather tried to take — *a city* (not Tigranakert). Lucullus, and Pompeius who followed, well knew of the fabulous wealth of the much-venerated temple. If the city had been Tigranakert, Cicero would surely have named it — it was the wealthy, southern capital of the Armenian empire and of primary military importance. The much-venerated temple was that of the great Armenian mother-goddess, Anahit at Acilisene, which was to be despoiled by Marcus Antonius in 34 BC. In spite of the critical necessity to cross the Euphrates in order to loot the holiest temple of ancient Armenia, the Romans were prevented by the Armenian archers whose arrows could kill at a range of about 200 metres (Plutarch, p. 236). To attack Tigranakert, Lucullus would have had to cross the Euphrates at Melitene which he well knew would be impossible in the face of the enemy, because of its depth, width and strong currents at that point. Cicero, who must have heard of the change of plan was perhaps trying to give the unpalatable news in diplomatic language to the Assembly at the Forum — the reason for not naming 'the city', which was not, after all, Tigranakert. Lucullus would try to reach the eastern bank of the Euphrates at Cabira and land in Acilicene, near the famous temple. An Armenian scholar writes:

> Against the mutinous soldiery of Rome stood the freehold farmers of Armenia, steeled by centuries of agricultural work and the consciousness of an invincible past. Described by Sallustius Crispus as 'remarkable by the beauty of their horses and armour', the Armenian cavalry was led by an hereditary landed aristocracy for whom personal honour, courage in the field, single combat, hunting and banqueting were the highest tests of manhood. Man for man, soul for soul, the Roman host, at best, was no match for the native Armenian, Georgian [Caucasian], Albanian or Kurd. The Romans were out for conquest and loot, the latter were defending their sacred native soil.[16]

In late 68 BC, having failed to penetrate Eastern Armenia, Lucullus retreated south and laid siege to Nisibis. The lack of plunder and the trials and privations of an advancing winter in the Armenian mountains, demoralised the Roman army to the point of mutiny. They were also unpopular among the natives of the cities they occupied. While Tigran invaded and occupied Cappadocia, and at the same time carried out mopping-up operations of pockets of Roman resistance in the south, Mithradates with 4000 of his own troops and 4000 Armenians, emerged from northern Armenia along the valley of the River Lycus, into the heart of his kingdom (67 BC). The natives of Pontus, having briefly experienced the merciless weight of the Roman yoke, welcomed the return of their king with delight. Lucullus had been unable to go to the relief of the Roman general in Pontus, Fabius Hadrianus, because of Tigran's harassment and the mutinous attitude of his troops, and had also been mortified to witness the Armenian occupation of Cappadocia.

Lucullus's failure to invade Armenia successfully, seems to have been largely due to his ignorance of the immensity of the country and the great distances he proposed to traverse with his legions. This exacerbated the mutinous discontent of his troops. But the true situation was not reported to the Senate in Rome. Plutarch (ibid., p. 233) again:

> He [Lucullus] kept them [the Fimbrian legion] indeed, with him, but without urging his authority upon them; nor did he lead them out to battle, being contented if they should but stay with him, though he then saw Cappadocia wasted by Tigranes [How could he have held Tigranakert in such circumstances?], and Mithridates again triumphing, whom not long before he reported to the Senate to be wholly subdued; and commissioners were now arriving to settle the affairs of Pontus, as if all had been quietly in his possession. But when they came, they found him not so much as master of himself, but contemned and derided by the common soldiers.

If Lucullus had indeed captured Tigrankert, its enormous wealth, including at least part of the king's personal treasure, would have made his army the most loyal in the world — at least long enough to follow Lucullus to the northern capital of Armenia.

Having received the command of Asia in 65 BC, Pompeius occupied Syria and put an end to the Seleucid dynasty wich had survived the changing political and military fortunes of a kingdom and an empire for 250 years. He then set out on his campaign against Mithradates of Pontus, not Tigran. He pursued the Parthian king, Phraates III, to invade Armenia. Phraates was unsuccessful and returned home. On receiving tidings of Pompeius's plan, Mithradates retreated beyond the Caucasus.

Pompeius did not think that his enemy, by now an old man,

would survive his trans-Caucasian march, and decided, instead of pursuit, to explore the unknown lands in the vicinity of the Caspian Sea where no Roman general had ever trod. Perhaps he thought of opening up a new trade route to the Far East. More likely, as was the way with Roman generals, he thought of the glory of being the first Roman to penetrate so far to the East, and such an adventure might lead to even more plunder than had already been taken from Asia to Rome. He reached the great inland sea at a point where it was a threatening desert and a colony of poisonous snakes. Back at Colchis, there was still no news of Mithradates.

At that juncture, an unexpected visitor, in the person of the crown prince of Armenia, Tigran the Great's third son[17], offered to lead Pompeius and his legions to Artashat (Artaxata), to invade the Armenian capital, depose the old king, his father, and usurp the throne. Of incidental but important interest is that not far from Artashat in the fortresses of Babyrsa and Olane were housed the royal and national treasures of Armenia (Strabo, XI.xvi.6). The outcome was that when the Imperator appeared at the city gates, they were thrown open and Tigran, now an old man of 75, submitted to him unconditionally. Tigran is described as having 'abjectly' prostrated himself at the knees of his conqueror. But this gesture is presented to a modern reader out of context with the immemorial Asiatic custom in such circumstances. Witness Alexander the Great in Persia, demanding prostration from his Greek courtiers to himself; and what of the 'abject' kneeling Roman Emperor Valerian, below his arrogant, mounted conqueror, Shapur I, depicted in relief on the rock-face at Naqsh-i Rustam! Also, let us come nearer home and remember the 'abject' genuflections of vassals to their lords in feudal medieval Western Europe!

Pompeius quickly raised the Armenian king, embraced him and sat him by his side. Tigran then gave away huge sums of money and treasure to satiate the greed not only of Pompeius himself and his masters in Rome, but that of every officer and legionary at that moment in camp outside the walls of Artashat. He gave to each military tribune 10,000 drachmas; to each centurion 1000 drachmas; to each soldier 50 drachmas and a talent to a Hipparch and a Chiliarch. To Pompeius himself, he gave 6000 talents of silver, which Pompeius added to the 20,000 talents he had already extracted from the wealthy bankers of Asia — after all, what is war all about? In short, Tigran bought off the

Roman host, which was much cheaper than fighting a war: 'Of the riches and power of this country, this is no slight proof' (Strabo, XI.xiv.10). Pompeius was so pleased at so easy a victory, with such riches to give and display back in Rome, that he could afford to be magnanimous. He let Tigran retain the whole of his kingdom, with the exception of Sophene, which he allotted to the traitorous son. Young Tigran, disappointed with his small province, when he had expected to receive a kingdom which extended from the Caspian to the western Euphrates, had the temerity to insult the great Imperator. Pompeius, remembering that the young man had married a Parthian princess, and offended by the insult, took him prisoner and displayed him at his Triumph in Rome as the son-in-law of the implacable enemy of Rome, the Parthian king. Then he had him imprisoned. Some say that he was strangled.

Thus, the whole of Armenia, including Sophene, reverted to its rightful ruler. Tigran retained even Gordyene and Nisibis, which Pompeius withheld from the Parthians. He was not a 'client of Rome' as it is sometimes averred. He had bought off Pompeius and was not in any sense a tribute-paying king. As to the city of Tigranakert, though allegedly, it was despoiled, and partially destroyed by Lucullus, it remained in fact a considerable city. We hear of it again when it was invested by the Roman general, Corbulo, in AD 58. Two hundred years later the Sassanid king, Shapur of Persia mentions it as the first major city of Armenia to be seen when travelling from the south. As late as the Islamic period, a general of the Faith prayed to have it without bloodshed. Immediately the eastern gates were thrown open by an invisible hand. Tigran the Great, King of Kings, died in his capital city of Artashat at the ripe old age of 84 years. His death marks the end of an epoch.

Historical Armenia had been in existence for some 500 years. Here is an example to belie the traditional view held by historians generally, that Armenia had been, for most of those centuries, a 'client state' of the Persian and later of the Seleucid or Parthian empires. That traditional view does not appear to be at all in line with historical facts. The following salient points emerge from a brief review of what has so far been recounted.

From Cyrus the Great (*c.*550 BC) down to Artaxerxes I (*c.*450 BC), a period of 100 years, there can be no doubt as to the vassalage of the infant Armenian state. However, such seems to have been the pressure of the people for their independence, that after the Persian palace revolution which placed Darius Hystaspis on the throne in 522 BC, there was an almost successful Armenian revolt (so early in its history!). Thenceforth, the Armenian position seems to have improved towards semi-autonomy. Hydarnes I, one of 'The Seven' (521–499 BC) was followed, perhaps, by Ervant the Short-lived (*c.* 499–494 BC) and Tigranes, the Achaemenid (*c.*494–480 BC). Hydarnes III (*c.*425 BC), like Hydarnes I, was undoubtedly satrap of Armenia. Under him and his namesake of the sixth century, Armenia was indeed a client state, as it was, perhaps to a lesser degree, under his son, Terituchmes (d. *c.* 402 BC). The sister of Terituchmes married King Artaxerxes I of Achaemenid Persia; their daughter married Ervand (Orontes), son of Artasyras. Ervand I inherited the Armenian satrapy (401–344 BC). But his allegiance to the Great King was very tenuous, so much so that he could more accurately be called 'King'. He was in supreme command of the Armenian militia, was ruler of Armenia (Eastern and Western, after the disgrace of Tiribazus, satrap of Western Armenia), as well as Mysia and much of western Asia Minor, including Pergamum; he was sufficiently powerful to assert his independence by coining his own gold. It would be fair to describe him more as an ally of Persia (when it suited him) than as a tribute-paying king, although officially he is described as a satrap.

After the brief satrapal reign of Codomannus, the Armenian government reverted to the Orontids. Ervand II (344–325 BC). The alliance continued, but the relationship between the two royal houses of Persia and of Armenia must have been weaker. For Ervand II was born in Armenia and, psychologically, he must surely have had much deeper associations with the people over whom he ruled than his father. The alliance with Persia, of course, continued; Armenian cavalry fought side by side with the Persian forces against Alexander the Great. But after Gaugamela (331 BC), when Persia, along with the whole of the Near East, except for the kingdoms skirting the Pontic coast, was part of Alexander's empire, Ervand declared himself King of Armenia. Alexander did not attempt to cross Armenia. His satrapal nominee, Mithranes, was rejected as satrap but accepted as crown prince, and on his father Ervand II's death, ascended the Armenian throne as King of Armenia. It is very unlikely that Mithranes paid tribute to Alexander's treasury. That is perhaps the reason for the attempt of Neoptolamus to usurp the throne.

The Armenian aristocracy must have made his position untenable, for he abdicated within a year (321–320).[18] That one year might well be ignored; Mithranes simply resumed his rule and died peacefully in *c.* 317 BC.

The conventional version of the history then continues in the same traditional strain of Armenian subservience to a foreign power; this time to the Syrio-Macedonian House of Seleucus. All the successors of Mithranes — Orontes III, Samus, Arsames, Xerxes and finally Orontes IV — are said to have been dominated by the Seleucids.[19] If this were indeed so, it could only have been a nominal status, perhaps invented by the arrogant Macedonians themselves and perpetuated by the Greek and Roman historians, who are the main sources of European scholars delving into the intricacies of Armenian history. The above-named Orontids were all acknowledged to be, and indeed entitled, 'king'. Two of them, in defiance of the Seleucids, gave refuge to client kings of Syria, and two others built cities right on the borders of the Seleucid empire, which they named after themselves. Around 210 BC, Antiochus the Great did indeed impose his suzerainty over Armenia, as a result of which the House of Orontes expired (*c.* 200 BC). If the Orontids had been 'clients' of the Seleucids, there would have been no need for Antiochus to have taken military action and upset a satisfactory situation, operating for nearly 100 years. Two scions of the House of Orontes, Artashes (Artaxias) and Zareh (Zariadris), were made *strategi* of Greater Armenia and Sophene, respectively; they must have paid tribute and they were certainly clients of the House of Seleucus — but for a mere 20 years. After the Peace of Apamea (189 BC), Artashes established a new royal line, the Artaxiad, which continued for over 150 years. The best that can be said of the Seleucids in the Armenian context, it seems, is that they *attempted* for 100 years to control the Orontids through their connections in Iberia, via Bactria–Sogdiana the Caspian and the Caucasus, where Seleucus I planned to build a canal to join the Black and the Caspian Seas. The plan did not materialise. Artashes and Zareh then, between them, ruled as kings from Iberia and Albania in the north to beyond the southern shores of the Caspian to the frontiers of Central Asia; and westwards to the confines of the ancient Armeno-Phrygian province of the true Lesser Armenia, almost to the River Halys. Artashes died peacefully in 159 BC.

About the middle of the second century BC, a people called the

Parthians, with perhaps Scythian antecedents, are introduced to history as a tribe occupying the region in eastern Iran that we now know as Khorasan. After the death of Alexander the Great, Seleucus I reorganised and strengthened some Macedonian outposts in Central Asia, where he might have encountered a people called the Parni (Strabo, XI.ix.1-3). The Parni appear to have migrated and settled in Parthia/Khorasan where they had become the ruling aristocracy. A certain Arsaces (Arshak), Parni governor of Macedonian Bactria, had unsuccessfully revolted and had fled to Khorasan (*c.*250 BC). He put himself at the head of the Parni, who had by that time identified themselves with the Parthians, and led a Parthian revolt against the Macedonian Seleucids. Success enabled him to establish a Parthian dynasty in the former Achaemenid lands. Claiming descent from the Achaemenid king, Artaxerxes II, Arses declared himself King of Parthia (*c.*247 BC). In the course of time (*c.* 150 BC), Parthia annexed all the former Persian lands from their Seleucid masters. On the eastern side of the River Tigris, Parthian progress was checked by Tigran the Great of Armenia, until his own empire in Mesopotamia fell to them when he submitted to Pompeius (*c.*63 BC). They then collided with the Romans. Tigran died in 55 BC, absolute and independent monarch of his vast homelands, acknowledged legitimate holder of the title of King of Kings.

Taking a strictly conservative estimate, the above review gives the kingdom of Armenia a period of 276 years of complete independence, from Mithranes to Tigran the Great (331–55 BC), with two or three very brief interruptions. Add to that period the 57 years of Orontes I's reign, who was king in all but name, and the 13 years of King Orontes II's rule, and two continuous, independent dynasties are revealed, spanning a period of 346 years.

The reader may judge for himself whether during that period the ordinary Armenian folk, populating those enormous territories, were aware of being anything but a free people — as free as, say, an ordinary Persian. Indeed, it might be suggested that the Armenians were in a happier situation than their southern neighbours, if for no other reason than that of the geophysical character of their land of mountains and valleys in which they could carry on their daily tasks without any interference. There were no armies marching to and fro across Armenia, in contrast to Mesopotamia and Persia/Parthia. Armenia's mountain districts were peopled by fierce tribes headed by powerful native nobility under recognised ruling kings, while in the valleys and plains the peaceful cultivator provided the necessary economic resources. The people had never known a strong foreign domination, had never been conquered. Punitive expeditions, it is true, had extorted from them admissions of conquest and tribute; but they had never been subject to a strange governor supported by a loyal army of barbarians. Whether their kings were descended from *nominal* satraps or not matters little; it suffices to say that they were representative of their people and ruled through the power and loyalty of their nobles. In fact, the kingdom of Armenia and (neighbouring) Pontus were the only two states which may be said to have born any resemblance to our idea of a nation; and although they may perhaps have been less democratic than the townships of Syria and western Asia Minor, they were undoubtedly more united and homogeneous than any of the other states or principalities in the tract of country under discussion.[20]

In the early centuries AD, the countries west of the Euphrates in Asia Minor had been integrated within the Romano-Byzantine empire. East of the Euphrates, Armenia remained, down to about the middle of the fifth century, the only country with a distinct identity and continuous national history stretching back over many centuries. This is not the impression that a reader of Armenian history in a standard text receives. It is true that Armenia was sometimes subservient to Rome/Byzantium or Persia/Parthia, which is the experience of most countries — perhaps all countries — *vis-à-vis* their neighbours. But there were long periods, ignored by most (but not all) classical writers and certainly by many European historians (whose sources are the classical writers), when Armenian diplomacy played off one dominant power against another, supporting with its military might, especially its celebrated cavalry, first one side then the other. But such policies have invariably been misinterpreted and, instead of crediting Armenia with its diplomatic astuteness in order to survive the aggressions of its powerful neighbours, it is persistently alleged to be a client state of Persia/Parthia, Macedonia or Rome; its brief periods of misfortune being thus emphasised, and ignored as if it were a colony of one or another power. This is stressed by the foreign royal dynastic names of the kings of Armenia.

If that principle of subservience were applied, say, to England, then we would see quite factual situations in which the Viking-Normans involved the English in their wars with France; the House of Orange involved England in its Franco-Dutch wars and the king of the House of Hanover took England into his country's wars with France, Prussia and Austria. But in every case the descendants of the foreign kings adopted England as the country of their primary concern, rather than those of their forefathers. The Armenian kings were no henchmen of Persia or Parthia; most of the time they were independent kings of an independent people. They were certainly closer in character to Achaemenid Persia and to the later Parthian Arsacids than to Rome. They were especially close to the Parthians in their relatively unaggressive attitudes and in honouring treaties and seeking peace rather than war, sometimes to the point of naivety by modern standards, educated as our diplomatists are in the principles laid down by Niccolò Machiavelli.

The ancient caravan routes were no doubt busy with the burdens of trade from China, India and Persia, travelling towards the ports of the Black Sea and the Mediterranean. The prosperity of Armenia in those circumstances was such that it stimulated the greed of its neighbours: its palaces so richly furnished, its temples so well endowed that Fame carried the knowledge to the Romans and spurred their unquenchable avarice. The temple of Anahit at Erez (near Erzinjan), for example, housed a golden statue of the goddess, where she was known as the 'Golden Mother'. This had been left intact, venerated and respected by all intruders, until the arrival of the rapacious Romans, in the person of Marcus Antonius (of whom more below), who stole it. As to the magnificent city of Tigranakert, because it had been populated largely by deportees (mainly Greeks from Cappadocia) after Tigran's death it seems to have been abandoned by large sections of its population. Irresponsible city councillors had allowed it to fall into decay and, in course of time, to disappear completely. Probably, little by little, its stone buildings and city walls were dismantled and the material used for other purposes. But for some centuries yet to come, it remained, by the very nature of its geographical position, an important bastion of war and commerce. We hear of it again a century later, as a target for Rome's general Corbulo campaigning against Armenia's King Trdat-Tiridates I.

Artavasd-Artavasdes II (55–33 BC)

Tigran's surviving son and successor, Artavasd (Artavasdes II, 55–33 BC), ascended the throne of still a powerful, independent state. His coins (see Plate 13B) show he continued to use his father, the emperor's title of King of Kings. He had, like so many of his predecessors and successors, to exercise his diplomatic skills to keep in check the superpowers — the foreigners from Rome and his more civilised neighbours, the Parthians. In Rome, the aged senator Crassus was at last granted his amibition to seek glory in the East. The Senate appointed him pro-consul of Syria. It did not give him a mandate for war with Parthia. But Crassus thought that it would be easy to break the power of Parthia; to make a fortune far surpassing those of Lucullus and Pompeius, by controlling, ostensibly on behalf of Rome, the trade of Asia, although at that time (*c.*54 BC) Parthia was at peace with Rome and had no aggressive intentions. On arriving in Syria he behaved more like a usurer than a general, whose first task might have been to secure the strategic fortresses of Babylon and Seleucia-on-Tigris. He wasted many days in computing the revenues of the cities and neglecting his duty as a general to see that his soldiers were disciplined and exercised.

The pompous Roman arrived in Asia, ignorant of the terrain over which he was to lead his legions, ignorant of the military strength of Armenia and Parthia, ignorant of military strategy in the Near East and too complacent to take advice, and ignorant, above all, of the manner in which the ephemeral Parthian cavalry harassed its enemies, led them into waterless deserts or swampy marshes, where they were smothered and suffocated in dust and sand or sunk into bogs of mud. In those distressing situations, hot, tired and laden with useless armour or heavy leather equipment, they would be shot at by arrows which could pierce steel, by veteran, mounted bowmen, galloping past like a tornado.

Crassus, a stubborn old man, with only his avarice for the gold of Asia in mind, ignored the Armenian king Artavasd's advice to march through northern Mesopotamia, through Edessa, to the riverlands of the Tigris and the mountain paths of Armenia, where Parthian cavalry could not tread, even if the king had permitted them to cross his frontiers. Crassus arrogantly brushed aside the friendly recommendation and chose, against all the protestations of his own counsellers, to go by the 'direct' route across the sandy wilderness of Syria and the wastelands of

Babylonia. Artavasd then knew of the disaster that was quite soon to overtake the Romans. So, as Plutarch puts it, 'he went his way' and quickly came to terms with his powerful neighbour, the Parthian king, Orodes II. Armenia was no 'client state', as some historians would have us believe. Artavasd, for example, in this instance could choose his friends or allies. He did so, and gave his sister in marriage to the Parthian crown prince, Pacorus.

Crassus's obedient legions followed their besotted leader, while the Parthian cavalry slaughtered them with their powerful arrows, fired from galloping horses and the lances and swords of their followers finished the slaughter. That was the decisive battle of Carrhae (53 BC), which told Rome that it could never occupy the lands beyond the Euphrates, marking the frontiers of Persia and Babylonia. The remnants of the army took shelter in Carrhae. Crassus was eventually captured, murdered and decapitated. The fate of Crassus in Asia would have assuaged the sorrows and pains of Spartacus, leader of the great slave revolt in Italy (73–71 BC). He would have rejoiced if he had witnessed the torments of Crassus when the Parthians flung his son's head amidst the Roman host. It was Crassus the Lean who had put down the slaves' revolt by the indiscriminate massacre of thousands of men, women and children. For good measure, he finished that work by lining both sides of the Appian Way with a thousand and more of crucified bodies, many of which were seen to be writhing in tortured pain three days after crucifixion. It sickened even the hardened hearts of those who had carried out his orders.

In the meantime, far away in the fastnesses of north-east Armenia, on the banks of the beautiful, fast-flowing Araxes, and behind the ramparts of the Armenian capital, Artashat (Artaxata), the marriage of Parthia and Armenia in the persons of their respective prince and princess, was being celebrated. Plutarch (Everyman II, *Crassus*, p. 302) describes the celebrations and the dramatic events that took place during the festivities:

> Their feastings and entertainment in Artaxata in consequence were very sumptuous, and various Grecian compositions, suitable to the occasion, were recited before them. For Hyrodes [Orodes] was not ignorant of the Greek language and literature, and Artavasdes was so expert in it, that he wrote tragedies and orations and histories, some of which are still extant. When the head of Crassus was brought to the door, the

tables were just taken away, and one Jason ... was singing the scene in the Bacchae of Euripides. ... He was receiving much applause, when Sillaces, coming to the room, and having made obeisance to the king, threw down the head of Crassus into the midst of the company. The Parthians receiving it with joy and acclamations. Jason ... taking up the head of Crassus, and acting the part of a bacchante in her frenzy, in a rapturous, impassioned manner, sang the lyric passages:

'We've hunted down a mighty chase to-day,
and from the mountain bring the noble prey,'

to the great delight of the company.

The historical narrative continues with the appearance of Mark Antony in Armenia, at the head of his victorious legions. The Armenian king, Parthia's ally since the year 53 BC, appeared to submit. There was no formal peace treaty — Armenia and Rome were technically still at war; there were no guarantees 'no towns were occupied, no hostages taken, no garrisons left [Antony probably could not spare any troops for garrisoning]; in spring 36 BC Antony struck a coin with the Armenian tiara, as though Armenia was his. Armenia's regular policy was to maintain independence by playing off Parthia against Rome, but as between them her sympathies, like her civilisation, were Parthian.' After his battle with Antony, Artavasd maintained an understanding with Phraates, the Parthian king. Antony's 'preparations had thoroughly alarmed Asia; the kings of Media had joined Parthia, as perhaps Elymais did also; Asia was closing her ranks against the Roman, and Armenia could not well hold aloof'[21] (ibid.). The defeated Artavasd was required to guide Antony over the Armenian mountains to enable the Romans to descend upon the Parthians from the north, in order to avoid a repetition of the disaster of Carrhae, which had resulted from the stubborn, mistaken strategy of Crassus. 'Artavasdes, whose troops formed the greater part of the escort, rode off home before the attack; the two legions were annihilated and their eagles added to the Parthian collection ... the siege-train was burnt or carried off; the victory was as decisive as could be.'[22] After a number of unsuccessful attempts to retrieve his losses, and with winter fast approaching, Antony had to retreat to Armenia, guided by a

244

Median who, taking them first to Tabriz, brought them to the Armenian frontier.

Here it must be emphasised that Artavasd had not 'betrayed' (Strabo, XI.xiii.4) Antony. Armenia was, as has already been stated, technically at war with Rome. In spite of that, the Romans were faithfully guided over Armenian territory to the Parthian field, and when Antony, defeated, weak and in need of help, fled into Armenia, he and the remainder of his troops could have been slaughtered to a man. Instead, they were received hospitably. Plutarch (Everyman III, *Antony*, pp. 303-4) describes the situation: 'But when they were got over on the other side (of the River Araxes) and found themselves in Armenia, just as if land was now sighted after a storm at sea, they kissed the ground for joy shedding tears and embracing each other in their delight. But taking their journey through a land that abounded in all sorts of plenty, they ate, after their long want, with that excess of everything they met with, that they suffered from dropsies and dysentries.'

In spite of this unexpected Armenian hospitality, and in order to present himself in Egypt to his beloved Cleopatra in a triumphant light, Antony inveigled Artavasd and his family to his tent on a pretext of a demonstration of friendship. He then treacherously 'seized him, bound him, and carried him (and his family) to Alexandria, and there led him in his Triumph in that city'.[23] Antony then presented the king and his family to Cleopatra. She tortured them mercilessly in unsuccessful attempts to discover the secret repository of the Armenian crown jewels, until they all died. Antony was not at all the romantic hero depicted by the genius of Shakespeare. In reality he personified the rapacious Romans in Asia quite as faithfully as the grasping Crassus Dives.

The shadowy figures that followed King Artavasd to the Armenian throne defied the Romans from time to time, and for brief periods seized the reins of royal power. Only two years after Antony's departure, Prince Artashes, Artavasd's eldest son, recovered the Armenian throne and promptly massacred all the Roman traders in Armenia. Armenia and Media were lost to Rome. The last ruler of the House of Artashes (Artaxias) was Queen Erato, who asserted her sovereignty, in spite of Roman intimidations. She was dethroned by the Romans for the second and last time in AD 14. The Artaxiads had by then been the royal house of Armenia, continously, for some 200 years. Antony commemorated his Asiatic campaign by striking a coin bearing on one side his own head and the legend 'Armenia Conquered'. That speaks volumes for the difficulties and failures that the Romans had experienced, over a long period, in their attempts to subdue Armenia.

The social and political organisation of Great Armenia in the Artaxiad epoch was to some extent a replica of that of the Urartian monarchy. Like it, the monarchy of Tigranes II [the Great] was a federation of States, great and small, Armenian and foreign, held together by the ties of political subordination. Overlord of numerous kings, Tigranes bore, in imitation of the Iranian emperors, the title of *Basileis Basileon* (King of Kings), which was also the exact equivalent of the Urartian *erili erilaue*, and, as in the case of his Urartian predecessors, his was a theophanic kingship. Moreover the dynasts who accepted the superior authority of the King of Kings appear to have formed, as in Urartu, two groups: the tributaries and the vassals. The rulers of the kingdoms outside Armenia belonged, obviously, to the former category. At the same time, we hear of 'many kings' paying court to Tigranes and among them of four in particular who remained in constant attendance on him. These, evidently, were not foreign monarchs of the calibre of those of Atropatene or of Commagene, but, plainly, local and lesser Armenian dynasts. The reference to the four kings, it will be seen, leaves no doubt of this, and is, besides, an important witness to the continued existence of the Armenian dynastic aristocracy under the Artaxiad Great King. These Armenian dynasts, and also temple-states of equally immemorial antiquity, formed thus the second group: the vassals. As for the rest of Armenian society, the crystallisation of its subdivisions at the non-dynastic levels in the Artaxiad epoch ... as in the Urartian polity, there existed a body of the ordinary, non-sovereign *noblesse*.[24]

Political chaos prevailed in Armenia after AD 14. Romans and Parthians fought over the possession of Armenia, supported respectively by pro-Roman and pro-Parthian Armenian factions. During the course of that struggle, the Armenian northern capital, Artashat (Artaxata) was put to the torch and the city of Tigranakert and a royal crown of Armenia were captured by the Roman general Corbulo (AD 60).[25] After nearly 50 years of struggle, the superpowers, Parthia and Rome, agreed at the

Peace of Rhandia (AD 63) that Prince Trdat (Tiridates), brother of King Vologases I (AD 51–80) of the Parthian Royal House of Arsacid (Arshakes), should rule Armenia under Roman tutelage: a face-saving scheme for both the warring powers. To that end, Tiridates (63–100) travelled to Rome, escorted by 3000 cavalrymen, nobles and dignitaries, where he received the crown of Armenia from the hands of Nero, amidst great pomp and ceremony and festivities and games in the Forum.

A fascinating possibility connected with this event in Armenian history is the suggestion that 'the episode of the pilgrimage of the Magi (from Persia-Parthia), which is recounted in the Matthaean prologue (Chapter ii) to the Gospels, has been precipitated by an impact which may have been made on the imagination of the internal proletariat of the Hellenic world by an historic visit of a party of Magi, not to the infant Jesus of Bethlehem, but to the adult Emperor Nero at Rome, in the suite of Tiridates, when the Arsacid King of Armenia came to pay his respects to his Roman suzerain in AD 66.'[26] On his return to Armenia, Tiridates rebuilt his capital, Artaxata.

Notes

1. Greater Armenia, as described. Lesser Armenia, in early history, was on the eastern side of the Euphrates.
2. R.N. Frye, *The Heritage of Persia* (Wiedenfeld & Nicolson, 1965), p. 277 n. 35.
3. The first monarchy of Armenia was that of Urartu; the second was that of the Orontids.
4. Toumanoff, *Studies in Christian Caucasian History* (Georgetown University Press, 1963) p. 74.
5. Arnold Toynbee, *A Study of History*, VII. p. 665.
6. Toumanoff, pp. 77-8 n. 86.
7. Khorenatsi (II.50) seems to have anticipated the attack of the Alani upon Armenia by at least a century. According to Jospehus (*Wars*, VII.viii.4) they invaded Armenia *c.* AD 70. But long before that, Pompey encountered them in his Mithradatic Wars. The Alani, a tribe of Scythians, perhaps the Sarmatians of Polybius, in southern Russia, are first heard of *c.*160 BC, only a year before the death of Artashes. Therefore, it is quite possible for an unrecorded (by classical writers) attack — recorded by Khorenatsi (whose source in this instance does not seem to be known, although Professor Robert Thomson ascribes it to Josephus, spuriously quoted by Khorenatsi, according to Thomson) to have taken place in the early years of the reign of Artashes and for him to have married, in accordance with the legend, the Alani princess, Satenik. In

which case she would probably have been Tigran the Great's grand-mother.

8. Here an example can be given of the way in which some Western European writers dismiss — indeed, reject — the existence of an independent Armenian kingdom to support their Graeco-Roman bias. The following quotation is from two co-authors of a work concerned with this period: 'Artaxias' pretensions to independence, though (Antiochus IV) allowing him to remain as a vassal king, subject to payment of annual tribute'. The authors make no mention of the Macedonian's dishonourable breaking of the Treaty of Apamea; also, they lead the reader to believe that the King of Armenia was a usurper without royal antecedents ('pretensions'), paying tribute not for a mere one year, when Antiochus died, but for many years. In fact Artashes was King of Armenia for 29 years, and outlived Antiochus by five years, paying tribute to no one, after the first year.

9. Tigran allowed Mithradates to retain Colchis, and after his marriage to Mithradates' daughter, Cleopatra, gave him Armenia Minor. René Grousset, (*Histoire*, p. 85) expresses the relationship of the two monarchs, succinctly: 'dans l'alliance qui fut alors conclus entre les deux souverains, Mithradates faisait un peu figure client de Tigran'.

10. Among the last of the 3000-year-old cuneiform scripts was that which dates Antiochus IV who was killed by a Parthian arrow in 129 BC.

11. M. Huniani, *Justini Epitoma Historiarum Philippicarum Pompei Trogi*, XL.1, 1-4, English translation by J.S. Watson (London, 1853, p. 271); R. Ghirshman, *Iran* (Penguin, London, 1965), p. 251.

12. Toumanoff, *op. cit.*, p. 202.

13. Archias is said to have written a poem (among other works) on the Mithridatic Wars in honour of Lucullus.

14. Arshak Safrastian, 'The Armenian Empire in Syria', *Arm. Rev.* 23, no. 4 (1970), pp. 15-18. 'The Reported Capture of Tigranakert by Lucullus in 69 BC', *Arm. Rev.* 22 (1969), p. 41. I am indebted to Mr E. Gulbekian for having brought Dr Safrastian's articles to my attention.

15. Ibid.

16. Ibid.

17. Tigran the Great had four sons: the first was killed in battle; the second was executed by his father for treason; the third was the traitorous prince introduced above; the fourth was Artavasd II who succeeded his father in 55 BC.

18. Tarn, 'The Heritage of Alexander', CAH VI.ii. pp. 464, 466, 468.

19. To have any hold at all over the infant Orontid monarchy, Seleucus I had to have the alliance of the ambitious Iberian royal house of the first Pharnabazids. Thus, the Armenian kings were briefly (some 50 years) obliged to pay, probably a nominal tribute to the Syrio-Macedonian Seleucus I and Antiochus I. As Professor Toumanoff puts it, 'the Iberian alliance ... needed by the Seleucids in order to hold the Orontid Monarchy within a pincer movement'. It was a 'tenuous' hold, p. 81 n. 104, p. 449.

20. Sir Mark Sykes, *The Caliph's Last Heritage* (London, 1915), p. 25.

21. Tarn 'The War of the East Against the West', CAH X.ii. pp. 72-4.

22. Tarn, 'The Dream of Empire', CAH X.ii. p. 79.

23. J.G.C. Anderson, 'The Eastern Frontier Under Augustus', CAH X.ix. p. 279.

24. Toumanoff, *op. cit.*, pp. 77-8.

25. Tacitus, *Annals*, XIV.25.

26. Arnold J. Toynbee, *A Study of History* (Oxford University Press, 1954) VI, pp. 455-6, quoting Pliny, *Historia Naturalis*, Book XXX, Ch. 2; cf. Suetonius, *Life of Nero*, Ch. 13.

23

The Royal House of Arshak (the Arsacids)

Trdat-Tiridates I (AD 63–100)

The Armenian branch of the Royal House of Arshak (Arsaces) of Parthia (the Arsacids) was thus established. It endured for 400 years, outlasting its Parthian parent by 200 years. Trdat I ruled for almost 40 years down to AD 100. The independence of his successors and the integrity of the Armenian frontiers had been maintained, only interrupted by brief periods, as, for example, in 115, when the Emperor Trajan (98–117) annexed Armenia as Rome's easternmost province for a mere two years. If Armenia had been a true and loyal client state of Rome, there would have been no need for Trajan to colonise it. The truth of the matter seems to be that after Trdat's Roman coronation (a diplomatic, face-saving, exercise, agreed between Vologases I of Parthia and Corbulo), Armenia reverted to her ancient close connections with Persia/Parthia where the roots of its royal dynasties were to be found from the earliest times (as in the cases of the foreign royal dynasties of some European countries, which do not markedly affect the continuity of the respective national histories). Parthia 'continued to include the large, *nominally* vassal kingdoms of Armenia, Media, Atropatene, Hyrcania, Sacastene and Persis, of which Armenia and Media were ruled by members of the Arsacid house'.[1]

Trajan died only two years after his invasion of Armenia. His successor, Hadrian (117–38), decided to set more easily accessible limits to the far-flung frontiers of the Empire; and Armenia, embattled in its Araratian mountains, was certainly not easily accessible. Rome's eastern frontier was fixed at the Euphrates, and 'to greater Armenia he [Hadrian] gave back its king'.[2] That

king was Valarsh I (alias Vologases, 117–42). But it was probably Valarsh II (*c*.215) who perpetuated the memory of his very
brief reign by giving his name to the new city of Kainipolis (Nor
Kagak), originally planned by Marcus Aurelius's general, Priscus,
in atonement (it is alleged) for the destruction by his forces of the
old capital of Artaxata in AD 163 — razed for the second time
Corbulo having destroyed it first in AD 58. Thus, Vagharshapat
(Kainipolis renamed) was established as the new capital of
Armenia (*c*.185) and eventually the seat of the Katholicos of all
the Armenians, which we now know as the holy city of
Echmiadzin (the Only-Begotten Descended) near Erevan.

Trdat-Tridates II usually called Khosrov I (Chosroes I) (217–52)

Long before the end of the Armenian Arsacid period, Persian
newcomers, the Sassanids, has expelled the Parthians from Persia
(*c*.225). The home of the Sassanids, as that of the great House of
the Achaemenids, was Fars, in south Persia. The traditions of
Iran and the teachings of Zoroaster had been stubbornly
preserved.

King Ardashir of the House of Sassan led a successful revolt
against King Artabanuz V of Parthia in AD 224, in which the
Parthian king was killed. Ardashir then seized Ctesiphon and the
crown of his Achaemenid ancestors (AD 226). The Parthians,
however, had friends among ruling kings and princes who, over
the far-flung empire of Parthia, saw dangers to themselves from
the new regime in Persia. The most closely involved, most
powerful and most influential of these rulers was the Arsacid
King Khosrov (Chosroes) I of Armenia also known as Trdat II
(217–52)[3] who

> opened the gates of the Caucasus in order to bring in Scythian
> aid and received support from Rome. The powerful king of the
> Kushans, at whose court members of the family of Artabanus
> had sought refuge, also placed forces at the disposal of the
> coalition. Only one of the great Parthian families, however —
> that of Karen — joined the movement against Ardashir; all the
> others hastened to assure the new sovereign of their loyalty.

Ardashir smashed the coalition in a series of battles, and by
bribery persuaded some of the allies to abandon what was

clearly a hopeless struggle. The Romans and Scythians withdrew, and the Kushan King retired after two years of hostilities (226–28). In the end, the king of Armenia was left to continue the fight alone. He put up a stubborn resistance and was defeated but only after no less than ten years of fighting. Ardashir was now master of an empire extending from the Euphrates to Merv, Herat, and Seistan ... Conflict with Rome ... ended ... in the reoccupation by the Persians of the two important fortresses of Nisibis and Carrhae.[4] Ardashir had much fighting to do to consolidate his rule ... His boundaries did not include Armenia.[5]

The thoughtful reader should be able to assess the strength of Armenia in the time of Khosrov, which could persist for 12 years (10 of them quite alone) against an enemy who had destroyed Parthian might and had demoralised not only the Kushan empire, but Rome itself. The Armenian defeat resulted only from the assassination of Khosrov by Anak Pahlavi (Parthian), who had been bribed by Ardashir to commit the murder.

The political events which preceded the reign and conversion to Christianity of Trdat III (286–342), son of Khosrov, are given at some length by Edward Gibbon in his splendid literary style: the Parthian abhorrence of the Sassanid usurpers overflowed into Armenia, where 'of the many princes of that ancient race, Chosroes (Khosrov), King of Armenia, had alone preserved both his life and his independence. He defended himself ... above all by his own courage. Invincible in arms during a thirty years' war, he was at length assassinated by the emissaries of Sapor (Shapur, son of Ardashir), King of Persia (252).'[6] The infant son of Khosrov, 'young Tiridates, the future hope of his country, was saved by the fidelity of a servant. [For the following twenty years] Sapor spread devastation and terror on either side of the Euphrates' (ibid.). Then came the Roman legions, led by their Emperor Valerian in person, to defend Rome's Asiatic provinces. In the ensuing encounter with the Persians near Edessa, Valerian was vanquished and taken prisoner (AD 260) by Shapur — an unprecedented defeat sustained by Rome, in which a Roman emperor was taken prisoner. He was then loaded with chains and, 'invested in the Imperial purple, was exposed to the multitude'.[7] Valerian died, an insulted and humiliated captive.

Trdat-Tiridates III, the Great (287–330)

King Trdat (or Drtad) III was educated in the court of Rome: 'He signalised his youth by deeds of valour and displayed matchless dexterity, as well as strength in every martial exercise.'[8] He was physically so powerful that (as told by Moses of Khoren (II.79)), he could seize two wild bulls by the horns and break the horns off with his bare hands. In a chariot race, when his opponent was about to overtake him, he leapt off his chariot and stopped the charging horses and the roaring chariot of his rival.

The purpose of quoting those tales, and such others of the same character that might appear in these pages, is to perpetuate some of the heroic legends which were (and perhaps are still) told to children in Armenian primary schools. There is, however, at least one authentic event in which Trdat held back, single-handed, a group of soldiers who sought to assassinate his bene-factor, Licinius. The latter's gratitude brought Trdat to the Emperor Diocletian's attention, and 'in the third year of his reign he [Trdat] was invested with the Kingdom of Armenia'. Finally, Agathangelus (I.4; fifth-century biographer of Trdat III) records that a Gothic chieftain challenged the Roman Emperor Dio-cletian to meet him in single combat. Trdat successfully stood in for the emperor. The latter gratefully gave Trdat an army with which to expel the Persians from Armenia, in his own right — not for Rome. The events influenced Rome to turn a blind eye to the introduction of the Christian faith by Trdat as the state religion of Armenia (301). During 26 years, Armenia had suffered the hardships of a foreign yoke. Led by Trdat, the loyal Armenian princes with their zealous troops, expelled the Persians from Armenian territory, and the warrior king carried his arms even into northern Mesopotamia. The boundaries of Armenia were extended to Media, which included the vast province of Atro-patene, down to the great city of Ecbatana.

In the meantime, the son of King Khosrov's assassin, Gregory, an Arsacid prince, had taken refuge in Caesara (Cappadocia), where, from his boyhood, he had been instructed in, and imbued by the Christian faith. Either because he was unaware of his father's crime or upon an impulse of evangelical vocation, he travelled to Armenia, to Vagharshapat, for the purpose of con-verting his boyhood friend, now King of Armenia, to the Christian faith. His identity as the son of Khosrov's murderer was promptly betrayed to the king, who threw him after torture, into a pit. However, he miraculously survived his 13 year ordeal, sustained with food provided by a pious widow. King Trdat the Great had no doubt witnessed the persecution of Christians in Rome during the reigns of Decius (249–51) and Valerian (253–60) and Diocletian (285–305). He brought with him to Armenia the ruthless practice of torture and death to those who defied a Caesar or king and refused to worship the effigies of traditional gods and goddesses. Before Gregory's appearance, the king's victims included the virgins of a convent in Rome who, led by their respected abbess, Gayanē, fled to Armenia from the lustful attentions of the Emperor. But in Armenia they were horrified to find a ruler in the image of Diocletian. The beautiful, high-born Hripsimē rejected and fled from King Trdat's passion for her (Agathangelus, XIX). She and her companions were pursued, overtaken, bound with cords and, with great cruelty, put to death.[9] These and other persecutions of the many Christians in Armenia finally brought divine retribution upon the king in the form which we recognise today as the frightful affliction of lycanthropy. He imagined himself to have been transformed into a beast, eating grass on all fours. That situation recalls a similar calamity experienced by King Nebuchadnezzar of Babylon (Dan. IV.33). His sister's entreaties at last persuaded Trdat to release Gregory from the pit, and he was immediately cured of his dreadful affliction. A rough punishment had shown a rough king the error of his ways. He embraced the Christian faith for himself and his people, forbade the worship of idols, and zealously set about destroying them. Many an Armenian monument of beauty and artistic interest to posterity were obliterated for ever, including the golden statue of the great mother goddess, Anahit of Erez (Acilisene).[10] First stolen by Mark Antony, it must have been among the other treasures carried off by him from Asia which were restored to their rightful owners by Augustus.[11]

Having vilified King Trdat for his initial scepticism of the new faith, we can turn again to the pages of Edward Gibbon's *History* for the more favourable comment: 'In Armenia, the renowned Tiridates had long enjoyed the peace and glory which he deserved by his valour and fidelity to the cause of Rome. The first alliance which he maintained with Constantine was productive of spiritual as well as temporal benefits; by the conversion of Tiridates the character of a saint was applied to that of a hero, the Christian faith was preached and established from the Euphrates to the shores of the Caspian' (II. p. 368).

While the story of the legendary events preceding the conversion of King Trdat are sacrosanct in Armenian folklore, a fragment of the Italian translation of Agathangelus (p. 145) which has
fortunately been preserved, records the original state of affairs
during Trdat's reign in Armenia. It seems that there was, at that
time, a series of great epidemics sweeping over the country,
afflicting large numbers of the people, including the king himself,
with such ailments as leprosy, palsy, dropsy or insanity. Then,
Gregory, whom everyone believed to be long dead, appeared,
and his faith cured the king. The news spread throughout the
kingdom, and the afflicted and invalids flocked to the capital
Vagharshapat, where on being cured and on being seen to be
cured, the whole nation embraced the Christian faith, introduced
by Saint Gregory, which had miraculously cured king and
people, and exorcised the evil spirits which had held sway over as
pagan land.

Now, the traditional date of the establishment of Christianity
by the Armenians as their state religion (which did not permit the
practice of any other religion) is the year 301. Recent scholarship,
however, has moved it to the year 314. This is highly controversial, but even if 314 were accepted, that would still maintain
the Armenian lead as the first state to embrace Christianity and
to legislate against the practice of paganism. For Constantine the
Great's Edict of Toleration (March 313) was more liberal, indeed,
diplomatic. It allowed the worship of the ancient pagan gods. But
the emperor and most probably all his courtiers (if they wished to
remain in favour at court) and large sections of the people
accepted the new faith. The soldiery who had taken part in the
successful and decisive battles before Constantine coud establish
his authority over the whole of the Roman empire, fought in the
name of Christ. Eusebius (*Vit. const.* I. xxviii-xxxii), personifying
the emotions of his own generation as well as those of the
converts to the new faith in the time of the Emperor, describes
Constantine's religious experiences, which ultimately led him
and his troops to victory.[12] The people who wished to follow the
precepts of the faith were openly allowed to do so. Christianity
was universally embraced and at least its ecclesiastical ceremonies, if not the teachings of Jesus, were observed. The introduction of the new religion was facilitated by the symbolism of
the Cross, common to both Christ and the Sun God. The state
tolerated all other religions within the vast empire until the edicts
of Theodosius the Great (381) initiated the persecution of the

adherents of the ancient religions, thenceforth described as 'pagans'.

Reference was made above to Constantine's diplomatic and unhurried approach to the introduction of the new religion into his vast realms. Conversely, Trdat savagely enforced it, mercilessly persecuting any dissidents. It is feasible that his fanaticism was not unmixed with a politically-oriented desire to unite the Armenians against the incursions of Persian Mazdaism. There was also peace during this period of transition because of Trdat's early alliance with Caesar Galerius (AD 296–7) against the Persians and his early friendship with Diocletian. Armenia remained unmolested during the reigns of Diocletian's successors, with the exception of a war with Caesar Maximin. But the appearance of Constantine (*c.*320) brought peace. Whereupon the Armenian king and his bishop St Gregory travelled to Constantine's court, at that time probably in Illyria (Agathangelus CXXVI points to the very distant city of Rome).[13] The aged visitors were received with the highest honours. The emperor prostrated himself at the feet of the saint. Then, with much pomp, the two Armenian leaders, of Church and state respectively, were escorted back to their native land, after having, perhaps, concluded a formal treaty with the great emperor, in order to confirm and strengthen relationships with their powerful neighbour (Agath. CXXVI).

Khosrov II, Kotak (the Young) 331–8

Trdat the Great was succeeded by his son, Khosrov II known as Kotak or the Young. The early years of his reign were peaceful. There followed a great Hunnish invasion which he repulsed, though Vagharshapat was destroyed by fire. Barely had he recovered from that encounter, when the Persians under Shapur II (310–79) invaded Armenia from the east. Khosrov was the victor of the first battle which took place near Lake Van. Thenceforth, with Byzantine assistance, the Armenians, led by their king, repulsed the Persian onslaughts until his death. His son Tiran (or Tigranes V) was a lukewarm Christian, while the Katholicos Yusik, was a pious and intransigent bigot, with an overmighty attitude towards his king. A bitter feud between Church and state, at a politically critical moment, resulted in a division of the people. On the king's orders, the Katholicos was beaten to death by a mob. The instability of the country following that event made it possible for the Persians to kidnap the Armenian king, to blind him and to hand him over to Shapur (350). (Faustus of Byzantium XII,XX).

Thenceforth, Armenia entered an era of over 400 years which might well be described as political oblivion. The Persians invaded, this time a leaderless and divided country, while at the same time (339–40) a great massacre of Christians in Persia was perpetrated. Then, the Byzantine emperor led the imperial troops from the west and achieved a decisive victory over the Persians. The peace treaty between the two great powers which followed (387), included a clause forbidding Byzantium from supporting the Armenian, King Arshak II (Arsaces), son of Tiran 350–67, in any future Armenian conflict with Persia. Unfortunately, too, Arshak was no diplomat, no statesman. The devious nature of his activities for or against his mighty Byzantine and Persian neighbours soon brought their joint wrath upon Armenia. It was forthwith dismembered, the larger portion falling under the suzerainty of the Persian Sassanids and the remainder becoming an extension of the Byzantine empire. This Arshak (Arsaces) II's successors were shadowy figures completely subservient to Byzantium or Persia. The Armenian Arsacid dynasty struggled on down to 428 when the last Arsacid king of Armenia, Artashes III, died. The Sassanian monarch installed a Persian governor — a *marzpan* — to rule the land.

The Dark Ages

In the meantime, while Byzantine policy aimed to absorb Armenia completely, Persia was at first more conciliatory, particularly as the Armenian armed forces would be more amenable under such a policy. The Armenian *marzpans* (or margraves), a status higher than that of a satrap, appointed by the Persian king, perpetuated the old feudal and the hereditary laws, and the estates of the *nakharars* (or feudal lords) were transmitted, as before, in accordance with the principle of primogeniture. The Byzantine emperors, however, passed laws over the parts of Armenia they ruled which replaced that principle of succession, gave rights over parts of the inheritance of the father's estates to younger sons as well as to daughters, and thus fragmented the great and powerful Armenian feudal estates.

In the fifth century, the Persian Sassanian king, Yazdagird II (439–57) tried to impose Mazdaism on Christian Armenia, in order to facilitate the absorbtion of the Armenians into the Persian hegemony. This brought to a head an already deteriorating relationship between the two countries. The Armenians, under their commander Vardan Mamikonian, fought valorously a decisive battle on the field of Avarayr (near Nakhichevan), on 26 May 451, in defence of their faith, against enormous odds. Although defeated amidst awful carnage, their persistent guerrilla tactics in the mountainous regions, for over 30 years, until 484, were at last rewarded with freedom of religious worship. That sacrifice was to be obstinately repeated again and again over the following centuries. The Battle of Avarayr is celebrated, and its valiant heroes mourned and honoured each May in every Armenian church, all over the world. The Armenian historian, Eghishe, a contemporary of Prince Vardan Mamikonian, describes those momentous events in his *History of Vardan and the Armenian Wars.*

After 590, when Byzantium was more powerful than Persia, the larger share of Armenia was seized by Byzantium — the territory, that is, west of a line from Tiflis down to Lake Urmia. Armenian rulers (Curopalates) were appointed by the emperor to rule the Armeno-Byzantine territories. This accelerated the slow disintegration of the Armenian polity which the first partition had signalised. It had serious, permanent effects on the historical direction of the country and its people. The wars of the seventh and eighth centuries across Persian Armenia, between the Arab Abbasids and the Byzantine empires, devastated the land. Those who were able, many *nakharars* and their households, and many commoners fled to western Byzantine territory. The *nakharars* were indeed, tempted by offers of great estates in Byzantium in exchange for their land in the east. Thus, the very foundations of the Armenian nation suffered a blow from which it never fully recovered. For so many of the aristocratic families abandoned their estates, that large sections of the people either followed them or found themselves leaderless and at the complete mercy of cruel and savage invaders. The situation improved somewhat from the second half of the ninth century, for about 150 years, when a few of the most powerful Armenian barons, such as the Bagratids and the Artsruni, who were still in Armenia, seized political opportunities to extend their already vast estates in the north and the east, including the Lake Van region. During that period,

Armenia was ruled by a strong territorial aristocracy, yet, it was only a sad shadow of the era when the nobility possessed their own independent kings of the House of Arsaces. Those nobles who stayed and fought

> maintained and perhaps increased their ascendency; they were supported by the obstinate patriotism of the people; and the interval between the overthrow of the ancient and the rise of the medieval kingdom is filled by the almost incessant clash of arms. From the east the pertinacity of the Armenian race is challenged at first by the Persians, eager to convert them to the religion of the Magi, and next by the Arabs, who, after supplanting the Sassanian dynasty, seek to impose upon them the precepts of Islam. The neighbours upon the west are scarcely less obtrusive; and we may discover beneath the religious controversies with their fellow-Christians of the Roman Empire the same fervid self-assertion which has enabled this strange people to preserve, in the face of odds which appear to us to have been overwhelming, the inflexible individuality of their race. While their clergy are resisting the menaces or the blandishments of the Church of the Empire, their nobles are combating the worship of the Persians or of the Mohammedans at the head of the native levies. It thus happened that, when the bonds relaxed which bound the subject states to the Arab caliphate, the Armenians possessed, in their class of nobles as well as in their patriarchate, institutions which had been tested in the furnace of adversity during a period of over 400 years.[14]

In the Arsacid and post-Arsacid period (after 428), 28 Armenian princes or *nakharars*, are named by Professor Cyril Toumanoff, with biographical data. Over the centuries, they were sometimes independent of, sometimes serving under, the Armenian king; sometimes tributaries of Persia, sometimes of Byzantium; sometimes united, sometimes at war with one another. The feudal organisation of Armenia, while it fragmented its defences against external enemies, enabled the country, in the long period, to survive; for neither Byzantines, Persians nor Arabs were able completely to control the whole country. There were always some independent, defiant *nakharars* in their impregnable fortresses. If they could have united, there is little doubt that they would have sustained the independence of the whole of their country. But they were people of their own times. They simply suffered from the medieval, world-wide tradition of individualism and separatism. Our nineteenth-century concept of nationalism, partly stimulated by swift communications between distant parts, was for good or ill, unknown. The following four great aristocratic houses have been chosen from Toumanoff's list (pp. 192–215), as examples and as assessments of the ancient status, privilege, prestige and power that they enjoyed.

The Mamikonian princes 'appear to have been the immemorial dynasts of Tayk, on the Armeno–Georgian confines' (Toumanoff, p. 209). The earliest recorded member of that dynasty seems to have been Mancaeus, who defended Tigranakert against the Romans in 69 BC. In the Armenian monarchy, the Mamikonids held the office of High Constable (*Sparapet*), that is, marshal of all the armed forces of the realm, including, above all, the princely cavalry contingents; which implies a pre-eminence among the kingdom's princes. By the fourth century, the House of Mamikonian had acquired, in addition to its homelands situated in the middle valley of the River Arsanias, half the province of Turuberan. The other half, too, was appended to the great estates when Hamazasp I Mamikonian married Sahak-anoysh, daughter and heiress of St Isaac, the Gregorid, chief prelate of Armenia and descendent of St Gregory the Illuminator, who is regarded as the founder of the Armenian Church. As a result of Hamazasp's marriage to Sahak-anoysh, the Mamikonids became holders of territories of the greatest extent under the Armenian monarchy. The eldest son of that marriage was St Vartan II who led the Armenian insurrection against the Persians and lost his life at the great Battle of Avarayr (451).

From 377 down to 750, eight Mamikonid princes ruled Armenia. Hamazasp II Mamikonian (655–58) was *Curopalates* under Byzantium. (The *Curopalates* were entrusted with the civil administration of the country, while the military command was held by an Armenian general of the armed forces.) In 655, Hamazasp II Mamikonian, acquired the principality of Bznunik from one of the other great Armenian princely houses, that of Rshtuni (see below). That period seems to represent the apogee of Mamikonid power and wealth. After 772, that traditionally Romanophile house began to decline, losing its great estates to the Bagratids in the ninth century, and to the Turks in the twelfth century. They then migrated to Armeno–Cilicia. 'Two Georgian princely Houses [the Liparitids and the T'umanitids] still extant, trace their descent from the Mamikonians. A branch of one of them, that of the Liparitids–Orbeliani, returned to Armenia in 1177 and subsequently formed the third dynasty of Siunia, reigning till the fifteenth century.' The Mamikonians, as implied above, were successfully involved with Byzantine royalty and aristocracy. Their connections with the emperor and his court include: Artabasuds, *comes obsequii,* Curopalates and son-in-law of the Emperor Leo III (717–802); Caesar Bardes (866); the Empress Theodora, consort of the Emperor Theophilus (829–42).

The Princes Rshtuni ruled over the canton of the same name on the southern shores of Lake Van, from their capital city of Vostan. Their territories included the fortified island of Akhtamar on Lake Van, the city of Tosp, on the site of the ancient Urartian capital, Tushpa on the east coast of Lake Van; and the principality of Bznunik (which was acquired by the Mamikonids in the year 655). It is of the utmost interest that the Rshtunis not only occupied the heartlands of ancient Urartu but also appear to derive their name from the Urartian kings, Rusa or Rusha. It is a fascinating conjecture and even a possibility that they were descendants of the Royal House of Urartu. 'Theodore Rshtuni was Ruling High Constable of Armenia, with the Roman title of Patrician (638–*c.*645), and then, having concluded in 653–4 the treaty of protectorate with the Caliphate [he was] Presiding Prince of Armenia', under the Arabs, until his downfall in 655. The estates of Rshtunik passed to the Artsrunis, and the dynasty died during the eighth century, in the Arab period.

The Bagratuni (the House of Bagrat): there are a number of legends concerned with the origin of the Bagratids, which are irrelevant in the context of this skeleton review of the history of Armenia. Bagratid, Viceroy of Syria (83–69 BC), under Tigran the Great, is the first known member of that distinguished family. Early in the fourth century, the Bagratids were reigning in Syspiritis (Ispir), on the south-eastern side of the Black Sea, from their great castle of Subatavan, and 'enfeoffed of the offices of Coronant (*T'agadir*) of Armenia and Guardian of the Moschic Mountains' in that region. From the seventh to the ninth centuries, 12 Bagratid princes held the office of Presiding Prince of Armenia, three of them holding the Byzantine office of *curopalate.* In the Arab period, the Bagratids lost some territories but gained others in their wars against the Arabs, as well as competing Armenian princes. Their gains included the important cities of

Bagaran and Ani, which were to become Bagratid capital cities.

The Artsruni Princes were, like the Artaxiads, related to the ancient Orontid line. They were dispossessed of their original lands in Sophene by the Artaxiads who gave them in exchange large estates on the Median border, in the vicinity of Lake Urmia. By the eleventh century, the Artsruni domains had expanded enormously: their territories included the region from the northern province of Ayrarat down to beyond Lake Urmia, taking in the province of Moxoene to the south of Lake Van. The whole princedom was known as Vaspurakan. The Artsrunis claimed descent from the patricide Assyrian prince Sharezer (Sarasar), son of King Sennacherib, who fled 'to the land of Armenia' (II Kings XIX.37).[15] In 908, Gagik Arsruni, Lord of Vaspurakan, was provoked by his Bagratid suzrain to break away from a rare medieval historical moment of a unified Armenia. Unwittingly, he became a political tool in the hands of his country's enemies for the destruction of Armenia, by accepting a crown from the Caliph of Baghdad, followed by a laudatory appendage of 'King of Kings' from the Byzantine emperor. In 1021, unable to face the dual pressures of the Turkish hordes on the one hand and Byzantine intrigues on the other, Sennacherib-John abdicated in favour of the Emperor Basil II. Byzantium compensated him with vast estates in Cappadocia, together constituting, none the less, only a province of the empire.

There is sufficient information to support the view that a feudal system seems to have come to full fruition during the Arsacid period. This should not be difficult to accept since a feudal, or quasi-feudal system had been established as far back, and beyond, the Achaemenid period, in Urartu, according to assumptions supported by scholarly argument (e.g. Dr Nicolas Adontz, *Histoire d'Arménie*). Feudal traditions in the Arsacid period (*c.* 60–*c.*430) had been so well established that they continued after the demise of the Armenian fourth monarchy (the Arsacid). That feudal hierarchy was headed by four hereditary lords, each holding vast domains, situated on the frontier territories of the kingdom; they were plenipotentiaries in their respective domains. Thus, they were primarily responsible for the defence of the realm, holding the highest offices at the king's court, his chief counsellors and promulgators of his decrees to the people. Plutarch identifies them (in a derogatory spirit, unworthy of a scholar) as the four kings who were always 'waiting on him [Tigran the Great]'.

Whereas that top stratum of the feudal pyramid seems to have disappeared with the end of the monarchy, the next in rank, the hereditary rulers of the princely houses, the *nakharars*, became increasingly important, both in the social organisation of Armenia and in political decision-making. They exercised their inalienable rights over their particular territories, which they jealously guarded, and they honoured their obligations to the king, particularly in time of war when they provided, if required, funds for its prosecution and, especially, contingents of the redoubtable Armenian cavalry. In Arsacid times, their numbers could exceed 100,000. Below the *nakharars* were the free noblemen (*azats*) who had particular functions in the organisation of their respective *nakharar's* domain. They, like all other social grades below them, were subject to taxation. Other classes included the serfs who, though personally free, were attached to their lord's estate; they constituted the infantry in wartime. The city-dwellers included merchants, artisans and craftsmen.

Notes

1. M. Rostovtzeff, 'The Sarmatae and Parthians', CAH XI.vi. p. 113.
2. Wilhelm Weber, 'Hadrian', CAH XI.ii. p. 301.
3. Rostovtzeff, *op. cit.*, p. 110; René Grousset, *Histoire de l'Arménie* (Paris, 1946), pp. 112-13; Toumanoff, p. 205.
4. Ghirshmann, *Iran* (Penguin Books, Harmondsworth, 1975), p. 291.
5. Frye, *The Heritage of Persia* (Weidenfeld and Nicolson, 1965)
6. Edward Gibbon, *The Decline and Fall of the Roman Empire* (London, 1862), I.403, II.70; Agathangelus II.13 (Victor Langlois, *Collection des Historiens Anciens et Modernes de l'Arménie* (Paris, 1881), I.p.168.
7. Gibbon, *op. cit.*, I.406; Agathangelus III.16 (Langlois, I.121-3).
8. Gibbon, *op. cit.*, II.78-9; Moses of Khoren, translations (into Armenian) of fragments of lost manuscripts of Byzantine historians, Langlois I. 397; Agathangelus. I.4.
9. This is the subject of the Armenian composer, Aram Khachaturian's opera 'Gayane'.
10. Agathangelus, CVIII-CX (Langlois, I. 164-8).
11. Tarn, 'The Triumph of Octavian', CAH X.i. p. 113.
12. Eusebius, *Vit. Const.*, I.xxviii-xxxii.
13. These dates are given by Langlois I. 211 n. 4, based on Faustus of Byzantium, III,iii.
14. Frédéric Macler, 'Armenia', CMH IV (ed. 1923) p. 155. The Armenian *curopalates* under the Byzantine emperors were entrusted with the administration of the country, while the military command was held by an Armenian general of the forces.
15. See also Toumanoff, p. 305; Adontz, pp. 125-28.

24

The Royal House of Bagrat (the Bagratids)

The 450 years or so between the end of the fourth and the beginning of the fifth monarchy of Armenia (428–885), might be described as the 'Dark Ages' of medieval Armenian history, from the political point of view. Disunity and treachery among the *nakharars*; wars for the possession of Armenian territories between Byzantium and Persia; Byzantium and Armenia; Persia and Armenia; the Arab invasion of Armenia. But in the midst of the general political and social instability, there were oases of peace, especially in the new churches and monasteries (which had replaced the ancient temples), where some of the early illuminated manuscripts (which like all subsequent activities of the same kind, incorporated literature and art) were produced. At the same time other intellectual activities were also being practised, mostly with a strong religious bias.

In the eighth century, the Abbasid Caliph, Harun ar-Rashid (786–809), who feared the resurgence of Byzantine power in central and eastern Anatolia, and the unrest of the Arab emirates, supported the Armenian Bagratids in their ambitions for power over the other Armenian princes. This they achieved, and at the end of the ninth century, Ashot I Bagratuni (Ashot of the House of Bagrat), son of Smbat the Confessor, Prince of Princes was crowned King of Armenia by his peers in 885; he also received a crown each from the Emperor Basil I of Byzantium (himself of Armenian descent) and from the Caliph al-Mu'tamid, as a mark of their recognition of the newly installed monarch. Thus, the independent Armenian monarchy, dormant since 428, the end of the Arsacid period, was re-established. That monarchy may be described as the fifth monarchy of Armenia. The Armenian royal title: 'King of Kings of Great Armenia' was recognised by Byzantium.

Ashot had already inherited the provinces of Tayk (or Taikh), Gughark and Turuberan; and the cities of Bagaran, Ani, Kars, Mush (Moxoene), together with their respective surrounding lands. On the death of Prince Mamikonian, he seized the province of Bagravandene. By the marriage of his daughters to princes of Siunia and Artsruni, Lord of Vaspurakan, he sealed an alliance which ensured the support of his powerful sons-in-law, to whose vast estates and immense wealth he must have had, at the very least, a vicarious access.

In the 'Dark Ages' between the fall of the Arsacids and the revival of the monarchy under Ashot Bagratuni, the Katholicos had been the only representative of the Armenian people. He was respected by the Persians and was the medium of communication between the Arab Caliph at Baghdad and the Armenian princes. When the monarchy was re-established, the Katholicos insisted upon perpetuating the ancient ceremonial religious rites, and of anointing the king at his coronation. He would, when possible, mediate between rebellious *nakharars* and their king; he might when politically necessary, lay his king's case before the Byzantine emperor; in the king's absence, he was the custodian of the keys of the capital's city gates. Sometimes, he would side with the king against the people when an important but unpopular measure had to be taken, as in the Cilician period (11th to 14th centuries) when the Katholicos supported his far sighted sovereign in saving a potentially disastrous situation by the temporary expediency of uniting the Armenian Church with that of Rome.

Figure 24.1: Stone carving on a wall of the Citadel of Ani: two knights confronting a dragon

Then, as now, the keystone of the ecclesiastical edifice was the person of the Katholicos. I do not know that we can instance among Christian organisations any counterpart of this high office. Beside it that of the king seems mere fable and tinsel. The office was hereditary in the family of [Gregory] the Illuminator; and that family had been endowed with territories extending over fifteen provinces and comprising several princely residences.... It was customary for the descendants of Gregory to marry into the king's family, and they were accorded many of the honours due to royalty alone. As often as the king aroused and probably deserved the censure of the Katholikos, that spiritual castigation was unflinchingly enforced. In a vacancy of the Chair ... it was not the priesthood who chose the successor but the king, the nobles and the army. In these several respects the office was identified with the existing institutions of the country, and it was perhaps indeed modelled upon that of the high priests among the polytheists.... Two descendants of the Illuminator, one in the fourth, the other in the fifth century, added new and peculiar lustre to the institution. Nerses the First introduced the refinements of hierarchical government; Sahak the Great gave to the people an alphabet of their own. The throne of the successors of Tiridates crumbled away in the course of about a century from the death of the first Christian monarch; that of the successors of St. Gregory has weathered the storms of sixteen centuries and remains a solid and impressive monument at the present day.[1]

As to the position of the monarch, he had to accept, and never forget, that he was only the leader among equals *vis-à-vis* his powerful and proud princes, if he was to retain their loyalty. The art of diplomacy was therefore indispensable in the psychological armoury of a king; generally, the Bagratids were masters of the art. But the son and successor of Ashot, Smbat (890–914), seems to have lacked it. Incredibly, he ceded the city of Nakhichevan, within the domains of Prince Artsruni, Lord of Vaspurakan, to the neighbouring Prince of Siunik. Thus, he lit the flames of civil war, disloyalty and treason, when the furious Gagik Artsruni invited the delighted Yusuf, the Arab Emir of Azerbaijan (Atropatene), to support him in his revolt against his sovereign. The Caliph of Baghdad at once sent a king's crown to Gagik in 908, and so the Kingdom of Vaspurakan, stretching from the province of Ayrarat in the north to Lake Urmia in the south, was born. Other princes followed Artsruni's example and also declared their independence. Yusuf's forces entered Armenia (914); they took King Smbat prisoner and, after torturing him, nailed him to a cross in Dvin, Yusuf's capital. His purpose was the conquest of the Kingdom of Armenia, aided and abetted by King Artsruni of Vaspurakan.

The danger of piecemeal annihilation was at last recognised by many of the *nakharars* who hastened to join Smbat's son and heir, Ashot II (915–28) in a courageous confrontation with the enemy. Even Gigik Artsruni, regretting his disastrous action against his king and compatriots, withdrew his support from Yusuf. More allies came to the assistance of Ashot and his barons: the Iberian and Albanian kings joined the Armenian forces. Ashot invited the intervention of his prelate, John the Historian, who was able to write the history of his times at first hand, after his imprisonment and release by Yusuf. John had been in correspondence with the Byzantine Orthodox Patriarch, Nicholas Mysticus, as well as with the Emperor Constantine Porphyrogenitus himself. John brought about a meeting between the Armenian king and the Byzantine emperor at Constantinople. Ashot returned to Armenia laden with gifts, but, above all, he headed a Byzantine contingent. The Arabs were routed. Ashot was hailed King of Kings, and Gagik Artsruni acknowledged Ashot as his suzerain.

The period between the tenth century and first quarter of the

Figure 24.2: The House of Bagrat

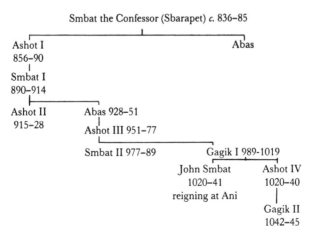

eleventh century was a time of relative peace and prosperity. The Abbasid Arabs were at war with Byzantium. There was a revival of confidence and trade in Armenia and the wealthy landowners seem to have endowed some monasteries with territories, the products of which enriched them. In particular, the monastery of Tat'ev was a beneficiary of the socio-political circumstances of its times. We have inherited from that monastery a legacy of illuminated manuscripts of the most extraordinary beauty. The reign of Gagik I Bagratuni (989–1020) is the high watermark of power and stability of at least one part of Armenia. In that period Armenia enjoyed the unaccustomed experience of unbroken peace and prosperity. The city of Ani (somewhat to the east of modern Kars) had been the Bagratid capital since 961. Strategically well situated for defence against attack from all sides, it was protected by walls of great strength and complexity, and endowed with palaces and many churches, and described as 'the city of 1001 churches'.[2] However, continuous internecine strife among the subjects of Gagik's successors, made Armenia an easy prey to Byzantine ambitions.

The last stand for a duration of three years, was made under the valiant leadership of the boy king Gagik II (1042–45) against the combined forces of Byzantium and the Emirat of Dvin. Gagik Bagratuni had been crowned king by a member of the ancient Armeno–Parthian aristocratic House of Pahlavuni. Marshal of all the armed forces or generalissimo, Vahram Pahlavuni (Gagik's Arsacid uncle) had repulsed three successive Greek armies (despatched by the Emperor Michael IV) which had spread desolation in Armenia. The fourth invasion, assisted by the Albanians (Aluans) was broken up with such fury, that the terrified Greeks and their allies fled in disorder, leaving 20,000 dead and wounded beneath the walls of Ani (1042). But, at last, Ani fell to the enemy, not as a result of defeat in war, but through the treachery of the Byzantine Emperor Constantine IX Monomachus and the young king's own ungrateful Armenian henchman and adviser, the traitor Vest Sarkis. The King was inveigled to Constantinople by the emperor, ostensibly to sign a treaty of peace. Once in his power, the emperor disregarded his vows on the cross of good faith, and imprisoned Gagik. He then, again through treacherous paths, seized the glorious city of Ani, the last bastion of Armenia.

The invasion of the Seljuk Turks began in 1048 and then, at last, weakened by her wars with the empires of Byzantium and

Arabia, Armenia ceased to be Christendom's eastern bastion against Turkish–Mohammedan invasions (1064). By so effectively helping Armenia towards her destruction, Byzantium forged the links of the chain of events which, beginning with a disastrous defeat at the hands of the Turks at the decisive Battle of Mantzikert (1071), when there was treason and treachery in the Byzantine ranks and the Emperor Romanus Diogenese was taken prisoner, ultimately led to Byzantium's own annihilation in 1453. The Turkī peoples overran not only Armenia and the whole of Anatolia, but also Eastern Europe, Mesopotamia and North Africa, destroying the accumulated inheritance of thousands of years of civilisation.

There was, indeed, a brief moment between the twelfth and early thirteenth centuries when Armenian feudal lords, with allegiance to Georgian princes, liberated and ruled the entire northern, central and eastern regions of Armenia. Art, architecture and other intellectual activities flowered once again. Although the Mongol invasions of the thirteenth century put an end to political semi-independence, life and culture continued in the monasteries until the advent of Timur and the worst horrors of Tartar depredations in the fourteenth century. They left a trail of ruins in their systematic looting and demolition of historic buildings and the slaughter of whole populations all the way to the western littoral of Anatolia, where they razed the great port of Smyrna which had been defended by the Knights of St John the Hospitallers.

Those who are familiar with the medieval history of the Near East respect the names of the valorous commanders bearing the titles of the great princely Houses of Armenia, who took leading parts in the affairs of foreign countries. I referred above to some members of the Armenian landed aristocracy who exchanged their territories for estates offered to them by Byzantium in southern and central Anatolia. From the following examples of many instances of Armenian involvement in Byzantine affairs, it would appear that the genius of those immigrants manifested itself in all walks of life within the empire — emperors, civil servants, army generals, navy commanders; in the world of literature, art and science, as well as, no doubt, in trade and commerce. It was the heroic struggle of the Bagratid sovereigns against Islam that paved the way for the rule of the Byzantine emperors, Nicephorus Phocas (963–69) and John Zimiskes (969–76), both soldiers of Armenian descent, which carried the empire to its furthest limits. The decline began after the death of Basil II (976–1025). Many of the emperors of Byzantium were Armenians or of Armenian descent. Leo V, the Armenian (813–20), defeated the Bulgars who were at the very gates of Constantinople when he ascended the imperial throne. He was supported in his iconoclastic zeal by John Hylilas (John the Grammarian), another Armenian, who was elevated to the patriarchate by Leo's son and successor, the Emperor Theophilus.[3] John's nephew, Leo the Mathematician, Archbishop of Thessalonica, was for a time Director of the University of Constantinople, under the Empress Theodora, consort of Theophilus, and regent after her husband's death, and herself an Armenian. It was her brilliant brother, Caesar Bardas, who re-established the University of Constantinople and initiated the renaissance of Byzantine art and learning, which continued to the end of Byzantium in spite of many political upheavals.[4] The important Macedonian dynasty was founded by Basil I (867–86), an Armenian.[5] So many of his successors and their army commanders, top administrators and intellectuals were either directly or indirectly of Armenian descent that his dynasty is sometimes called the Armenian dynasty, and the era of his dynasty, the Graeco-Armenian period.[6]

From the seventh century, for a period of some 500 years, Armenians were to be found in every walk of life in Byzantium: in commerce and industry as well as in cultural activities. They were to be found in the army among the common soldiers (there were Armenian legions) as well as among the officers and generals, the most celebrated in the last category (before this period) being Narses, successor of the great Belisarius, under the Emperor Justinian. (The Emperor Heraclius (610–41), the first of the Graeco–Byzantines who followed the earlier Romano–Byzantine emperors was of Armenian descent.) In the navy, too, there must have been various categories of Armenian sailors and commanders, the best known being Admiral Alexius Musele (Mushegh) possibly a member of the Mamikonian family, in the reign of Romanus I Lecapenus (919–44). They were also civil servants and among the top administrators of the empire. In the ninth and tenth centuries 'they [the Armenians in Byzantium] dominated the social, military and political life of the empire and were largely responsible for its greatness ... [their] role, moreover, [was] of world-wide historical significance.'[7]

The ninth and tenth centuries represent the zenith of the

Graeco–Byzantine period, when Byzantium triumphed every-where 'and its scholars resurrected Greek antiquity, thus making possible the preservation of its literature. Herein lies perhaps the most important part of the legacy of the Armenian civilisation'.[8] That legacy was, of course, in addition to: the earlier Urarto–Armenian contributions to bronze art, certain aspects of architec-ture, and the introduction of a system of voluntary political federation of neighbouring states, which, in modern terms, might be described as the United States of Urartu; Great Armenia's art in the form of impressive illuminated manuscripts from its monasteries, dating from the seventh century (the earliest actually dated Armenian manuscript is the Moscow Manuscript (887)), an original form of church architecture which, according to some scholars influenced that of Byzantium, the legacy of Armenian historians from the fourth century onwards, whose works are of international significance since they throw light on Armenian affairs as well as those of the ever-changing neigh-bouring peoples and nations; the monasteries of the Armeno–Cilician kingdom (see below), which for 300 years, down to 1375, produced illuminated manuscripts of superb artistic merit, which may be compared with the best of those produced in Western Europe in the same period; the special part that kingdom played in assisting the unruly western crusader lords in Outremer, in their wars against Islam.

In case the foregoing account of deep and extensive Armenian involvement in important Byzantine affairs should give the impression that Byzantium simply swallowed up and integrated within its socio-political bosom — in short, Graecofied — the Armenians living within its territories, the following quotation from an eminent French scholar, should disabuse or, at any rate, modify, such a conception:

> The Armenian was never able to fraternize completely with the Greeks. However high he may have risen in the empire, however great his fortunes may have been, however devoted the services which he may have rendered in the army and in the administration, the Armenian never became a Byzantine like others. He kept at least for himself and his private life, his language, his habits, his customs and his national religion; grouped with him were other Armenians, immigrants like him; instead of Hellenizing himself in Greece, he Armenized the Greek territories where he settled; he remained in the

Byzantine empire an unassimilated foreign element, which on occasions became dangerous.[9]

This somewhat sweeping statement might not be wholly true, but it does serve to emphasise the existence of an obstinate Armenian characteristic — that of retaining his national identity against overwhelming odds.

And what of those valorous Armenian commanders bearing the titles of the great princely Houses of Armenia, to whom I referred above (p. 269) — what became of them? The senior members, as already described, held great estates within the Byzantine Empire in the west. In the eleventh century, the Bagratids, with the co-operation of other Armenian princes, founded a new kingdom in Cilicia (see below) which endured for over three hundred years — an important Christian bastion of the Crusaders. It seems, from a similarity of names of Armenian princes and the later Kurdish chieftains, quoted below, that some relatives of those rulers, scions of the princely houses, accompanied by their wives, children, relatives and armed retainers, retreated into the mountain fastnesses, inaccessible to any but those who were born and bred in the region, where they became the leaders of the nomadic mountain tribes, probably the descendants of the Karduchai, whom Xenophon encountered in 401 BC, on his celebrated journey through Armenia. Now known as Kurds, they have carried on to this day an incessant guerrilla warfare against the lowlanders, be they Turks, Armenians, Persians or Iraqis. Groups of them in turn achieved independence to varying degrees from time to time and from place to place.

It is unfortunate from the point of view of the Armenians, a Christian people, surrounded by Mohammedans, that the mountain people adopted Islam; the descendants of their originally Armenian leaders, were naturally brought up as Mohammedans. The suggestion that the Kurdish rulers are of Armenian descent is convincingly supported by their names, between which and those of the great medieval Armenian ruling Houses 'there is more than a chance resemblance', such as Mamikonian (Kurdish Mamikanli), Bagratuni (Kurdish Begranli), Rushduni (Kurdish Rushkotanli) and Mandikanian (Kurdish Mendikanli).[10] Arabian authors of the Middle Ages refer to princes, bearing Kurdish versions of those names, as Moslem emirs, appointed by the Caliphs in certain Armenian or Turkish districts. Their descendants are today fighting a chronic war with Iraq and Iran, sometimes more fiercely than at others, but fighting constantly. In recent years they have again started troubling the Turks. They are claiming territories in eastern Turkey, that is, the lands of ancient and medieval Armenia.

Notes

1. Lynch, *Armenia* (Longmans and Co., 1901; reprinted Beirut 1966), I, pp. 298-300.
2. On a tour of eastern Turkey, I visited the site of Ani. Its disintegrating city walls, the crumbling structure of its marvellous churches and the still visible but fast-peeling frescoes, were indeed distressing to witness.
3. Charles Diehl, 'From Nicephorus I to the fall of the Phrygian Dynasty', CMH IV. ii. p. 43.
4. Ibid.
5. Abbé Albert Vogt, 'The Macedonian Dynasty 867–976', CMH, IV, iii. p. 49.
6. P. Charanis, *The Armenians and Byzantine Empire* (Lisbon, 1963), p. 57.
7. Ibid.
8. Ibid.
9. J. Laurent, 'Les origines mediévales de la question arménnienne', *Revue des Etudes Arméniennes* 1 (1920), 47, quoted by Charanis, p. 56 n. 218.
10. Sykes, *The Caliphs' Last Heritage* (Macmillan, 1915), p. 252.

25

The Kingdom of Armenia in Cilicia

There is yet one last chapter of events in the history of independent Armenia which took place in Cilicia, demonstrating the persistent nature and the adaptable character of its people. In spite of much blood-letting and distress after the depredations of the Orthodox Byzantine Greeks (who abhorred the heretical Armenians) and the Mohammedan Turks, many Armenians followed some of their princely leaders to the deep valleys of the Taurus and the narrow coastal plain of Cilicia, where they carved out for themselves a number of Armenian principalities, on Byzantine territory. A number of Armenian princes had been obliged by Byzantium to exchange their extensive native lands in the east for estates in the west, within the Byzantine empire in Anatolia even before the onslaught of the Seljuk Turks. Sir Steven Runciman[1] succinctly explains the political positions of the main Armenian contenders for territories in Cilicia:

> Between the Turks of Anatolia and the Frankish states of Northern Syria, was a group of Armenian principalities. (Many of which were established long before the appearance of the First Crusaders.) There was Oshin, who controlled the central Taurus mountains, and to the east of him the prince of the house of Roupen (Ruben). There was Kogh Vasil (the Robber Baron Vasil) in the Anti-Taurus, Thatoul at Marash and Gabriel at Melitene. Thatoul and Gabriel belonged to the Orthodox Church and were therefore inclined to co-operate with Byzantium. They and Oshin based their juridical position on titles conferred on them by the Emperor. But the Roupenians (Rubenids), who alone of the Armenians succeeded in founding an enduring state, were traditionally hostile both to Byzantium and the Orthodox Church.

Figure 25.1: The Royal House of Armeno-Cilicia

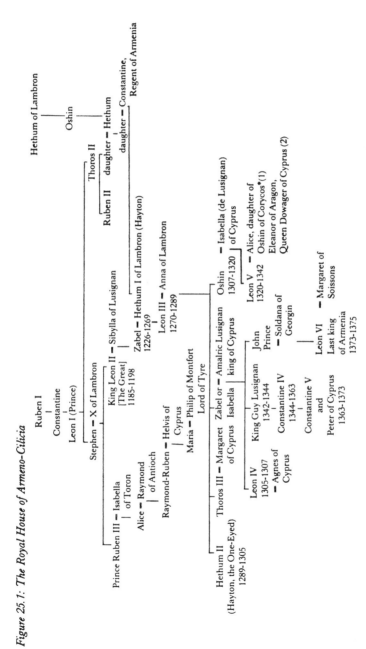

* Oshin of Corycos: Son of Constantine Hethumian-Lambron, Regent of Armenia during Zabel's infancy 1219-1226

275

The Armenian Kingdom of Cilicia, called Lesser or Little Armenia, after the ancient, defunct first Armenian homeland on the west bank of the River Euphrates, was founded by Prince Ruben the Great (1080–95), of the Royal House of Bagratids (Ruppen Pakraduni), when he, with a few determined friends and loyal followers, took shelter from Byzantine and Turk in the gorges of the Taurus in Cilicia and captured the fortress of Partzer-pert (some 15 miles north of Sis). Other Armenian *nakharars* had already set up semi-independent principalities or chieftainships in the Cilician mountains. The most successful among these was Oshin, who founded the princely house of Hethum. He was supported by his friend, a prince of the ancient Armenian Artsruni royal family, at that time the Byzantine governor of Tarsus, who influenced the Emperor Alexius Comnenus to give Oshin the hereditary fiefdom of the fortress of Lampron (north of the Gulf of Tarsus).

These events coincided with the appearance of the first crusaders in 1097. The crusading leaders had a variety of relationships with the new Armenian principalities: sometimes they supported them against Byzantine and Turk; at others they fought them. They used their roads, were helped by Armenian troops, received their embassies and established feudal governments near their frontiers. The crusaders, as is well known, also fought each other when they should have been united as fellow crusaders with Christian Armenia, in fighting the common enemies — the Turks and Arabs (Saracens). There was also strife between the two main Armenian ruling families, the House of Ruben and the House of Hethum. Over a period of 100 years, the more militant Rubenid princes increased their territories at the expense of the Hethumids, in spite of the help the latter received from their Byzantine masters.

In the meantime, Constantine, son of Ruben the Great, established himself in the fortress city of Vahké, which he had seized from the Greeks. The first crusaders, led by Godfrey of Bouillon, were welcomed by Constantine and his subordinate lords. Armenians saw in the European newcomers (as naively as so often in the centuries to come, particularly in the nineteenth and twentieth centuries) brothers of a similar religion and allies against the common enemy, the Turks and the Arabs, as well as the Byzantine Greeks. The historian, Matthew of Edessa, records Pope Gregory XIII's comment that 'no nation came more generously to the aid of the Crusaders than the Armenians, who gave them food, men, horses and arms'. At the siege of Antioch, the Armenian prince Oshin and his brother Pazouni, and Constantine, as well as the Armenian monks of the Black Mountains and the local Armenian populace, all came to the aid of the crusaders, and the conquest of Antioch by the Franks was thus secured. Celebrations took the form of the marriage of Prince Constantine's daughter to Joscelin of Courtenay, Count of Edessa, who had inherited that Armenian principality from Count Baldwin of Boulogne (initially an ill-gotten gain after the latter had been crowned King of Jerusalem). The daughter of Prince Thoros I, Constantine's grand-daughter, married Count Bauduin, brother of Godfrey. These unions drew Armenians and Franks closer together.

The ordinary Armenians thrived in Cilicia and the neighbouring Frankish principality of Antioch, not only in war but also in peaceful trading, as well as the arts and crafts. There was already a powerful group of Genoese traders in Cilicia around the year 1100, who had their own viscount and their own court of justice. Although the crusaders were past masters in the manufacture and the handling of siege weapons, in 1123, when unsuccessfully besieging Tyre, the Franks and Venetians had to summon an Armenian engineer from Antioch to build military engines for them. As a result Tyre fell to the crusaders the following year (7 July 1124), a serious setback for Islam.

The Rubenid Thoros II (1148–68) seems to have been heir to the most successful line of Armenian princes struggling against the Byzantine Greeks, Turks, Arabs and the western crusaders, in maintaining their hold of Cilician territories, Sis, Anazarbus, Manistra, Adana, Tarsus and the whole of eastern Cilicia. It was the nephew of Thoros, Ruben III (1175–85) who succeeded in at last freeing his country from foreign occupation, until he could claim to rule over the provinces extending from Isauria in the west to the Amanus mountains in the east, although he could not completely quell the strife that continued between the Armenian barons within those domains. In 1185 he retired to the monastery of Tradog ceding the rule of the principality to his brother Leon II (1185-1219) who had served him loyally during his reign.

Figure 25.2: Gold seal (obverse and reverse) of Leon II, the Magnificent

Leon the Magnificent (1185–1219)

Having consolidated his brother's conquests, Leon then subdued the turbulent Armenian princes. He is described by
Armenian historians as Leon (Levon) the Magnificent, and by
others as Leon the Great. His reign inaugurated Armenia's Silver
Age, which closed with the death of King Hethum I in 1269. He
maintained the unity of his country, kept powerful and hostile
Byzantium at bay and defeated in 1187 a Turkish horde under a
certain Rustam (killed in battle) and the united forces of the
Sultans of Aleppo and Damascus. He contrived to deal diplomatically with the swashbuckling western lords, particularly with
Bohemond III, Prince of neighbouring Antioch, who was his
overlord. Leon's troops also took part in the siege of Acre, and he
was among the lords who assisted Richard I Coeur de Lion of
England in the conquest of Cyprus (1191) from the Byzantine
renegade Isaac Ducas Comnenus. In the same year, according to
an English chronicle, Leon was the chief of the bridegroom's
friends at Richard's wedding to the beautiful but unfortunate
Princess Berengaria of Navarre. Subsequently (1192) Richard
sold Cyprus to Count Guy de Lusignan and it remained in the
possession of that family for almost 200 years. They then briefly
inherited the throne of the remnants of the Kingdom of Armeno–
Cilicia, before it was completely overwhelmed by Islamic forces.
Of incidental interest is the romantic background of Hugh de
Lusignan who inherited the kingdom of Cyprus in 1205. While
still in France, Hugh had been betrothed to Isabella, the

beautiful, fourteen-year-old daughter of the Count of Angoulême. The count as well as Hugh were vassals of King John of England. John was already married to Howisa of Gloucester, but as that wealthy lady was his cousin, the marriage had taken place by a special papal dispensation, under stricture that the marriage was never to be consummated. John therefore easily dissolved that non-marriage and demanded and obtained the hand of the tearful Isabella in 1200. The equally disconsolate Hugh went off to drown his sorrow in the wars and intrigues of Outremer, becoming King of Cyprus in 1205. Such was the background of the Lusignans, kings of Cyprus and, almost at the end of the crusades, briefly also kings of Armenia.

In 1191, Leon seized the fortress of Baghras which guarded the northern side of Antioch. At first in the possession of the Templars, it had been captured by Saladin and dismantled. Leon, though a feudatory of Antioch, refused to hand it back to the Templars and, what is more, he rebuilt it. This aroused the suspicions of Bohemond III, Lord of Antioch, as to Leon's designs on his principality. Exasperated, he signed a separate peace treaty with Saladin, the arch-enemy of Christendom, and drew his attention to Leon's actions. Saladin was too urgently occupied elsewhere to concern himself with Bohemond's troubles. These events, and the fact that Bohemond had not yet repaid Leon the sums of money he had lent him in 1188, did not improve the relationship of the two neighbouring principalities. When Saladin died in 1193, Leon discovered and pre-empted a ruse of Bohemond against him. He invited Bohemond and his family to a banquet at Baghras, ostensibly to try to resolve their differences. Then just as in the past, Bohemond had invited Leon's brother Ruben III to Antioch, broken the laws of hospitality, made him prisoner and forced his suzerainty over Ruben and his House, so now Leon emulated Bohemond's misdeeds. He seized and imprisoned him, his family and his retinue of courtiers. Bohemond then had no alternative but to bow to Leon's demands and to surrender Antioch to him. Armenian troops under Leon's nephew-in-law, Hethum of Sassun, entered Antioch and lodged themselves in the palace. Although Antioch's aristocracy, many of whom were blood relations of the Armenian nobility, were happy enough to accept their new suzerain (Bohemond having been an unpopular ruler), the Antiochean bourgeoisie could not bring themselves to accept the heretical Armenian as their ruler. Many of them also (and perhaps more to the point) were Italian merchants and it was not in their interests to have an Armenian master. There were riots in the streets. At the end, the citizens formed a commune for the interim administration of the city, and hailed Bohemond's son, Raymond, as their suzerain, until his father should return. At the same time, they appealed to his brother, Bohemond of Tripoli, and to Henry of Champagne, King of Jerusalem, for help. Henry went to Sis, the Armenian capital, and in 1194, Leon allowed Bohemond to return to Antioch, on condition that he renounced his lordship over Armenia, and that Leon retained the fortress of Baghras and the surrounding country. The treaty between the two princes was sealed by the marriage of Leon's niece and heir-presumptive, Alice, to Bohemond's son and heir, Raymond.

The Third Crusade (1189–92) was led by the Emperor (of the Holy Roman Empire) Frederick Barbarossa. There was consternation in the ranks of Islam on hearing of that expedition against them, led by such a powerful warrior. Leon promised Frederick every facility for his journey through Armenian territory. In return, Frederick pledged to give him a crown. As is well known, Barbarossa was unfortunately drowned while crossing the River Calicadnus. It was not until 1198, at the Feast of the Epiphany, that Leon's coronation took place, amidst splendour and pageantry, in the cathedral church of Tarsus. He was annointed by the Armenian Katholicos, Grigor VII, in the presence of various ecclesiastical dignitaries and many princes and lords, including Byzantine and Frankish feudatories who held lands under the Armenian ruler. Leon received the crown from the hands of the papal legate, Conrad Wittelsbach, Archbishop of Mainz, who also represented Henry VI of the Holy Roman Empire. Alexius Angelus, Emperor of Byzantium, also sent Leon a crown to confirm his recognition of Armenian suzerainty over the former Byzantine territories in Cilicia. The sixth and last monarchy of Armenia was thus established.

Continuing his policy of association with the western leaders around him, to safeguard his kingdom against the Greeks and Turks, Leon repudiated his first wife, Isabelle of Austria, and married Sibylla, daughter of Amalric de Lusignan, recently crowned King of Cyprus. The marriage of his niece and heir-presumptive Alice, to Bohemond's heir, Raymond, produced a son, christened Ruben-Raymond. Raymond died in 1197, before his father, Bohemond; the heir to the principality of Antioch was then his son, Ruben-Raymond. On Bohemond's death in 1201, a war of succession broke out between the claimants to the lordship of Antioch, the Armenian king supporting his niece's son, Ruben-Raymond, against the latter's uncle, the Count of Tripoli. After 15 years of war, Ruben-Raymond was crowned prince of Antioch but three years later, in 1219, he was ousted by his uncle. Thus, Raymond's untimely death frustrated Leon's ambition to join his vigorous kingdom by marriage, to the robust principality of neighbouring Antioch (and probably making Antioch, at the same time, a vassal of Armenia). The combined forces of the two would then have made it possible for Leon to face the powerful Mohammedan sultans and possibly also the Frankish–Byzantine Emperor's threats from Constantinople. He had, however, achieved peace between the aristocratic factions within his own realm. He himself had made peace with his princely rival, Hethum, and sent him as his ambassador to the Pope. With a view to strengthening the political status of his country, he was prepared to recognise the Pope as head of all Christendom, including that of the Armenian Holy Apostolic Orthodox Church, with some important reservations. There was much correspondence with the Holy See on the one hand and the Armenian Katholicos and his king on the other. 'In the principality of Antioch the separated Armenian Church was powerful and was encouraged by the princes who found it a useful counter against the Orthodox'. On the other hand, 'many Armenian bishops came to recognise papal supremacy, and some attended the Synods of the Latin Church, forgiving in the Latin doctrines what they thought impardonable in the Greek.'[2] But the Armenian people would not be party to any compromise. However, those negotiations between a willing king, the leader of his Church and many of his nobles, with the successor of St Peter, would have established, in the eyes of the Franks, the sincerity of the Armenians in their support of the Latin cause. That in its turn must have helped to bring about a closer understanding between Armenians and Franks.

At the Armenian court at Sis, Leon entertained leaders and captains from various parts of Western Europe — England, France, Germany, Italy — who came to serve under his banner against Islam. He emulated the protocols, the fixing of taxes and the tribunals of his Frankish neighbours. He adopted the Assizes of Antioch as the law of his own Kingdom. They were later translated into Armenian, and since the original is lost, the Armenian translation is the scholar's source of information in that field of jurisprudence. By his second marriage, the Armenian king was the son-in-law of Amalric de Lusignan, King of Cyprus; his daughter, Rita, ('Stephanie') was married to John de Brienne, King of Jerusalem; his niece Philippa was the wife of Theodore I Lascaris, Emperor of Nicaea. By granting the port of Seleucia, the castles of Norpert (Castellum Novum) and Camardias to the Hospitallers and some other castles in western Cilicia to the Teutonic Knights, he won their friendship. On the other hand, he seized the Armenian lands that the Templars had occupied, and drove them out of his country. Thus, he strengthened his frontiers with the aid of foreign powers and at the same time he put at their disposal his own considerable military potential, the most stable in Outremer, against the growing strength of Islam. For the County of Edessa had been lost in 1144, Jerusalem in 1187 and Saladin's forces were at the gates of Tyre, Tripoli and Antioch, three major bastions of Christendom in Syria. To promote commerce, he allowed privileges to, and cultivated good relations with, Genoa and Venice, thus making Armeno–Cilicia, with its port of Ayas (Lajazzo) and Corycos the entrepôt between Europe and Asia. He also remembered the needy, and founded orphanages, hospitals and schools. In the numerous monasteries, calligraphy and the arts were greatly encouraged. A number of illuminated manuscripts which have come down to us add lustre to the era of his reign. King Leon II appears to have been a liberal-minded monarch, perhaps with advanced ideals. This is evident in his diplomatic and flexible religious attitude, which helped the survival of his country in the midst of a multitude of enemies and predatory warlords.

The foundations of social and political stability thus laid were taken up after Leon's death, in 1219, by the Hethumid baron, Constantine. He was elected as protector and regent of Leon's four-year-old daughter, Zabel (Isabella), to whom Leon had bequeathed his crown, rather than to his weak protegé and grandnephew, Ruben-Raymond. For the following seven years, Constantine set himself up as king-maker. First he imprisoned Ruben-Raymond, who had proclaimed himself King of Armenia. He died in prison. Then, Constantine passed the crown to Philip (fourth son of Bohemond IV of Antioch) who, with the consent of the Armenian nobles, had married the child-Queen Zabel. But Philip was more in sympathy with the western Catholic crusaders than with the heretical Armenians. Worst of all, he stole the royal and national treasure (the crown jewels) of Armenia and sent them to his father. Constantine imprisoned Philip and demanded the return of the treasure in exchange for his release. But Bohemond preferred to have the jewels to his son, and so Philip likewise died in prison. In 1226, Zabel was given in marriage to a more worthy husband, Constantine's own son, Hethum I (1226–69), and so at last, the Rubenid and Hethumid dynasties, with their respective military and cultural talents, were united.

Hethum the Great (1226–69)

The first part of King Hethum's reign was relatively peaceful, but the rumblings of the oncoming Mongol invasions might easily have been heard in Armenia. Having overrun the whole of Central Asia and Persia, Jenghiz Khan died in 1227, a year after Hethum's accession to the Armenian throne. Under his son, Ogdai Khan, the Mongolian empire expanded into Europe: Kiev was destroyed in 1240; an army of Poles and Germans was annihilated at Liegnitz (Lower Silesia, Poland) in 1241. At the same time the Mongols had swarmed through Greater Armenia and Georgia and ravaged Asia Minor. Then, in 1242, Ogdai Khan died, and Guyuk his son ruled until his own death (1250). His successor was another of Jenghiz's grandsons, Mongka Khan (1251), who installed his brother, Kublai, in Peking as ruler of China. Mongka, like his brother Kublai, was a military genius and great administrator. He must also have been a consummate diplomat, with liberal ideas. The last attribute expressed itself in his toleration of all religions within his vast empire. King Hethum must have realised that, beset though he was by his Turkish–Seljuk neighbours, the real and immediate danger was that of the Mongols. If only he could foster their friendship! It is here that the Armenian monarch proved himself to be a worthy successor of Leon the Magnificent. Just as his great predecessor had seen the expediency of putting aside his national pride and religious prejudices for the sake of the safety — indeed, the survival — of his country, to cultivate the friendship of the ferocious western knights, and to negotiate at the same time with Catholic Rome for a prudent compromise, so Hethum I recognised the wisdom of voluntary submission to the Great Khan, before the Mongol hordes overran his country, Lesser Armenia, as they had overrun Greater Armenia. In 1247, he despatched his brother, the Constable Smbat,[3] commander-in-chief, historian and legislator, to the Mongolian court at Karakorum where, as the ambassador of the Armenian king, Smbat made his submission to the Great Khan. He returned to the Armenian capital, Sis three years later, in 1250, with a charter guaranteeing the integrity of his country. A brief account of his journey is to be found in a letter from Smbat to his brother-in-law, Henry I of Cyprus, quoted by William of Nangis in his *Vie de Saint Louis*. 'It was a full year's travel [from Antioch], riding 10 leagues a day, to reach the great king of the Tartars'.[4]

In 1253, King Hethum himself undertook the 3500-mile journey to Karakorum in Outer Mongolia. As a king who had come voluntarily in friendship, he was received by the Great Khan Mongka with many honours. Karakorum at that time could be described as a great capital, a centre to which ambassadors and diplomats, travellers on a variety of missions made their way — merchants, adventurers, churchmen, evangelists. Some settled in the Mongolian capital where their skills appear to have been welcomed. When the Flemish Franciscan friar William of Rubruck arrived there as the ambassador of St Louis of France in 1254 (in the same year as King Hethum), the first Christian he met was an Armenian monk serving in his small chapel. He then found 'a swarm of Christians'[5] including Nestorians and other Monophysites, Greek Orthodox, Muslim Turks and Persians as well as Buddhists from Tibet and Taoists and Confucians from China. There were diplomats from the Byzantine court, from the Arab Caliph and the Seljuk Sultan and from other parts of the medieval world including Delhi, Kurdistan and, of course, the Russias. The religious brotherhood from Europe would represent the Pope and Catholicism, and in speaking of the extent to which Christianity was practised as a state religion, they would of course describe the countries and royal courts of Western Europe. Among the ordinary foreigners who had settled in the Great Khan's capital were Alans, Ruthenians, Georgians and Armenians; a Hungarian woman married to a French goldsmith from Paris, another woman from Metz in Lorraine married to a Russian carpenter. There was neither racial nor religious discrimination at Karakorum. This is where the Armenian king had his interview with Mongka Khan. The latter not only renewed his predecessor's promises and assurances of alliance with Armenia, but he broadened the terms of the treaty: the Armenian *and all other Christian churches and monasteries* within the Mongolian empire were to be freed from taxation, and King Hethum is reported to have discussed with the Great Khan the possibility of Mongol assistance to liberate the Holy Land from Moslem domination. That idea was a practical demonstration of the Armenian monarch's valuable service to the Christian institutions of his day, and his zeal (and that of his people), as a member of the crusading warriors on whose behalf he was in effect negotiating.

Laden with gifts and encouraged by the friendship of the mighty Mongolian Khan, Hethum on his way back in 1256, passed through Greater Armenia where he was welcomed by many local Armenian princes, bishops and other prelates. For Leon the Magnificent had set a precedent of authority over Greater Armenia as well as his native Lesser Armenia–Cilicia — together constituting Great Armenia — by stamping upon his coins: 'King of All the Armenians'.

In his biography of St Louis, Joinville (Jean, Lord of Joinville, King Louis IX's Seneschal in Champagne) recounts how

the King of Armenia went to the King of the Tartars, and to obtain help from him became his vassal. On his return to Armenia the king brought back with him so great a number of men-at-arms that he was in a strong position to make war on the Sultan of Iconium. The struggle between them lasted for a very long time, but in the end the Tartars killed so many of the sultan's men that their ruler ceased to be of any further consequence. In the meantime, so many exciting reports of the coming battle had been circulating in Cyprus that some of our sergeants, attracted by the chance of a fight and in the hope of gaining booty, had crossed over into Armenia; but not one of them ever came back.[6]

Hethum, in fact recovered some fortresses that had been taken from him by the Seljuks, as well as territories that once belonged to the Armenian chieftain, Vasil, Lord of Kaisun, before the petty, independent baronies of Armeno–Cilicia had been welded together into a kingdom. In 1259 King Hethum defeated a great Turkish army under Kilij Arslan Sultan of Rum and expelled it from his western frontiers; in 1263, he freed the Syrian port of Seleucia (opposite indispensable Cyprus) and its hinterland from the Turks.

The history of many of the peoples of the Near East might have been quite different if the western princes in Syria and

Palestine had subdued their arrogance and personal ambitions, lent a favourable ear to Hethum's pleas and joined the Armenians and the Mongols in an all-out attack upon the Arabs and particularly against the Mamluks of Egypt. The Latins were also afraid of fostering a power they could not control. They preferred to continue as before, to fight the Moslems, whose ways they had come to understand, and whose strength they could measure. Many of them had adopted the oriental way of life. Thus King Hethum's scheme fell upon deaf ears. He did, however, succeed in persuading his son-in-law, Bohemond VI, Prince of Antioch, Count of Tripoli, to join him and his Mongol allies. By his marriage to the Armenian princess, Sibylla, Bohemond had become, to some degree, Hethum's vassal.

Since the Mamluks were ultimately the force which destroyed the crusading enterprise as well as the Mongolian threat in the Near East (thus changing the course of history), a few words here about their origin would not be out of place. They were composed basically of young Kipchak slaves, bought by the Venetian Azov traders from the Tartars, who rounded up the unlucky young people between the Volga and the Don (*c.* 1220). The Venetians sold them to the Egyptian Arabs, who used them as army conscripts, thus nurturing a serpent which ultimately turned upon its masters and fathered the ruling warlords in a foreign land; they were known as Mamluks.[7] Between 1250 and 1517, they were the unchallengeable masters in Egypt, one of the most war-torn and troubled regions of those times. Mamluk power was founded by (possibly) an Armenian woman, Shajar-al-Durr (the Tree of Pearls), a bondmaid in the service of the Ayyubid Sultan al-Salih (*c.* 1249). When she bore him a son, he gave her her freedom. On al-Salih's death, Shajar-al-Durr assumed sovereign power and ruled for 80 days, striking her own coins; she had herself mentioned in the Friday prayer. When she married her commander-in-chief, 'Izz-al-Din Aykab, her Egyptian emirs nominated him sultan. However, she remained queen and took care to keep her husband as her subordinate. When she heard that he was planning a second marriage, she had him murdered in his bath in the Citadel of Cairo; whereupon, 'she was herself battered to death with wooden shoes by the slave women of Aykab's first wife, and her body was cast from a tower'. Thus, through Shajar, Aykab was the first Mamluk sultan (1250–57).[8] The Mamluk sultan of Egypt represented the temporal, the military as well as the spiritual power of Islam:

no matter how base his origin, [he] had among his employees the exalted person of the Commander of the Faithful [the Caliph], who could give spiritual sanction to military and civil projects. The first of these re-established Caliphs attempted to return to Baghdad and to assert his power once again in Mesopotamia, but he not only lost his life but also the army the Mamluk Sultan had lent him, and thenceforth the only active operation that his successors were allowed to perform unaided was the investiture of their servant and master, the ruler of Egypt.[9]

In January 1258, the formidable Il-Khan Hulagu, ruler of the Middle East and brother of the Great Khan Mongka, besieged, took and destroyed the Arab capital, Baghdad, said to have been impregnable, with frightful massacre of its Moslem citizens — men, women and children — the ordinary townsfolk as well as the palace courtiers. The Abbasid Caliph himself was executed only after he had been made to reveal the hiding-place of his hoard of treasure. The Christian citizens, who had taken refuge in their churches, were spared. Then Hulagu set out to repress the arrogant Ayubid prince, al-Kamil of Mayafarkin (Martyropolis), in northern Mesopotamia. That city was 'besieged and captured early in 1260, largely thanks to the help of Hulagu's Armenian and Georgian allies. The Moslems were massacred and the Christians spared. Al-Kamil was tortured by being forced to eat his own flesh till he died'.[10] In the same year, Nisibis, Harran, Edessa and Aleppo in Syria were taken; whereupon, Damascus surrendered. On 1 March 1260, the Mongol general Kitbuqa, a Christian, accompanied by King Hethum of Armenia and Prince Bohemond VI of Antioch, rode with the Mongol army into Damascus in triumph. When Hethum joined forces with the Il-Khan at Edessa in an attempt to capture Jerusalem from the Mamluks, the two united forces defeated Nasir, Sultan of Aleppo and they divided his land between them. All might have gone well but for the sudden death of the Great Khan at Karakorum, which obliged Hulagu to hasten to his eastern frontiers to meet possible invasions of his territories by other Mongol Khans, especially that of the Golden Horde in southern Russia. He put his son Abaga in charge of his Mesopotamian forces. Hulagu died in 1265. An interesting comment is offered by Arnold Toynbee: that 'Hulagu's expedition appears to have been suggested to the mind of Hulagu's overlord, Khaqan

Mangu, by the Uniate-Catholic King Hayton of Little Armenia'.[11] Another interesting piece of information pertaining to these times and to some extent involving Armenia, by the same writer (Toynbee, *A Study of History*, VII, p. 313) states: in the reign of Hulagu Khan's descendant, Gaykhātū Khan (AD 1291–95), 'in the year 1294, an issue of printed paper [money] notes, with a bilingual inscription in Chinese and Arabic, was uttered in the commercial capital, Tabriz.' But the protests of the business community 'were so violent' that the issue had to be withdrawn after only two or three days' trial. This 'printed paper money may have been unloaded on the hands of the Venetian and Genoese merchants in Tabriz at the time' or via Armeno–Cilicia, which was an entrepôt between Europe and Asia.

In 1266, Hethum, anticipating a Mamluk invasion of his country, went personally to the Il-Khan's court at Tabriz to seek help. War broke out in his absence. His two sons Leon and Thoros led the greatly outnumbered Armenian forces against the Mamluks, under Sultan Baibars. The Armenians were routed; Prince Thoros was killed; Ayas, Adana and Tarsus were sacked; at Sis, the palace was looted and the cathedral burnt to the ground; thousands were massacred; 40,000 captives, including Prince Leon, and an enormous amount of booty were carried off. It was a disaster of irreparable magnitude which met Hethum's eyes on his return from Tabriz. The Il-Khan was unable to help him, but he did send him a high-ranking Mamluk captive. The Armenian king was able to exchange the Mamluk prisoner for his heir, Leon, on agreeing to cede to the Moslems four important fortresses. Then he abdicated his throne in favour of Leon and retired to a monastery, after a distinguished, indeed, illustrious, reign of 44 years. He died a year later in 1269.

The Last 100 Years

The subsequent history to the end of the Armenian Kingdom of Cilicia in 1375, must be told briefly. By the end of King Hethum I's reign (1269), Mongolian power in western Asia was waning. A combined Mongol, Armenian and Georgian force had been defeated in 1260 at the decisive battle of Ain Jalud (the Pools of Goliath), near Nazareth, by the Mamluks, assisted, as they had been, with food and the free passage of their army, by the crusading lords of Palestine. In 1261, the Greeks had reconquered

Constantinople and had put an end to Roman rule in Byzantium. In the same year, the Abbasid Caliphate had been established in Cairo. St Louis of France who had led the Fourth Crusade, died in 1270. In that year, Leon III (1270–89), son of Hethum I, came to the throne. He was successful against both the Mamluks of Egypt and the Turks of Iconium, and by 1281, in spite of serious setbacks, had re-established Armenian independence in Cilicia. On his death in 1289, his son, Hethum II (1289–1305) succeeded him. Without the powerful Mongolian support his predecessors had enjoyed, neither Armenia nor, for that matter, Outremer, could withstand the hammerings of the Mamluk sultans of Egypt. In the last decade of the thirteenth century, their attacks intensified. In 1291, with the fall of Acre and Tyre, the crusaders' power in Syria–Palestine was destroyed forever, leaving Armenia, under King Hethùm II, as the last Christian bastion on the Asiatic mainland, supporting and supported by Cyprus. There was much intermarriage between members of the royal houses of the two countries. Hethum II's sister, Zabel (Isabella) married Amalric de Lusignan, King of Cyprus and titular Lord of Tyre in 1295.

But the political events in King Hethum II's reign, coinciding in 1291, with the destruction of Outremer, might collectively be described as a losing struggle for survival. In 1292, the See of the Armenian Katholicos at Hromkla fell to the Mamluks. The Katholicos himself was taken prisoner and the church treasures were looted. The only remaining port of any importance on the Asiatic mainland was that of Armenia's Ayas (Lajazzo), the only available entrance into Asia from the eastern Mediterranean. It was indispensable for the trade of the Venetians, Genoese and Pisans with Central Asia and the Far East.

Marco Polo had passed through Ayas in 1271, collecting from the Armenian authorities the great Khan's credentials or safe conduct, without which, at that time, there was no guarantee of safety to travellers in Central Asia. In his *Travels*, he writes that

> the king [of Armenia] rules his dominions with strict regards to justice. There are numerous towns, fortified places and castles, and an abundance of all necessaries of life, as well as of those things which contribute to its comforts.... The port of Laiasus (Ayas) has considerable traffic and it is frequented by merchants from Venice, Genoa and many other places, who trade in spiceries and drugs of different sorts, manufactures of silk

and of wool, and other rich commodities. Those persons who design to travel into the interior of the Levant, usually proceed in the first instance to this port of Laiasus.[12]

Ayas fell to the Mamluks in 1345, but its docks had been dismantled and its fortifications destroyed in 1337. Apart from the Mamluk danger, no king after Hethum II (1289–1305) could control either the ambitious and unruly Armenian barons — some pro- others anti-Latin — nor the religious dissension rife among the populace — some pro- but most anti-Rome. The king himself entered a Franciscan monastery and many members of the nobility embraced Catholicism, in the vain hope that their country might receive help from the West. The main body of the Armenian people remained faithful to the Armenian Holy Apostolic Orthodox Church and they turned against their rulers.

One of the fundamental causes of Armeno–Cilicia's destruction seems to have been the religious intransigence of the Armenian people. One distressing example, which appears to have provided the slippery political slope which plunged the Kingdom of Armenia to its extinction supports this statement: towards the end of the troubled years of Hethum II's reign, and after the loss of his alliance with the Mongols, he took up once more the efforts of his predecessors, to win western help, by attempting, through his Katholicos Grigor VIII Anavarzetsi, to introduce ritual changes into the Armenian Church, to conform more closely to the Church of Rome. In the midst of negotiations, the Katholicos died, and Hethum, always prone to retire to a monastery, chose that occasion to abdicate the throne in favour of his nephew, Leon IV (1305–07). Leon then, in cooperation with his uncle–adviser, called a council of ecclesiastics and princes. A profession of faith, written by the late Katholicos, was adopted. When the people heard of this, their fury knew no bounds. They called upon the Mongol chief, Bilarghu, against their own king and his uncle. Bilarghu treacherously invited them to a banquet at Anazarbus, where he put them and their entourage of princes and nobles to death (13 August 1307).

Oshin (1307–20), brother of Hethum II (some say brother of Leon IV), connected by his two marriages to King Hugh III of Cyprus and King Robert of Naples, as well as to Philip II, titular Latin Emperor of the East, followed Leon IV to the throne. His first task was successfully to expel Bilarghu and his Mongols from Armenia. In 1316, at a Council in Adana, Oshin and his

Katholicos adopted for Armeno–Cilicia his predecessor's ecclesiastical conformity to the Roman persuasion, in the face of the anger of his subjects. In spite of this and his Roman connections, his appeals for help to Pope John XIII and Philip de Valois, King of France, were ignored. However, he appears to have defended his country without anyone's help, for 13 years — the full period of his reign — before a natural death. He had, during his reign, and in spite of his perpetual wars, built and restored the various fortresses and churches, in Armeno–Cilicia, in particular those of Tarsus, where he built a magnificent church, which still stands, although it is converted to a mosque and is now known as Kilisa-cami.

His stepson and successor, Leon V (1320–42), came to the throne during his minority. The regency, led by a nationalist, Oshin of Corycos, expelled the Latin courtiers. Oshin married Leon's mother, and arranged the marriage of his own daughter by a previous marriage to the young Leon V. These measures counteracted all Latin influence and, on the face of it, re-established the Armenian Church.

However, when Leon V came to his majority, he undid all Oshin's work, married a Spanish lady with Lusignan connections, and put his stepfather, Oshin, to death. In the absence of a male Armenian heir, the throne was inherited by Guy de Lusignan, King of Cyprus, son of Leon V's aunt, Zabel and Amalric de Lusignan. He reigned for only two years (1342–44) and on his death was followed by a usurper, Constantine IV (1344–69), son of Baldwin, Marshal of Armenia. With help from Cyprus and Rhodes, he expelled the Mamluks from Armenia and, later, even added the port of Alexandretta to his kingdom. Much to his credit, he also succeeded in suppressing the chronic religious dissensions in his country. Peace was thus restored and perpetuated until Constantine's death in 1369. His successor Constantine V, another usurper (1369–73), son of a Cypriot serf, had risen to the rank of a baron of Armenia of great wealth. He had offered the crown to Peter, King of Cyprus, but when Peter was assassinated in 1369, he declared himself King of Armenia. In 1373, he, too, was assassinated.

Leon VI (1373–75), reigned for only two years down to 1375. In 1375, the capital, Sis, fell to the Egyptian Mamluks and the last King of Armenia, Leon VI, grandson of Zabel (sister of Hethum II) and Amalric de Lusignan, was taken prisoner, and the Armenian kingdom of Cilicia ceased to exist, except for the stronghold of Corycos, with its architecturally pleasing castle, somehow built out at sea, joined to a land castle by a causeway. Corycos held out for over 70 years, until taken by the Turks in 1448.

The West had long since turned its back on crusading adventures, as shown by their prevarications when the ambassador, representing *Christian* Mongolia, visited in turn, Rome, Genoa, Paris and Bordeaux (Edward I of England's capital in France), vainly seeking their help to crush Islam and free the Holy Places of Christendom. Leon VI was held captive in Egypt until 1382 when, through the intervention of John of Castile and Peter of Aragon, he was given his freedom. He travelled to Paris and London seeking in vain the help of the French and English kings to liberate his country. According to Sir John Froissart's *Chronicles*, Leon arrived in France in 1385. He was well received by Charles VI and his lords who, Froissart writes, said: 'We will that the King of Armenia, who has come to us in hopes of assistance, have allowed him wherewithal to maintain his dignity ... and if we are able, he shall have men at arms to aid him in the recovery of his kingdom.'[13] The French monarch allowed Leon an annual pension of 6000 francs, in recognition of his rank.[14] War between England and France, which had come to an uneasy end at the beginning of Richard II's reign, still seems to have been in the air, and according to Froissart, the King of Armenia offered to intercede between the two countries. He sailed to England and landed at Dover. 'He found there the English king's uncles, the earls of Cambridge and Buckingham. He told them the purpose of his visit ... "For," he said, "the long continuance of the war has greatly emboldened and raised the pride of the Turks and Saracens. No one now make any opposition to them." '[15] He was taken to London. 'It was before the highest assembly of the realm, held by Richard II at Westminster, that Leon advocated the cause of his country, and that of peace. In a document dated 3 February 1386, Richard, referring to the ambassadors of "peace" consents to appoint representatives, and confesses to "yielding to the entreaties, prayers and requests made to us by our royal cousin the King of Armenia".'[16] But at a purely formal council, his pleas for peace were rejected by an elegant speech delivered by the Archbishop of Canterbury. The war between England and France in fact petered out, and peace was ensured by Richard's marriage to a French princess. Richard entertained Leon at a great banquet and offered him costly gifts which, however, the King of Armenia courteously refused, accepting only a ring worth about 100 francs. But Richard generously settled the considerable pension of £1000 a year on him. The latter expressed his gratitude by making Richard II of England his testamentary executor.

Leon VI, last King of Armenia, died in 1393, in the palace of Tournelles, opposite the royal hotel of St Pol, where the kings of France usually resided. He was buried in the Church of the Celestins. After the manner of his own country, his friends clothed him in white, carrying torches of white wax: his body, dressed in royal robes of the same colour, was placed upon a white bed of state, with a golden sceptre in his hand and his head encircled with a crown of gold. The funeral was attended by many of the princes and great lords and watched by crowds of common people. His monument may be seen today in the Abbey Cathedral of St Denis, next to those of the French monarchs.

After the death of Leon, the kings of Cyprus were the nominal kings of Armenia, until 1489, when the title passed to Venice. Almost at the same time (1485), by reason of the marriage of Anne de Lusignan with Duke Louis I of Savoy, the rulers of Piedmont assumed the empty claim to a kingdom of the past.

Notes

1. Steven Runciman, *A History of the Crusades* (Penguin, 1951), 3 vols, II. p. 14.

2. Ibid., p. 323.

3. It was the Constable Smbat who translated the Assizes of Antioch into Armenian.

4. Joinville and Villehardouin, *Chronicles of the Crusades* (Penguin, 1963), p. 283.

5. M. Komroff, *Contemporaries of Marco Polo* (Cape, London, 1928), pp. 120-1, 126-7, 149-50, 172. Translated from *Itinerarium Fratris Willielmi de Rubruquis, de Ordine Fratrum Minorum, Galli, Anno Gratiae 1253, ad Partes Orientales*; Komroff, *The Journal of Friar William of Rubruck*, pp. 98-9, quoted by Arnold Toynbee, *A Study of History* (Oxford University Press, 1954), vol. V, pp. 114-15.

6. Joinville and Villehardouin *op. cit.*, p. 200.

7. Mamlūk (pl. mamālīk), possessed. (Philip K. Hitti, *History of the Arabs* (London, 1937), p. 235 n. 1.)

8. Philip K. Hitti, *The Arabs* (Macmillan, London, 1937), p. 672.

9. Mark Sykes, *The Caliphs' Last Heritage* (Macmillan, London, 1915), p. 276.

10. Kirakos of Gantzag, *History*, trans. Brosset (St Petersburg, 1870),

pp. 177-9; Vartan, *History of the World*, in Armenian (Moscow, 1861), p. 199; Rashid ad-Din Ibn Abdazzhir, *History of the Mongols of Persia*, ed. with French trans. by Quatremère (Paris, 1836). Quoted by Runciman, *op. cit.*, III, p. 305.

11. Toynbee, *op. cit.*, II, p. 451.

12. Marco Polo, *Travels* (Dent, Everyman's Library), p. 31.

13. John Froissart, *Chronicles of England, France, Spain and the Adjoining Countries*, trans. from the French by Thomas Johnes (London, 1839), vol. II, pp. 137, 144 n. by Sauval, 199, *Antiquities of Paris*, vol. II, p. 251, quoting Juvenal des Ursine; R. Curzon, *Armenia* (London, 1854).

14. Pope Gregory XIII in a Bull promulgated in 1384, instructed that 'No nation and no people were so prompt or so full of zeal as the Armenians to lend their aid, be it in men, in horses, in provision, or in counsel; with all their forces and with the greatest gallantry and fidelity they came to the aid of the Christians in their holy wars.' Quoted from Aram Raffi, 'Armenian Culture and Characteristics', in Noel and Herold Buxton, *Travel and Politics in Armenia* (Smith, Elder, 1914).

15. Froissart, *op. cit.*

16. Raffi, *op. cit.*

26

Religion

The religion of pre-Christian Armenia had much in common with that of its neighbours and the most ancient peoples of Mesopotamia. There was Vahagn, the counterpart of the Iranian Verethragna or Vahram and the Greek Heracles; his wife was Astghik, the Greek Aphrodite, goddess of love. Nanē is the counterpart of Athena-Minerva, goddess of power and wisdom, preserver of the state and a divinity of a purely ethical character. Tir-Apollo was the patron of Augurs, interpreter of dreams (*Erazahan*); the god of the arts and sciences and the recorder of man's morals for his master, Aramazd (see below). Dreams were interpreted by his temple priests. Moses of Khoren (II.14) writes of the effigies of these gods and goddesses as well as one of a Syrio–Seleucid god, of Assyrian origin, 'the statue of Barshamin (Moses I.14) embellished with ivory, crystal and silver [Anania of Shirak refers to that Assyrian god as Parsham]; [and] the tablet with a horoscope made of ivory and crystal',[1] that were brought over to Armenia from Greece and Syria, and of the Greek priests who accompanied the statues of their respective deities. His chronology, however, was often confused and unreliable, and it is difficult to establish the dates of certain parts of his history. In this instance, too, the part that is credible is that of the arrival of the Greek priests in Armavir, where Greek inscriptions have been discovered. They probably arrived in the first century BC, because of the possibility that it was King Tigran the Great who brought at least the Greek and Syrio–Macedonian statues, especially that of Barshamin to Armenia.

Principally, there was the worship of a mother or fertility goddess, which has been a universal and eternal religious concept down to our own times. In Iran and especially in Armenia, she was worshipped under the name of Anahit, the equivalent of the Babylonian Ishtar and the Greek Artemis. She appears to have been greatly venerated and had a place in the topmost area of the Armenian pantheon of deities. Her feast-days were in the spring and autumn equinoxes. Many temples in Armenia seem to have been dedicated to her, but the main temple was at Erez (Erzinjan) where, under the eyes of her celebrated golden statue 'they [the Armenians] dedicate to her service male and female slaves ... the most illustrious men of the tribe [at Acilisene (Erez)] actually consecrate to her their daughters while maidens; and it is the custom for these first to be prostituted in the temple of the goddess ... and after this to be given in marriage.... However, they do not admit any man that comes along, but preferably those of equal rank with themselves' (Strabo, XI. xiv. 16). This was a common custom in the ancient world: Herodotus mentions the Lydians in this context and the Babylonians, too, who sacrificed the virginity of their daughters to their goddess.

Anahit appears to be one of a great trinity, the second of which was the Armenian Aramazd, the Iranian Ahura-Mazda, the Babylonian Bel Merodach, the Greek Zeus or more properly, Cronos creator of heaven and earth, god of the most fundamental elements in nature, fire, air and water; father of all the gods. The effigy of Aramazd was housed in a great temple at Ani-Kamakhos (Western Armenia). The third god of the trinity was also widely worshipped and he appears to have been the most ethically advanced of all earlier teachers, who could be described as the forerunner, in some important respects, of Christian ethics. Mithra was worshipped under the name of Mihr in Armenia. He can be identified in some respects with the Sumerian Shamash, the sun god, the god of destiny, the god of justice and the enemy of wrong and the friend of righteousness. Mihr hated sin and, as the sun-god, his rays penetrated every quarter; he saw all things and read the thoughts of men. Nothing could be concealed from Mihr. Thus, Christian ethics overlap some important Mithraïc ethics (as, indeed, Buddhist, as well as those of a number of pre-Christian secular philosophers) — justice, righteousness, truth and, by implication and evolutionary thought, love and compassion.

Mithra is linked with Varuna in the Hindu Rigveda. Mithraism, writes H.G. Wells, 'began to spread very widely under the Caesars and Antonines. It promised immortality. Its followers were mainly slaves, soldiers and distressed people. In its methods of worship, in the burning of candles before the altar and so forth, it has a certain superficial resemblance to the later developments of the ritual of the third great religious movement in the Roman world, Christianity. Christianity also was a doctrine of immortality and salvation, and it too spread at first chiefly among the lowly and unhappy.' Perhaps a syncretism of the causes for the universalism of Christianity in the times of its teacher might be expressed by pointing to the pessimism of the last phases of the Hellenistic world, resulting from the failure of the rationalism of classical Greece and the debility of the hoary, institutionalised, authoritarian religions of ancient Mesopotamia–Babylonia and India. These situations left a serious vacuum in man's religious aspirations which could only be filled by an entirely new concept of a source which could appear to offer succour to those in distress and want, and others who felt 'lost'; a saviour above reason, above law — a saviour of faith. There were several 'saviour' and 'faith' versions for a new religion; Christianity prevailed over them all.

The Armenian Church is described as the Holy Apostolic Orthodox Church of Armenia. The founder apostles are said to have been St Thaddeus, one of 'The Seventy', and St Bartholomew, the sixth in order of the apostles; the brother and son respectively of St James. Tradition[2] has it that King Abgar of Edessa (Urfa) (*c.* 5 BC–AD 32), wrote to Jesus begging Him to cure him of a malady. The allegedly written reply from Jesus, preserved together with His portrait (painted by Abgar's messenger, Ananias), purports to inform the king that one of His disciples would visit him, after the Writer's ascension. On the arrival of St Thaddeus, the king, having been cured, together with his wonderstruck people, was converted to Christianity.[3] Soon after that momentous event, the king died (*c.* 32). His nephew, Sanatruk, king of another province in Great Armenia, embraced Christianity when St Thaddeus visited him, in spite of his fear of the wrath of his nobles. His anxiety was justified when he was compelled to apostatise and to martyrize St Thaddeus. He was then murdered, according to Moses of Khoren (II. 30-6) in Shavarsham (Ardaz) on the slopes of Mount Ararat. St Bartholomew, too, was martyred by King Sanatruk in Armenia in the city of Arevpan.[4]

It is manifest that Christianity was being preached, and gaining many adherents, long before the appearance of Trdat the Great and St Gregory the Illuminator. Indeed, writers of the third and fourth centuries refer to the throne of the Armenian pontiffs as 'the Chair' of St Thaddeus. A third-century bishop, Merujan (Meruzanes) is mentioned by Eusebius.[5] This name connects its bearer with the great Artsruni family who acquired extensive estates in the huge province of Vaspurakan, some of whose descendants became kings of Armenia in the Middle Ages. Even earlier than Merujan (by *c.* 100), the apostles and their disciples in Armenia seem to have had a substantial following, for there were persecutions during the reign of Khosrov I (217–52) and his predecessors.

The Holy Apostolic Orthodox Church of Armenia adheres to the Nicaean creed, as defined at the Council of Nicaea in 325: 'Christ is a *very God*, begotten of God, but not a creature of God; *Son of God*, of *one nature with the Father*, who came down from heaven, and took flesh and *became Man*, and suffered and ascended into heaven; Who was, before He was begotten and Who has always been.' In plain language, God became man, in the fullest sense. To a layman, the Nicaean creed seems to uphold the single nature of God, as well as God manifesting Himself in three natures — the latter being a Trinitarian statement and its official interpretation.

The Nicaean formula was questioned and the following compromise was adopted at the Council of Chalcedon in 451: Jesus Christ according to His Godhead is of *one nature with the Father*, according to His humanity is, apart from sin, *of one nature with man*. Thus, one and the same Christ is recognised in *two natures* indissolubly united but yet distinct. Thus the Greek Orthodox *adopting the Chalcedonian dogma* believes in the dual nature of Christ. He is God manifest on earth in the holy person of Christ, as well as in the secular person of vulnerable man.

The dogmatic gulf between the Armenian Church and that of Rome is even wider: in common with the Greek Church, the Armenian Church rejects the *Filioque* (= and from the Son) and, of course, denies the infallibility of the Pope. As the concept of the *Filioque* is today the main stumbling-block between the union of the Roman and Greek Churches (apart from the ambitions of priests), its interpretation ought to be stated:

The older creed had declared that the 'Holy Ghost proceeded from the Father.' The Latins wanted to add, and they did add '*Filioque*', and placed the Greeks out of their communion because they would not follow this lead.... Latin Christendom believes that the Holy Ghost proceeds from the Father *and the Son*; Greek and the Eastern Christians, that the Holy Spirit proceeds from the Father, without any mention of the Son ... and the two words *filio que*, which had been added to the Latin creed, had split off the Byzantine Christians [from Rome].[6]

Filioque, the double procession of the Holy Ghost added by the Western Church to the Nicaean Creed, is no part of the original Creed. It is first met at the Third Council in 589. After 800, it was generally chanted throughout the Frankish empire. The initial Great Schism (or separation) came when the Frankish monks in Jerusalem introduced it in their liturgy. It was officially adopted by Rome after the year 1000.

'The Armenian Church expressly rejects Chalcedon ... The Armenians therefore differ both with the Greek and with the Roman Church in their expression of the mystery of Christology. They will not hear of two natures. They hold that in Christ there is one person and one nature, one will and one energy; and their liturgy presents this dogma in an impressive manner in the Trisagion, which runs: "O God, holy God, mighty God, everlasting God, *who wast crucified for us*".'[7] Edward Gibbon defines his view of the Armenian position concisely: 'The Armenians alone are the pure disciples of Eutychus. They alone persevere in the opinion that the manhood of Christ was created, or existed without creation, of a divine and incorruptible substance.'[8] But Eutychus was anathemetised as a heretic at the Council of Dvin (Armenia) in 506. Of incidental interest, Gibbon remarks: 'Our bishops will hear with surprise that the austerity of their [the Armenian priesthood's] life increases in just proportion to the elevation of their rank.'[9] Dr V. Nersessian states the Armenian position:

The Armenian Church recognises the doctrinal and canonical validity of the first three Ecumenical councils, of Nicea (325), Constantinople (381) and Ephesus (431) as adequate for 'the basis of life and guide to the path leading to God' and rejects the decisions of the council of Chalcedon (451). Because of this rejection, both Orthodox and Roman Catholic Churches have erroneously considered the Armenian Church as being Monophysite. The Armenian Church has always rejected the mingling or the confusion of the two natures of Christ and recognised in Him a divine and a human nature, adopting the definition 'One nature in the Incarnate God'. It is for this reason that the Armenian Church celebrates the Baptism (the manifestation of Divinity) and the Birth (Manifestation in the flesh) of Christ on the same day (6 January), whereas the Greeks and others celebrate the same events on two separate days (25 December and 6 January).[10]

It is interesting that, perhaps only coincidentally, the 'Dark Ages' of Armenian political history of some 450 years, set in only *after* the destruction of the nation's ancient religious institutions, and therefore the destruction of its social pattern. It was after Trdat the Great and his adoption of Christianity as the Armenian state religion, that Armenian society seems to have begun its slow disintegration; in that time the land was abandoned by many of the aristocratic families for one or another reason, and its people were left without leaders, at the mercy of Rome and Persia. Armenia never really recovered its ancient glories, even under the Bagratids.

The emergence of Christianity added religious dissenssions to political discord. The Armenian Holy Apostolic Church was opposed to the Greek Orthodox (the Byzantine version of Christianity) no less (indeed, a good deal more) than to the pagan fire-worshipping Mazdaism of Persia, or the Mohammedanism of the Arabs of the seventh century. The hatred inherent in those religious differences and dogma was one of the most important causes of centuries of warfare and bloodshed. Another important cause militating against the growth of a powerful state, was the perpetual disunity of the Armenian princes whose independent spirit and personal ambition were fostered by the mountainous character of their country. The prince of each deep valley recognised no law but his own. In the end, this proved to be the undoing of Armenia, for its geographical position, astride a great highway of Eurasia, combined with its natural wealth, always excited the rapacity of its powerful neighbours. Only the united forces of its aristocracy could have held back its enemies, and such unity was seldom experienced. In medieval England and France, too, disunity among the petty princes and barons was rife, no less than in Armenia; they, too, sometimes sided with the enemies of their respective countries. But they eventually achieved stable nationhood, helped by the geographical situation of their particular kingdoms — England as an island; France at the western extremity of the Eurasian continent, backing upon a vast ocean, the limits of which were unknown. On the other hand, it can be argued that Armenia's history as an independent or quasi-independent nation, might have been shorter by a thousand years, if its defence depended entirely upon the forces of a central government. For, once defeated, the whole country would have at one blow succumbed to the enemy; whereas, ruled as it so often was, by independent and powerful princes, each in his own daunting mountain fastness, there were always a number of parts which together constituted the independent land of Armenia.

Notes

1. Moses of Khoren I. 14; II. 12; Agathangelus, CVIII (Langlois I, p. 164), CIX n. 2, n. 3 (Langlois I, p. 167).
2. Moses of Khoren II. 14. Langlois (I. 164, n. 1) translates and expands upon '*Erazmoin* songe, et *mouin* (cf. Emin, *Recherches sur le pag. armen.*, p. 18 from the French translation): 'Cet endroit se trouvait dans la province d'Ararat'. Cf. Indjidji, *Arm. anc*, p. 497 *et seq.*; Agathange CIX. 132 (Langlois I. 167 n. 3 also): Lerubna of Edessa (Langlois I, pp. 317, 328, 330).
3. Eusebius, *Hist. eccl.*, X I. xiiil Lerubna of Edessa I and VI (Langlois pp. 327 and 328 respectively).
4. Lerubna of Edessa, IX (Langlois, pp. 330-1). Langlois, I. p. 331: 'Leroubna, fils de scribe Apschatar a recueille tous les faits qui se sont passés du temps d'Abgar et de Sanadroug, et les a déposés dans les archives d'Edesse'.
5. Eusebius, *op. cit.*, VI. 46.
6. H.G. Wells, *Outline of History* (London 1937), pp. 530, 649, 663.
7. Lynch I, pp. 281, 312, 313, 315.
8. Gibbon, VI, p. 58.
9. Ibid.
10. V. Neressina, *The Christian Orient* (British Museum Publications, 1978).

27

Language and Learning

Although the Armenians assimilated the Urartian culture, their language eventually became that of the new kingdom. The Armenian language might be mainly a late off-shoot of the Indo-Hittite group of languages, of which the Indo-European Hittite is one. Only some 400 words in the Armenian language today belong to the original, the remaining being loan words.

Basic Armenian appears to be closest to Greek. Its vocabulary consists of more Indo-European words with Greek than with any other dialect. The next highest number of lexical parallels is to be found in Sanskrit, with only 300 shared words. It is also suggested that Armenian shares so many grammatical and lexical elements with Hittite that it is much more reasonable to suppose that Armenian developed naturally from Hittite dialects of Asia Minor, west of the Upper Euphrates. In fact, there are so many characteristics of Armenian which remind one of Hittite that it is highly improbable that they can be separated.

However, Hittites, Luwians, Phygians and the people of Hayasa, with whom the Armenians were associated, spoke Indo-European languages. Also, it is less open to argument to accept that the Armenians emerged from the west, probably with the Phrygians, than either that they were authochthonous people of Asia Minor or that they emerged from the east.

For a thousand years, down to c.AD 400, the Armenians used the script of their neighbours — the Persians and the Syrians (Aramaic) as well as Greek, to record business transactions and matters of state. When Hellenistic culture penetrated Asia, c. 330 BC, the Armenian aristocracy was already familiar with the Greek language. The Armenian alphabet was invented in AD 406 by Mesrop-Mashtots, a learned cleric, during the pontificate of Sahak the Great (c. 390–439), in the reign of King Vramshapuh (392–414), the penultimate Arsacid king of Armenia. Mashtots appears to have been commissioned to undertake that historic task, by Katholicos and king, as a tool to greater national unification and Christian identity of the Armenian people; and particularly as an additional barrier against the infiltration into Armenia of Persian Mazdaism. Anania of Shirak, geographer, astronomer and mathematician, records that an existing set of 29 consonants were 'arranged in order' by Daniel, a Syrian scholar. The missing seven vowels were supplied to Mashtots by Hayek, a nobleman of Taron. Ruphinos of Samosata, a gifted scribe, appears to have incorporated those seven vowels with the consonants and shaped the letters and thus given unity of character to the complete alphabet of 36 letters.[1] St Gregory the Illuminator had preached in the Armenian language and the native language was commonly used throughout the land.[2]

Before the invention of the alphabet, such inscriptions as have been found in the Armenian language are in the Greek, Syriac, or Persian script. An important role of the new alphabet was to propagate the Christian religion throughout Armenia. Down to that time the liturgy was performed and the mass celebrated in Greek or Syriac, but the lessons from the Scriptures were declaimed by the priests in Armenian. The introduction of the new alphabet demanded the enormous task, which was undertaken, of translating the Bible from a Syrian original and later from the Greek text of the Septuagint. That scrupulous translation (edited yet again soon after by a Church Father) ranks high among the different versions of the Bible for accuracy as well as for literary refinement.

Of secular learning, there were, no doubt, libraries of the works of the ancient philosophers, in their original language, mainly Greek. For example, King Artavasd, son of Tigran the Great, a scholar of considerable talent, must have had such libraries in his various palaces as, indeed, during the Armeno–Cilician period, the scholarly royal house of Hethum. These, a variety of secular texts, were translated from Greek and Syriac during the course of the following two centuries and beyond. Examples of these are the *Chronicle* of Eusebius, The Alexander *Romance* of the Pseudo-Callisthenes and many philosophical works, including those of Plato. Callisthenes, nephew of Aristotle, was among the many scholars who accompanied Alexander the Great on his wars and explorations in the East. He was Alexander's official historian. His original Graeco–Egyptian, fourth-century manuscript was lost, but a copy of it, made in the thirteenth century and known as Pseudo-Calisthenes, has preserved an Armenian translation made from the Greek (Eusebius, 'Chronicon') in the fifth century. The thirteenth-century Armenian copy was discovered in Constantinople and published by Aucher in Venice in 1818.[3] There is also extant an English translation. Thus we have the good fortune to be able to read, as if fresh from fifth-century Egypt, this Armenian version (the admitted best translation) of the Alexander epics. Its style and essence is strangely modern.

Manetho's *History of Egypt from the Beginning* is lost; but a list of the dynasties is preserved in Julius Africanus and in Eusebius (most correct in the Armenian version). Manetho lived in the reign of Ptolemy I (323–285 BC).

Aristotle's works seem to have been of particular interest to the Armenian educated classes; the measure of that interest can be assessed by the great collection of that philosopher's works, some 300 manuscripts, which are to be found in the huge national library at Erevan, called the Madenataran together with more than 10,000 Armenian manuscripts, miniatures, parchments and palimpsests, dating from the ninth century, and other ancient and priceless literary works. Among those important translations, of which in some cases the originals are now lost (thus leaving the Armenian version as the source work in each such case) there are many original works by Armenian scholars. In particular, a number of Armenian, and other historians with very close Armenian connections, of the fourth and fifth centuries must be mentioned. First place must be given to the Herodotus of the Armenians — Movses Khorenatsi (Moses of Khoren), whose general history of Armenia, down to his own times (fifth century) is, in spite of many inaccuracies, of primary importance. At the very least, it could be a starting point for research and criticism. Other notable historians of that early period are Agathangelos, Faustus of Byzantium, Eghishé, Lazarus of Pharb, Bardesan, Zenob of Glag and John Mamikonian (the last flourished in the seventh century but is included here because he continued the work of Zenob). These are source writers of their respective periods and regions in and around Armenia. Of secular (folk) learning, there was, no doubt, an oral transmission down the ages consisting of epic poems, songs, legends and folk-tales, which were collected and housed in the palaces of the Armenian kings and the libraries of the monasteries (Langlois I, p. 25, n. 2). Much of this busy activity took place, evidently with **great** enthusiasm and inspiring excitement, during the fifth century, which is consequently described as the Golden Age of Armenian literature. Armenian scholars travelled to Greece in order to translate classical works into the new Armenian script. Armenian philosophers of international repute were to be found in Athens and Rome: David the Invincible (in philosophical disputations) lived in Rome; statues were erected in their honour both in Athens and Rome. As in Europe, so in Armenia, monasteries were centres of learning and schools of scribes, lay as well as religious, included women; a remarkably advanced attitude, even by modern standards.

In the middle centuries of medieval Armenia, many other scholars flourished, among the most prominent of whom were Sebeos (*Primary History of Armenia*, among other works, eighth century); Katholicos John V and Prince Artsruni (tenth century); the seer-poet Grigor Narekats'i, Aristakes of Lastivert and Asoghik of Taron; Prince Gregory Majistros translated from the original Euclid's *Elements* and Plato's *Timaeus* and *Phaedon* (eleventh century). It seems that Homer was also translated: the Imperial Library, Paris, possesses an Armenian vocabulary, obviously intended for scholars wishing to translate the *Iliad*; Stepan Orbelian, Bishop of Siunik, chronicler and historian (thirteenth century).

During the existence of the revived Kingdom of Armenia in Cilicia (eleventh–fourteenth centuries), important literature was contributed by Grigor Arkantsi, Matthew of Edessa, the Constable Smbat and Prince Hethum (Hayton). The ecclesiast and poet in that period (eleventh century), the Katholicos Nerses Shnorhali (Nerses the Gracious) must also be mentioned.

This brief catalogue of names (for it would be beyond the limited scope of this work to do more than list the authors' names and their periods) is intended for those who might wish to go further and discover and read their works for themselves.

The works of the above writers are in classical Armenian, and many of them have been translated into French and increasingly more of them are being translated into English. But some (probably) itinerant teachers (thirteenth century), wrote and recited in the vernacular. They describe the sufferings of the people during the Mongol invasions and particularly their distress at the hands of the feudal lords and the landholding clergy. Many poems and legends and fragments of history, scattered among the people, still await collection and publication. They would throw more light on Armenian social and political history of the Middle Ages.

Some of the wealth resulting from trade, especially from transit dues on goods travelling through Armenia from east and west, might well have been used to endow the monasteries where much of the scholarship of those and later times was expressed in many beautiful illuminated manuscripts.

The manuscripts housed in the National Library, Madenataran, at Erevan, have been regarded as holy, some even as miraculous. A copy of one such mystical work of the tenth century, a confession of guilt and atonement, is still put under the pillow of the sick to hasten recovery. Manuscripts are decorated with gold adhered to the paper or parchment with garlic, the often dominant colour, red, made from a cochineal dye, prepared from a species of shell-insect, found in Karapagh (not Coccus Cacti, but Porphysophora Hamelii), each insect providing only one drop of colour. Strabo (XI. xiv) writes: in Armenia 'there are also other mines, in particular those of sandyx (an earthy ore containing arsenic, which yields a bright red colour) as it is called, which is called "Armenian" colour, like chalcê [a purple dye, usually spelt Chalchê]'. In the Madenataran, a fifteenth-century calendar, one inch square, rests upon a huge, thirteenth-century book of collected sermons, weighing 80 lb and comprising 632 pages of calf skin. It was found by two Armenian women in a deserted Armenian monastery in Turkey, during the First World War. As it was too heavy for them to carry, they split it into two, buried one half wrapped in a cloth, and carried the other to Georgia, whence it eventually reached Armenia. Two years later, a Polish officer found the first half and sold it to another officer in Baku, and it too reached Armenia, where the two parts were reunited.

The Madenataran has preserved the earliest examples of Armenian miniatures. Four of these (seventh century) respectively depict the Annunciation to Mary; the Annunciation to Zachariah, the Adoration of the Magi and the Baptism of Christ. They are the remains of a manuscript and they were incorporated into the famous tenth-century (989) Gospels of Echmiadzin. Of the two oldest miniatures, each with its own precise date, the first is the Gospel of Queen Mlkhe (862) and the second is the 'Moscow' Manuscript (887). Thenceforth, many hundreds, indeed thousands, of miniatures and illustrated Gospels were produced in monasteries in various parts of Armenia: in Sebastia by Grigor Akoretsi (eleventh century); at Haghbad by Markare in Taron by Thoros. There was an explosiion of religious art, incorporating secular art, in Lesser Armenia of Armeno–Cilicia, which attained its apogee in the thirteenth century, when Thoros Roslin produced beautiful illustrations depicting aspects of Armenia's social, political, economic and religious life. His work is considered to be far superior to Giotto's (*c.* 1267–1337) predecessors and contemporaries in Italy. There were many other artists in Great Armenia continuing from the thirteenth century onwards, in Nakhichevan, Gladsor (Siunik) and Tatev, in which following earlier Armenian tradition, the colophons depicted activities in war and peace. They have become valuable documents for historians and sociologists. In spite of great losses during the Seljuk invasions in the eleventh and twelfth centuries, when over 10,000 manuscripts were destroyed, there still remain some 24,000 examples in various libraries, monasteries and museums, such as the madenataran (Erevan), St James's Monastery (Jerusalem), at the Catholic monasteries of the Mkhitarist Fathers at Venice and Vienna, in the great museums in Europe and America as well as among private collections.[4]

In the field of science, contributions to geography, astronomy and mathematics were made by Anania of Shirak, Bishop of Siunik (seventh century), a celebrated scholar of his time, who has already been mentioned above in connection with the invention of the Armenian alphabet. Although in the seventh century there were no centres of higher education in Armenia (Anania went to Trebizond for his studies), after the ninth century, some of the great monasteries, such as those at Haghbad, Ani, Siunik and Tatev, offered competent teachers and comprehensive libraries to Armenian scholars. Prince Gregory Majistros (Krikor Pahlavuni, descendant of the royal house of the Arsacids, late tenth century) was held in high regard as a scholar and philosopher and translator of the classics, both by the Byzantine court of the emperors and the sultans and emirs of the Arab world. He might be seen as an example of Armenian scholars who saved for posterity some parts of their country's cultural heritage, down to his own time. We know (among many other contributions) of the fragments of an elegy on the death of King Artashes, which he wrote down, on hearing it in a peasant's song. He translated Euclid's *Geometry* but among many other translations, only Plato's *Timaeus* and *Phaedo* have survived. His many manuscripts (as many as 80), are preserved in the library of the Armenian monastery of St Lazare, Venice.

Thus, in spite of a tumultuous history and the sea of armies which ebbed and flowed around the walls of the monasteries and castles of medieval Armenia (of which there still remain many dramatic ruins), considerable activity took place within them. During brief periods of calm, or when the fighting was at a distance, architects, artists, poets, philosophers, and, as we have seen, historians and writers on religious subjects and translators of Greek classics into Armenian, produced in turn new cities, cathedrals and churches with architectural innovations of great beauty and originality, important historical works, and miniature paintings of the first order which are to be found in the illuminated gospels, of which there are many examples in the great national library at Erevan, at the Mkhitariants monastery of St Lazare, Venice and scattered in many museums (e.g. the British Museum) and private libraries (see Plates 15 and 16).

I have already referred to the wholesale, terrible destruction of the ancient Armenian temples, monuments and works of pagan art, wrought by King Trdat the Great, when he adopted Christianity for himself and his country. The king, with St Gregory the Illuminator at his side, led his troops from Vagharshapat down the valley to Artashat (Artaxata). The temple priests and their fully armed followers, some on horseback, some on foot, likened to 'demons', were put to flight.

> But the swarm took refuge in the temple of the great goddess, Anahid at Artaxata where from the roof they discharged arrows and precipitated a hail of stones upon the advancing host. Gregory, making the sign of the Cross, ran to the gate of the edifice, which dissolved into its foundations, wreathed in flames. The dusky troop vanished like a puff of smoke from the face of the land, to Caucasus and Chaldia [the Pontic regions] in the north. The treasures of the temple were distributed among the needy; some of the priests were selected or accepted for the service of the Church, to which body was also allotted the confiscated land. The king and minister travelled the country in all directions, preaching (the king himself preached), overthrowing temples and endowing the Church with their rich possessions. One after another the most famous sanctuaries succumbed to the royal zeal ...

Every temple, every shrine, every statue of gods and goddesses (some of which had been looted by the Romans, particularly those under Mark Antony, but returned to Armenia by Augustus), were shattered. 'A more personal delight may have thrilled the saint — if saints be capable of such emotions — as he shattered the golden statue of the goddess Anahid at Erzinjan (Erez), and watched the lofty walls of her numerous shrines sinking to the level of the ground. They were the most magnificent of all the sacred edifices in Armenia and they were defended to the last by quite an army of dusky foes. Within the vacant enclosures were erected the sign of the Cross.'[5] These violent methods to substitute Christianity for polytheism were essentially similar to those employed in Europe. The most fundamental difference was the impetuosity and brevity of time in relatively narrow boundaries, where conversion from paganism to Christianity was imposed upon an ignorant people; there was no time allowed, as in Europe, for maturity to restrain the savage destruction of pagan monuments.

> We learn from the Armenian writer ... how the ancient festival in honour of the god was converted into the festival of a martyr, and how, in fact, while the myth was new and unfamiliar, much of the ritual and all the surroundings remained the same. The sacred groves were taken by storm amid scenes of carnage ... The lands and slaves of the heathen fanes were made over to the Church; ... The children of the priests were distributed among the newly founded seminaries, where they were ... introduced to the literature of the Church ... Such was the nature of the revolution accomplished by St Gregory (and King Trdat) with a thoroughness and decision which we cannot but admire.[6]

Christianity put an end to the heroic tradition of the *gusan* (minstrel) who had travelled and informed while entertaining; not unlike the much later European troubadours.

Notes

1. Gorioun, *Biographie de saint Mesrob* (Langlois II. p. 10); Lazare de Pharbe, *Histoire d'Arménie* (Langlois II, p. 266); Moise de Khorène, *Histoire d'Arménie* LIV (Langlois II, p. 162).
2. Agathangelus CXXIII (Langlois I. p. 182).
3. Victor Langlois, *Le Pseudo–Calisthènes*, I., p. 399.
4. V. Nersessian, *Armenia, The Christian Orient,* British Museum (London, 1978).
5. Agathangelos CVIII-CX (Langlois I, pp. 164-9).
6. Agathangelos XCIX-CXX (Langlois I, pp. 178-9).

28

Armenia's Wealth of Ecclesiastical Architecture

The great Apostolic Cathedral of Holy Etchmiadzin, near Erevan was founded in the fourth century, on the site of a fire-worshippers' temple. That 'legend' was validated in 1957 when archaeologists from the Armenian State Academy, revealed the fire-basket or grate and alter of the temple below the crypt of the cathedral, where a perpetual fire provided suitable incense to Ahura-Mazda. The building is of immense architectural interest, especially because of the many alterations and additions that have been made to it since its foundation. Thus, at the present day, the cathedral building incorporates more than one style of architecture. A scheme for its restoration was carried out by the Patriarch Kirakos in 1441. The west door and main entrance were added in 1658, whilst the sacristy at the end of the building was added in 1882. The cathedral is set in the centre of monastic buildings and the residence of the Katholicos.

Armenian architecture is of international historical importance. Its serious study is less than a century old. There were, indeed, travellers and explorers in the nineteenth century, such as H.F.B. Lynch, who recorded, in writing and by illustrations, the buildings, particularly the medieval churches, which he discovered in Armenia. But these were not systematically studied by professional architects until the very end of the nineteenth and beginning of the twentieth centuries. I refer especially to French and German writers, such as Auguste Choisy (1899) and G. Millet (1916); and to J. Strygowski's great work: *Die Baukunst der Armenier und Europa* (1918). The additional contributions of Russian and Armenian scholars down to 1939, established the importance, on an international scale, of the Armenian contribution to architectural styles. Many early Armenian churches, recognisable by the Ashlar stonework (masonary or squared stones in regular courses in contradistinction to rubble work) with which they are faced, are often found on the site of pagan temples. The groundplan of those temples seem to have been square, and the Christian church architects used that original ground plan to erect a building suitable to its own Christian character.

The original Etchmiadzin cathedral-building was, early in its history, extended by four semicircular apses. To appreciate the elegant external proportions of the building, one needs to let one's eyes travel along the top of the walls, below the cupolas and campaniles and the eaves, when the artistically conceived perspective immediately becomes strikingly apparent. Graceful, false or blind arches embellish sometimes the interior and at others the exterior of the walls.

[The] domed-cross type of church spread to Greece and through most of Anatolia. More distant parts of the Byzantine Empire, however, retained much of their earlier styles of church design or developed new styles of their own which were largely independent of early Byzantine architecture. Thus, sixth and seventh-century churches in Mesopotamia and Egypt differed but little from fourth and fifth century examples in those areas; in plan they were oblong basilicas, and domes were rarely, if ever, used. In Bulgaria and Armenia, on the other hand, far more sophisticated styles emerged, suffused with a richness of architectural effects not found in typical Early Byzantine churches. These styles depended to some extent on the basilica plan, but they were also often based on circular or octagonal plans.[1]

Those who are interested in the architecture of this area and period, are familiar with the perennial discussions between Graecophiles and Armenophiles, as to whether it is the Armenian styles which influenced the Byzantine or the converse. That Christianity was first adopted as its state religion by Armenia nearly a century before Byzantium is a basic argument that might be advanced by Armenophiles.

Some claim for Armenian contribution to European Gothic architecture might legitimately be made. The slender columns which support the pointed arches, flanking the façade of the monastic church of Haghbad (tenth century) is an example.

More evidence of such a claim is found in the design of the great cathedral at Ani (eleventh century). It was not until the thirteenth century that Gothic art first appeared in the cathedrals of southern Europe.[2]

The Cathedral of Ani: in spite of its small proportions, if judged by European standards, the Cathedral at Ani has still a certain grandeur, and such beauty that its appeal is universal and cannot fail to arouse at the same time a sense of awe and delight (see Plate 18).

> The apse is only indicated by two niches which recess back from the face of the wall on the east. Two similar niches are seen on the south and, I think, on the north side; but their purpose is ornamental and to secure uniformity of design.... The remainder of the space is diversified with the lightest of false (blind) arches, which rise almost to the roof, embraces the niches and extends to all four walls.... One remarks the tall and slender pillars of the false arcades, the cushion form of the capitals with their richly chiselled faces, the low spring of the rounded arches which curve inwards at the base, but scarcely suggest, so slight is the curve, the horseshoe shape.... And the bold arched moulding of *pointed form* which envelop the door and window, takes the eye above the tops of the neighbouring arches and leads it upwards to the loftier roof of the transept.[3]

The interior is remarkable for its artistic concept as well as for its historic innovation. Here again we have examples 'of many characteristics of the Gothic style, of which it establishes the Oriental origin.... The roofs as well as walls are composed of stone, and, as usual in Armenian churches, no wood or metal has been used.... In no case do we discover any trace of (artistic or architectural) barbarism; the designs are sober and full of grace, the execution is beyond praise ... a monument of the highest artistic merit, denoting a standard of culture which was far in advance of the contemporary standards in the West.'[4] Several inscriptions in Armenian appear on the walls, of which the earliest (1010 AD) records that the cathedral, founded by King Smbad, had been completed by Queen Katranideh of Armenia, to meet the wishes of her husband, Gagik, King of Kings of Armenia and Georgia (989–1020).[5]

The Church of St Gregory the Illuminator (church of the patron saint of the Armenians (see Plate 17)) is situated in a dramatic position at the eastern end of what was once the city of

Ani 'upon the side of the cliff which breaks away to the bed of River Arpa by a series of black crags.... The stream hisses in a gloomy ravine of grey and lichened rock. Subterraneous passages lead inwards into the town.' If the ruinous porch were removed, the architectural characteristics with which we are familiar would be revealed, such as: the oblong figure of unbroken walls; graceful blind arches; 'the roof scene of nave, and transept and aisles, surmounted by a polygonal dome with a conical roof. Tall, double shafts support the arches of the false arcades which extend around the building ... the slender pillars suggest the Gothic.'[6] Writing in the years 1880–85, H.F.B. Lynch found the interior of the church in 'almost perfect preservation; the plaster adheres to the walls and ceilings, and [even] the frescoes with which they were adorned are still intelligible.'[7] The design of the interior resembles that of the cathedral; the dome rests on four piers, the apse is flanked by diminutive side chapels. The frescoes upon the façade, represent Biblical subjects.[8]

The Chapel of St Gregory, a circular building, with a drum-shaped dome and a conical roof, rises upon the summit of a cliff in full view of the city. 'It is a charming monument which, like the cathedral, blends elements of Byzantine and (what we now recognise to be the later, European) Gothic art.... The inside diameter is approximately 10 metres.... It seems to have been used as a place of burial by the Pahlavuni or Pahlavid family, which furnished one of the most illustrious names in Armenian history. The great noble who led the faction which opposed the cession of Ani to the Byzantines was a Pahlavid — Vahram Palavuni, whose name figures in inscriptions over the door.'[9]

The Church of Zvartnots (named after the heavenly hosts), situated east of Holy Echmiadzin, near Erevan: its ruins were discovered by archaeologists in 1900–4. It was built by the Katholicos Nerses III (641–61) Patriarch of Armenia. He is known as Nerses of Tayk, with the honorary title of Shinol (builder) (Lewond, p. 159, n. 11). This is corroborated by a Greek inscription on a stone slab found lying on the ground, which states: 'Built by Nerses, remember.' It is dedicated to the Felicitous Angels who had appeared to St Gregory the Illuminator in a vision. 'It has a circular foundation, cruciform interior, three storeyed exterior and a central dome, originally fifty metres high. The dome rested upon the second storey which rose on a projecting, round, arched arcade, carried on pillars and decorated with ornamental capitals; the whole structure supported by four massive [basalt] piers. It was magnificently decorated, with splendid carvings both within and without.'[10] It is the largest round church in the world. It is said that in the tenth century the Arabs who at that time occupied that part of Armenia, pulled it down so that no building should be taller than their new mosque. However, it is more likely to have been destroyed by an earthquake. The discovery of such a monumental piece of architecture encouraged archaeologists to search for other remains of architectural interest and to restore and study them. 'In 1931, excavations were made near Zvartnots Church. Half a kilometre from the Church, excavations revealed a massive wall surrounding the site of a medieval city and seventh century town-type settlement with the remains of buildings, orchards and irrigation canals.... In Armenia, there are numerous monumental relics of architecture — the work of remarkable artists who developed their own individual style. A study of these monuments is giving us a fuller picture of Armenian art in Medieval times.'

The Church of The Holy Cross at Aght'amar, was built by the architect Manuel for King Gagik of Vaspurakan between the years 915 and 921. The church is on an island in Lake Van and is unexpectedly unique in that it is decorated with reliefs of biblical subjects, on the *outer* face of its walls. It is today the best preserved of the many medieval churches in what is now Turkish-occupied territory (see Plate 19).

Notes

1. P. Sherrard and the editors of Time-Life Books, *Byzantium* (USA, 1971), pp. 139-40.
2. Eric King, *The Sphere Magazine*, 2 September 1939.
3. Lynch I, 371-2, 374, 381, 382.
4. Ibid.
5. Ibid.
6. Ibid.
7. Ibid.
8. Ibid.
9. The State Historical Museum, Erevan, Armenia.
10. A.L. Mongait, *Architecture in the USSR* (Pelican, 1961).

Epilogue

In 1453 the Turks at last broke into Constantinople and thus destroyed the last vestiges of the Byzantine empire. At first the indifference, and later the political interests of the western powers, perpetuated the ever-tottering throne of the Turkish Caliphs and Padishahs and prevented their expulsion from Graeco–Armenian administration which continued to maintain the essential government-machinery of empire, for which they had been responsible to the Byzantine emperors. Moreover, it was the commercial acumen and industry of the Armenians which greatly helped to keep the Turkish treasury solvent. The Turks expressed their gratitude by a number of massacres of genocidal proportions at the close of the nineteenth and the early part of the twentieth centuries, which obliterated the Armenians from their ancient homelands in central and eastern Anatolia.

Today the Soviet Socialist Republic of Armenia comprises a small part of its former extensive northern provinces. It is about the size of Belgium, with a population of some 3½ million. Parts of its highlands could be described as fragments of the roof of the world. Lake Sevan, which is bigger than all the lakes in Switzerland put together, is more than 1¼ miles above sea-level. The whole country stands high above sea level empty in nature and large areas of it arid. The latter disadvantage was overcome in ancient times by canals, some of which still function; new ones have been built as well, within the shrunken territories of the modern state. And, of course, people have moved in to cultivate every possible acre.

This brief account of the history of Armenia should be concluded with the important reminder of its several phases of greatness and independence, which tend to be forgotten or misinterpreted when they emerge for several centuries at a time, out of the folds of a continuous narrative covering 4000 years. After over 500 years of subservience, there is once more a national home for the Armenians, and administered by them, where the courageous vitality of that people, expressed in legends, and ancient and medieval art and literature, is being regenerated and developed by dedicated scholars at the University of Erevan as well as at other universities in various parts of the world.

Since the end of Achaemenid Persia (331 BC), the Orontid,

315

Artaxiad, Arsacid, Bagratid and Rubenid sovereigns of Armenia had ruled their country, with fluctuating fortunes, altogether for over 1500 years down to 1375. The main periods of the history of Armenia might be classified as follows:

		Number of years (in round figures)
1.	The nascent kingdom of Urartu amidst Hurrian chieftainships and principalities, in the land of Armenia from 2300 BC to 1300 BC	1000
2.	The Urartian period *c.* 1300–*c.*600 BC; first monarchy of Armenia	700
3.	Period in which Armenian insurgents and invaders were expelling or absorbing the Urartians *c.* 590–530 BC	60
4.	First Achaemenian satrapies in Armenia, under Cyrus the Great (530 BC) to the end of the Achaemenids (331 BC)	200
5.	The royal house of Orontes *c.* 330–*c.* 190 BC; second monarchy of Armenia	140
6.	The royal house of Artaxias 190 BC–AD 14; third monarchy of Armenia	200
7.	A period of change, confusion and revolution AD 14–63	50
8.	The Royal House of Arsaces AD 63–428; fourth monarchy of Armenia	350
9.	The Dark Ages, 428–885	450
	(428–633 Persian rule through military *marzpans* 623–693 Byzantine rule through civil *curopalates* 693–862 Arab rule through *ostikans* (governors) from Baghdad)	
10.	The Royal House of Bagratids 885–1064 (fall of Ani); fifth monarchy of Armenia	180
11.	The Royal House of Ruben (Armeno–Cilicia); sixth monarchy of Armenia	300
		3630
12.	Under the yoke of the Ottoman Empire, 1400–1920	500
13.	The Armenian Soviet Socialist Republic	60
	The history of Armenia, spans a period of over 4000 years	4190

Sir John Maundevile (*d.* 1382), *Travels into Great Armenia*, records his impressions:

Men go to Trebizond toward Armenia the Great, unto a City that is clept [called] Erzeroum, that was wont to be a good City and a plenteous; but the Turks have greatly wasted it. Thereabout groweth no Wine nor Fruit, or else little or none. In this Land is the Earth more high than in any other and that maketh great Cold. And there be many good Waters and good Wells that come under Earth from the River of Paradise, that is clept Euphrates, that is a Day's Journey from the City. And that River cometh towards Ind under Earth, and cometh out into the Land of Altazar. And so pass Men by this Armenia and enter the Sea of Persia.

From that City of Erzeroum go men to ... an Hill that Men called Ararat ... where Noah's Ship rested, and yet is upon that Mountain. And Men may see it afar in clear Weather. And that Mountain is well a 7 Mile high.... So that no Man may go up there. Nor never Man did, since the Time of Noah, save a Monk that, by the Grace of God, brought one of the Planks down, and yet is in the Minster at the Foot of the Mountain.

And beside is the City of Dain that Noah founded. And fast by is the City of Any [Ani] in the which were a 1000 Churches.

Later on in his travels, the adventurous knight re-enters Armenia from Persia: 'And then after is Armenia, in which were wont to be 5 Kingdoms, that is a noble Country and full of Goods. And it beginneth at Persia and stretcheth toward the West in Length unto Turkey.... In this Armenia be full many good Cities but Taurizo (Tabreez) is most in Name.

Sir John also recorded an interesting legend in his *Travels*:

In that country is an old castle that stands upon a rock, which is called the Castle of the Sparrow-Hawk, beyond the city of Layays [Lajazzo or Ayas], which belongeth to the rich Lordship of Cruk, a good, Christian man; where a 'Fair Lady of Faerie' keeps a sparrow-hawk upon a perch. 'And who that will watch that sparrow-hawk seven days and seven nights, without company and without sleep, that fair Lady shall give him his first earthly wish. And one time it befell that a King of Armenia, that was a worthy knight and doughty man, and a noble prince, watched that Hawk for seven days and seven nights, and the Lady came to him and bade him wish, for he had well deserved it. And he answered that he was great Lord enough, and well in Peace, and had enough of worldly Riches; and therefore he would wish none other Thing, but the Body of that fair Lady, and to have it at his Will. And she answered him, that he knew not what he asked, for she said that he should not ask but an earthly Thing, for she was none earthly Thing but a ghostly Thing.... 'But since that I may not withdraw you from your lewd Courage, I shall give you without Wishing, and to all them that shall come of your Lineage, Sir King! ye shall have War without Peace, and always to the 9th Generation ye shall be in Subjection of your Enemies, and ye shall be in Need of all Goods.' And never since then, neither that King of Armenia nor the Country were ever in Peace; neither had they ever since then Plenty of Goods; and they have been since then always under Tribute to the Saracens.

The curse of the Fair Lady of Faerie was only, too well substantiated, alas.

Index

Note: The term 'city' is applied to all place names, to distinguish them from personal names.

320

Index

Ervand I, Satrap of Armenia, 209-18, 237, 239
Ervand II, King of Armenia, 214-16, 237, 239
Ervand III, King of Armenia, 216-17, 238
Ervand IV, King of Armenia, 217-21, 238
Ervand V, King of Armenia, 226
Ervand the Short-lived, 209, 237
Ervandashat, city of, 219, 222
Erzerum, 36, 66, 75, 128, 136, 317
Erzincan, 96, 99, 115, 128, 136
Esarhaddon, King, 100, 196, 205
Etchmiadzin, *see* Echmiadzin
Etius, Kingdom of, 65, 72-3
Etruria, 84, 128, 141, 162-74, 196
Etruscans, 21, 157, 162, 166-72
Euclid, 304, 307
Eusebius, historian, 255, 298, 303
Eutychus, 299
Ezekiel, 205

Fabius Hadrianus, general, 234
Fars, city of, 251
Faustus of Byzantium, historian, 67, 202, 257, 304
Filioque, 298-9
Fimbrian legion, 234
Firat river, 21, 204, 221
Flandin, Eugène, 34
Flood, the Great, 42
Fort Shalmaneser, *see* Til Barsip
France, the French, 33, 84, 164, 178, 196, 241, 281, 284, 292, 300, 305
Frankish empire, 299
Franks, 277, 280-1
Frederick Barbarossa, Emperor, 280
Froissart, Sir John, historian, 292

Gabriel of Melitene, prince, 274
Gagik Artsruni, King of Armenia, 262, 266-7, 314
Gagik Bagratuni I, King of Armenia, 268, 312
Gagik Bagratuni II, King of Armenia, 288
Galerius, Emperor, 256
Gamir(k) (Cimmerians), 100
Ganjak, city of, 113
Gayane, Mother Superior, 254
Gaugamela, battle of, 214-15, 219n.5, 237
Gaul(s), 1, 206
Gavin de Beer, Sir, 171-2
Gaykhatu Khan, Mongol chieftain, 288
Gaza, the city of, 6
Genoa, -oese, 277, 282, 288-9, 292
Georgia(ns), 228, 233, 269, 283-4, 287-8, 306
Gerizim, mt., 195
German(s), -ny, 27, 281, 283
Gibbon, Edward, historian, 252, 254, 299
Gilgamesh, epic of, 42
Gilu-khepa, princess, 14-15
Gilurani, grove of, 97n.3
Gilzani, kingdom of, 55, 64, 194
Giotto, Italian painter, 306

Girik Tepe, 75
Gladsor, city of, 306
Glasgow, city of, 169
Glass, 138
Gnuni, princely house of, 95
Gobi desert, 127
Godfrey of Bouillon, of the First Crusade, 276
Goek Tepe, 158
Gogarene, province of, 222
Gold, 17, 42, 69, 73, 78-9, 96, 128, 136-40, 166, 216, 226, 237
Gold ingots, 138
Golden Hord, the, 287
Gordion, the city of, 121, 162, 167, 169
Gordios, King of Phrygia, 95, 167
Gordyen(ians), 226, 230, 236
Gospels (illustrated) and miniatures of:
  Echmiadzin, 306
  Grigor Akoretsi, Sebastia, 306
  Haghbad, 306
  Moscow Manuscript, 306
  Queen Mikhe, 306
Gothic architecture, 311-13
Grand Comneni, empire of, 115
Greece and Greeks, 5, 13, 21, 66-7, 79, 84, 102, 120-1, 128, 157, 162-9, 174, 179, 195-202, 212-13, 218, 221, 229, 235, 238, 243, 268, 271, 276-7, 288, 295-7, 304, 311
Greek Orthodox Church, 274, 284, 298-300
Gregory, the Illuminator, *see* St Gregory
Gregory Majistros, Armenian prince, and philosopher, 304, 307
Gregory XIII, Pope, 276, 294n.14
Grigor VII, Katholicos, 280
Grigor VIII, Anavorzetsi, Katholicos, 290
Grigor Arkantsi, chronicler, 305
Grigor Narekatsi, poet, 304
Gudea of Lagash, 6, 136, 140
Gugarkh, province of, 265
Gulbekian, E.V., 4, 248n.16
Gurdi, prince, 95, 222
Gurgum, kingdom, 66, 79, 85, 193
Gusan, Armenian minstrels, 309
Guy de Lusignan, *see* Lusignan
Guyard, Stanislas, M., 36, 102
Gyges, King of Lydia, 100

Haay, 204
Hadrian, Emperor, 250
Hadrianus, Fabius, 234
Haghbad, monastery, 307, 311
Haik, *see* Hayk
Hakkari mts., 3, 28, 57
Haldi(ans), *see* Khaldi(ans)
Halys river, 16, 112, 197, 206, 222, 238
Hamadan, *see* Ecbatana
Hamath, city of, 54, 57, 194
Hammamat, wadi of, 8
Hammurabi, King, 7, 12, 13, 141, 142, 144, 145
Han emperors, 127, 225
Hannibal, 221, 223

323

Index

Index